The Allocation of Multinational Business Income: Reassessing the Formulary Apportionment Option

Series on International Taxation

VOLUME 76

Series Editors

Prof. Ruth Mason, University of Virginia School of Law
Prof. Dr Ekkehart Reimer, University of Heidelberg

Introduction & Contents

The Series on International Taxation deals with a wide variety of topics in the global tax arena. The authors include many of the field's leading experts as well as talented newcomers. Their expert views and incisive commentary have proven highly useful to practitioners and academics alike.

Objective

The volumes published in this series are aimed at offering high-quality analytical information and practical solutions to international tax practitioners.

Readership

Practitioners, academics and policy makers in international tax law.

Frequency of Publication

2-3 new volumes published each year.

The titles published in this series are listed at the end of this volume.

The Allocation of Multinational Business Income: Reassessing the Formulary Apportionment Option

Edited by

Richard Krever
François Vaillancourt

Wolters Kluwer

Published by:
Kluwer Law International B.V.
PO Box 316
2400 AH Alphen aan den Rijn
The Netherlands
E-mail: international-sales@wolterskluwer.com
Website: lrus.wolterskluwer.com

Sold and distributed in North, Central and South America by:
Wolters Kluwer Legal & Regulatory U.S.
7201 McKinney Circle
Frederick, MD 21704
United States of America
Email: customer.service@wolterskluwer.com

Sold and distributed in all other countries by:
Air Business Subscriptions
Rockwood House
Haywards Heath
West Sussex
RH16 3DH
United Kingdom
Email: international-customerservice@wolterskluwer.com

ISBN 978-94-035-0614-2

e-Book: ISBN 978-94-035-0615-9
web-PDF: ISBN 978-94-035-0620-3

Editors

Richard Krever is a professor at the University of Western Australia Law School, Perth and an International Fellow at the Centre for Business Taxation at the University of Oxford, Oxford. He has previously held tax law drafting, design and interpretation roles with the IMF, World Bank, Australian Treasury and Australian Taxation Office and provided tax law design and drafting assistance on behalf of international organizations in many Asian, African, Caribbean, South American, Pacific and eastern European nations. Professor Krever was made a member of the Order of Australia in recognition of his contributions to tax academia in Australia.

François Vaillancourt is an emeritus professor in the Faculty of Economic Sciences, Université de Montréal and Fellow in the Center for Interuniversity Research and Analysis of Organizations (CIRANO), Montréal. He has acted as a consultant on public finance issues for the Canadian and Québec governments as well as for the IMF and the World Bank. He has worked in particular on intergovernmental finance, tax incidence and tax complexity and associated costs.

Contributors

Richard Bird is an emeritus professor in the Rotman School of Management, University of Toronto, Toronto.

Yariv Brauner holds the Hugh Culverhouse Eminent Scholar Chair in Taxation and is Professor of Law in the Levin College of Law, University of Florida, Gainesville.

J. Clifton Fleming, Jr. is Professor of Law and holder of the Ernest L. Wilkinson chair in the Brigham Young University Law School, Provo. He has held the Fulbright Distinguished Chair at the Vienna University of Economics and Business, Vienna; and the Freeland Chair in the Levin College of Law at the University of Florida, Gainesville; and has been Professor-in-Residence in the IRS Office of Chief Counsel.

Fei Gao is a research fellow in the University of Sydney Business School, University of Sydney, Sydney.

Itai Grinberg is a professor in the Law School, Georgetown University, Washington D.C.

Walter Hellerstein is Distinguished Research Professor & Francis Shackelford Distinguished Professor in Taxation Law Emeritus in the School of Law, University of Georgia, Athens.

Joe Huddleston is a managing director in the Indirect State and Local Tax group of the National Tax Office of EY LLP. He is based in Washington, D.C. Prior to working with EY, Mr Huddleston was Executive Director for the Multistate Tax Commission.

Peter Mellor is a research fellow in the Faculty of Business and Economics, Monash University, Melbourne.

Jack Mintz is the President's Fellow of the School of Public Policy at the University of Calgary, Calgary; and National Policy Advisor, EY Canada.

Robert J. Peroni is the Fondren Foundation Centennial Chair for Faculty Excellence and Professor of Law at the University of Texas School of Law at Austin. He previously was the J. Landis Martin Visiting Professor of Law and Business and the Jack N. Pritzker Distinguished Visiting Professor of Law at the Northwestern University School of Law, Chicago; the Robert Kramer Research Professor of Law at the George Washington University Law School, Washington D.C.; and Professor-in-Residence in the IRS Office of Chief Counsel.

Kerrie Sadiq is Professor of Taxation in the School of Accountancy, QUT Business School, Queensland University of Technology, Brisbane.

Stephen E. Shay is a senior lecturer in Law at Harvard Law School, Cambridge, United States. Mr Shay previously was Deputy Assistant Secretary for International Tax Affairs in the United States Department of the Treasury in the Obama Administration and a tax partner with Ropes & Gray, LLP, Boston.

Shirley Sicilian is a managing director in the State and Local Tax group of the Washington National Tax practice of KPMG US LLP and serves as the firm's National Director for State and Local Tax Controversy. She is based in Washington, D.C. Prior to working with KPMG LLP, Ms Sicilian was General Counsel for the Multistate Tax Commission.

Michael Smart is a professor in the Department of Economics at the University of Toronto, Toronto.

Antony Ting is an associate professor at the University of Sydney Business School, University of Sydney, Sydney.

John Vella is Associate Professor of Taxation at the Faculty of Law, University of Oxford, Oxford; Assistant Director of the Oxford University Centre for Business Taxation, Oxford; and a Non-Tutorial Fellow of Harris Manchester College, Oxford.

Joann Martens Weiner is an associate professor and Director of the Applied Economics master's programme at the George Washington University, Washington D.C.

Summary of Contents

Table of Contents

Acknowledgements

The research in this volume was supported by generous contributions by Center for Interuniversity Research and Analysis of Organizations (CIRANO), Montréal, and the Université de Sherbrook by a symposium at which the research was tested and critiqued and the Australian Research Council by way of a Discovery Project Grant DP180101837.

Introduction: Reassessing the Formulary Apportionment Option

Richard Krever & François Vaillancourt

The rapid spread of income taxation across developed countries and their colonies in a relatively small window of time before, during and after the First World War, coinciding with the growth of worldwide trade in a period of rapid improvements in global communication, and transport, created the conditions for emerging tax conflicts. A significant number of new income tax laws levied tax on the worldwide income of residents and domestic source income derived by non-residents. Overlapping tax claims were inevitable in the case of cross-border transactions with both the source jurisdiction in which profits were generated and the recipient's jurisdiction claiming the right to tax the same income.

Both residence and source-based tax claims were recognized as legitimate exercises of sovereignty in international law, leaving investors facing the prospect of double taxation if they earned income abroad and lived in a country that imposed residence-based taxation. The rationale for imposing tax on the global income of individual residents was relatively straightforward - personal income was often subject to a progressive tax rate scale with the aim of redistributing increments in economic capacity, a concept indifferent to the source of income. The logic behind taxing resident companies on their worldwide income was less obvious, with the common indicators of corporate residency - place of incorporation or place of central management and control - only tangentially, if at all, related to the generation of income in other jurisdictions.

The double tax problem was of serious concern to the business community, and governments responded to those concerns by asking the League of Nations to find a satisfactory resolution. Only a few months after its formation, the League appointed a committee of experts to develop mechanisms to address the problem The Committee concluded there was no principled solution - the problem arose because two jurisdictions sought and had the legal jurisdiction in international law to tax the same income.

The answer, the Committee said, was political compromise – countries could enter into bilateral treaties and agree to share the tax collection.

Separately, the Committee looked at how the source of income could be determined when the same enterprises operated across multiple jurisdictions with the many arms of the firm all contributing to the profits through intra-group transactions. Two approaches were considered. The first was to treat the many arms of the enterprise, be they branches or separate subsidiaries, as parts of a single business and determine the source of total income derived by the enterprise by reference to the factors in each jurisdiction in which it operated that contributed to gross profits: capital, labour and sales. Under this approach, intra-group transactions were ignored and intangible property owned by parts of the enterprise was disregarded. Only the presence of income-generating factors was determinative of the source of income.

The second approach, now known as separate accounting or arm's length methodology, treated each part of a multinational enterprise as if it were a separate unrelated entity and substituted arm's length prices for those used by the taxpayers. The arm's length pricing was based on comparables – the price that would be charged for comparable goods or services if the parts of an enterprise were truly independent and operating at arm's length.

Apportioning profits of cross-border enterprises by reference to a formula had long been used in subnational tax systems and for a shorter time for some national income taxes. As the international community looked in the 1930s for a consensus approach to allocating global profits, both formulary apportionment and separate accounting had reasonable prospects of adoption. However, as Richard Krever and Peter Mellor note in Chapter 1, at the international level, the pendulum swung firmly in the direction of separate accounting when the League of Nations accepted the recommendation of a US expert and incorporated separate accounting in its model treaty. Since that time, the arm's length methodology has been incorporated into all tax treaties and universally applied for international tax purposes in the domestic legislation of national governments.

I FORMULARY APPORTIONMENT IN PRACTICE

The adoption of separate accounting at the international level has not displaced the use of formulary apportionment as the preferred method of allocating profits of multi-jurisdiction enterprises at the subnational level. Decades of experience with formulary apportionment in the United States and Canada, documented by Shirley Sicilian and Joe Huddleston and Michael Smart and François Vaillancourt in Chapters 2 and 3, respectively, provide valuable lessons on both technical aspects of a formulary apportionment system in practice and, equally and perhaps more importantly, the political economy of establishing and maintaining a successful formulary apportionment regime.

While the use of factors as surrogate indicators of the place value is created or the source of income on its face sets the stage for an objective profit allocation system, policymakers enjoy significant discretion in the choice and weighting of factors. As

Michael Smart and François Vaillancourt show in Chapter 3, looking at the Canadian provincial systems, when formulary apportionment is used to divide source between multiple jurisdictions, it can be tailored to create a sustainable formula to which all parties can sign up. At the same time, the US state experience catalogued by Shirley Sicilian and Joe Huddleston in Chapter 2 shows agreements can fragment over time where some jurisdictions conclude an existing formula favours other jurisdictions at the expense of the former group.

The US and Canadian experiences demonstrate how current systems evolved. Looking forward, the very slow, but seemingly steady, march by the EU towards formulary apportionment for the allocation of profits within the Union under its Common Consolidated Corporate Tax Base (CCCTB) proposal, described by Joann Martens Weiner in Chapter 4, provides an ongoing example of the issues that must be addressed to bring different jurisdictions on board to a common formula, if that is the desired outcome.

Two models exist in respect of entities included in a formulary apportionment regime. The simpler applies separately to each legal entity but includes all branches of the entity. The broader alternative, formulary apportionment with unitary combination (or combined reporting), includes all entities within a larger economic group. The narrower formulary apportionment system, used by Canadian provinces, is relatively easily circumvented if branches are converted to separate entities. The wider unitary combination approach avoids this problem but raises a separate question of which entities should be considered part of a unitary enterprise. The experience of US states with unitary combination discussed by Walter Hellerstein in Chapter 5 provides useful lessons on applying formulary apportionment to economic entities that enjoy complete flexibility in terms of their choice of legal structures.

II ALTERNATIVES TO UNIVERSAL FORMULARY APPORTIONMENT

Despite the apparent success of formulary apportionment at the subnational level, separate accounting has prevailed at the national level since the international community chose that alternative nearly a century ago. The limited impact of advocates for a shift to formulary apportionment has led to proposals for more limited, and perhaps politically palatable, alternatives. In the absence of coordinated international agreement, one possibility is unilateral adoption of formulary apportionment. The study by J. Clifton Fleming, Jr., Robert J. Peroni and Stephen E. Shay in Chapter 6 shows that unilateral adoption of formulary apportionment can address some problems but throws up new ones to replace them. Much will depend on the design of the tax base, they suggest, and the choice of arm's length or formulary apportionment cannot therefore be considered separately from the base.

While universal adoption of formulary apportionment across the board may be elusive for the moment, a shift to a formulary approach may be feasible if limited to particular sectors, as Kerrie Sadiq explains in Chapter 7. One candidate, she notes, is digital enterprises that are particularly difficult to fit into a traditional arm's length model. This approach has received attention recently following suggestions by the

Organisation for Economic Co-operation and Development (OECD) that formulary apportionment might be the optimal way to allocate profits of digital companies. Another possible candidate might be the banking industry. In almost all jurisdictions, prudential rules require banks to segregate their pure banking operations from other activities and international agreements set out guidelines for conformity of the main elements of the service across all jurisdictions, leaving this a logical nominee for formulary apportionment applied to a sector.

III APPROACHING THE MIDDLE

The central tenet of separate accounting is the application of arm's length pricing based on the market value of comparable supplies between unconnected persons. The supposition that an uncontrolled market price exists for all intra-enterprise transactions has long been dismissed as a myth by critics who pointed out the *raison d'être* for a multinational enterprise is the synergy that derives from transactions and arrangements which could never take place between unconnected firms. This observation was long resisted by advocates of arm's length transfer pricing methodology but a shift came in the wake of the 2008-2009 global financial crisis when the leaders of the Group of 20, aware of the revenue costs of international tax avoidance, delegated to the OECD responsibility for devising measures to counter transfer pricing solutions. The 'base erosion and profit shifting' (BEPS) project devised by the OECD in response to the call for action retained the foundations of the separate account system but opened the door to innovative variations of traditional transfer pricing methodologies. These included the incorporation of formulary-like attributes into the 'profit-split' method of devising a transfer price, an approach that arguably provided arm's length advocates with cover for a de facto retreat from true separate accounting. Whether the changes amount to a gradual morphing of arm's length methodology into a quasi-formulary apportionment approach is explored by Yariv Brauner in Chapter 8.

Seeking an inclusive outcome, at an early stage the OECD opened the BEPS project to all jurisdictions, not just OECD members, and deliberately adopted vague principles, most notably the allocation of income to the jurisdiction in which 'value was created', sufficiently flexible to accommodate almost all variations that different parties to the project might wish to adopt. China, the most important economic power outside the OECD, used this flexibility to move well beyond traditional arm's length approaches to map out new profit-split methodologies that arguably go beyond formulary apportionment, bringing new factors such as inputs by users of digital social media into the calculation of profit source. The impact of this new approach is explored by Fei Gao and Antony Ting in Chapter 9.

IV FORMULARY APPORTIONMENT IN A WIDER CONTEXT

The allocation of multinational enterprise profits by means of separate accounting or formulary apportionment methodologies does not take place in a tax vacuum and determining the source of income – the place where value giving rise to profits is created – may be a suboptimal priority in the wider context of tax goals. John Vella in Chapter 10 suggests the two alternatives are better evaluated by reference to traditional tax criteria such as economic efficiency, fairness, ease of administration, robustness to avoidance and incentive compatibility.

As illustrated by the case of China noted earlier, one by-product of the OECD's extension of its 'action plans' to include much of the rest of the global community, an outreach described by the body as an 'inclusive framework', has been the development of many other hybrid and separate proposals for allocating profits. These proposals raise numerous conceptual and practical issues. Itai Grinberg in Chapter 11 suggests the principal attributes of formulary apportionment are sufficiently settled for it to serve as a benchmark for evaluating the alternative approaches that have emerged in recent years and provides guidelines as to how this might be done.

V THE PROSPECTS

However attractive formulary apportionment might appear in theory as a solution to the avoidance, distortions and unfairness of current allocation systems, its value as a global solution will only be realized if proponents can successfully navigate it through the political minefield of tax reform. It is a particularly treacherous minefield in the case of international taxation, where agreement is needed across multiple jurisdictions. Richard Bird and Jack Mintz set out a possible path forward in Chapter 12, drawing on lessons from current formulary apportionment systems and contemporary international tax developments. Central to a programme for success is recognition by advocates for formulary apportionment of the need for compromise to achieve widespread support; this may require financial transfers between winners and losers. Consensus can only be achieved with a formulary apportionment system with features that offer some benefits to all nations. The result will no doubt deviate from purists' view of a model formulary apportionment regime but can nevertheless still yield important improvements over the status quo.

Part I The Story to Date

CHAPTER 1

History and Theory of Formulary Apportionment

Richard Krever & Peter Mellor

§1.01 INTRODUCTION

From the time income taxes were first widely enacted, tax designers have been concerned with the question of how to allocate profits in transactions that incorporated labour, capital or sales inputs across several jurisdictions if each jurisdiction wished to tax the income that was 'sourced' in that jurisdiction. The intuitive solution adopted almost universally for the earliest income and predecessor taxes when an enterprise operated across borders was to allocate a share of the profits to each jurisdiction that contributed to the total profits by reference to formulas incorporating the factors that were presumed to contribute to the generation of those profits. Most commonly, the first formulas were applied unilaterally on a jurisdiction-by-jurisdiction basis and often applied on a sectoral basis to particular industries.

Formulary apportionment faded into insignificance internationally in the early part of the twentieth century as countries increasingly turned to the accounting records of enterprises to determine income within a jurisdiction, giving rise to the water's edge approach to income allocation. Starting with accounting profits, tax authorities were empowered to substitute an arm's length price based on the value of comparable transactions between unrelated persons if this differed from the transfer price nominated by a business in transactions between related parties. The water's edge approach received a significant boost internationally when the League of Nations model tax treaty endorsed this approach in the 1930s, followed by the Organisation for Economic Co-operation and Development (OECD) model treaty in 1963 and the UN model treaty in 1980.

Formulary apportionment did not disappear, however, when separate accounting emerged as the preferred system internationally. Rather, it developed into the preferred methodology for allocating business profits between states in Australia and the United States and between provinces in Canada. In the last three decades of the twentieth century, as the emergence of tax havens and the practice of associated profit shifting transfer pricing grew,[1] theoretical support for formulary apportionment at the international level also grew, with a large school of academics and tax theoreticians advocating a shift from the water's edge separate accounting system of profit allocation to a formulary apportionment approach. In contrast, the OECD and OECD members remained firmly behind the water's edge - hypothetical arm's length price system - and when California attempted to unilaterally apply formulary apportionment to find its share of the global profits of multinational firms, many countries opposing the use of formulary apportionment systems in the international sphere supported suits by taxpayers seeking to challenge the rules on constitutional grounds.

Interest in formulary apportionment picked up again in the first years of the twenty-first century when the European Union proposed to use a variation of formulary apportionment to allocate company profits among Member States signing up to the EU's proposed Common Consolidated Corporate Tax Base (CCCTB). Reactions outside the EU to the proposal were mixed. While some saw a possible renaissance of support for international formulary apportionment, others regarded it as another internal profit allocation system within a multi-jurisdiction single market akin to the US state or Canadian provincial regimes. The EU proposals turned out to be short-lived in any event as internal politics and distractions led to the effective shelving of the CCCTB programme in 2011, when the EU Commission shifted its recommendation on the CCCTB to make formulary apportionment optional,[2] a move that undoubtedly dampened the spirits of formulary apportionment advocates.

The trigger for formulary apportionment's next international revival was the global financial crisis (GFC) of 2008-09. In the 1990s, work by the OECD on what it labelled 'harmful tax competition' had made world leaders aware of the significant revenue costs of profit shifting by means of transfer pricing within multinational groups and the events of September 11, 2001 impressed upon G20 leaders the security risks posed by easy access to tax havens. The OECD's ongoing work subsequent to the terrorist attacks in New York provided G20 leaders with a fuller understanding of the links between tax havens, tax avoidance and the declining share of tax revenue collected from multinationals. Acutely aware of revenue needs, G20 leaders meeting soon after the first GFC shock agreed to delegate to the OECD responsibility for developing a comprehensive response to tax avoidance, a call that led the organization to develop its Base Erosion and Profit Shifting (BEPS) programme.

1. A comprehensive study of the growth of tax havens can be found in Vanessa Ogle, *Archipelago Capitalism: Tax Havens, Offshore Money, and the State, 1950s–1970s*, 122(5) Am. Hist. Rev. 1431 (2017).
2. European Commission, *Proposal for a Council Directive on a Common Consolidated Corporate Tax Base (CCCTB)*, COM (2011) 121/4, 16 March 2011; the European Parliament resolution of 19 April 2012 provided for a mandatory apportionment system after a transition period but the proposal in its entirety subsequently stalled in the European Council: *see* Joann M. Weiner, *The Dream is Alive: EU Tax Policy with a Common Consolidated Corporate Tax Base and Formulary Apportionment* §4.05 (this volume).

The OECD sought to use the BEPS programme as a way of reinforcing its commitment to the arm's-length system but discovered there were strong reservations by some in the wider group of external states invited to participate in the BEPS project. The organization settled on a simple but clever way of resolving the different views with the adoption of an agreement by all that the arm's length rules should be interpreted in a manner that facilitates taxation by states in which there has been 'value creation' by a multinational group[3] while leaving the core concept of 'value creation' undefined. This provided common ground for higher-level agreement on the principle while allowing participants to adopt their own interpretations of how the principle should be applied. The approach in turn has led to what some might regard as a back door to formulary apportionment through new interpretations of the profit-split transfer pricing methodology, a methodology that the OECD considered to fall within the notion of arm's length pricing. A dramatic development later in the BEPS process was the release of two documents in 2019 that foreshadowed the possible recommendation of an explicit formulary apportionment system for allocating the profits of digital enterprises (*see* further §1.06[A], below).

Concurrently, the revival of the CCCTB initiative in Europe may lead to the adoption of another formulary apportionment regime, admittedly in a single economic market but for the first time involving participation by sovereign nations. This, along with the possibility of unilateral or sectoral adoption, and the appearance of formulary apportionment-like interpretations of arm's length methodology suggest the story of formulary apportionment may still have some chapters to be written.

This chapter examines the historical development of the formulary apportionment approach in key jurisdictions.

§1.02 FORMULARY APPORTIONMENT IN THE NINETEENTH CENTURY

The earliest predecessors to today's multinational corporations long predate the modern independent state. Created by royal charters in the opening years of the seventeenth century, companies such as the Dutch East India Company and English East India Company established footprints in colonies across the globe, but always operating within the confines of an empire or home state. The creation of modern limited liability companies in the mid-nineteenth century followed by the growth of international commerce in the later part of that century and decolonization in the twentieth century laid the foundations for the modern multinational enterprise. The gradual rise of income tax from the late 1800s until the First World War, when it quickly spread across much of the globe, led to the question of how the income of a multi-jurisdiction business should be allocated to the jurisdictions in which the business operated if each levied an income tax.

As early adopters of both income taxation and predecessor taxes, the US subnational states provided useful illustrations of early design choices in the case of

3. OECD, *Actions 8-10 – 2015 Final Reports, Aligning Transfer Pricing Outcomes with Value Creation*, OECD/G20 Base Erosion and Profit Shifting Project (OECD Publishing 2015).

cross-jurisdictional enterprises. The treatment of these businesses was considered by US states first in the context of property taxes levied on businesses owning assets such as railways or telegraph lines that crossed several jurisdictions and later state corporate 'capital taxes' applied to companies within the jurisdiction.

The apportionment of taxing rights over multistate businesses involving property such as railroads and telegraph lines was relatively straightforward. Rather than seek to determine precisely where revenue was derived, jurisdictions simply applied a 'unit rule' that looked at the length of track or lines in the state relative to the total length of track or lines of the business. Apportionment of general capital taxes was more nuanced. These taxes were adopted by a number of states in the decades following the end of various state corporate income tax laws and the repeal of the US federal income tax after the Civil War. While notionally based on the 'capital stock' of a business in a state, in effect the taxes were imposed on a share of distributed profits equal to the proportional value of the total assets of a company that were used in the course of transacting business in the state.[4] Originally levied only on companies incorporated in the state, the Pennsylvania tax was widened in 1868 to any company doing business in the state, regardless of its place of incorporation,[5] and New York followed with a similar extension in 1880.[6]

Abroad, a similar approach was used for an 1884 corporation tax in the German state of Baden, which apportioned income to the jurisdiction based on the proportion of the business' capital employed in the state.[7] The French dividend tax of 1872 taxed dividends of foreign companies with branches in France according to a 'taxable quota' based on factors determined by a special governmental commission including the proportion of assets in France compared to total assets and the turnover in France compared with total turnover.[8]

4. *Commonwealth v. Standard Oil Company*, 101 Pa. 119, 146 (20 November 1882). *See* Edwin R. A. Seligman, *Taxation of Corporations III*, 5(4) Pol. Sci. Q. 636, 648 (1890). The US Supreme Court described the tax in *obiter* as a 'franchise tax in the nature of an income tax': *Mercantile Bank v. New York*, 121 US 138, 158 (4 April 1887), referred to in Edwin R. A. Seligman, *Taxation of Corporations II*, 5(3) Pol. Sci. Q. 438, 445 (1890).
5. Edwin R. A. Seligman, *Taxation of Corporations I*, 5(2) Pol. Sci. Q. 269, 299 (1890), citing Pa. Laws of 1868, no. 69, ss. 4 and 6.
6. New York Laws of 1880 c. 542 (enacted on 1 June 1880), s. 3; Seligman, *Taxation of Corporations I*, *supra* n. 5, at 301. This era was one 'marked by the expansion and development of large scale business, and the corporate form of organization', and the new forms of corporation tax involved some political controversy in New York at least: Merlin Harold Hunter, *The Development of Corporation Taxation in the State of New York* 22 (PhD thesis, Faculty of the Graduate School, Cornell University, 1917). While Pennsylvania also maintained significant state tax exemptions for manufacturing companies, the policies of the states in many instances during this period (the Progressive Era) have also been seen as evidencing a reversal in the 'race to the bottom' policy competition between them up to that point to favour corporations at the expense of the state revenue: Dante J. Scala, *Taxing the Intangibles: How States Pursued Corporate Wealth in the Early Twentieth Century*, 27(2) Bus. & Econ. Hist. 431 (1998).
7. Seligman, *Taxation of Corporations III*, *supra* n. 4, at 660.
8. Mitchell B. Carroll, *Observations on the Report of the Committee of the National Tax Association on Uniformity and Reciprocity in State Tax Legislation, Especially with regard to the Allocation of Income of International Enterprises*, 24 Proceedings of the Annual Conference on Taxation under the Auspices of the National Tax Association 333, 337 (1931).

The use of a formula to determine income sourced within the jurisdiction for income tax purposes first appeared in the Australian colonies in the late nineteenth century. A company tax based on distributed dividends adopted in Tasmania in 1880 was followed by income taxes imposed by South Australia, Tasmania, Victoria, New South Wales and Western Australia. Queensland imposed a tax on distributed dividends to the extent profits were attributable to business in that colony. Profits attributed to South Australia, Tasmania and New South Wales for the purpose of their income taxes were determined using water's edge separate accounting, but the taxes in other colonies (states after 1901) were determined initially using unilateral formulas adopted by each colony. The Queensland tax was based on the proportion of property in the colony,[9] while the Victorian income tax was levied on the basis of receipts from the state.[10] Western Australia first proposed to follow the Queensland model but ultimately used water's edge separate accounting following concerns about loss companies.

§1.03 FORMULARY APPORTIONMENT AND SUBNATIONAL TAXES IN THE TWENTIETH CENTURY

The spread of state income taxation in Australia and the United States in the early years of the twentieth century provided the basis for modern formulary apportionment theory. The debate and consideration of these rules took place in parallel with debate over the optimal method to allocate international taxing rights over investment and business income (discussed further in §1.04), a debate that involved many of the same experts but ultimately followed a different path, recommending adoption of a separate accounting arm's length model.

[A] Early US Formulary Apportionment

Wisconsin was the first US state to impose a general income tax with the tax applying to worldwide income of residents and income 'derived from sources within the state' by non-residents. Income 'sourced' in Wisconsin was calculated on the basis of the proportion of a company's capital assets within the state and business conducted in the state.[11] T. S. Adams, the University of Wisconsin-Madison and later Yale University economics professor who played an important role in the drafting of the Wisconsin tax (and who later designed the US foreign tax credit regime and was one of the first theorists to propose a value added tax), described the calculation of Wisconsin-source income as 'both intricate and perplexing'.[12] He subsequently proposed in 1917 replacement of the ambiguous and difficult to calculate 'business' factor with a formula

9. Dividend Duty Act 1890 (Qld), s. 9. The relevant proportion of average capital was defined by reference to the corresponding proportion of the total assets of the company wherever situated.
10. Income Tax Act 1895 (Vic.), s. 10(4) and Income Tax Regulations 1895, reg. 17.
11. L. 1911 c. 658, s. 3; Corporations Act, c. 85.
12. T. S. Adams, *The Significance of the Wisconsin Income Tax*, 28(4) Pol. Sci. Q. 569, 578-579 (1913).

based on the proportion of a company's property and payroll located in the state, with payroll acting as a proxy for a range of activities that contribute to business income including production, marketing, purchasing and sales. In the short term, he suggested that an arbitrary weighting of factors would be necessary, but he thought eventually the weighting could be determined more 'scientifically'.[13]

The precedent for unilateral adoption of a formula to determine the source of income based on an arbitrary weighting of factors had been established and the approach was followed by other states. Two years after Adams' call for a more scientific approach to state formulary apportionment, Massachusetts unilaterally adopted a three-factor apportionment formula,[14] based on the proportion of a company's tangible property, labour costs and sales receipts attributable to the state. Significantly, in the course of upholding the constitutional validity of the unilateral formulary apportionment approach, the US Supreme Court suggested it was technically impossible to determine precisely what share of the profits of a multistate enterprise was attributable to a state, justifying the measurement by use of a surrogate formula.[15]

The proliferation of unilateral and differing approaches across states prompted the National Tax Association in 1920 to appoint a committee charged with investigating options for the allocation of income by source where enterprises operated across states. The committee reported at the 1922 National Tax Association conference, favouring a uniform mathematical formula over water's edge separate accounting, which it labelled 'specific allocation'. The most serious problem with specific allocation, the committee concluded, was the significant administrative and compliance costs entailed in case-by-case determinations. A formula, the committee suggested, would yield appropriate results 90% of the time while alternatives for the remaining 10% were investigated.

The National Tax Association committee recommended a formula with equal weighting given to property and 'business', with the latter including both sales and amounts paid for labour and material.[16] This approach was based on Treasury data that indicated business returns were usually twice the return on government bond rates, leading the committee to conclude that half of the profits realized by a business were attributable to the property employed in the business and the other half due to the labour and material inputs. Unlike the Massachusetts three-factor formula, the formula

13. T. S. Adams, *The Taxation of Business*, 11 Proceedings of the Annual Conference on Taxation under the Auspices of the National Tax Association 185, 193-194 (1917). Cited by the author (in support of the source principle as a tax on business affecting producers) in T. S. Adams, *Fundamental Problems of Federal Income Taxation*, 35(4) Q.J. Econ. 527, 541-542 (1921). Also cited as a significant development in William E. Tuttle, *The Proposed Uniform State Taxation Statute*, 16 Proceedings of the Annual Tulane Tax Institute 796, 797 (1966).
14. General Acts 1919 c. 355, s. 6, https://archive.org/details/actsresolvespass1919mass/page/442; National Industrial Conference Board, *State Income Taxes, Vol. I: Historical Development* 14-15 (New York 1930).
15. Brandeis J., at 120-121 in *Underwood Typewriter Co. v. Chamberlain*, 254 US 113 (15 November 1920).
16. Carl S. Lamb, H. H. Burbank, W. S. Elliott, R. M. Haig, Alexander Holmes, Henry B. Nelson, Frank D. Strader & J. F. Zoller, *Report of the Committee on the Apportionment Between States of Taxes on Mercantile and Manufacturing Business*, 15 Proceedings of the Annual Conference on Taxation under the Auspices of the National Tax Association 198, 206 (1922).

proposed by the National Tax Association committee attributed no share of the profits to a sales factor. The formulary approach recommended by the committee was endorsed by T. S. Adams at the time, though he was wary about the equal weighting used in the formula.[17]

The matter was far from settled, however, with a 1931 meeting of the National Tax Association focusing on the merits of separate accounting in interstate allocation,[18] a reconsideration supported indirectly by a US Supreme Court decision that cautioned against the use of arbitrary formulas that were 'out of proportion' to the actual business carried on in the state.[19] T. S. Adams once again supported a general apportionment formula, subject to a right for the Commissioner to call for separate accounting to be provided.[20]

By 1933, the National Tax Association had swung completely behind formulary apportionment and endorsed the Massachusetts formula.[21] Significantly, the rationale for favouring formulary apportionment was not that it provided an effective means of sourcing income across jurisdictions but rather that it could approximate the outcome of separate accounting with less expense, implying separate accounts would produce the most accurate measurement.[22]

[B] The Shift to Unitary Taxation

The spread of formulary apportionment across the United States raised a further conceptual and legal question in addition to the question of which formula to use to allocate profits where an enterprise operated across several states. This was whether the formula should be applied separately to each entity in a company group or on a combined basis, consolidating the accounts of legally separate enterprises that in a commercial or economic sense formed part of a single unitary business.

---

17. T. S. Adams in *Discussion – Apportionment of Taxes Between States*, 15 Proceedings of the Annual Conference on Taxation under the Auspices of the National Tax Association 215, 221 (1922).
18. Charles W. Gerstenberg, *Allocation of Business Income*, in Seth T. Cole, Franklin S. Edmonds, Charles W. Gerstenberg, John S. Edwards, Morris Frey, Fred R. Fairchild, Mark Graves, Henry F. Long, Harley L. Lutz, Blaine F. Moore, Ray L. Riley, James L. Sayler, H. P. Sneed & J. T. White, *Report of the Committee of the National Tax Association on Uniformity and Reciprocity in State Taxing Legislation*, 24 Proceedings of the Annual Conference on Taxation under the Auspices of the National Tax Association 294, 308 (1931).
19. The Supreme Court reached this conclusion in respect of a North Carolina formula that looked only at the proportion of real estate and tangible property in the state without regard to sales or labour costs: *Hans Rees' Sons, Inc. v. North Carolina*, 283 US 123, noted in Gerstenberg, *supra* n. 18, at 309, n. 2.
20. T. S. Adams, *Allocation versus Apportionment*, 24 Proceedings of the Annual Conference on Taxation under the Auspices of the National Tax Association 345, 347 (1931).
21. Franklin S. Edmonds, John S. Edwards, William S. Elliott, Fred R. Fairchild, Charles W. Gerstenberg, Mark Graves, Robert Murray Haig, Henry F. Long, Harley L. Lutz, A. J. Maxwell, Blaine F. Moore, Ray L. Riley & J. T. White, *Report of Committee on Uniformity and Reciprocity in State Taxing Legislation*, 26 Proceedings of the Annual Conference on Taxation under the Auspices of the National Tax Association (Phoenix, Arizona) 259, 261-263 (1933).
22. Edmonds *et al.*, *Report of Committee on Uniformity and Reciprocity in State Taxing Legislation*, *supra* n. 21, at 262-263.

The initial moves towards applying formulary apportionment in state income taxation on a combined unitary basis came in the early 1920s when the state of New York sought to assess the income of car manufacturer Studebaker's subsidiary responsible for all sales in that state calculated as a proportion of the combined profits of the group. The New York tax commission argued that it should be able to calculate the subsidiary's profits using unitary accounting on the basis that intra-group transfer prices had been deliberately set to avoid tax. The accounts of the subsidiary responsible for sales in New York revealed a loss as a result of intra-group transfer prices insufficient to offset overheads or other selling expenses. The state lost its bid, however, when the New York Court of Appeals ruled there was no statutory basis for the use of combined unitary accounting proposed by the tax commission.[23]

The theoretical basis to extend formulary apportionment to combined unitary group companies was set out not long afterwards in an important paper by former Treasury official and Columbia law professor Roswell Magill.[24] The implementation breakthrough came in 1936 when Californian tax officials moved to counter profit shifting by Hollywood movie production businesses using separate distribution entities in Nevada.[25] Unlike the earlier New York initiative, the Californian move was founded in statutory authority that provided the tax office with authority to adopt procedures necessary to determine income attributable to the state.[26] Combined unitary taxation had arrived.

[C] The Path to Uniformity in US State Formulary Apportionment

The inconsistent rules for US state formulary apportionment that developed during the interwar years prompted attempts at the national level to mandate a uniform state formulary apportionment system across the United States in 1945 and again in 1947 but neither led to federal legislation.[27] Further efforts at the state level followed. A Governors' Conference of 1953 adopted a resolution requesting the Council of State Governments to study the problem of non-uniform formulas and interpretations, and

---

23. *People ex rel. Studebaker Corp. v. Gilchrist*, 155 N.E. 68 (N.Y. 1926) (New York Court of Appeals). *See further* George T. Altman & Frank M. Keesling, *Allocation of Income in State Taxation* 165-166 (Commerce Clearing House Inc. 1946) and Joel S. Newman, *Two New York Cases*, 34(1) Touro L. Rev. 301 (2018).
24. Roswell Magill, *Allocation of Income by Corporate Contract*, 44(6) Harv. L. Rev. 935 (1931), citing *Cliffs Chemical Co.* case, 193 Wis. 295, 214 N.W. 447 (1927). This was based on the issue of whether a shareholder of the local subsidiary could object to a contract 'on the ground that the corporation was being deprived of profits to which it is legitimately entitled'. Indicia would include repeated losses, a contract price no higher than cost or materially lower than market, a rate of return less than for similar businesses and rate of return less than that before the contract.
25. The initiative is discussed in Joe Huddleston & Shirley Sicilian, *History and Considerations for Combined Reporting: Will States Adopt a Model Combined Reporting Statute?*, [2008] St. & Local Tax Law.: Symposium Edition 3, 7-8 and Frank M. Keesling, *California's Contributions to State and Local Taxation*, [1979] 4 B.Y.U. L. Rev. 809, 831, 833; see also Frank M. Keesling, *A Current Look at the Combined Report and Uniformity in Allocation Practices*, 42(2) J. Tax'n 106 (1975).
26. Nancy Foran & Dahli Gray, *The Evolution of the Unitary Tax Apportionment Method*, 15(1) Accounting Historians J. 65, 72-74 (1988).
27. Tuttle, *supra* n. 13, at 798-799.

the following year the Controllership Foundation (the research arm of the Controllers Institute, an organization representing financial executives) issued a research report finding compliance cost savings from a uniform formula.[28] Finally, in 1957, the National Conference of Commissioners on Uniform State Laws (Uniform Law Commission) developed a model Uniform Division of Income for Tax Purposes Act (UDITPA) that proposed universal adoption of the Massachusetts three-factor apportionment formula, to be applied separately to entities (including branches) with no provision for unitary combination with associated corporate entities. UDITPA also provided a right for a taxpayer to petition for separate accounting or the Commissioner to require it if the apportionment did not give rise to a fair reflection of business activity.

The UDITPA proposal was met with substantial criticism from a number of bodies including the National Tax Association and Controllers Institute and prompted a campaign by a variety of organizations launched to achieve uniformity on terms favoured by the organizations' sponsors.[29] As one commentator put it, small business sought 'a uniform system in which there were no taxes', big business, 'one which would permit separate negotiation with each of the states, with different conclusions reached in each jurisdiction' and administrators, a system 'produc[ing] the revenues demanded for sound budgetary purposes ... [with,] to the extent possible, a complete lack of controversy and litigation'.[30]

A greater take-up of UDITPA by states in the mid-1960s occurred as a pre-emptive move to avoid federal intervention in state income tax systems. Responding to significant business pressure, Congress in 1959 had acted to negate one element of a state law that the US Supreme Court decision had upheld[31] and at the same time initiated a Congressional committee process that yielded a recommendation for sweeping and far-reaching federal legislation to govern state income tax laws.[32] The prospect of federal intervention based on the power of the federal government to

28. Arthur D. Lynn, Jr., *Formula Apportionment of Corporate Income for State Tax Purposes: Natura Non Facit Saltum*, 18(1) Ohio St. L.J. 84, 87-88 (1957).
29. The Controllers' Institute, which had originally reported compliance cost savings from a uniform formula (*see* Lynn, *supra* n. 28, at 87, n. 19), was critical of the proposed formula in terms of the 'throwback rule' included in UDITPA reassigning sales to the state of production where a state of sale did not tax corporate income: *see* Arthur D. Lynn, Jr., *The Uniform Division of Income for Tax Purposes Act Re-Examined*, 46(6) Va. L. Rev. 1257, 1266 (1960). For further discussion of the throwback rule, see Vernon B. Savoie & Michael L. Burr, *The Throwback Rule: Concepts, Components and Planning Opportunities*, 2(1) J. St. Tax'n 19 (1983).
30. Tuttle, *supra* n. 13, at 800. The author was then Director of Individual Income Tax in the Louisiana Department of Revenue.
31. Public Law 86-272 (Interstate Income Law), reversing the effect of *Northwestern States Portland Cement Co. v. Minnesota*, 358 US 450 (24 February 1959). *See further* Note, *State Taxation of Interstate Commerce: Public Law 86-272*, 46(2) Va. L. Rev. 297; Joe B. Huddleston & Shirley K. Sicilian, *Should UDITPA be Revisited?*, [2009/10] St. & Local Tax Law.: Symposium Edition 191, 194-195.
32. Jerome R. Hellerstein, *Federal Legislation on State Taxation of Interstate Commerce: Key Areas of Controversy*, 12th Annual Tax Conference 21, 23 (1966).

oversee interstate commerce greatly worried state legislators,[33] prompting widespread adoption of UDITPA, a move that successfully forestalled Congressional action.

The three-factor formula set out in UDITPA was viewed with favour in states that housed employees, capital and customers. It produced significantly less revenue in those states hosting only customers, prompting some states to shift to a single sales factor apportionment formula, a practice that was upheld by the Supreme Court in 1978.[34] Later variations that appeared in different states were also validated by the Supreme Court, which also affirmed the right of states to apply formulary apportionment on the basis of a combined report for all entities in a single business group.[35]

The growing fragmentation of a uniform formula prompted the Multistate Tax Commission to revise UDITPA, and a new version of the Act adopted in 2015 recommended adoption of a three-factor formula including double-weighting of sales but ultimately left to each state the determination of the factors to use in the apportionment formula and the weighting of each factor.[36]

[D] Australian and Canadian Subnational Developments

[1] Australia

All of the Australian states had imposed general income taxes by 1907. The diversity in Australian colonial approaches used prior to federation in 1901 continued in the early years of the twentieth century, with formulary apportionment often provided for by statute as a fallback method where separate accounting could not be used. The inconsistencies and resulting double taxation of some multistate businesses led to pressure for a more uniform approach to be developed, and in 1929 the Melbourne Chamber of Commerce proposed a formula as a solution to the problem. It suggested that in the case of goods manufactured in one state and sold in another, two-thirds of the profit should be allocated to the manufacturing state and one-third to the destination state, while half the profits on goods sold by a wholesale or retail vendor through an agent or branch in another state should be taxed in the buyer's state.

This apportionment scheme recommended by the Melbourne Chamber of Commerce was subsequently adopted by South Australia and Victoria in 1930 and 1931,

---

33. Among other things, the federal law may have established, in the words of one expert, 'a roadmap for the creation of "nowhere income", income that no state subjects to tax'. *See* Charles E. McLure, Jr., *Understanding Uniformity and Diversity in State Corporate Income Taxes*, 61(1) Nat'l Tax J. 141, 149 (2008).
34. *Moorman Mfg. Co. v. Bair*, 437 US 267 (1978) endorsing Iowa's single sales factor formula.
35. *See, e.g., Mobil Oil Corp. v. Commissioner of Taxes of Vermont* 445 US 425 (1980) (inclusion of dividends received by a non-resident company in its apportionable income).
36. Multistate Tax Commission, *Model Compact Article IV, Division of Income (UDITPA), as revised by Multistate Tax Commission July 29, 2015*, art. 9, http://www.mtc.gov/Uniformity/Article-IV. *See further* §1.06[D], *infra*.

respectively,[37] and then in 1936-37 incorporated into harmonized state income tax laws adopted by all the states following the recommendations of a Royal Commission report in 1934.[38] Separately the harmonized income tax laws included on a contingent basis (subject to universal adoption) a specific formulary apportionment rule for banks.[39] The uniform formulary apportionment experiment came to an end soon afterwards when the federal government in 1942, as a 'temporary' wartime measure, effectively appropriated the state income tax systems for the duration of the world war. The federal government subsequently declined to reinstate room for state income taxation after the war and has enjoyed a monopoly in the field since that time.

Separately from state developments, a quasi-formulary apportionment was also adopted in Australia for federal income tax purposes in respect of exporters. Prior to 1930, resident taxpayers in Australia were subject to tax only on Australian-source income. Pressure for a formula apportionment came not from tax authorities concerned about transfer pricing but rather exporters seeking exemption for a portion of profits attributable to sales abroad. The success of a manufacturing firm in obtaining a 50% allocation of profits on export sales to foreign sources (and hence exempt from Australian taxation)[40] was followed by a similar 50% allocation for a wool and skins exporting business.[41]

[2] Canada

As noted elsewhere in this volume,[42] the Canadian provinces entered the field of corporate income taxation in various years between the late nineteenth century and 1939. Taxes were generally levied on income sourced in the province, though Ontario's 1932 corporate income tax imposed liability without any territorial limitation,[43] with a 1935 amendment extending the tax to any business having an office in the province or conducting business in the province.[44] The resulting double taxation was partially mitigated by the adoption in 1939 of a measure allowing Ontario companies a

37. Taxation Act 1930 (SA); Income Tax Acts Amendment Act 1931 (Vic.). *See* Richard Krever & Peter Mellor, *The Development of Centralised Income Taxation in Australia, 1901-1942*, in *Studies in the History of Tax Law, Vol. 7*, 363, 375 (Peter Harris & Dominic de Cogan eds., Hart Publishing 2015).
38. Royal Commission on Taxation (Justice David Ferguson, chair), *Second Report of the Royal Commission on Taxation* 83, 84 (5 February 1934).
39. *See, e.g.*, Income Tax (Management) Act 1936 (NSW), Pt. III, Div. 11.
40. 1 CTBR Case 42 (c. 1926); the High Court declined to decide on the Commissioner's appeal holding the question of source of income was a question of fact, not law, that had been decided at the lower-level tribunal. This High Court decision is apparently the case on that issue (referring to an appeal from an unspecified Board of Review decision) reported at *Federal Commissioner of Taxation v. Lewis Berger & Sons (Australia) Ltd* (1927) 39 CLR 468 (Starke J.).
41. *Michell v. Federal Commissioner of Taxation* (1927) 46 CLR 413 (Starke J.).
42. *See* Michael Smart & François Vaillancourt, *Formulary Apportionment in Canada and Taxation of Corporate Income in 2019: Current Practice, Origins and Evaluation* §3.03 (this volume).
43. *See* (Ontario) Corporations Tax Act s. 3a (from 1932). *See also*, by contrast (Quebec) Corporation Tax Act s. 5a (tax on 'profits earned in the Province') (from 1932).
44. (Ontario) Corporations Tax Act s. 3a(1) and (2) (from 1935).

deduction, but not credit, for taxes paid in other provinces.[45] Not long afterwards, this and other problems resulting from inconsistencies in provincial legislation disappeared as the Canadian federal government appropriated the income tax field during World War II in a similar way to that taken by the federal government in Australia.

Unlike the case in Australia, the Canadian federal government agreed after the war to relinquish some of its taxing rights to allow provinces to resume provincial income taxation, which they did on a staggered basis, in many cases under arrangements involving federal collection of the tax. The post-war resumption of provincial income was eventually harmonized in 1956 under a 'standard corporation income tax' model[46] that allocated a company's profits to a permanent establishment in different provinces on the basis of sales and payroll, with fiscal equalization between provinces removing any significant pressure for provinces to make any unilateral departures from this formula.[47] The Canadian provinces have never taken up combined reporting, though it was recommended in 1993 by an Ontario government-appointed tax review commission.[48]

§1.04 THE LEAGUE OF NATIONS, OECD AND THE TRIUMPH OF ARM's LENGTH SEPARATE ACCOUNTING ALLOCATION OF PROFITS AT THE INTERNATIONAL LEVEL

The divergence between international practice and subnational approaches to the allocation of income derived by enterprises operating in multiple jurisdictions is to a large extent explicable by the fundamentally different concerns of the designers of the two systems. Subnational income taxes were mostly enacted as source-based taxes, and the primary concern was the allocation of business income to various sources. The prompt for international income allocation rules was a concern over the prospect of double taxation as nations levied tax on both a residence and source basis. In the absence of unilateral relief measures, enterprises operating across borders would face separate taxes in the home state and the foreign jurisdictions in which the business had operations.[49] The problem became a serious international issue with the rapid expansion of national income taxes across developed countries during and shortly after the First World War and elsewhere during the interwar years.

---

45. *See, e.g.* (Ontario) Corporations Tax Act s. 14(7)(d) (from 1939); *see also* (Quebec) Corporation Tax Act ss. 6 and 9 (from 1947).
46. Federal-Provincial Tax-Sharing Arrangements Act 1956 (Can.), 4-5 Eliz. II, c. 29, s. 2(1)(d). *See* D. B. Perry, *Financing the Canadian Federation, 1867 to 1995: Setting the Stage for Change* 54-61 (Canadian Tax Foundation 1997).
47. *See* Smart & Vaillancourt, *Formulary Apportionment in Canada and Taxation of Corporate Income in 2019: Current Practice, Origins and Evaluation* §3.04[C] (this volume).
48. Ontario, Fair Tax Commission, *Fair Taxation in a Changing World* 415-416 (University of Toronto Press 1993). A subsequent study in 2015 again downplayed the risks of tax planning by corporate groups on the basis that such decisions would involve a range of factors in addition to tax: Canada, Ministry of Finance, *Interprovincial Tax Planning by Corporate Groups in Canada: A Review of the Evidence*, in *Tax Expenditures and Evaluations 2014*, 71, 87 (24 February 2015).
49. The literature on this historical development of the tax treaty system at the international level is extensive. *See, e.g.*, recently, Michael J. Graetz & Michael M. O'Hear, *The 'Original Intent' of US*

The switch in the United States in 1918 from a deduction for foreign taxes to a full credit removed the risk of double taxation for US enterprises, but the problem remained in other major economic powers such as the United Kingdom. At the same time, the unilateral foreign tax credit effectively stripped away an important part of the US tax base by ceding taxing rights to source jurisdictions and leaving the United States with only a residual taxing power if its tax rates were higher than those of the source country. Pressure grew for relief from double taxation where the home state provided no credits for foreign taxes and for a more even distribution of taxing rights where it did.

Shortly after the formation of the League of Nations in early 1920, an International Financial Conference in Brussels recommended that the League of Nations consider the issue of double taxation[50] and the League referred the issue to its Financial Committee which commissioned four economists (Professor Bruins from France, Professor Einaudi from Italy, Professor Seligman from the United States and Sir Josiah Stamp from the United Kingdom) to study the issue. Prior to the release of their report in 1923,[51] the League established a committee whose work led to the publication in 1927 and 1928 of draft bilateral tax treaties. Both the 1923 report and later draft treaties reflected a view held by most committee members that profits derived from active businesses were attributable to inputs by the source jurisdiction and that country should have first and primary taxing rights over this income, while profits from passive investments should be taxed mostly by the residence country, with negotiated caps setting the maximum source country tax that could be levied on this income. An alternative approach that would tax profits based on the destination of outputs (sales) rather than the source as indicated by the location of inputs used to generate the goods or services sold elsewhere developed by the International Chamber of Commerce at its Second Congress in Rome in March 1923 gained no traction with the designers of the model income tax treaties.[52]

The 1923 report that forms the foundation for much of our modern international tax system suggested that each country should be entitled to tax 'the portion of the income produced' in the territory of that state but largely left open the question of how business income should be attributed to individual jurisdictions where an enterprise

International Taxation, 46(5) Duke L.J. 1021 (1997); Sol Picciotto, *Is the International Tax System Fit for Purpose, Especially for Developing Countries?* (International Centre for Tax and Development Working Paper 13, September 2013); Sunita Jogarajan, *Double Taxation and the League of Nations* (Cambridge University Press 2018); Rebecca M. Kysar, *Unraveling the Tax Treaty*, Minn. L. Rev. (2019, forthcoming); Michael Kobetsky, *International Taxation of Permanent Establishments: Principles and Policy* (Cambridge University Press 2011); Richard Woodward, *The Evolution of the International Corporate Tax Regime, 1920-2008*, in *Business, Civil Society and the 'New' Politics of Corporate Tax Justice: Paying a Fair Share?* 22 (Richard Eccleston & Ainsley Elbra eds., Edward Elgar 2018).

50. Ke Chin Wang, *International Double Taxation of Income: Relief Through International Agreement 1921-1945*, 59(1) Harv. L. Rev. 73, 81 (1945).
51. Professors Bruins, Einaudi, Seligman & Sir Josiah Stamp, *Report on Double Taxation Submitted to the Financial Committee of the League of Nations* (Economic and Financial Commission, League of Nations, Geneva, 5 April 1923).
52. Bret Wells & Cym H. Lowell, *Income Tax Treaty Policy in the 21st Century: Residence vs. Source*, 5(1) Colum. J. Tax L. 1, 15-16, 18 (2014); Kysar, *supra* n. 49, at 4, citing Wells & Lowell.

operated across two or more countries. It suggested the fallback rule should be separate accounting for each entity or branch but indicated there could be agreements between countries on the rules for apportionment where separate accounts did not exist (as might be the case with branches of foreign companies). The commentary to the 1928 draft model treaty based on a 1927 report by a Committee of Technical Experts of the League was more ambiguous, bringing in the concept of a 'permanent establishment' as the basis for taxing rights of a source country[53] and in the case of a taxpayer with a permanent establishment in more than country suggesting only that the tax administrations of treaty partners should 'come to an arrangement as to the basis for apportionment' if the enterprise operated in both jurisdictions.[54]

Recognizing the need for more concrete guidance, the League commissioned a study on income allocation by international tax lawyer Mitchell B. Carroll. Carroll had previously studied the use by many jurisdictions of formulas to allocate global income,[55] but his report,[56] published in 1933, recommended the calculation of business income in each jurisdiction as if each branch were an independent taxpayer dealing at arm's length with all other parts of the enterprise. As Carroll later explained, referring to the treaty as it was revised immediately after the publication of his report,[57] the net income of each branch was calculated as 'if it were an independent enterprise engaged in the same or similar activities under the same or similar conditions'.[58] The incorporation of separate accounts and arm's length methodology in the model treaty was, Carroll noted, a 'decided victory' for the advocates of separate accounting as the basic method for allocating taxable income over the supporters of fractional apportionment.[59]

In the course of his 'headlong rush' to secure the separate accounts or water's edge system of income allocation,[60] Carroll acknowledged, but largely dismissed, observations that the system was not without problems. Central to the separate accounts system is the use of the hypothetical arm's length price or comparable that an independent unrelated entity would use for sales and purchases. Carroll conceded that

53. *See* Wang, *supra* n. 50, at 77-78, citing the *Report Presented by the Committee of Technical Experts on Double Taxation and Tax Evasion*, Draft of a Bilateral Convention for the Prevention of Double Taxation (1927).
54. League of Nations, *Report Presented by the General Meeting of Government Experts on Double Taxation and Tax Evasion, Double Taxation and Tax Evasion* 5 (Economic and Financial Commission, Geneva, October 1928).
55. Mitchell B. Carroll, *A Brief Survey of Methods of Allocating Taxable Income Throughout the World*, in *Lectures on Taxation* 131, 151-153 and 168-170 (Roswell Magill ed., Commerce Clearing House 1932).
56. Mitchell B. Carroll, *Taxation of Foreign and National Enterprises, Vol. 4: Methods of Allocating Taxable Income* (League of Nations, Geneva 1933).
57. The triumph of separate accounting over formulary apportionment in the League of Nations model treaty is set out in Wells & Lowell, *supra* n. 52, at 39.
58. Mitchell B. Carroll, *Allocation of Business Income: The Draft Convention of the League of Nations*, 34(3) Colum. L. Rev. 473 (1934), referring also to the 1933 draft Convention.
59. *Ibid.*, 473; for a fuller accounting of Carroll's role, *see* Sara L. McGaughey & Pascalis Raimondos, *Shifting MNE Taxation from National to Global Profits: A Radical Reform Long Overdue*, 50(9) J. Int'l Bus. Stud. 1668 (2019).
60. Stanley I. Langbein, *The Unitary Method and the Myth of Arm's Length*, 30 Tax Notes 625, 634-637 (1986).

the hypothetical arm's length price could not be readily established in many cases, necessitating a case-by-case determination by the taxpayer and tax officials,[61] and further accepted the case for fractional apportionment in subnational income taxation.[62]

The ascendancy of separate accounting in the international income tax system was cemented in 1963 when the OECD published its first model income tax treaty largely based on the League of Nations precedents. Disquiet by capital importing countries over the recognition in the OECD model of source country taxing rights for business income attributable to a permanent establishment but exclusive residence country taxing rights for all other business income and very limited (capped) taxing rights for source countries for most types of investment income led the UN to issue an alternative model in 1980. However, it, too, accepted separate accounting as the basis for profit allocation of a multinational enterprise.

The apparent triumph of arm's length methodology over formulary apportionment did not mean the end of consideration of the formulary apportionment option. In the United States, one prompt for further consideration of formulary apportionment, somewhat ironically, was the promulgation in the early 1960s by the US Treasury of transfer pricing regulations intended to reinforce the arm's length methodology used by the federal government. The strengthened arm's length rules prompted the House of Representatives to pass an amendment of the transfer pricing provision providing for a three-factor formula apportionment of gains from sales of goods. The measure failed to pass the Senate, however, which instead invited the Treasury to make further regulations on transfer pricing methodology. Those rules affirmed traditional transfer pricing methodology based on the use of comparables or arm's length pricing, relegating alternative profit-split methods to calculate appropriate transfer prices to a last choice.[63] Separately, parts of the business community began to advocate in favour of formulary apportionment in the hope of forestalling rules that would eliminate deferral of tax on foreign source income derived through foreign subsidiaries.[64] Those proposals also failed to win the support of legislators.

§1.05 PRELUDE TO THE GLOBAL FINANCIAL CRISIS

Two stories on the allocation for tax purposes of profits realized by enterprises operating across borders ran in parallel in the closing decades of the twentieth century and the first years of the current one prior to the global financial crisis of 2008-2009. One concerned the use of formulary apportionment to allocate taxing rights within countries such as the United States, Canada and Switzerland where subnational governments levied income taxes. Experience in the first two jurisdictions in particular

61. *Ibid.*, 482.
62. *Ibid.*, 488, 494.
63. *Ibid.*, 639, 644, 646. *See also* Reuven S. Avi-Yonah, *The Rise and Fall of Arm's Length: A Study in the Evolution of US International Taxation*, 15(1) Va. Tax Rev. 89, 107-108 (1995).
64. Nir Fishbien, *From Switzerland With Love: Surrey's Papers and the Original Intent(s) of Subpart-F*, 38(1) Va. Tax Rev. 1, 27, n. 125 (2018).

contributed to the ongoing debate about identifying the source of income at the international level, with the Swiss experience having far less impact. Formulary apportionment was also used within jurisdictions such as Germany[65] and, for a time, Ukraine[66] as a factor to distribute revenues collected under national income taxes. The international story was far different with the growth of tax treaties in this period effectively reinforcing the water's edge/arm's length rules for determining the source of income.

At the same time, however, three developments over this period helped set the stage for a resurgence of support for formulary apportionment in the post-financial crisis period. The first was a new theoretical analysis in the academic world that established a more robust conceptual base for the adoption of formulary apportionment. The second and third were developments in California and the EU that provided new insights into the technical issues arising in formulary apportionment and the political hurdles a move from arm's length methodology would entail.

[A] Developing the Conceptual Case for Formulary Apportionment

The foundation for much of the modern literature supporting the use of formulary apportionment was a 1972 paper on rules and principles for inter-nation equity in taxation by US-based economists Richard and Peggy Musgrave.[67] Allocating income to source jurisdictions on the basis of operations of permanent establishments was, Musgrave and Musgrave argued, conceptually inferior to allocation based on a formula. They suggested the location of capital should be the primary factor when determining the source of income, with some adjustment for factors leading to excess returns in a particular location. The use of separate accounting at the international level, they suggested, was both 'exceedingly difficult' and 'arbitrary' in terms of its division between establishments. They conceded, however, that the complexities of an apportionment formula that accounted for regional variations in capital returns were problematic, ultimately concluding the optimal system would be an international-level corporate income tax with revenue sharing.[68] Whatever the theoretical merits of the proposal, it clearly was not achievable at the political level.

---

65. *See, e.g.*, Ulrich Schreiber, *Evaluating the Common Consolidated Corporate Tax Base*, in *A Common Consolidated Corporate Tax Base for Europe* 113, 123 (Wolfgang Schön, Ulrich Schreiber & Christoph Spengel eds., Springer 2008); Dieter Biehl, *Fiscal Federalism in Germany*, in *Economic Union in Federal Systems* 152, 175-176 (Anne Mullins & Cheryl Saunders eds., Federation Press 1994).
66. Jorge Martinez-Vazquez, Charles E. McLure, Jr. & Sally Wallace, *Subnational Fiscal Decentralization in Ukraine*, in *Decentralization of the Socialist State: Intergovernmental Finance in Transition Economies* 281, 304-305 (Richard M. Bird, Robert D. Ebel & Christine I. Wallich eds., World Bank 1995).
67. Richard A. Musgrave & Peggy B. Musgrave, *Inter-Nation Equity*, in *Modern Fiscal Issues: Essays in Honor of Carl S Shoup* 63 (Richard M. Bird & John G. Head eds., University of Toronto Press 1972).
68. *Ibid.*, 85.

The Musgrave and Musgrave study was followed in 1974 by three technical papers prepared separately by Professors Carl Shoup, Peggy Musgrave and Charles McLure[69] on taxation issues in support of a broader United Nations study on the impact of multinational enterprises on economic development. While the study by Shoup noted a number of difficulties that would arise through use of formulary apportionment at the international level (as discussed further in the US context in the report by McLure), it concluded that the potential for administrative benefits called for further study of the formulary apportionment option, in particular for developing countries.[70]

The case for formulary apportionment was strengthened significantly in the course of the early 1980s with a series of papers supporting the economic foundations of the system following the lead of Charles McLure.[71] As an income tax apportioned according to factors is economically equivalent to a tax on those factors,[72] an important point in the discussion was whether formulary apportionment might distort multinationals' decisions on the allocation of production factors, an issue not raised by separate accounting where profits could be shifted without moving actual production factors.[73] Balancing the impact on the allocation of resources against source jurisdictions' need for more realistic allocation of profits to the factors that generate them, economists generally favoured formulary apportionment over separate accounting.[74]

---

69. Carl S. Shoup, *Taxation of Multinational Corporations*; Peggy B. Musgrave, *International Tax Differentials for Multinational Corporations: Equity and Efficiency Considerations*; Charles E. McLure, Jr., *State Income Taxation of Multistate Corporations in the United States of America*; in United Nations Department of Economic and Social Affairs, *The Impact of Multinational Corporations on Development and on International Relations, Technical Papers: Taxation* 1, 43 and 58 respectively (United Nations 1974).
70. Shoup, *Taxation of Multinational Corporations*, *supra* n. 69, at 35.
71. Charles E. McLure, Jr., *Defining a Unitary Business: An Economist's View, 30 Years Later*, 73 St. Tax Notes 875 (2014).
72. Charles E. McLure, Jr., *The State Corporate Income Tax: Lambs in Wolves' Clothing*, in *The Economics of Taxation* 327 (Henry J. Aaron & Michael J. Boskin eds., Brookings Institution, 1980). This finding was later noted as affecting 'only slightly' the analysis as to impact of the corporation tax on mobile capital and investment decisions, in that the impact will be felt in accordance with the sensitivity of each factor to taxation rather than of those capital investment decisions as a whole: Charles E. McLure, Jr., *Assignment of Corporate Income Taxes in a Federal System*, in *Tax Assignment in Federal Countries* 101, 110 (Charles E. McLure, Jr. ed., Centre for Research on Federal Financial Relations in association with the International Seminar in Public Economics 1983).
73. Roger Gordon & John D. Wilson, *An Examination of Multijurisdictional Corporate Income Taxation under Formula Apportionment*, 54(6) Econometrica 1357 (1986).
74. Richard M. Bird, *The Interjurisdictional Allocation of Income*, 3(3) Austl. Tax F. 333 (1986); Richard M. Bird & Donald J. S. Brean, *The Interjurisdictional Allocation of Income and the Unitary Taxation Debate*, 34(6) Can. Tax J. 1377 (1986).

Academic interest in formulary apportionment continued into the 1990s, mostly positive,[75] but also some critical.[76] Among the contributions was what has become an often-cited paper that proposed a model tax treaty for the Asian-Pacific region and which proposed, based on the growing interdependence between parts of multinational enterprises, a departure from in the traditional treaty approach with an expanded role for formulary apportionment, relegating separate accounting to a subordinate method.[77] Meanwhile the struggle to contain tax minimization by way of transfer pricing continued, prompting administrative responses[78] and sustaining some federal government interest in the United States in the adoption of a formulary apportionment system.[79]

As support for the adoption of formulary apportionment at the international level in academic literature grew,[80] scholars investigated the revenue consequences of a

---

75. *See, e.g.*, Stanley I. Langbein, *A Modified Fractional Apportionment Proposal for Tax Transfer Pricing*, 54 Tax Notes 719 (1992); Dan R. Bucks & Michael Mazerov, *The State Solution to the Federal Government's International Transfer Pricing Problem*, 46(3) Nat'l Tax J. 385 (1993). While supportive of a formulary approach to determination of source, later Nobel laureate in economics William Vickrey was at this time critical of the Massachusetts formula ('has all the earmarks of having been concocted by a committee of lawyers who had forgotten anything they were taught about statistics or economics') and also suggested that sales did not have an appropriate role to play in the allocation: William Vickrey, *The Corporate Income Tax in the US Tax System*, 73 Tax Notes 597, 602 (1996) (publication of a report presented in 1992), quoted by the hearing officer at the 2012 public consultations of the Multistate Tax Commission on the revisions to UDITPA as noted in Richard D. Pomp, *Reforming a State Corporate Income Tax*, 32(2) J. St. Tax'n 21 (2014).
76. Charles H. Berry, David F. Bradford & James R. Hines, Jr., *Arm's Length Pricing: Some Economic Perspectives*, 54 Tax Notes 731 (1992). *See also* later criticism of formulary apportionment in James R. Hines, Jr., *Income Misattribution under Formula Apportionment*, 54(1) Eur. Econ. Rev. 108 (2010).
77. Richard J. Vann, *A Model Tax Treaty for the Asian-Pacific Region? (Part 1)*, 45(3) Bull. Int'l Tax'n 99, 107 (1991) and *A Model Tax Treaty for the Asian-Pacific Region? (Part 2)*, 45(4) Bull. Int'l Tax'n 151 (1991).
78. *See, e.g.*, US General Accounting Office, *International Taxation: Problems Persist in Determining Tax Effects of Intercompany Prices* (1992), concluding (at 93-94) also that formulary apportionment 'does not appear to be a practical alternative' due to the need for multilateral agreement on the formula.
79. In 1995, for example, Congress commissioned a study from the General Accounting Office (now Government Accountability Office) on steps that would have to be taken for the federal government to adopt a formulary apportionment system based on the Californian model; *see Tax Policy and Administration: California Taxes on Multinational Corporations and Related Federal Issues* (Letter Report, 07/11/95, GAO/GGD-95-171). In that year, the General Accounting Office also reported that, in IRS advance pricing agreements 'started and/or finished without being withdrawn as of July 7, 1994 and that had decided upon methodologies', over one-third of the methods used to determine arm's length prices involved 'different profit measures or formulary or allocation apportionment', though it was noted that 'Treasury officials told us that they would be surprised if IRS was using formulary apportionment in the sense of applying the same formula to different companies' and the IRS officials indicated that the method had 'been used only in difficult cases and only after obtaining the agreement of affected treaty partners': US General Accounting Office, *International Taxation: Transfer Pricing and Information on Nonpayment of Tax* 33-34 (1995).
80. Reuven S. Avi-Yonah, *Slicing the Shadow: A Proposal for Updating US International Taxation*, 58 Tax Notes 1511 (1993) (background drawn from Robert Reich, *The Work of Nations* (1991)); Avi-Yonah, *The Rise and Fall of Arm's Length*, *supra* n. 63; Daniel Sandler, *Slicing the Shadow – The Continuing Debate over Unitary Taxation and Worldwide Combined Reporting*, [1994] 6 Brit. Tax Rev. 572. *But see* Chantal Thomas, *Customary International Law and State Taxation of*

change. Predictions of significant revenue increases for source countries from a three-factor allocation formula stimulated further interest in the option.[81] Ironically, at the same time interest in formulary apportionment at the national level grew, a number of taxpayers were successful appealing against unitary formulary apportionment assessments at the state level, albeit on technical and not higher-level conceptual grounds.[82] Those who saw merit in a shift to formulary apportionment often looked for more gradual paths to adoption such as incorporation in a free-trade agreement,[83] in the context of an economic union of national (as opposed to subnational) governments,[84] or by means of more limited application to particular sectors.[85]

While OECD-based commentators continued their support for separate accounting[86] and a core of scholars remained critical of the formulary apportionment concept,[87] theoreticians' support for formulary apportionment grew as advances in

Corporate Income: The Case for the Separate Accounting Method, 14 Berkeley J. Int'l L. 99 (1996) arguing separate accounting is more consistent with customary international law.

81. Douglas Shackelford & Joel Slemrod, *The Revenue Consequences of Using Formula Apportionment to Calculate US and Foreign-Source Income: A Firm-Level Analysis*, 5(1) Int'l Tax & Pub. Fin. 41 (1998) suggested US-based multinationals would see their US tax liabilities rise by 38%, with an 81% increase for oil and gas firms.
82. *See further* Paul R. Koppel, *A Long Goodbye to the Unitary Method of Income Computation in Massachusetts: Polaroid Corp. Revisited through Gillette Co. v. Commissioner*, 4 St. & Loc. Tax Law. 145 (1999).
83. Paul R. McDaniel, *Formulary Taxation in the North American Free Trade Zone*, 49(4) Tax L. Rev. 691, 740 (1994); Michael J. McIntyre, *Commentary: The Design of Tax Rules for the North American Free Trade Alliance*, 49(4) Tax L. Rev. 769, 770 (1994), citing James W. Wetzler, *Should the US Adopt Formula Apportionment?*, 48(3) Nat'l Tax J. 357, 360 (1995).
84. The argument in favour of formulary apportionment in the European Union was set out in Charles E. McLure, Jr., *Replacing Separate Entity Accounting and the Arm's Length Principle with Formulary Apportionment*, 56(12) Bull. Int'l Tax'n 586, 588 (2002); Charles E. McLure, Jr. & Joann M. Weiner, *Deciding whether the European Union Should Adopt Formula Apportionment of Company Income*, in *Taxing Capital Income in the European Union: Issues and Options for Reform* 243, 272 (Sijbren Cnossen ed., Oxford University Press 2000), and Malcolm Gammie, *Corporate Taxation in Europe – Paths to a Solution*, [2001] 4 Brit. Tax Rev. 233, 249. *See also* Michael J. McIntyre, *The Use of Combined Reporting By Nation States*, 35 Tax Notes Int'l 917, 946 (2004), noting the possibility for a water's edge limitation to be included in national reforms, as either a temporary measure during the broader take-up phase or operated in conjunction with strong anti-avoidance measures.
85. Kerrie Sadiq, *The Taxation of Multinational Banks: Alternative Apportionment through a Unitary Taxation Regime Aligning with Economic Reality*, 13(4) N.Z. J. Tax'n L. & Pol'y 640 (2007); Ilan Benshalom, *Taxing the Financial Income of Multinational Enterprises by Employing a Hybrid Formulary and Arm's Length Allocation Method*, 28(3) Va. Tax Rev. 619 (2009).
86. John Neighbour & Jeffrey Owens, *Transfer Pricing in the New Millennium: Will the Arm's Length Principle Survive?*, 10(4) Geo. Mason L. Rev. 951 (2002); Jeffrey Owens, *Should the Arm's Length Principle Retire?*, 12(3) Int'l Transfer Pricing J. 99 (2005).
87. Julie Roin, *Can the Income Tax Be Saved? The Promise and Pitfalls of Adopting Worldwide Formulary Apportionment*, 61(3) Tax L. Rev. 169 (2008); Rosanne Altshuler & Harry Grubert, *Formula Apportionment: Is It Better Than The Current System and Are There Better Alternatives?*, 63(4/2) Nat'l Tax J. 1145 (2010); Antony Ting, *Multilateral Formulary Apportionment Model – A Reality Check*, 25(1) Austl. Tax F. 95 (2010); on the benefits of an incremental approach to reform, Susan C. Morse, *Revisiting Global Formulary Apportionment*, 29(4) Va. Tax Rev. 593 (2010).

communication and transport paired with the growing importance of services and the enhanced value of intangible property in the economy.[88]

[B] Formulary Apportionment in California

Although discussion of formulary apportionment subsided at the federal income tax level in the United States after the early 1960s, it was kept alive at the state income tax level. Since the early 1940s, California had allowed multinational enterprises the option of using worldwide unitary data when calculating their California income tax liability, an option that was used when enterprises determined this would lead to a lower in-state allocation of income.[89] Following California's adoption of UDITPA in 1966, Californian authorities looked to extend the mandatory unitary taxation to include worldwide affiliates and in the 1970s began to assess income tax on this basis.[90] Eventually, twelve US states would use worldwide income in their formula.[91] The change was strongly criticized by multinationals, the US federal government and foreign governments,[92] several of which joined litigation to declare the approach unconstitutional. California ultimately prevailed in the courts in 1983,[93] a finding reaffirmed at the Supreme Court a little over a decade later,[94] but succumbed to external pressure including threats by foreign governments of retaliation[95] and re-treated in 1986,[96] allowing multinationals the option of using an optional water's edge unitary combination.[97] In most cases, worldwide combination would give rise to higher

88. Kimberly A. Clausing & Reuven S. Avi-Yonah, *Reforming Corporate Taxation in a Global Economy: A Proposal to Adopt Formulary Apportionment* (Brookings Institution Discussion Paper 2007-08, June 2007); Michael Kobetsky, *The Case for Unitary Taxation of International Enterprises*, 62(5) Bull. Int'l Tax'n 201 (2008); Reuven S. Avi-Yonah, Kimberly A. Clausing & Michael C. Durst, *Allocating Business Profits for Tax Purposes: A Proposal to Adopt a Formulary Profit Split*, 9(5) Fla. Tax Rev. 497 (2009); Elizabeth King, *Transfer Pricing and Corporate Taxation: Problems, Practical Implications and Proposed Solutions* (Springer 2009).
89. Benjamin F. Miller, *Worldwide Unitary Combination: The California Practice*, in *The State Corporation Income Tax: Issues in Worldwide Unitary Combination* 132, 138-139 (Charles E. McLure, Jr. ed., Hoover Institution Press 1984).
90. *Ibid.*, 139.
91. Franklin C. Latcham, *Worldwide Combination and the* Container *Case: A Perspective on Unitary Taxation*, 2(1) Int'l Tax & Bus. Law. 29, 30, n. 4 (1984).
92. *See, e.g.*, R. F. Edmonds, *Unitary Tax*, 18(9) Tax'n in Australia 898 (1984); Paul Latimer, *Objections to American State Unitary Taxation of Multi-Jurisdictional Corporations*, 21(4) Tax'n in Australia 220 (1986); Paul Latimer, *The Demise of American State Unitary Taxation of Multi-Jurisdictional Corporations*, 21(7) Tax'n in Australia 517 (1987).
93. *Container Corp. v. Franchise Tax Board*, 463 US 159 (1983).
94. *Barclays Bank plc v. Franchise Tax Board of California*, 512 US 298 (1994).
95. Robert D. Wallingford, *British Retaliation Against the California Unitary Tax: The Needed Impetus for a Federal Solution*, 8(3) J. Comp. Bus. & Cap. Market L. 345 (1986).
96. The saga of California's attempt to apply international unitary formulary apportionment is described in Charles E. McLure, Jr., *Economic Integration and European Taxation of Corporate Income at Source: Some Lessons from the US Experience*, 29(8) Eur. Tax'n 243 (1989).
97. Greer C. Bosworth, *Taxation: Reform of California's Unitary Tax – 1986 Cal. Stat. ch. 660*, 22(2) Stan. J. Int'l L. 421 (1986); Bronwyn J. F. McNeill, *California's Recent Legislation on Unitary Taxation and Barclay's Bank plc v. Franchise Tax Board of California*, 48(1) Tax Law. 231, 237-238 (1994). Importantly, the option only applied on a prospective basis from 1 January

state taxes,[98] but in some instances, companies could benefit from worldwide unitary formulary apportionment.[99]

Although the Californian experiment with worldwide unitary taxation ultimately proved to be short-lived, it helped prompt new interest and discussion of the merits of extending formulary apportionment from subnational taxes to national income taxes. The observation of Brennan J. in the first decision to consider the constitutionality of the Californian unitary worldwide formulary apportionment that allocating income among taxing jurisdictions was like 'slicing a shadow'[100] became a catchphrase for those advocating a uniform formulary solution.

[C] Tentative Moves Towards Formulary Apportionment in the EU

The path towards formulary apportionment in European Union somewhat ironically can be traced to the release in 1992 of an EU-commissioned report that recommended continued reliance on separate accounting and arm's length pricing to determining the source of income in EU Member States.[101] The committee under the chairmanship of former Dutch finance minister Onno Ruding had been appointed in 1991 to provide advice on the convergence of EU company tax systems following failed attempts in the 1970s and 1980s to harmonize EU company tax systems.[102] The committee's final report recommended greater harmonization of company tax systems but no convergence on a single formula to allocate profits.[103]

The political and economic environment began to shift, however, not long after the release of the Ruding Report. The most significant development, arguably, was the adoption in 1993 of the Maastricht Treaty (Treaty on European Union) which set the European Community on the path to economic and monetary union, eventually leading to the establishment of the single currency on 1 January 1999. The growing integration

1988, and the option was revocable by the revenue authority, prompting continued litigation over assessments for previous years. Legislation providing for a broader option was passed in 1993.

98. George N. Carlson & Harvey Galper, *Water's Edge Versus Worldwide Unitary Combination*, in *The State Corporation Income Tax: Issues in Worldwide Unitary Combination* 1, 2 (Charles E. McLure, Jr. ed., Hoover Institution Press 1984).

99. Karen S. Hreha & Peter A. Silhan, *Tax Base Differences Between Worldwide and Water's Edge Methods of Unitary Taxation: A Survey of Fortune 500 Companies* (University of Illinois at Urbana-Champaign College of Commerce and Business Administration Working Paper 1369, July 1987), https://www.ideals.illinois.edu/bitstream/handle/2142/28914/taxbasedifferenc1369hreh.pdf?sequence=1.

100. *Container Corp. v. Franchise Tax Board*, 463 US 159, 192 (1983).

101. McLure & Weiner, *supra* n. 84, at 272.

102. *Ibid.*, 272-273.

103. Committee of Independent Experts on Company Taxation (Onno Ruding, chair), *Report of the Committee of Independent Experts on Company Taxation* (European Communities 1992).

of European economies inevitably revived discussion on the desirability of harmonizing company income tax systems, including proposals for the adoption of formulary apportionment.[104]

An initial 2001 internal report on European company tax systems prepared for European Commission, the executive body of the EU, proposed greater harmonization of company tax systems and canvassed the adoption of formulary apportionment as one option for allocating tax revenue, among Member States, though it stopped short of recommending formulary apportionment over separate accounting as a means of allocating revenues.[105] A subsequent 2003 internal report prepared by the EU's Directorate-General for Taxation and Customs Union provided stronger support for the formulary apportionment approach[106] and backing for the idea began to build as the work of the European Commission evolved into a specific policy proposal in 2004 for a Common Consolidated Corporate Tax Base (CCCTB) in Europe. Initially, the CCCTB focused on the development of a common tax base, leaving questions concerning consolidation and formulary apportionment for future attention.[107] Work on the issue led to extensive CCCTB working group meetings over the period 2004 to 2008 and two working papers on the CCCTB in 2007.[108] The gradual evolution of the CCCTB proposals towards a system of harmonized tax laws assessing profits allocated using a formulary apportionment system was scrutinized and largely supported by academic

104. Weiner, *The Dream is Alive* §4.03 (this volume). *See also* Joann Weiner, *Implementing Formulary Apportionment in the Single European Market* (US Department of the Treasury Office of Tax Analysis Paper, 30 December 1993).

105. European Commission, *Commission Staff Working Paper: Company Taxation in the Internal Market* COM(2001)582; discussed in Weiner, *The Dream is Alive* §4.04 (this volume).

106. European Commission, *Communication from the Commission to the Council, the European Parliament and the European Economic and Social Committee, An Internal Market without Company Tax Obstacles: Achievements, Ongoing Initiatives and Remaining Challenges,* COM(2003)726 final, 24 November 2003 (Bolkestein Report). Outside observers were generally supportive of the direction the Europeans appeared to be taking, recommending a clean start that avoided some of the missteps in existing formulary apportionment regimes. *See further* Walter Hellerstein & Charles E. McLure, Jr., *The European Commission's Report on Company Income Taxation: What the EU Can Learn from the Experience of the US States,* 11(2) Int'l Tax & Pub. Fin. 199-220 (2004) (generally adopting the recommendation, 'Don't Do What We Do', as appropriate for the EU); Jack Mintz, *Corporate Tax Harmonization in Europe: It's All About Compliance,* 11(2) Int'l Tax & Pub. Fin. 221 (2004).

107. European Commission, *Commission Non-Paper to Informal Ecofin Council, 10 and 11 September 2004, A Common Consolidated EU Corporate Tax Base* 3 (7 July 2004).

108. European Commission, *Common Consolidated Corporate Tax Base Working Group (CCCTB WG), CCCTB: Possible Elements of a Technical Outline,* CCCTB/WP057\doc\en (26 July 2007); European Commission, *Common Consolidated Corporate Tax Base Working Group (CCCTB WG), CCCTB: Possible Elements of the Sharing Mechanism,* CCCTB/WP060\doc\en (13 November 2007). This latter document envisaged a possible role for number of employees to be included in the payroll factor; the proposed mechanism also involved formulary apportionment of income-generating elements to each separate legal entity in the consolidated group, rather than geographically across a unitary enterprise: on this distinction, *see, e.g.,* Clemens Fuest, *The European Commission's Proposal for a Common Consolidated Corporate Tax Base,* 24(4) Oxford Rev. Econ. Pol'y 720, 723 (2008). Overall weighting of the factors was, however, considered to be an issue that should be dealt with at the political level.

studies,[109] though emerging work on possible winners and losers from the change foreshadowed the political challenges that change would involve.[110]

§1.06 FORMULARY APPORTIONMENT AFTER THE GLOBAL FINANCIAL CRISIS

In 2008-2009, a little less than a decade into the new century, the world's worst financial crisis since the great depression of the 1930s led to dramatic changes in international financial regulation and taxation. Subsequent changes to arm's length methodology by the OECD, the revival of formulary apportionment plans in the EU and the growth of international tax justice bodies reinvigorated support for formulary apportionment. Renewed academic discussion prompted, in part, by these three developments also played a role.

[A] Changes to the OECD's Transfer Pricing Methodology

One of the most important triggers for a resurgence of interest in formulary apportionment following the GFC has been the post-GFC revision of the OECD's transfer pricing methodologies used by almost all tax authorities to determine acceptable transfer prices for transactions between related enterprises. The chain of events leading to a rethink of arm's length methodology began with the inaugural G20 summit in November 2008, two months after the collapse of financial services firm Lehman Brothers triggered the GFC. The first step was truly modest, a request to the OECD by

109. *See, e.g.*, Joann Martens-Weiner, *Company Tax Reform in the European Union: Guidance from the United States and Canada on Implementing Formulary Apportionment in the EU* (Springer 2006); Joann Martens Weiner, *Practical Aspects of Implementing Formulary Apportionment in the European Union*, 8(7) Fla. Tax Rev. 629 (2007); Joann M. Weiner, *Combined Reporting and the Unitary Business Principle: A Doctrine That Has Not Yet Made the Atlantic Crossing*, [2008] St. & Local Tax Law.: Symposium Edition 179; Ulrich Schreiber, *Consolidation, Allocation and International Aspects*, in *A Common Consolidated Corporate Tax Base for Europe* 113 (Wolfgang Schön, Ulrich Schreiber & Christoph Spengel eds., Springer 2008); Stefan Mayer, *Formulary Apportionment for the Internal Market* (IBFD 2009).

110. *See* Fuest, *supra* n. 108. Studies from this time and following variously found potential for some slight overall revenue decline, though with gains and losses for particular states and the potential for substantial increases in tax payments under a mandatory approach (with gains going to the large, high-tax states); *see, e.g.*, Michael P. Devereux & Simon Loretz, *The Effects of EU Formula Apportionment on Corporate Tax Revenues*, 29(1) Fiscal Stud. 1 (2008). The potential for greater revenue stability for Member States under the CCCTB was also noted: Weiner, *Practical Aspects of Implementing Formulary Apportionment in the European Union*, *supra* n. 109. A number of countervailing considerations in the use of the labour factor were also seen: Patrick J. Weninger, *The Labour Apportionment Factor for a Common Consolidated Corporate Tax Base: A Double-Edged Sword*, 15(5) Int'l Transfer Pricing J. 213 (2008). Later studies would find the possibility for enforcement variations in the CCCTB to take the place of tax competition: Johannes Becker & Clemens Fuest, *Tax Enforcement and Tax Havens under Formula Apportionment*, 17(3) Int'l Tax & Pub. Fin. 217 (2010), but also more optimistically find the potential for significant revenue gains under different formula-setting scenarios: Marco Runkel & Guttorm Schelderup, *The Choice of Apportionment Factors under Formula Apportionment*, 52(3) Int'l Econ. Rev. 913 (2011). *See further* §1.06[B].

government leaders attending the summit that the Organisation strengthen its measures to combat tax evasion through tax havens. Following a second G20 meeting in April 2009, the OECD began to expand its anti-evasion work to incorporate tax avoidance, a subject that included tax minimization through the manipulation of transfer prices in intra-group transactions.[111]

The expanded agenda was endorsed by the G20 at their 2012 summit and the OECD embarked on what it termed a 'base erosion and profit shifting' (BEPS) project. A proposal to develop fifteen BEPS 'action plans' was announced the following year. Details of the action plans were released in 2015 and included three programmes to reform transfer pricing methodologies. Changes to the OECD's transfer pricing manual, setting out transfer pricing methodologies in more detail, followed.

Traditionally, the OECD recognized five core transfer pricing methodologies, including two described as 'transactional' methods, the transactional net margin method and the profit-split method. The focus of the expanded guidelines was the expanded use of profit-split methodologies. Supporters of separate accounting argued the revised guidelines reflected a continuing endorsement of the arm's length principle, with the changes best characterized as administrative reinforcement of separate accounting.[112] Critics of separate accounting viewed the changes differently, suggesting they amounted to an implicit acknowledgement by the OECD of a fundamental flaw in the principle upon which traditional arm's length pricing methodologies rested, namely that it was possible to establish an independent arm's length price for transactions that would only take place in a multinational business.[113] In effect, some suggested, the revisions to profit-split methodologies amounted to a shift by the OECD towards formulary apportionment by the back door.[114] The reality is that while the revised methodologies added new hurdles for companies to overcome when setting acceptable intra-group prices, they did not alter the basic structure of the system that allows multinational enterprises to shift profits between jurisdictions without a parallel shift in actual economic activity.

In addition to the problem of tax avoidance through transfer pricing, one issue the OECD hoped to tackle in its BEPS programme was the difficulty of updating the world's

111. *See* Kerrie Sadiq & Richard Krever, *Actions to Counter Base Erosion and Profit Shifting: A General Report*, in *Tax Design and Administration in a Post-BEPS Era: A Study of Key Reform Measures in 18 Jurisdictions* 1, 2 (Kerrie Sadiq, Adrian Sawyer & Bronwyn McCredie eds., Fiscal Publications 2019).
112. *See, e.g.*, Sol Picciotto, *Taxing Multinational Enterprises as Unitary Entities*, 82 Tax Notes Int'l 895, 906-907 (2016).
113. Tommaso Faccio & Valpy Fitzgerald, *Sharing the Corporate Tax Base: Equitable Taxing of Multinationals and the Choice of Formulary Apportionment*, 25(2) Transnat'l Corp. 67, 69 (2018).
114. Robert Robillard, *BEPS: Is the OECD Now at the Gates of Global Formulary Apportionment?*, 43(6-7) Intertax 447, 451 (2015). For a contrasting view that the OECD has maintained a strict adherence to the arm's length approach even though it had conceded at the outset of the BEPS project that 'there may be instances where the existing arm's length based norms cannot be effective', *see* Yariv Brauner, *Formula Based Transfer Pricing*, 42(10) Intertax 615 (2014); similarly, Yariv Brauner, *Transfer Pricing in BEPS: First Round – Business Interests Win (But, Not in Knock-Out)*, 43(1) Intertax 72, 84 (2015). *See generally* also Giammarco Cottani, *Formulary Apportionment: A Revamp in the Post-Base Erosion and Profit Shifting Era?*, 44(10) Intertax 755 (2016).

thousands of tax treaties when changes were required to address commercial changes in the global economy. It concluded the most efficient solution would be a multilateral treaty that simultaneously updated all bilateral treaties between signatories to the multilateral treaty. A key element in the success of the multilateral treaty was the 'inclusive framework' extension by the OECD of its BEPS programme to all non-Member States.

To achieve consensus among the wide array of economies participating in the BEPS project, the OECD described the principle on which its revised transfer pricing methodologies were based as recognizing profits in the jurisdiction in which 'value is created', a concept sufficiently vague to be endorsed by all participants. That vagueness opened the door to creative interpretation of the methodologies, particularly by some non-OECD members. Jurisdictions such as China have announced that in their view value creation is not aligned with economic activities exclusively and transfer prices should accordingly look beyond traditional criteria for determining an arm's length price. In particular, China has argued that multinationals benefit from location-specific advantages such as labour cost savings, local infrastructure, and selective markets willing to bear higher markups.

The diversity in approaches to interpreting the separate accounts system has led to renewed questions on whether traditional separate accounting continues to be appropriate for complex modern economies and prompted reconsideration of the formulary apportionment alternative in unexpected quarters. The speed at which views are evolving is remarkable, as illustrated by the OECD's evolving approach to the allocation of profits derived by digital companies. In early February 2019, the OECD commenced a project on the allocation of digital profits with a call for views on options it canvassed to apply arm's length rules to the sector.[115] By October 2019, when it issued a consultation paper on the topic, alternatives for allocating profits of digitalized businesses presented for consideration had been expanded to include a formulary apportionment option. The paper conceded there are 'increasing doubts that the arm's length principle can be relied on to give an appropriate result in all cases' and 'there seems to be agreement that the arm's length principle is becoming an increasing source of complexity'.[116] Once lost in the OECD's 'blind spot',[117] formulary apportionment has finally been recognized as a possible legitimate response to transfer pricing.

[B] The Stalling and Revival of Formulary Apportionment in the EU

The global financial crisis stalled, but did not derail, the EU proposals for a CCCTB that included an allocation of profits on a formulary apportionment basis. Following a

115. OECD, *Public Consultation Document: Addressing the Tax Challenges of the Digitalisation of the Economy, 13 February – 6 March 2019* (OECD 2019).
116. OECD Secretariat, *Public Consultation Document: Secretariat Proposal for a 'Unified Approach' under Pillar One, 9 October 2019 – 12 November 2019*, paras. 17-18 (OECD 2019).
117. Yariv Brauner, *BEPS: An Interim Evaluation*, 6(1) World Tax J. 10, 16 (2014).

workshop in 2010,[118] the European Commission moved in 2011 to recommend implementation of the CCCTB[119] with an optional formulary apportionment system built on an equally weighted three-factor formula with labour based on wages and number of employees.[120] The European Parliament amended the proposal in 2012 to provide for a 45% weight to each of payroll and assets and only 10% to sales.[121]

Few saw the proposal as a risk-free panacea to European company tax problems, and there was a concern in some quarters that the problems of transfer pricing could be replicated under the CCCTB if the system were abused by means of selective enforcement by tax-friendly jurisdictions.[122] As proposals for alternative solutions appeared,[123] studies appeared with predictions of winners and losers as tax burdens shifted under the formulary approach.[124] Not surprisingly, political resistance grew in some quarters, and many welcomed the release in 2013 of the OECD's BEPS action plan which quickly diverted the attention of European politicians.[125]

As the BEPS project progressed towards the implementation stage, European interest in formulary apportionment was revived, and in 2016, the European Commission renewed plans for a CCCTB[126] with formulary apportionment for the Union, based on a three-factor formula, with labour comprising both payroll cost and headcount. The proposal called for mandatory use of the formulary apportionment system by large multinational enterprises.[127] The revival prompted opposition from tax

118. *See* European Commission, *Preparation of the 2011 CCCTB Proposal*, https://ec.europa.eu/taxation_customs/business/company-tax/common-consolidated-corporate-tax-base-ccctb/preparation-2011-ccctb-proposal_en (accessed 10 Oct. 2019).
119. European Commission, *Proposal for a Council Directive on a Common Consolidated Corporate Tax Base (CCCTB)*, COM (2011) 121 final/2 (3 October 2011).
120. The formula had been mooted in one of the two 2007 working papers. *See* n. 108, *supra*; Weiner, *The Dream is Alive* §4.05 (this volume).
121. European Parliament legislative resolution of 19 April 2012 on the proposal for a Council Directive on a Common Consolidated Corporate Tax Base (CCCTB), COM(2011)0121-C7-0092/2011-2011/0058(CNS).
122. Johannes Becker & Clemens Fuest, *Tax Enforcement and Tax Havens under Formula Apportionment*, 17(3) Int'l Tax & Pub. Fin. 217 (2010).
123. Erik Röder, *Proposal for an Enhanced CCTB as Alternative to a CCCTB with Formulary Apportionment*, 4(2) World Tax J. 125 (2012).
124. One impact assessment found that effective tax burdens would be likely to 'considerably increase' in Portugal, Romania and Switzerland while Cyprus, Ireland and Italy would see the largest burden reductions. *See* Christoph Spengel, Martina Ortmann-Babel, Benedikt Zinn & Sebastian Matenaer, *A Common Corporate Tax Base for Europe: An Impact Assessment of the Draft Council Directive on a CC(C)TB*, 4(3) World Tax J. 185 (2012).
125. *See* European Council, *Note from Presidency to Permanent Representatives Committee/Council, Proposal for a Council Directive on a Common Consolidated Corporate Tax Base (CCCTB) – State of Play*, 1 December 2015.
126. *See* Jan van de Streek, *Some Introductory Remarks on the Relaunched CCTB/CCCTB Proposals from a Policy Perspective*, in *The EU Common Consolidated Corporate Tax Base: Critical Analysis* 1 (Dennis Weber & Jan van de Streek eds., Kluwer Law International 2018).
127. European Commission, *Proposal for a Council Directive on a Common Corporate Tax Base*, 25 October. 2016 COM(2016) 685 final 2016/0337(CNS). For some continued reservations about the desirability of the formulary apportionment under the relaunched proposal, *see, e.g.*, Sijbren Cnossen, *Corporation Taxes in the European Union: Slowly Moving Toward Comprehensive Business Income Taxation?*, 25(3) Int'l Tax & Pub. Fin. 808 (2018); attention to the scope for alternative tax-shifting strategies has also been emphasized: Dirk Kiesewetter, Tobias Steigenberger & Matthias Stier, *Can Formula Apportionment Really Prevent Multinational*

advisors[128] and academics noted it could impact negatively on fiscal relations between the EU and the United States given the latter's 'zealous commitment' to arm's length methodology.[129] Interest in Europe remained high, however, and on 1 March 2018, the European Parliament issued a report endorsing a slightly amended CCCTB proposal.[130] The proposal remains very much alive.

[C] Tax and Justice Organizations

The third development that prompted renewed interest in formulary apportionment was the significant expansion after 2000 of tax justice and development organizations and growth of tax justice advocacy groups. The issue of tax havens had received attention from groups such as Oxfam as early as the 1970s but follow-up was limited given limited resources and the complexity of the issue.[131] However, a flurry of disclosures of evasion and avoidance in more recent times following Panama, Paradise, Luxembourg, Swiss and other well-publicized leaks of tax avoidance files helped to foster global interest in, and support for, tax justice bodies raising awareness of international tax avoidance by multinational companies. Support was reinforced when the EU brought well-publicized actions to reverse illegal 'state aid' tax concessions for a number of internationally known companies. Organizations such as the UK's Tax Justice Network, the Global Alliance for Tax Justice and the Independent Commission for the Reform of International Corporate Taxation, along with a wide range of aid organizations such as Oxfam and aid advocacy bodies such as Action Aid, all pressed the case for international tax reform. The success of the Tax Justice Network, in

Enterprises from Profit Shifting? The Role of Asset Valuation, Intragroup Debt, and Leases, 88(9) J. Bus. Econ. 1029 (2018); Sebastian Eichfelder, Frank Hechtner & Jochen Hundsdoerfer, *Formula Apportionment: Factor Allocation and Tax Avoidance*, 27(4) Eur. Acct. Rev. 649, and the potential for definition of the labour factor to have adverse factor migration impacts: Eva Eberhartinger & Matthias Petutschnig, *CCCTB: The Employment Factor Game*, 43(2) Eur. J.L. & Econ. 333 (2017). Corporate responses to an option to use apportionment under various conditions are also explored in Thomas A. Gresik, *Allowing Firms to Choose Between Separate Accounting and Formula Apportionment Taxation*, 138 J. Pub. Econ. 32 (2016).

128. *See, e.g.*, the view of the Fiscal Committee of the Confederation of European Tax Advisers arguing the formula would impact on the tax burdens of service industries and digital businesses, sectors the European Union wished to promote. *See* CFE Fiscal Committee, *Opinion Statement FC 3/2017 on the Proposed Directives for the Introduction of a Common Corporate Tax Base and Common Consolidated Corporate Tax Base*, 57(11) Eur. Tax'n 504 (2017).
129. Pasquale Pistone & Yariv Brauner, *The European Union and the United States: The Good Old Tax 'Frenemies' in the Shadows of Reforms*, 71(6a) Bull. Int'l Tax'n 61 (2017).
130. European Parliament, Report on the Proposal for a Council Directive on a Common Consolidated Corporate Tax Base (CCCTB), A8-0051/2018 (1 March 2018). Amendments intended to address subsidiarity concerns of smaller states such as Denmark, Ireland, Luxembourg and Malta included a phase-out of the threshold for mandatory application to large groups over seven years and provision for a dispute resolution mechanism to address disputes on the formula.
131. Leonard Seabrooke & Duncan Wigan, *Emergent Entrepreneurs in Transnational Advocacy Networks: Professional Mobilization in the Fight for Global Tax Justice* 3 (GR:EEN Working Paper 41, University of Warwick, 2013), www.greenfp7.eu/papers/workingpapers, citing interview with UK tax activist in March 2013. For a more general discussion of the development of tax justice advocacy, see also Leonard Seabrooke & Duncan Wigan, *Powering Ideas Through Expertise: Professionals in Global Tax Battles*, 23(3) J. Eur. Pub. Pol'y 357 (2016).

particular, led to the establishment of similar bodies around the world and a global umbrella body. Through studies, social media and the press, these organizations have increased public awareness of the problems of tax avoidance under the current arm's length system and often pressed the case for formulary apportionment as a fairer system.[132]

Significantly, those advocating for formulary apportionment for smaller and less developed economies are concerned about the revenue implications if factors and weightings advocated for developed countries were applied in developing countries.[133] One issue, for example, is whether a labour factor should be based on payroll or number of employees in jurisdictions with high labour forces and low wages.[134] Technical questions of this sort have not distracted advocates from pursuing the broader reform agenda, and tax justice organizations remain a potent force in the development of formulary apportionment.

132. *See, e.g.*, Sol Picciotto, *Towards Unitary Taxation of Transnational Corporations* (Tax Justice Network 2012); Sol Picciotto, *Unitary Alternatives and Formulary Apportionment*, in *Taxing Multinational Enterprises as Unitary Firms* 27 (Sol Picciotto ed., Institute of Development Studies 2017); Seabrooke & Wigan, *Emergent Entrepreneurs*, *supra* n. 131, at 20. *See*, in this regard, Tax Justice Network, *Ending the Offshore Secrecy System: An Action Programme to Strengthen International Financial and Fiscal Regulatory Cooperation* (March 2009), http://www.taxjustice.net/cms/upload/pdf/TJN_0903_Action_Plan_for_G-20.pdf; Mark Bou Mansour, *IMF Support for Radical Overhaul of International Tax Rules Welcomed by Tax Justice Network, Tax Justice Network* (10 March 2019), https://www.taxjustice.net/2019/03/10/imf-support-for-radical-overhaul-of-international-tax-rules-welcomed-by-tax-justice-network/ (accessed 30 Sep. 2019), referring also to Tax Justice Network, *Consultation Response to OECD Consultation on Addressing the Tax Challenges of the Digitalisation of the Economy* (6 March 2019), https://www.taxjustice.net/wp-content/uploads/2019/03/Tax-Justice-Network-submission-OECD-consultation-March-2019.pdf. The approach taken by organizations such as the Tax Justice Network is to pursue incremental changes in political awareness to achieve 'constructive change' in the longer term; *see* Jamie Morgan, *Corporation Tax as a Problem of MNC Organisational Circuits: The Case for Unitary Taxation*, 18(2) Brit. J. Pol. & Int'l Rel. 463, 474-475 and references there cited (2016).

133. ActionAid International, *Submission to the International Monetary Fund's Consultation on Economic 'Spillovers' in International Taxation* 19 (March 2014), https://www.actionaid.org.uk/sites/default/files/publications/actionaid_international_submission_to_imf_tax_spillovers_consultation1.pdf (accessed 30 Sep. 2019); *see also* Alex Cobham & Simon Loretz, *International Distribution of the Corporate Tax Base: Implications of Different Apportionment Factors under Unitary Taxation* (International Centre for Tax and Development Working Paper 27, November 2014); Prem Sikka & Richard Murphy, *Unitary Taxation: Tax Base and the Role of Accounting* (International Centre for Tax and Development Working Paper 34, April 2015). *See also* Independent Commission for the Reform of International Corporate Taxation, *A Fairer Future for Global Taxation, A Roadmap to Improve Rules for Taxing Multinationals* (February 2018), following which a specialist conference, *Splitting the Riches: The Present and Future of Taxation by Formula*, was also held on 22 April 2018 to study the advantages and disadvantages of formulary taxation: https://www.icrict.com/icrict-events/2018/4/22/splitting-the-riches-the-present-and-future-of-taxation-by-formula.

134. Picciotto, *Towards Unitary Taxation of Transnational Corporations*, *supra* n. 132, at 13.

[D] Academic Literature

Academic work in the field of formulary apportionment since the global financial crisis has continued to add extensively to the understanding of the method and its appropriate application in practice. Changes to the OECD transfer pricing methodologies, developments in the EU and growing advocacy by tax justice bodies have contributed to continuing academic interest in the subject. Another important factor has been developments in the subnational formulary apportionment system in the United States. Particularly important, in addition to changes to tax bases and rates, has been continuing debate over the weighting of the three-factor profit apportionment formula, modified in the uniform act in 2014,[135] changes made by way of regulations to the uniform rules on the place at which services are provided[136] and the many unilateral departures from the rules by different states. These changes have yielded ideal case studies for empirical analysis on the impact of US state corporate tax policies on economic activity[137] and corporate revenues,[138] the effect on profits of multijurisdictional firms of formula uncertainty caused by local variations[139] and the impact of a switch to sales factor apportionment on employment levels.[140]

More generally, important studies have continued to emphasize the arguments in favour of a move to formulary apportionment and worldwide unitary combination at the international level,[141] and areas in which current US state systems can be

135. *See* Joe Huddleston & Shirley Sicilian, *The Project to Revise UDITPA*, Proceedings of the New York University Institute on State and Local Taxation (2009), http://www.mtc.gov/uploadedFiles/Multistate_Tax_Commission/Uniformity/Minutes/The%20Project%20to%20Revise%20UDITPA.pdf (accessed 30 Sep. 2019). *See also* John A. Swain, *Reforming the State Corporate Income Tax: A Market State Approach to the Sourcing of Service Receipts*, 83(2) Tul. L. Rev. 285 (2008).

136. Multistate Tax Commission, *Model General Allocation and Apportionment Regulations With Amendments Submitted for Adoption by the Commission, February 24, 2017*, http://www.mtc.gov/Uniformity/Project-Teams/Section-17-Model-Market-Sourcing-Regulations. *See further* Michael S. Schadewald, *Apportionment Issues: MTC Approves Changes to Model Apportionment Regulations*, 35(3) J. St. Tax'n 15; Walter Hellerstein, *The Transformation of the State Corporation Income Tax into a Market-Based Levy*, 130(5) J. Tax'n 4 (2019); Shirley Sicilian & Joe Huddleston, *The US States' Experience with Formulary Apportionment* (this volume), detailing among other changes the introduction of market-based sourcing methods for services and intangibles.

137. Kimberly A. Clausing, *The US State Experience under Formulary Apportionment: Are There Lessons for International Reform?*, 69(2) Nat'l Tax J. 353 (2016).

138. *Ibid.*

139. Regina Ortmann, *Uncertainty in Weighting Formulary Apportionment Factors: How Does Weighting Uncertainty Impact After-Tax Income of Multinational Groups?*, 2015/3 Die Betriebswirtschaft 161.

140. Charles W. Swenson, *The Cash Flow and Behavioral Effects of Switching to a Single Sales Factor on State Taxation*, 37(2) J. Am. Tax'n Assoc. 75 (2015).

141. *See, e.g.*, Darien Shanske, *White Paper on Eliminating the Water's Edge Election And Moving to Mandatory Worldwide Combined Reporting*, 89 St. Tax Notes 1181 (2018); Dan R. Bucks, *The Case for Worldwide Unitary: Stronger and Better Than Ever*, 91 St. Tax Notes 663 (2019); McGaughey & Raimondos, *supra* n. 59; Antony Ting & Sidney J. Gray, *The Rise of the Digital Economy: Rethinking the Taxation of Multinational Enterprises*, 50(9) J. Int'l Bus. Stud. 1656 (2019); that the reform should be considered: James W. Wetzler, *Is It Time to Consider*

strengthened.[142] Other studies suggest the formulary apportionment approach needs to be reinforced by other complementary measures[143] or rejected in favour of alternative reforms.[144] At the same time, pessimists argue that even the entire suite of available policy measures may not be sufficient to ensure states obtain an appropriate share of taxes on the profits of multinational enterprises.[145]

§1.07 CONCLUSION

Water's edge separate accounting for each branch or subsidiary of a multinational company operating a seamless enterprise across multiple jurisdictions is accepted today as a norm of international taxation. The approach was not given a century ago when national income taxes first spread across developed nations. Subnational governments, sometimes following a path through property taxes on business assets that stretched across jurisdiction borders and capital or franchise taxes levied on company profits measured indirectly through capital or distributions, had often moved into the income tax field before their national governments. Building on apportionment approaches used in predecessor taxes, subordinate governments almost invariably settled on formulary apportionment to measure the share of an entity's profits, and later, in many cases, a unitary group's profits sourced within their borders.

Proponents favouring the adoption of a similar approach for international allocations of income confronted another group favouring separate accounting for this purpose. Largely through the influence of the OECD, separate accounting prevailed at the international level, codified in the global tax treaty network built upon the OECD model treaty. Were it possible to apply accurately rules substituting arm's length prices for those used within a business for intra-group transactions, the two systems might have yielded similar results. Experience soon revealed, however, the artificiality and limitations of the arm's length concept when applied to multinational enterprises that built on internal synergies to operate a unitary business across borders and connected entities. The system facilitated and arguably even encouraged the shifting of profits out of the jurisdiction through intra-group transfer pricing arrangements. Countries sought

---

Worldwide Consolidation?, 163 Tax Notes 253 (2019). For a recent discussion of the development of business views on formulary apportionment, see also Helen Rogers & Lynne Oats, *Emerging Perspectives on the Evolving Arm's Length Principle and Formulary Apportionment*, [2019] 2 Brit. Tax Rev. 150.

142. Richard Phillips, Nathan Proctor & David Morse, *A Simple Fix for a $17 Billion Loophole: How States Can Reclaim Revenue Lost to Tax Havens*, St. Tax Notes 863 (11 March 2019).

143. Darien Shanske, *Expanding State Fiscal Capacity, Part I: Combining an Entity-Level Consumption Tax, Improved Sales Factor Apportionment, and a Tax on a Federal Windfall (the QBI Deduction)*, 22(2) Fla. Tax Rev. 448 (2019).

144. J. Clifton Fleming, Jr., Robert J. Peroni & Stephen E. Shay, *Formulary Apportionment in the US International Income Tax System: Putting Lipstick on a Pig?*, 36(1) Mich. J. Int'l L. 1 (2014) (noting the potential for real economic distortions under formulary apportionment and proposing worldwide taxation as a neutral alternative); J. Clifton Fleming, Jr., Robert J. Peroni & Stephen E. Shay, *Getting Serious About Cross-Border Earnings Stripping: Establishing an Analytical Framework*, 93(3) N.C. L. Rev. 673 (2015).

145. Joseph Bankman, Mitchell Kane & Alan Sykes, *Collecting the Rent: The Global Battle to Capture MNE Profits* (Stanford Law School Working Paper No. 527, November 2018).

to mitigate, if not prevent, this outcome through specific and general anti-avoidance rules and continual refinement of arm's length pricing methodologies but inevitably found multinational taxpayers remained several steps ahead of new measures to reduce transfer pricing. In the face of these difficulties, support for formulary apportionment remained strong in many tax policy circles.

Following the global financial crisis in 2008-2009, the pendulum has slowly, but unmistakably, been shifting away from orthodox separate accounts allocation. Development agencies and academic authors have embraced or continue to support a shift to formulary apportionment, and one important economic community may soon be the first to use the system across national borders. Ongoing modifications to transfer pricing rules and particularly the growth of profit-split methodologies are seen by some as moves to formulary apportionment by the back door. Taken together, these moves give reason to wonder if Mitchell B. Carroll's 'decided victory' might yet prove to be a long-lived but ultimately temporary phenomenon.

CHAPTER 2

The US States' Experience with Formulary Apportionment

Shirley Sicilian & Joe Huddleston[*]

§2.01 INTRODUCTION

US states have used formulary apportionment as their primary means of avoiding multiple taxation of business income since the early 1900s. This chapter provides a high-level sense of what 'formulary apportionment' means in the US state income tax context; how, and why, it developed and changed over the decades; and some of the factors that bear on its longevity and workability as an income attribution method. This chapter proceeds as follows. Section 2.02 considers the meaning of 'formulary apportionment' in the context of US state income taxes, examining the basic concept, the scope of income subject to apportionment, the specifics of the apportionment formula, and the issue of jurisdiction to tax. Section 2.03 examines how formulary apportionment developed in the US states. Section 2.04 concludes with observations as to why formulary apportionment perseveres as the income attribution method for US states.

Our purpose is to provide a simple and direct overview of the US states' experience with their predominant method of business income attribution, formulary apportionment – focusing on aspects of that experience which may be relevant for comparison or contrast to income attribution methods in the international tax context.

* The information in this chapter is not intended to be 'written advice concerning one or more federal tax matters' subject to the requirements of section 10.37(a)(2) of Treasury Department Circular 230 because the content is issued for general informational purposes only. The information contained in this chapter is of a general nature and based on authorities that are subject to change. Applicability of the information to specific situations should be determined through consultation with your tax adviser. This chapter represents the views of the authors only and does not necessarily represent the views or opinions of KPMG LLP or EY LLP. The authors wish to thank Nicole Bossert, a senior associate in the State and Local Tax group of the Washington National Tax practice of KPMG LLP, for her invaluable assistance.

§2.02 WHAT DOES 'FORMULARY APPORTIONMENT' MEAN IN THE CONTEXT OF US STATE CORPORATE INCOME TAXES?

[A] The Basic Concept

Forty-five US states and the District of Columbia impose a net income tax or a franchise tax measured by net income, and sometimes both, on corporations with which they have a sufficient connection, i.e., nexus.[1] One key feature of these taxes is how they determine the share of a multistate or multinational taxpayer's tax base that is attributable to the state. Fundamentally, every one of these US jurisdictions applies the same basic, two-part approach for all corporate taxpayers, both those domiciled in the state and those domiciled outside the state.

Under this basic approach, state laws first distinguish 'non-business' income from 'business' income. The two types of income are attributed differently. States typically attribute non-business income - i.e., income arising from transactions, activities, or assets that *are not* operationally related to the taxpayer's trade or business - using direct allocation rules. For example, most state tax laws directly allocate income or gain from a non-business intangible asset, such as dividends or interest, to that state if the taxpayer is domiciled there. Similarly, state laws often directly allocate income or gain from a non-business physical asset, such as land or a building, to that state if the asset is physically located there.

As for the second type of income, states typically attribute business income - i.e., income arising from transactions, activities, or assets that *are* operationally related to the taxpayer's trade or business - using formulary apportionment. Under the US states' method of formulary apportionment, a taxpayer's total business income becomes the pool of income to be apportioned. The state then estimates its taxable share of this total business income based on the share of certain income-producing activities taking place in the state. In essence, formulary apportionment in the context of US state corporate income tax is a method of estimating something that is hard to geographically locate - the share of a corporation's income attributable to a state - using a formula based on things that are easier to geographically locate. Traditionally, these things have been in-state property, payroll, and sales, and traditionally, they have been given equal weight.[2] A simple formula, below, illustrates the general concept.

1. CCH Smart Charts, State Tax Smart Charts, ¶10-510, Starting Point for Computation. Nevada, Ohio, South Dakota, Washington, and Wyoming are the five states that do not impose a net income tax or franchise tax measured by net income. However, Nevada, Ohio, and Washington each impose a gross receipts-based tax.
2. National Conference of Commissioners on Uniform State Laws, Uniform Division of Income for Tax Purposes Act (1957) (UDITPA) § 9.

US States' Traditional Formulary Apportionment Formula

$$\text{Taxpayer's total business income} \times \left(\frac{\left(\frac{Prop_{St}}{Prop_{All}}\right) + \left(\frac{Payroll_{St}}{Payroll_{All}}\right) + \left(\frac{Sales_{St}}{Sales_{All}}\right)}{3} \right) = \text{Taxpayer's business income apportioned to the state}$$

Where:
$Prop_{st}$ = Taxpayer's property in the state
$Prop_{All}$ = Taxpayer's property in all jurisdictions
$Payroll_{st}$ = Taxpayer's payroll in the state
$Payroll_{All}$ = Taxpayer's payroll in all jurisdictions
$Sales_{st}$ = Taxpayer's sales in the state
$Sales_{All}$ = Taxpayer's sales in all jurisdictions

As can be seen, two critical aspects of how any particular state applies formulary apportionment will be how it defines 'business income' and how it constructs the apportionment formula. Both aspects are subject to significant US constitutional limitations, primarily arising under the due process and dormant commerce clauses.[3] And both aspects have been moulded by significant nationwide trends, starting in the early 1920s when states first began adopting corporate income taxes and continuing through today.

Equally critical are the circumstances under which a state has jurisdiction to tax the corporation or its income in the first place. This aspect of state taxation is also subject to significant limitations under the due process and commerce clauses of the US Constitution. States' statutory language describing the circumstances under which tax applies must, or must be interpreted to, fit within those constitutional parameters.

[B] The Income Subject to Apportionment

[1] US Constitutional Parameters: The Unitary Business Principle

The US Constitution generally prohibits a state from taxing income that arises from an activity outside its borders.[4] Essentially, the state would not have jurisdiction to tax that income. However, if an in-state taxpayer's out-of-state activity has some 'concrete connection' with its in-state activity, then the in-state and out-of-state activity are part of a 'single economic enterprise' – i.e., a unitary business – and the state has nexus to tax an apportioned share of the total income arising from that entire unitary business,

3. US Constitution art. I, § 8, cl. 3; US Constitution, amendment XIV, § 1.
4. *ASARCO Inc. v. Idaho State Tax Comm'n*, 458 US 307, 315 (1982), quoting *Miller Brothers Co. v. Maryland*, 347 US 340, 344-345 (1954).

wherever conducted.[5] Vertically integrated businesses (potentially creating economies of scope)[6] and horizontally integrated businesses (potentially creating economies of scale)[7] are examples of businesses with activities that have a 'concrete connection', even if conducted both within and without a state.

This is the 'unitary business principle'. It holds that if income arises from transactions or activities of *a single economic enterprise*, parts of which are conducted in the state, the state has sufficient constitutional nexus with the entire business to apply formulary apportionment for determining the share of that business' total income attributable to the state.

Because the unitary business principle derives from clauses of the US Constitution, the contours of the principle have developed in large part as a result of decisions by the US Supreme Court, which is constitutionally charged with the interpreting those clauses. The US Supreme Court most commonly uses the '*Mobil* three factors' test to determine whether income or gain(loss) is arising from an activity of the unitary business.[8] Under the *Mobil* test, the question is whether contributions to income or gain resulted from 'functional integration, economies of scale, and centralized management'.[9] However, when it comes to limning the edges of a unitary businesses, the Court has tacitly approved many other statements of the unitary test as 'variations on the theme' that are 'not, so to speak, unitary', but which are nonetheless 'logically consistent with the underlying principles motivating the approach'.[10] The Court's most general statement of the unitary test is that there be ownership or control, and a 'flow of value'.[11] Table 2.1 lists a few of the most common statements of the test. Whether income or gain is arising from a single asset, multiple assets, transactions and activities, or the transactions and activities of an ongoing affiliated business, the assets, transactions, or activities must be part of the unitary business for the income to be considered apportionable business income.

5. *See Mobil Oil Corp v. Commissioner of Taxes of Vermont*, 445 US 425, 436-437 (1980); *Container Corp. of Am. v. Franchise Tax Bd.*, 463 US 159, 166 (1983) ('[T]he out-of-State activities of the purported "unitary business" [are required to] be related in some concrete way to the in-State activities').
6. *Exxon Corp. v. Wisconsin Dep't of Revenue*, 447 US 207, 224 (1980); *Underwood Typewriter Co. v. Chamberlain*, 254 US 113, 118-119 (1920); *Bass, Ratcliff & Gretton v. State Tax Comm'n*, 266 US 271, 278-279 (1924).
7. *E.g.*, *Container Corp.*, 463 US at 171-173; *Butler Brothers v. McColgan*, 315 US 501, 504 (1942).
8. *Mobil Oil Corp. v. Comm'r of Taxes of Vermont*, 445 US 425, 438 (1980).
9. *Ibid.* Note that in application, courts have sometimes read the 'and' more like an 'or'.
10. *Container Corp.*, 463 US at 167.
11. *Ibid.*, 178.

Table 2.1 Various Accepted Tests for Unity

US Supreme Court Cases	*Landmark State Cases*
Mobil 3 Factors (1980)[a] - Functional Integration - Economies of Scale, and - Centralized Management *Container* (1983)[b] - Flow of Value, or - Substantial mutual interdependence; and - Unity of ownership *Butler Bros.* 3 Unities (1942)[c] - Unity of ownership - Unity of operation, and - Unity of use	*Edison Cal. Stores* (1947)[d] - Contribution, or - Dependency *Hoechst Celanese* (2001)[e] - Material contribution Multistate Tax Commission(MTC) Model Regulations[f] Indicators of a unitary business: - Same general line of business - Vertical Integration - Strong central management Functional Integration defined as: - Transfer of assets or value - Pooling of assets or value

Notes:

[a] Mobil Oil Corp. v. Comm'r of Taxes of Vermont, 445 US 425, 438 (1980).

[b] *Container Corp. of Am. v. Franchise Tax Bd.*, 463 US 159, 178-179 (1983).

[c] *Butler Brothers v. McColgan*, 315 US 501, 508 (1942).

[d] *Edison Cal. Stores v. McColgan*, 30 Cal.2d 472 (1947).

[e] *Hoechst Celanese Corp. v. Franchise Tax Bd.*, 25 Cal.4th 508 (2001).

[f] Model General Allocation and Apportionment Regulations, MTC Model Reg. IV.1.(b) §§ 2(B)(1)(c)3 (as revised through 29 July 2010).

Whichever test is used, the US Supreme Court has established the unitary business principle as the 'linchpin of apportionability'.[12] The metaphor makes clear that the income and factors used in the apportionment calculation must be associated with the activity of a single economic enterprise, i.e., a unitary business.

[2] State Law Applying the Unitary Business Principle

Separate vs. Combined Reporting

The single *economic* enterprise being conducted by a unitary business may or may not correspond to a single *legal* enterprise. For example, a unitary business could be carried

12. *Mobil*, 445 US at 439.

out through, and entirely contained within, a single corporate entity.[13] But a unitary business could also be carried out through several related entities, including foreign affiliates, operating together.[14]

A state may not constitutionally require a taxpayer to include in its apportionment calculation the income and factors of an entity that is not part of the unitary business. But states routinely limit the calculation to exclude income and factors of some entities that are part of the unitary business. States that choose to limit the apportionment calculation to a single legal entity (i.e., only the income and factors of one corporate taxpayer itself) are 'separate reporting' states. States that allow, or require, the apportionment calculation to be applied to multiple legal entities, if engaged together in a unitary business, are 'combined reporting' states. Indeed, no state generally requires a taxpayer to determine its apportioned share of unitary business income based on the income and factors of the entire unitary business. Only Alaska mandates worldwide combined reporting, and only for oil and gas producers and pipeline companies.[15] Even states that use combined reporting typically either limit or allow taxpayers the option to limit application of the formula to a combined group of unitary affiliates that will usually fall short of the entire 'worldwide' unitary group. For example, almost all combined reporting states exclude, or allow taxpayers to elect to exclude, unitary foreign affiliates, resulting in a 'water's edge' combined report.

Today, over half of the US subnational jurisdictions with a corporate income or franchise tax require some degree of combined reporting.[16] Combined reporting can be described as follows.

US States' Traditional Worldwide Combined Reporting Apportionment Formula

$$\text{Total combined group members' business income} \times \left(\frac{\left(\frac{Prop_{St}}{Prop_{All}}\right) + \left(\frac{Payroll_{St}}{Payroll_{All}}\right) + \left(\frac{Sales_{St}}{Sales_{All}}\right)}{3} \right) = \text{Taxpayer's business income apportioned to the state}$$

Where:
$Prop_{st}$ = Taxpayer's property in the state
$Prop_{All}$ = Total combined group members' property in all jurisdictions
$Payroll_{st}$ = Taxpayer's payroll in the state
$Payroll_{All}$ = Total combined group members' payroll in all jurisdictions

13. *Butler Brothers*, 315 US at 504. Note, it is possible, if rare, that a single legal entity could also be conducting more than one unitary business.
14. *Bass*, 266 US.at 278-279, 281; *Container Corp.*, 463 US at 171; *Barclays Bank plc v. Franchise Tax Bd. of California*, 512 US 298, 302 (1994).
15. Alaska Stat. § 43.20.072.
16. CCH Smart Charts, State Tax Smart Charts, ¶10-550, Mandatory Combination (providing that twenty-nine jurisdictions require some form of combined reporting); *See* Figure 2.1.

$Sales_{st}$ = Taxpayer's sales in the state
$Sales_{All}$ = Total combined group members' sales in all jurisdictions

Because combined reporting simply sums the business net income of the combined unitary affiliates to determine the corporate taxpayer's pre-apportioned tax base, there is no need for a transfer pricing analysis to specifically identify which affiliate 'earned' the income. Under combined reporting, it does not matter where the business net income 'sits' on paper. Whether it has been retained by one affiliate or paid to the other, it will be thrown into a single pool of income to be apportioned.

But to the extent some unitary affiliates are excluded from the apportionment calculation, states' concerns addressed by transfer pricing analyses remain. For example, water's edge combined reporting states exclude most foreign affiliates, even if unitary. And separate reporting excludes all unitary domestic and foreign entities other than the one specific taxpayer. If the excluded unitary affiliate has nexus and is filing with the state on a separate basis, the state's intercompany pricing concerns may be lessened. But states have been paying increasing attention to transfer prices in situations where an excluded affiliate does not have nexus and is not filing. In these situations, if by some measure the transfer prices for a taxpayer's purchases are too high relative to a market price, or the transfer prices for a taxpayer's sales are too low relative to a market price, then states may argue the pool of income subject to apportionment could be smaller than it should be. Most states with a corporate income or franchise tax have enacted some sort of authority to adjust prices to prevent evasion of tax or clearly reflect income, similar to, or at least based on, Internal Revenue Code § 482.[17] Various water's edge combined reporting states have also created exceptions to the water's edge limitation in order not to exclude a unitary foreign entity from the apportionment calculation if it is domiciled in a 'tax haven'.[18]

Definitions of 'Business Income'

Whether a state restricts the scope of apportionable income and factors to that of a single legal entity or looks to the entire unitary business, the next step is to – within that scope – separate the apportionable income from the non-apportionable income. For this purpose, about half the US states use the model Uniform Division of Income for Tax Purposes Act (UDITPA) definition of 'business income', which was promulgated by the Uniform Law Commission in 1957:[19]

17. Internal Revenue Code § 482; Shirley Sicilian, *Comment Now While Multistate Transfer Pricing Group Forming Proposals*, 24(9) J. Multistate Tax'n & Incentives 31 (2015).
18. *See* Shirley Sicilian, *A Slow Motion Trend Toward Tax Haven Exceptions to Water's-Edge Combination*, 25(5) J. Multistate Tax'n & Incentives 36 (2015).
19. Uniform Law Commission (ULC), *Division of Income for Tax Purposes Act*, https://www.uniformlaws.org/committees/community-home?CommunityKey=f2ef73d2-2e5b-488e-a525-51be29fbee47 (accessed 26 Sep. 2019). The ULC (also known as the National Conference of Commissioners on Uniform State Laws) was established in 1892 and provides states with non-partisan model legislation intended 'to bring clarity and stability to critical areas of state statutory law': Uniform Law Commission, *Overview*, https://www.uniformlaws.org/aboutulc/overview (accessed 26 Sep. 2019). BNA Tax Management Portfolios, State Tax Portfolios: Corporate Income Taxes, 1140-2nd: Income Taxes: The Distinction Between Business and

> [I]ncome arising from transactions and activity in the regular course of the taxpayer's trade or business and includes income from tangible and intangible property if the acquisition, management, and disposition of the property constitute integral parts of the taxpayer's regular trade or business operations.[20]

A majority of states that have adopted this definition have interpreted it to include two types of income: transactional and functional. Transactional income refers to 'income arising from transactions and activity in the regular course of the taxpayer's trade or business'.[21] It focuses on the frequency and regularity of the transaction that produces the income. For example, income from the sale of the taxpayer's products to its customers would meet the transactional test. Functional income refers to 'income from tangible and intangible property if the acquisition, management and disposition of the property constitute integral parts of the taxpayer's regular trade or business operations'.[22] The functional test focuses on the property that is being disposed in the transaction that produces the income. For example, income from the sale of machinery or equipment that the taxpayer used to produce its product, or otherwise used in its unitary business, would meet the functional test. The Supreme Court has noted that the UDITPA rule is 'compatible' with the Constitution.[23]

Other states either categorize income by type or apportion income to the full extent allowed under the US Constitution.[24] Some of the latter group follow the more recent model developed by the Multistate Tax Commission (MTC or Commission).[25] The MTC model updates the 'transactional' and 'functional' provisions of the UDITPA model and adds that business income - called 'apportionable income' in the MTC model - includes 'all income that is apportionable under the Constitution of the United States'.[26] This MTC definition reflects a US state trend over recent years to achieve as broad a state statutory definition of apportionable 'business income' as would be allowed under the US Constitution.

To a large degree, this trend began after a number of state court decisions that interpreted the UDITPA language narrowly to require the transactional test be met even for functional income[27] or to exclude gain from the liquidation of a

Nonbusiness Income; Worksheet 2 Adoption of UDITPA, Apportionable Income, Conformity with MTC Regulations, and MTC Membership.

20. UDITPA § 1(a).
21. *Ibid.*
22. *Ibid.*
23. *See Allied-Signal, Inc. v. Dir., Div. of Taxation*, 504 US 768, 786 (1992) ('[i]n the abstract, [business income and non-business income] may be quite compatible with the unitary business principle').
24. *E.g.*, Colo. Rev. Stat. § 39-22-303.6(1)(a)(I) ('"Apportionable income" means: Any income that would be allocable to this state under the United States constitution, but that is apportioned rather than allocated pursuant to the laws of this state').
25. Multistate Tax Commission, Model Multistate Tax Compact Article IV (MTC Art. IV).
26. *Ibid.* § 1(a)(i).
27. *See, e.g., Uniroyal Tire Co. v. State Dep't of Rev.*, 779 So.2d. 227 (Ala. 2000); *Appeal of Chief Industries, Inc.*, 875 P.2d 278 (Kan. 1994); *Phillips Petroleum Co. v. Iowa Dep't of Rev. and Fin.*, 511 N.W.2d 608 (Iowa 1993); *Associated Partnership I, Inc. v. Huddleston*, 889 S.W.2d 190 (Tenn. 1994).

business.[28] In those states, the legislatures generally followed up with a statutory amendment to clarify the functional test or to include all income apportionable under the US Constitution.[29] The MTC model reflects this trend to broadly define apportionable income.

[C] The Apportionment Formula

[1] Constitutional Parameters: Fair Apportionment

The US Constitution requires that an apportionment formula be 'fair', and the US Supreme Court has said that for a formula to be 'fair' it must be internally and externally consistent.[30]

Internal consistency means that 'if applied by every jurisdiction, [the formula] ... would result in no more than all of the unitary business's income being taxed'.[31] Any formula that uses one or more of the three factors, regardless of the weightings, would meet the internal consistency test, including a single factor formula.[32] Note that this test posits a hypothetical: it imagines that every other state uses the same formula. Only if a state's formula creates multiple taxation of interstate commerce under this hypothetical will the formula fail this internal consistency test. Of course, states do not all use the same formula, and there may be multiple taxation in fact. But if the US Supreme Court were to concern itself with multiple taxation that arises simply from the fact that two-state formulas are different, then it would need to choose which formula should take precedence from among the many otherwise fair and non-discriminatory state formulas. To do so would, according to the Supreme Court, improperly place the Court in the role of a legislature.[33] Instead, the hypothetical approach allows a court to isolate multiple taxation that results from discrimination against interstate commerce that is inherent in the apportionment formula.[34]

---

28. *Lenox, Inc. v. Tolson*, 548 S.E.2d 513 (N.C. 2001); *Laurel Pipe Line Co. v. Commonwealth of Pennsylvania Board of Fin. & Rev.*, 642 A.2d 472 (Pa. 1994); *Kemppel v. Zaino*, 746 N.E.2d 1073 (Ohio 2001); *Blessing/White, Inc. v. Zehnder*, 768 N.E.2d 332 (Ill. App. Ct. 2002).
29. *See, e.g.*, H.B. 7, 4th Spec. Sess. (Ala. 2001) (amending Ala. Code § 40-27-1 subsequent to the decision in *Uniroyal Tire Co. v. State Dep't of Rev.*, 779 So.2d. 227 (Ala. 2000)); H.F. 548, 76th Gen. Assemb. (Iowa 1995) (amending Iowa Code Ann. § 422.32 subsequent to the decision in *Phillips Petroleum Co. v. Iowa Dep't of Rev. and Fin.*, 511 N.W. 608 (Iowa 1994)); H.B. 2949, Reg. Sess. (Kan. 2004) (amending Kan. Stat. Ann. § 79-3271 subsequent to the decision in *Appeal of Chief Industries, Inc.*, 875 P.2d 278 (Kan. 1994)); H.B. 1676, 101st Gen. Assemb., Reg. Sess. (Tenn. 1999) (amending Tenn. Code Ann. § 67-4-804 (now Tenn. Code Ann. § 67-4-2004) subsequent to the decision in *Associated Partnership I, Inc. v. Huddleston*, 889 S.W.2d 190 (Tenn. 1994)).
30. *Container Corp.*, 463 US at 169. State apportionment formulas must also be non-discriminatory; i.e., they may not discriminate against interstate commerce in favour of in-state commerce.
31. *Ibid.*
32. *Ibid.*, 183-184.
33. *Moorman Mfg. Co. v. Bair*, 437 US 267, 278 (1978).
34. *Comptroller of Treasury of Md. v. Wynne*, 575 U.S. ___ (2015), 135 S. Ct. 1787 (2015) ('[b]y hypothetically assuming that every State has the same tax structure, the internal consistency test allows courts to isolate the effect of a defendant State's tax scheme. This is a virtue of the test because it allows courts to distinguish between (1) tax schemes that inherently discriminate against interstate commerce without regard to the tax policies of other States, and (2) tax

External consistency requires that 'the factor or factors used in the apportionment formula must actually reflect a reasonable sense of how income is generated'.[35] Undoubtedly, all activities of a unitary business contribute something to the realization of its income.[36] But no apportionment formula could, or even attempts to, include all factors reflecting all activity. And a requirement to do so would certainly defeat the usefulness of formulary apportionment as a 'rough approximation'.[37] Even the model UDITPA three-factor formula includes only three types of taxpayer activity: property, payroll, and sales. These three factors do not exhaust the entire set of factors arguably relevant to the production of income. And none of these three factors is included in its entirety. For example, the property factor typically does not include intangible property; the payroll factor may exclude independent contractors; and the sales factor typically reassigns sales made to the US government on the basis of origination rather than destination.

Despite these omissions, the Supreme Court has acknowledged that '[t]he standard three-factor formula can be justified as a rough, practical approximation of the distribution of either a corporation's sources of income or the social costs which it generates'.[38] Having said that, the Supreme Court recognized that '[s]ome methods of formula apportionment are particularly problematic because they focus on only a small part of the spectrum of activities by which value is generated'.[39] A single sales factor formula may be an example of such a narrow spectrum. Nonetheless, even a single factor formula can provide a reasonable 'rough approximation' of income attributable to a state, and the Supreme Court has 'generally upheld the use of such formulas ...'.[40]

Any formula, whether a single sales formula or the 'benchmark' UDITPA three-factor formula, will occasionally over-reflect or under-reflect income attributable to a state for a particular taxpayer. To be sure, the more narrow the spectrum of activity included in an apportionment formula, the more likely the formula will fail to adequately reflect the share of a particular taxpayers' activity in the taxing state. The Supreme Court has held that 'when the [jurisdiction] has adopted a method *not* intrinsically arbitrary, it will be sustained until proof is offered of an unreasonable and arbitrary application in particular cases'.[41] Indeed, the Court has 'on occasion found the distortive effect of focusing on only one factor so outrageous in a particular case as to require reversal'.[42] So, as long as the formula is not 'intrinsically arbitrary', it will be

schemes that create disparate incentives to engage in interstate commerce (and sometimes result in double taxation) only as a result of the interaction of two different but nondiscriminatory and internally consistent schemes').

35. *Container Corp.*, 463 US at 169.
36. *See, e.g., Hans Rees' Sons, Inc. v. North Carolina*, 283 US 123, 133 (1931).
37. *Moorman*, 437 US at 271.
38. *General Motors Corp. v. D.C.*, 380 US 553, 561 (1983).
39. *Container Corp.*, 463 US at 182.
40. *Ibid.* (citing *Moorman*, US 267 at 275 (upholding single sales factor formula and its application to specific taxpayer)); *Underwood*, 254 US at 120 (upholding a single property factor formula, which did not include intangible property, and its application to a specific taxpayer). *See also*, *Hans Rees' Sons*, 283 US at 134 (holding a single tangible property factor to be 'fair on its face', but rejecting its application to a specific taxpayer in a particular case as distortive).
41. *Hans Rees' Sons*, 283 US at 133 (emphasis added).
42. *Container Corp.*, 463 US at 182-183 (referring to *Hans Rees' Sons*, 283 US at 134).

applied unless, with respect to a particular taxpayer, it is 'out of all appropriate proportion to the business transacted by the [taxpayer] in that State'.[43] The narrower the formula, the more likely the formula will produce distortion as applied to particular taxpayers, and the more frequently a state may be required to provide distortion relief.[44]

[2] State Laws Applying the Fair Apportionment Standard

[a] Factor Weighting

The model UDITPA, finalized by the Uniform Law Commission in 1957, calls for an apportionment formula with equal-weighting of property, payroll, and sales factors:

> All business income shall be apportioned to this state by multiplying the income by a fraction, the numerator of which is the property factor plus the payroll factor plus the sales factor, and the denominator of which is three.[45]

The property and payroll factors are intended to reflect contributions of taxpayers' production assets and activities to the earning of income, while the sales factor is intended to reflect contributions of taxpayers' market activities. During the drafting of UDITPA, some states perceived themselves to be primarily production states, and others perceived themselves to be primarily market states. Both were keen to make sure the benefits and protections they provided for the conduct of those activities were reflected in the model formula for sourcing the resulting income.[46]

In 1942, prior to the widespread adoption of UDIPTA, the US Supreme Court reviewed a similar formula then in use by California and explicitly found that the formula met the US constitutional due process requirement that a state's tax be fairly related to benefits the state provides and the US constitutional commerce clause requirement that income of multistate businesses be fairly apportioned.[47] Nearly forty

43. *Hans Rees' Sons*, 283 US at 135.
44. *Moorman*, 437 US at 274.
45. UDITPA § 9.
46. *See, e.g.*, comments by George V. Powell, chairman of the Uniform Law Commission on allocation and apportionment, responding to concerns by state representatives: '[w]e now have many states with an income tax which is imposed upon multi-state businesses, and the formula used in those states varies a great deal from state to state, with very disastrous results in some instances. A corporation may be doing business in several states, and because of the variance in the formulas may pay tax on considerably more than 100 per cent of its net income. The purpose of this Act is to select a formula which is believed to be fair and then every state use the same formula so that, theoretically, only 100 per cent of the corporation's net income will be subject to income tax by the states'. National Conference of Commissioners on Uniform State Laws, *UDITPA Proceedings in Committee of the Whole* 28 (22 August 1956).
47. *Butler Bros. v. McColgan*, 315 US 501, 505, 506 (1942) ('[The California] percentage was determined by averaging the percentages which (a) value of real and tangible personal property, (b) wages, salaries, commissions, and other compensation of employees, and (c) gross sales, less returns and allowances, attributable to the San Francisco house bore to the corresponding items of all houses of appellant.' ... '[w]e read [California's three factor apportionment formula] as calling for a method of allocation which is "fairly calculated" to assign to California that portion of the net income "reasonably attributable" to the business done there').

years later, in 1983, the Court confirmed its approval and seemed to praise the formula: 'not only has the three-factor formula met our approval, but it has become ... something of a benchmark against which other apportionment formulas are judged'.[48] The Court observed that '[t]he three-factor formula ... has gained wide approval precisely because payroll, property, and sales appear in combination to reflect a very large share of the activities by which value is generated'.[49] At one point in the mid-1970s, virtually all states that imposed an income tax had enacted the UDITPA equal-weighted, three-factor formula.[50]

But as of 2019, only nine jurisdictions still require the equal-weighted, three-factor formula for general corporations.[51] Although states are moving away from using an equal-weighted formula, notably, they are moving away in the same direction – towards more heavily weighting the sales factor. Thirty-seven states now at least double-weight the sales factor.[52] And twenty-four of those use the sales factor only.[53] A primary motivation for this trend is that emphasizing the sales factor, and de-emphasizing (or eliminating) the property and payroll factors, is thought to encourage economic development.[54] Reducing the weight given to property and payroll reduces a potential tax disincentive of locating capital investment and jobs in the state. A formula that uses only the sales factor eliminates that potential. Of course, if all states use the single sales formula, the economic development advantage for any particular state would disappear.

A single sales factor formula is still a type of formulary apportionment and not a form of direct allocation. The sales factor includes gross receipts from all revenue streams, each with potentially different profit margins, to apportion income arising from all of the taxpayer's assets and activities – from production of various products to marketing them, and including income from operational investments such as investment of working capital. The single sales factor formula can be shown as follows.

48. *Container Corp.*, 463 US at 170.
49. *Ibid.*, 183.
50. *See Moorman*, 437 US at 276 (noting that in 1978 'most States use the three-factor formula that Illinois adopted in 1970').
51. CCH Smart Charts, State Tax Smart Charts, ¶11-520, General Apportionment Formula, 2019 Tax Year; *see* Figure 2.2.
52. *Ibid.*
53. *Ibid.*
54. *E.g.*, the Maryland legislation adopting single sales factor came as a recommendation from the Maryland Economic Development and Business Climate Commission. *See Report of the Maryland Economic Development and Business Climate Commission, Phase II: Taxes* 37-38 (January 2016) (primary contributors to the report Mathew J. Bennett, Department of Legislative Services and J. Ryan Bishop, Department of Legislative Services): '[Single Sales Factor] will help reduce overall corporate income tax liabilities for corporations headquartered in the State or with significant amounts of property and payroll in the State.' *See also*, Michael Mazerov, *The 'Single Sales Factor' For State Corporate Taxes: A Boon to Economic Development or a Costly Giveaway?* 1 (Center on Budget and Policy Priorities 2005): 'This change [to single sales factor] is being advanced as a way to stimulate job creation and investment'; and Shirley Sicilian, *Exhibit 2: Multistate Tax Compact Article IV Recommended Amendments*, Memorandum to Cory Fong (Chair), Multistate Tax Commission 22 (3 May 2012), http://www.mtc.gov/uploadedFiles/Multistate_Tax_Commission/Events/2013-14_Committee_Meetings/Exhibit%202%20Memo%20from%20Shirley%20Sicilian%20to%20Cory%20Fong%20Art%20IV%20%20(05-03-2012).pdf (accessed 8 Oct. 2019).

Single Sales Factor Apportionment Formula

$$\text{Taxpayer's total business income} \times \left(\frac{\text{Sales}_{St}}{\text{Sales}_{All}} \right) = \text{Taxpayer business income apportioned to the state}$$

Where:
Sales_{St} = Taxpayer's sales in the state
Sales_{All} = Taxpayer's sales in all jurisdictions

[b] Definition of 'Sales'

UDITPA defines 'sales' as 'all gross receipts [of the taxpayer related to business income]'.[55] As discussed above, 'business income' is income that meets either the transactional test ('income arising from transactions and activity in the regular course of the taxpayer's trade or business') or the functional test ('income from tangible and intangible property if the acquisition, management and disposition of the property constitute integral parts of the taxpayer's regular trade or business operations'). Gross receipts associated with the transactional test include, for example, receipts from the sale of the taxpayer's product - its goods or services - to its customers. Gross receipts associated with the functional test include, for example, receipts from the sale of production plant, machinery, or equipment that the taxpayer used to produce its product. The functional test also includes dividends, or receipts associated with capital gain on the sale of a business, in some states.[56]

But the MTC model, in contrast to the UDITPA model, defines the sales factor to include only those receipts derived by the taxpayer from 'transactions and activity in the regular course of the taxpayer's trade or business'.[57] This language mirrors the description of transactional income contained within the definition of apportionable income. The language reflecting the description of functional income is not included.

Most state statutes contain the broader, UDITPA definition of 'sales'. The narrower, MTC model definition runs counter to the notion that if income from a sale is included as apportionable income, then the receipts from that sale should be included in the sales factor. However, there is also a notion that the sales factor should reflect the taxpayer's market activity, not its production activity. If that is the state's theory, then the type of receipts that are included in the sales factor might reasonably be limited to those that reflect the contribution of the taxpayer's market to the earning of income. Under this line of thinking, it would be unnecessary, and possibly

55. UDITPA § 1(g).
56. *See, e.g.*, *Jim Beam Brands Co. v. Franchise Tax Bd.*, 133 Cal.App.4th 514, 523 (2005).
57. Multistate Tax Commission, Model General Allocation and Apportionment Regulations § 2(a)(6) (2017 MTC Regs) (current as of 2017). Note the Model Multistate Tax Compact uses the term 'receipts factor' rather than 'sales factor'.

counterproductive, to include receipts from transactions involving the taxpayer's production property - such as plant, machinery, and equipment - in the sales factor, even though income from the sale of such property is included in the pool of apportionable income. Including receipts from these types of assets would not reflect the market for the taxpayer's product and could essentially double count the property factor. In a three-factor apportionment formula, the sales factor could reasonably be limited in this way so that it is focused on reflecting the contributions of market states, rather than amplifying the contributions of the production states. If a state has adopted a single sales factor, however, then this analysis may be different. In that case, the state may find it reasonable to provide for some reflection of the contributions of the production state, even if that is accomplished through the sales factor.

[c] Sales Factor Numerator Sourcing

Under both the UDITPA and the MTC models, receipts from the sale of tangible personal property are included in a state's sales factor numerator if the property was 'delivered ... to a purchaser' in the state.[58] If the state to which the property was delivered does not have nexus or jurisdiction to tax the seller, then a 'throwback' rule applies, and the sale is sourced instead to the state from which the property was delivered.[59]

Under UDITPA, sales 'other than sales of tangible personal property' are attributable to a state's sales factor numerator if: '(a) the income-producing activity is performed in this State; or (b) the income-producing activity is performed both in and outside this State and a greater proportion of the income-producing activity is performed in this State than in any other State, based on costs of performance'.[60] This rule is known as the 'cost of performance' (COP) rule. There is no 'throwback' rule for sales of services and intangibles. It would be difficult to know where to 'throw back' a sale of services or intangibles. But more importantly, it is unlikely that a state would not have jurisdiction to tax when there are 'costs of performance' there, since these types of costs generally arise from property and employees, which create a physical presence.

One issue some states have had with the COP rule is that the rule does not do what a sales factor is supposed to do: it does not reflect the taxpayer's market. In 1957, when UDITPA was adopted, place of performance may have been a reasonable proxy for market location. But today, advances in computer and communications technology and expanding markets allow many services to be provided remotely.[61] Instead, the COP rule tends to source receipts to the production states where the costs of performance are incurred in the form of property and payroll. Thus, there has been a concern among some states that the COP rule may duplicate the function of the property and payroll factors. Such duplication of the property and payroll factors could

58. UDITPA § 16(a); MTC Art. IV § 16(a).
59. UDITPA § 16(b).
60. UDITPA § 17.
61. John A. Swain, *Reforming the State Corporate Income Tax: A Market State Approach to the Sourcing of Service Receipts*, 83(2) Tul. L. Rev. 285 (2008).

be counterproductive for states that have tried to more heavily weight the sales factor as a means of encouraging economic development.

The UDITPA drafters acknowledged from the beginning that the COP rule was given short shrift.[62] But their focus on sales of tangible personal property reflected the practical realities of the time. In 1957, most of the economy was mercantile and manufacturing. Major service industries of the day, financial organizations and public utilities, were excluded from UDITPA altogether. Regarding what was left of the service economy, William Pierce - the primary drafter - wrote in 1957 that he expected frequent resort to the UDITPA distortion relief provisions.[63]

Over the years, shortcomings in the COP rule became increasingly problematic, as the service and intangible property sectors grew and became a much greater share of the economy. In addition, significant portions of the major industries that were excluded from the rule - financial services and public utilities - have arguably fallen within UDITPA's scope as they have been deregulated. Thus, a considerably higher percentage of the economy is subject to the UDITPA COP rule today than was the case in 1957.

At the same time that more of the economy is falling under COP numerator sourcing, the trend towards heavily weighting the sales factor magnifies the COP provision's significance. These trends combine to place increasing emphasis on whatever shortcomings there may be with COP sourcing. Some states that could live with COP in the 1960s began to view it as a risk in terms of growing uncertainty over its application, administrative burden, and revenue loss. In the early 2000s, a number of states began to address these concerns by adopting new sales factor numerator sourcing rules for services and intangibles based on where the 'market' is for these products.

The states' shift to single sales factor and market-based sourcing may have come earlier if not for US Supreme Court decisions in 1967 and 1992 suggesting that some form of physical presence may be constitutionally required for state imposition of a tax.[64] If state tax bases were apportioned using sales alone, and there was no physical property or payroll in the state, a good part of state tax bases might not be subject to any state's taxing jurisdiction. The states' caution, as applied to corporate income and franchise taxes, began to erode in the late 1990s and was nearly extinguished by the mid-2010s, as a result of several state court decision that permitted the imposition of corporate income taxes based solely on economic connections to the state.[65] Around

62. John S. Warren, *UDITPA – A Historical Perspective*, 38 St. Tax Notes 133 (2005); *see also* William J. Pierce, *The Uniform Division of Income for State Tax Purposes*, 35(10) Taxes 781 (1957).
63. Pierce, *supra* n. 62, at 780.
64. *See Nat'l Bellas Hess, Inc. v. Dep't of Revenue of State of Ill.*, 386 US 753 (1967); *Quill Corp. v. North Dakota*, 504 US 298 (1992). Note, these are sales and use tax cases, but the question was the extent to which they might also apply to imposition of income and franchise taxes.
65. *KFC v. Iowa Dep't. of Revenue*, 792 N.W. 2d 308 (Iowa 2010), cert. denied, 132 S. Ct. 97 (2011); *Geoffrey, Inc. v. Comm'r of Revenue*, 899 N.E. 2d 87 (2009.), cert. denied, 129 S.Ct. 2853 (2009); *Lanco, Inc. v. Dir., Div. of Taxation*, 879 A.2d 1234 (App. Div. 2005), aff'd 188 N.J. 380 (2006), cert. denied, 127 S. Ct. 2974 (2007); *Geoffrey, Inc. v. South Carolina Tax Comm'n*, 437 S.E.2d 13 (1993), cert. denied, 114 S. Ct. 550 (1993); *A&F Trademark, Inc. v. Tolson*, 605 S.E. 2d 187 (2004), cert. denied, 126 S.Ct. 353 (2005); *Tax Comm'r of State v. MBNA Am. Bank, N.A.* 640

this time, the state trend away from COP towards market-based sourcing intensified. A physical presence requirement was definitively rejected by the US Supreme Court in 2018.[66] So today it is clear that sales in a state over some *de minimis* amount may indicate the seller is conducting a business there and has a sufficient presence - virtual or economic if not physical - to satisfy the commerce clause nexus requirements of the US Constitution.

It can be difficult to identify the 'market' for a sale, particularly when the buyer is itself a multistate business. And as states began moving away from the UDITPA COP provision, they did not necessarily define 'market' in a uniform manner. In 2006, the MTC stepped in to provide a forum for its member states in developing a model market-based sourcing rule for services and intangibles. The MTC states' aim was to help maintain a reasonable level of uniformity by giving state legislatures something to draw on as they modernized their apportionment statutes.[67] The MTC market-based sourcing model, completed eight years later in 2014, eliminates the COP rule and instead sources sales factor numerator receipts for services to where the services are 'delivered' and for intangibles to where the intangibles are 'used'. Model MTC Regulations adopted in 2017 provide extensive detail on how 'delivered' and 'used' should be interpreted.

i. Market-Based Sourcing for Sales of Services

Today, more than three-quarters of the states with a corporate income or franchise tax use some form of market-based sourcing for services.[68] States variously source service receipts to where the taxpayer's customer received a benefit, where the service is delivered, where the customer is located, or where the service is received. The most widely used approach is to source where 'the customer received the benefit of the service'.[69] The MTC chose a different approach for its model, however. Under the MTC approach, receipts from the sale of a service are included in the sales factor numerator

S.E. 2d 226 (2006), cert. denied, 127 S. Ct. 2997 (2007); *FIA Card Services, N.A. v. Tax Comm'r of W. Virginia*, 127 S. Ct. 2997 (2007); *Capital One Bank & Capital One F.S.B. v. Comm'r of Revenue*, 899 N.E.2d 76 (2009), cert. denied, 129 S. Ct. 2827 (2009); *Comptroller of the Treasury v. SYL, Inc.*, 825 A. 2d 399 (2003), cert. denied 124 S. Ct. 478 (2003); *Sec'y, Dep't. of Revenue, State of La. v. GAP (Apparel), Inc.*, 886 So. 2d 459 (LA Ct. App. 2004); *Bridges v. Geoffrey, Inc.*, 984 So. 2d 115 (LA Ct. App. 2008), writ denied sub nom. 978 So. 2d 370; *Geoffrey, Inc. v. Oklahoma Tax Comm'n*, 132 P. 3d 632 (2005). *But see In the Matter of the Income Tax Protest of Scioto Insurance Co.*, Supreme Court of Oklahoma Case Number 108943 (1 May 2012) (no due process nexus with second-tier intellectual property holding company whose only contact with state was receipt of royalty payments from an Oklahoma taxpayer - the first-tier royalty recipient - under a contract not made in Oklahoma) and *J.C. Penney Nat'l Bank v. Johnson*, 19 S.W. 3d 831 (Tenn. Ct. App. 1999) (court applies physical presence nexus rule without deciding whether Commerce Clause compelled such a standard).

66. *See South Dakota v. Wayfair, Inc.*, 138 S. Ct. 2080 (2018).
67. *See* Sicilian, *Multistate Tax Compact Article IV Recommended Amendments*, supra n. 54, at 22. *See also* Joe B. Huddleston & Shirley K. Sicilian, *Should UDITPA be Revisited?* (2009/10) St. & Local Tax Law., Symposium Edition 191, 196.
68. CCH Smart Charts, State Tax Smart Charts, ¶11-525, Sales Factor; *see* Table 2.2.
69. *See, e.g.*, Cal. Rev. & Tax. Code § 25136(a)(1) ('[s]ales from services are in this state to the extent the purchaser of the service received the benefit of the services in this state').

'if the taxpayer's market for the sales is in this state'.[70] The taxpayer's market for sales is relevantly in the state 'if and to the extent the service is delivered to a location in this state'.[71] The MTC expressed its belief that, in most cases, the benefit will be received where the service is delivered, so the two rules should achieve the same sourcing result.[72] Further, the MTC explained it saw three possible advantages of the 'delivered' rule over the 'benefits received' rule:

> The first is that the 'delivered' rule is evaluated more from the perspective of the taxpayer as opposed to the perspective of the taxpayer's customer. Taxpayers may be more likely to know where their services were delivered than where their customers received the benefit. Second, it may also be easier for an auditor to determine, years later, where a taxpayer delivered a product than where the taxpayer's customer received a benefit. And third, using the same 'delivered' rule for services as is used for tangible personal property avoids having to determine whether the taxpayer's product is more of a service or a good, which is increasingly a difficult distinction to make (e.g., electric utilities, research reporting services, or digital products).[73]

MTC model regulations define 'delivery' location for three different categories of services: in-person services,[74] services delivered to the customer or on behalf of the customer or delivered electronically through the customer,[75] and professional services.[76] The first and third categories are fairly straightforward. The second category is recognized as a 'catch-all'. There are special rules for related party transactions involving services delivered electronically.[77] If the taxpayer does not have sufficient information to make a determination, it can make a reasonable approximation. If the taxpayer is not taxable in a state where the receipt would otherwise be sourced, or if the source cannot be reasonably approximated, the receipt is thrown out of the sales factor denominator.[78]

ii. Market-Based Sourcing for Sales or Licences of Intangibles

The situation is similar for sales factor numerator sourcing of receipts from the sale or licensing of intangibles. Today, about half of the states with a corporate income or franchise tax use some form of market-based sourcing for transactions involving intangibles.[79] The remainder use COP, another rule, or do not provide specific guidance. States that use market-based sourcing for intangibles have defined the market fairly uniformly, and consistently with the MTC model, as location of 'use'.

---

70. MTC Art. IV 17(a).
71. MTC Art. IV 17(a)(3).
72. Sicilian, *Multistate Tax Compact Article IV Recommended Amendments*, *supra* n. 54, at 22.
73. *Ibid.*
74. 2017 MTC Regs. IV.17(d)(2).
75. 2017 MTC Regs. IV.17(d)(3).
76. 2017 MTC Regs. IV.17(d)(4).
77. 2017 MTC Regs. IV.17(d)(3)(B)2.b.v.
78. 2017 MTC Regs. IV.17(d)(2)(C).
79. CCH Smart Charts, State Tax Smart Charts, ¶11-525, Sales Factor. *See* Table 2.3.

Under the MTC approach, receipts from a transaction involving intangibles are included in the sales factor numerator 'if the taxpayer's market for sales is in this state'.[80] When the transaction is a rental, lease, or licence, the taxpayer's market for the intangible is in the state 'if and to the extent the property is used in this state, provided that intangible property utilized in marketing a good or service to a consumer is "used in this state" if that good or service is purchased by a consumer who is in this state'.[81] This has been called a 'look-through' rule. The MTC theory in adopting the 'look-through' rule for marketing intangibles was that, regardless of where the licensee is located, the licensor is able to enter into that licence agreement because there is consumer demand for its intangible in the state of the ultimate consumer, and in many cases, the licensor may focus its marketing efforts in that consumer state, as opposed to the state of the licensee. 'Marketing intangibles' include trademarks and trade names used to commercially exploit a product or service; customer lists; distribution channels; and unique names, symbols, or pictures with important promotional value; film, television or multimedia productions, or events for commercial distribution; or franchise agreements.[82]

By model regulation, the MTC has also defined 'use' for rental, lease, or licence of production intangibles and mixed intangibles. 'Production intangibles' include patents, copyrights, or trade secrets to be used in a manufacturing process, where the value of the intangible lies predominately in its use in that process. MTC model regulations presume that the use of a production intangible takes place in the state of the licensee's commercial domicile (if the licensee is a business) or the licensee's state of primary residence (if the licensee is an individual).[83] For mixed intangibles, where the fees are not separately stated in the contract, the MTC model regulation creates a presumption that the licensing fees are paid entirely for the licence of the marketing intangible.[84]

Because a taxpayer may be unlikely to know where an intangible is 'used' if it is sold outright, receipts from the *sale*, as opposed to the licence, of an intangible are 'thrown out' of both the numerator and denominator under the MTC model, with two exceptions.[85] The first exception is for the sale of a contract right or government licence that relates to a specific geographic area.[86] The second exception is for circumstances where the taxpayer makes a contingent sale and thus does have a continuing relationship with the purchaser.[87] Essentially, contingency sales are treated as licences

80. MTC Art. IV 17(a).
81. MTC Art. IV 17(a)(4)(i).
82. MTC Model Reg. IV.17(e)(2).
83. MTC Model Reg. IV.17(e)(2).
84. MTC Model Reg. IV.17(e)(3).
85. MTC Art. IV 17(a)(4)(ii)(C).
86. MTC Art. IV 17(a)(4)(ii)(A).
87. MTC Art. IV 17(a)(4)(ii)(B). A contingency sale is a transaction in which certain terms, such as price, depend on future events. An example of this is a sale of an intangible patented process where the purchaser agrees to make monthly payments to the taxpayer based on the purchaser's volume of production using the patented process. Essentially, contingency sales are treated as licences because they resemble licences.

because they resemble licences. Both exceptions are motivated by the fact that the taxpayer is more likely to know where the intangible is 'used' even after it is sold.

Under the MTC model regulations, receipts from sale or licence of digital goods or services are sourced by special rule as if the product were a service, rather than an intangible.[88] Digital products that are delivered electronically are sourced to a state 'if and to the extent that the taxpayer's customer receives the service in [the state]'.[89] Digital products that are delivered electronically 'on behalf of' the customer (e.g., digital advertising delivered to a customer's market) are sourced to a state 'if and to the extent that the end users or other third-party recipients are in [the state]'.[90] Under the model rule, it is not relevant what the terms of the contractual relationship are, or whether the sale or licence product could be characterized as intangible property rather than a service. At this point, though, only a handful of states have adopted specific guidance for digital products.

If the taxpayer does not have sufficient information to make a determination, it can make a reasonable approximation. If the taxpayer is not taxable in a state where the receipt would otherwise be sourced, or if the source cannot be reasonably approximated, the receipt is thrown out of the sales factor denominator.[91]

[D] Jurisdiction to Tax

[1] US Constitutional Parameter: Nexus

To apply its taxing jurisdiction in the first place, a state must have a sufficient connection, or 'nexus', with the corporation. Both the due process and commerce clauses of the US Constitution set criteria for determining nexus. In a nutshell, the focus of the due process clause is on 'fundamental fairness', while the commerce clause is focused on 'structural concerns about the effects of state regulation on the national economy'.[92]

The US Supreme Court described the limits imposed by the due process clause in the following terms:

> That test is whether property was taken without due process of law, or, if paraphrase we must, whether the taxing power exerted by the state bears fiscal relation to protection, opportunities and benefits given by the state. The simple but controlling question is whether the state has given anything for which it can ask return.[93]

The Court ruled in later cases that states meet the jurisdictional requirements of the due process clause where a business has 'certain minimum contacts with it such that the maintenance of the suit does not offend "traditional notions of fair play and

88. 2017 MTC Regs. IV.17.(g).(2).
89. 2017 MTC Regs. IV.17.(d).(3)(B)2.
90. 2017 MTC Regs. IV.17.(d).(3)(B)3.
91. 2017 MTC Regs. IV.17(d)(2)(C).
92. *Quill Corp. v. North Dakota*, 504 US 298, 325 (1992).
93. *Wisconsin v. J.C. Penney*, 311 US 435, 444 (1940).

substantial justice"'.[94] 'Due process requires some definite link, some minimum connection, between a state and the person, property or transaction it seeks to tax.'[95] The Court's cases applying this 'minimum contacts' test have focused on whether an out-of-state business 'purposefully avails' itself of the benefits of the economic market in the forum state.[96] If so, the due process clause is not a bar to that state's taxing jurisdiction. In *Quill v. North Dakota*, the Court made it clear that a physical presence is not required for due process purposes. Rather, in-state sales alone potentially indicate the seller has 'purposefully avail[ed]' itself of the state's market in satisfaction of due process clause requirements.[97]

In its recent *South Dakota v. Wayfair* decision, the US Supreme Court overturned the physical presence requirement for commerce clause nexus purposes. Many states had already taken the position that the commerce clause physical presence requirement only applied for sales and use tax purposes and did not apply for income or franchise tax purposes. In *Wayfair*, the Court removed all doubt by eliminating the requirement even in the context of sales and use tax. The Court held that imposition of state tax satisfies the 'substantial nexus' requirement of the commerce clause if the taxpayer is 'carrying on business' there.[98] It then further found that having 'sales' in a state may indicate the seller is 'carrying on business' there, which could mean it has some form of connection – economic or virtual, if not physical – sufficient to establish a 'substantial nexus' and authorize the state to require payment of a tax.[99]

[2] State Law Applying the Nexus Standard

Most states have enacted a statutory threshold for imposition of corporate income and franchise taxes that reflects some variation of the US constitutional due process 'fiscal relation' standard labelled 'doing business in the state' or 'deriving income from an in-state source'. Today, only one state explicitly restricts its imposition of corporate income or franchise taxing authority to taxpayers with a physical presence.[100] The rest either explicitly recognize the potential for 'economic nexus' or have not explicitly taken a position.

Ten of the 'economic nexus' states have also adopted some form of the MTC's model 'factor presence' test to set a bright-line nexus standard with *de minimis* thresholds using in-state dollar values of property, payroll, or sales as the threshold measures.[101] Under these tests, the same definitions and numerator sourcing rules used

94. *Int'l Shoe Co. v. State of Wash., Office of Unemployment Comp. & Placement*, 326 US 310, 316 (1945) (quoting *Milliken v. Meyer*, 311 US 457, 463 (1940)).
95. *Miller Brothers Co. v. Maryland*, 347 US 340, 344-45 (1954).
96. *See, e.g., Burger King Corp. v. Rudzewicz*, 471 US 462, 475 (1985).
97. *Quill Corp. v. North Dakota*, 504 US 298, 307 (1992).
98. *South Dakota v. Wayfair, Inc.*, 138 S. Ct. 2080, 2099 (2018).
99. *Ibid.*
100. Texas requires an out-of-state business to have a physical presence in the state to have franchise tax nexus with Texas. Tex. Tax Code Ann. § 171.001(a); Tex. Admin. Code § 3.586.
101. Multistate Tax Commission, *Factor Presence Nexus Standard for Business Activity Taxes* (17 October 2002), http://www.mtc.gov/Uniformity/Adopted-Uniformity-Recommendations (accessed 8 Oct. 2019). *See* CCH Smart Charts, State Tax Smart Charts, ¶10-075, Nexus P.L.

for apportionment apply for the factor presence thresholds. Some of the factor presence states use single sales factor for apportionment purposes, yet still use these three traditional factors to test for more than a *de minimis* presence.

Under a factor presence statute, the state may assert jurisdiction based on some threshold level of in-state sales. When is a sale 'in' a state? Sales of tangible personal property are typically sourced for sales factor numerator purposes to the location where the property is 'delivered'. It is reasonably clear, and states are fairly uniform, when it comes to sourcing these sales - in both a legal and practical sense. But there may not be as high a degree of uniformity and clarity when it comes to sales or licensing of services and intangible property, especially when the customer itself is a multistate business.[102]

Further, unlike a sales tax, an income tax is not a tax on a transaction that occurs in the state. It is a tax on income and, specifically, on income arising from the activity of the taxpayer. The sales factor is based on an assumption that in-state sales are indicative of in-state taxpayer activities - generally, market activities. But that assumption may not hold in all cases under certain sourcing rules. For example, as noted above, some states source receipts from the sale or licence of certain intangibles to the location of the taxpayer's customer's customer (i.e., the location of the ultimate consumer or 'end user') - a 'look through' approach. And the taxpayer may not always be 'carrying on business' in the state of its customer's customer.[103]

§2.03 HOW DID FORMULARY APPORTIONMENT DEVELOP IN THE US STATES?[104]

In their early days, US states relied heavily on property taxes. Formulary apportionment arose in that context. Only after the US federal government imposed an income tax in the early 1900s did most US states follow suit. States then borrowed the apportionment method developed for property tax purposes and applied it to their new business income taxes.

86-272-Doing Business in the State (Alabama, California, Colorado, Connecticut, Michigan, New York, Tennessee, Virginia, Washington (B&O)); CCH Smart Charts, State Tax Smart Charts, ¶14-030, Nexus (Ohio Commercial Activity Tax); CCH Smart Charts, State Tax Smart Charts, ¶60-025, Nexus-Doing Business in the State (Washington Business & Occupation Tax).

102. Shirley Sicilian, Wayfair *in the Context of Corporate Income Tax*, 29(2) J. Multistate Tax'n & Incentives 34 (2019). *See also* Shirley Sicilian, Raj Lapsiwala & Sarah Vergel de Dios, *After* Wayfair, *A Focus on Sourcing*; 28(7) J. Multistate Tax'n & Incentives 39 (2018). *See* Tables 2.2 and 2.3.
103. Sicilian, Wayfair *in the Context of Corporate Income Tax*, *supra* n. 102.
104. This section was developed from the brief history of combined reporting discussed in a prior work of the authors. Joe Huddleston & Shirley Sicilian, *History and Considerations for Combined Reporting: Will States Adopt a Model Combined Reporting Statute?* (2008) St. & Local Tax Law., Symposium Edition 3.

[A] Late 1800s: Genesis of the Unitary Business Principle in the Context of Property Tax

In the late 1800s, property tax was the dominant form of state taxation, and the railroads were one of the few types of businesses that typically operated in more than one state. Railroad property, tracks, and travelling cars physically spanned across state lines. State and county governments felt that the value of the railroad property which formed their tax base was not simply the stand-alone value of rail and cars in the state. They argued, essentially, that the value of the whole was greater than the sum of the parts. The US Supreme Court agreed and explained:

> [A] railroad must be regarded for many, indeed for most purposes, as a *unit*. The track of the road is but one track from one end of it to the other, and, except in its use as one track is of little value. In this track as a whole each county through which it passes has an interest much more important than it has in the limited part of it lying within its boundary. Destroy by any means a few miles of this track within an interior county ... its effect upon the value of the remainder of the road is out of all proportion to the mere local value of the part of it destroyed. . . . It may well be doubted whether any better mode of determining the value of that portion of the track within any one county has been devised than to ascertain the value of the whole road, and apportion the value within the county by its relative length to the whole.[105]

[B] 1910–1920s: Application of the Unitary Business Principle to Corporate Income Tax

In 1909, the federal government enacted a Corporation Excise Tax Act,[106] and states soon followed. The same sort of multistate apportionment issues then naturally arose in the context of an income tax. In *Underwood Typewriter Co. v. Chamberlain*, the US Supreme Court considered a case where the taxpayer earned its income through 'a series of transactions beginning with manufacture in Connecticut and ending with sale in other states. ...The legislature, in attempting to put upon this business its fair share of the burden of taxation, was faced with the impossibility of allocating specifically the profits earned by the processes conducted within its borders. It, therefore, adopted a method of apportionment ...'.[107] The Court upheld the state's logic of applying the unitary concept of formulary apportionment, developed under property tax, to the income tax. A few years later, in *Bass, Ratcliff & Gretton v. State Tax Commission*, the Court was faced with the same issue but in a case where the taxpayer was a foreign corporation, with all of its manufacturing and a large part of its sales in England. The taxpayer imported a portion of its product into the United States which it sold through branch offices in New York and Chicago. The Court relied on *Underwood Typewriter* and found the state was justified in attributing to itself a portion of the income earned

105. *Taylor v. Secor*, 92 US 575, 608 (1875) (emphasis added).
106. Corporation Excise Tax Act of 1909, ch. 6, 36 Stat. 11, 112-117 (1909).
107. *Underwood Typewriter Co. v. Chamberlain*, 254 US 113, 120-121 (1920).

by this multinational corporation from the conduct of its unitary business partly within and partly outside the state. Thus, the Court confirmed that the unitary business and formulary apportionment concepts could apply in the context of an income tax on a worldwide, as well as domestic, basis.[108]

[C] 1930s–1940s: California Combined Reporting

By the 1930s, more corporations were choosing to separately incorporate segments of their business that might have once been distinguished only as divisions of a single corporation. Because most states applied the apportionment calculation separately to each separate corporation (i.e., separate reporting), this raised the question of whether, and if so how, to apportion the income of a unitary business when the business was carried out through separate affiliated taxpayers, rather than through divisions of a single taxpayer. California faced the issue with the movie industry during the 1930s. Movies were produced in California and then sold to out-of-state affiliate distributors. As a result of the pricing, virtually all of the income from film-making was reflected by the out-of-state affiliates and essentially none of it by 'Hollywood'. The California tax agency took the position that the income attributable to the in-state activities should not vary depending on the corporate structure in which a business chose to operate and that prices charged between commonly owned affiliates should not drive the apportionment result. Rather, production and distribution of a film were two parts of a single unitary business. Thus, some share of the income from that entire single business should be attributed to the in-state taxpayer and apportioned to the state. So in 1937, without explicit statutory authority, California determined that taxpayers should apportion income based on a combined report that included the income and factors of all separately incorporated unitary affiliates in order to properly reflect that taxpayer's share of the entire unitary business income attributable to the state.

The state argued combined reporting was implicit in the apportionment statutes, based on the unitary business principle. Under combined reporting, the entire unitary business' income was included in the pool of income to be apportioned and the entire unitary business' factors were included in the denominators of the apportionment factors. Because the numerator of the apportionment factors included only the taxpayer's own California-sourced factors, the California combined report did not calculate the income attributable to the state from the entire unitary business, but only the taxpayer's share of the entire unitary business' income attributable to the state. The movie industry did not challenge the California position. It was not until 1947, in *Edison Cal. Stores v. McColgan*, that the California Court of Appeals upheld the application of formulary apportionment to a unitary business conducted through separate affiliated entities – i.e., combined reporting.[109] And it was another sixteen years before the same California court held in *Superior Oil Co. v. Franchise Tax Board* that the use of a combined report was not something to be imposed at the discretion of

108. *Bass, Ratcliff & Gretton v. State Tax Commission*, 266 US 271 (1924).
109. *Edison Cal. Stores v. McColgan*, 30 Cal.2d 472 (1947).

the tax administrator, but was mandatory in all unitary situations in order to properly apportion income under the unitary business principle.[110] This latter development is an important point, because - depending on the distribution of factors across unitary entities, and on whether those entities are experiencing positive or negative net income - combination can reduce the amount of income attributable to a state as well as increase it.

[D] 1950s–1960s: Widespread Adoption of Uniform Formulary Apportionment

The 1950s and 1960s were characterized by the widespread adoption of uniform formulary apportionment across the states. After decades of attempts by various organizations to draft model state corporate income tax apportionment formulas, the National Conference of Commissioners on Uniform State Laws promulgated its model UDITPA in 1957. It took the states some time to warm up to it. But by the mid-1960s, the states rallied. Congress was seriously considering pre-emptive federal legislation due to a lack of state uniformity, which had become a serious issue in the face of a US Supreme Court decision that broadened the nexus standard beyond most taxpayers' expectations at the time.[111] Many states adopted UDITPA directly into their statutes. Some adopted the Multistate Tax Compact, Article IV of which incorporated UDITPA nearly word for word and Article III of which allowed taxpayers an election to apportion under either Article IV or the existing state apportionment statute. The Compact became effective in 1967 when the required minimum of seven states had enacted it.[112] The Compact also created the MTC as its intergovernmental administrative agency and charged the Commission with several responsibilities.[113] One of these responsibilities is interpretation of Article IV of the Compact through promulgation of proposed model uniform regulations and other laws.[114] Today, Commission membership includes forty-nine states and the District of Columbia, sixteen of which have enacted the Compact.[115]

110. *Superior Oil Co. v. Franchise Tax Bd.*, 60 Cal.2d 406 (1963).
111. H.R. Rep. No. 952, 89th Cong., 1st Sess., Pt. VI, at 1139 (1965). *State v. Northwestern States Portland Cement Co.*, 358 US 450 (1959).
112. The US Supreme Court upheld the validity of the Multistate Tax Compact in *U.S. Steel Corp. v. Multistate Tax Comm'n*, 434 US 452 (1978).
113. *See* Multistate Tax Commission, *MTC History*, http://www.mtc.gov/The-Commission/MTC-History.
114. Model Multistate Tax Compact, Art.VII.1.
115. Sixteen jurisdictions are members of the Compact: Alabama, Alaska, Arkansas, Colorado, District of Columbia, Hawaii, Idaho, Kansas, Missouri, Montana, New Mexico, North Dakota, Oregon, Texas, Utah, and Washington. Another thirty-four states have joined the Commission as either sovereignty or associate members. Sovereignty members are: Georgia, Kentucky, Louisiana, Michigan, Minnesota, New Jersey, Rhode Island, and West Virginia. Associate members are: Arizona, California, Connecticut, Delaware, Florida, Illinois, Indiana, Iowa, Maine, Maryland, Massachusetts, Mississippi, Nebraska, New Hampshire, New York, North Carolina, Ohio, Oklahoma, Pennsylvania, South Carolina, South Dakota, Tennessee, Vermont, Virginia, Wisconsin, and Wyoming. Multistate Tax Commission, *Member States*, http://www.mtc.gov/The-Commission/Member-States.

[E] 1970s–1980s: Other States Consider Combined Reporting

With UDITPA now widely in place, the 1970s and 1980s saw other states pick up on California's lead from the 1930s and consider whether combined reporting was inherent in UDITPA and unitary apportionment. Courts in Idaho, Illinois, Kansas, Montana, Nebraska, and Oregon found that it was.[116] But the tide seemed to turn in the later 1980s, as state courts in Maine and Massachusetts held there must be either explicit statutory authority or distortion in order for the state to require combination.[117] By the end of this period, implicitly or explicitly, sixteen states had adopted combined reporting, and the litigation slowed. It was 2007 before another state, North Carolina, took the position that combination was inherent in formulary apportionment. The state's position was upheld on appeal.[118]

[F] 1980s–1990s: Worldwide Combined Reporting

In 1983, California was once again at the forefront. This time, the state was before the US Supreme Court, in *Container Corporation of America v. Franchise Tax Board*, on the question of whether formulary apportionment could be applied to an international unitary business even if the foreign aspects of the business were separately incorporated.[119] Recall that one of the Court's earliest precedents upholding formulary apportionment, *Bass, Ratcliff & Gretton v. State Tax Commission*, involved a business operating in both England and the United States.[120] The *Container* Court agreed that California could include the income and factors of separately incorporated foreign operations in calculating the share of entire unitary business income attributable to that California taxpayer's (Container Corp.'s) activities in California. Then, in 1994, California was once again before the Court in *Barclays Bank plc v. Franchise Tax Board*.[121] There the Court upheld California's application of combined reporting even though the parent of the unitary business was a foreign corporation.

After the *Container* and *Barclays* cases, a number of states began to show interest in worldwide combined reporting. The international business community and foreign governments became concerned, in part because unitary apportionment was not the standard for United States' or foreign governments' taxation of international income at the national level. The US Treasury formed a Working Group, with state, federal, and business community representatives. The twenty members of this Working Group included chairs of large corporations, state legislators (such as the house speakers from

116. *Am. Smelting & Refining Co. v. Idaho State Tax Comm.*, 592 P.2d 39 (Idaho 1979); *Caterpillar Tractor Co. v. Lenckos*, 417 N.E.2d 1343 (Ill. 1981); *Pioneer Container Corp. v. Beshears*, 684 P.2d 396 (Kan. 1984); *Mont. Dep't of Rev. v. Am. Smelting & Refining Co.*, 567 P.2d 901 (Mont. 1977); *PMD Investment Co. v. State Dep't of Rev.*, 345 N.W.2d 815 (Neb. 1984); *Coca Cola Co. v. Or. Dep't of Rev.*, 533 P.2d 788 (Or. 1975).
117. *Sears, Roebuck & Co. v. State Tax Assessor*, 561 A.2d 172 (Me. 1989); *Polaroid Corp. v. Comm. of Rev.*, 472 N.E.2d 259 (Mass. 1984).
118. *Wal-Mart Stores E., Inc. v. Hinton*, 676 S.E.2d 634 (N.C. Ct. App. 2009).
119. *Container Corp. of Am. v. Franchise Tax Bd.*, 463 US 159 (1983).
120. *Bass, Ratcliff & Gretton v. State Tax Comm.*, 266 US 271 (1924).
121. *Barclays Bank plc v. Franchise Tax Bd.*, 512 US 298 (1994).

Florida and New Hampshire), governors (from Utah, Illinois, and California), and high-level federal staff (including the US Secretary of the Treasury and an Under Secretary of State). Although no agreement was reached, the Working Group Chairman's Report ultimately recommended states adopt water's edge combination that included only those foreign entities doing business in a tax haven.[122] As a result of the report and the extreme unpopularity of the concept among businesses and major US trading partners, the states stepped away from mandatory worldwide combined reporting.

[G] 2000s–2020: Trends in Evidence Today

The early 2000s have been marked by states expanding the scope of income included in the taxpayer's apportionment calculation and narrowing the factors used to apportion that income.

The scope of apportionable income expanded over this period in two ways. First, the number of states requiring combined reporting doubled. A second wave of interest in combined reporting took hold in 2004 when Vermont became the first state in almost twenty years to enact it. Before 2004, only sixteen states used combined reporting. Almost every year since 2004, one or two states have enacted combined reporting. The MTC adopted a model combined reporting statute in 2006 and most states that have adopted combination after that date have largely used the model.[123] States continue to move towards combined reporting today. For example, in 2019, three states adopted mandatory combined reporting: Kentucky, New Jersey, and New Mexico. Today, over half of the forty-six jurisdictions with an income or franchise tax require some form of combined reporting.[124] Second, as described in detail above, many states adopted a definition of 'business income' intended to reach the full extent allowed under the US Constitution.

Meanwhile, states have steadily narrowed the factors used to apportion this income by moving away from the three-factor equal-weighted apportionment formula towards a single sales factor. States have also redefined the sales factor method for numerator sourcing to reflect the market, rather than the costs of performance. The primary motivation behind these two movements has been to remove a disincentive for taxpayers to locate jobs and capital investment in the state.[125]

As noted above, this trend towards market sourcing did not take off until a series of state court cases in the 1990s and early 2000s gave states comfort with the position that physical presence was not required for imposition of an income or franchise tax; rather, economic nexus – i.e., an economic or virtual presence in the state as evidenced

122. US Dep't of the Treasury, Office of the Secretary, *Worldwide Unitary Taxation Working Group: Chairman's Report and Supplemental Views* (August 1984).
123. Multistate Tax Commission, Proposed Model Combined Reporting Statute (29 July 2011), http://www.mtc.gov/uploadedFiles/Multistate_Tax_Commission/Uniformity/Uniformity_Projects/A_-_Z/Combined%20Reporting%20-%20FINAL%20version.pdf (accessed 8 Oct. 2019).
124. CCH Smart Charts, State Tax Smart Charts, ¶11-550, Combined Reports. *See* Figure 2.1.
125. *See* §2.02[C], text at n. 54, *supra*.

by sales in the state – could be sufficient. Today, only one state explicitly restricts its imposition of corporate income or franchise taxing authority to taxpayers with a physical presence.[126] The rest either explicitly recognize the potential for 'economic nexus' based on the presence of in-state sales, or have not explicitly taken a position.[127]

§2.04 WHY DOES FORMULARY APPORTIONMENT PERSEVERE AS THE DE FACTO INCOME ATTRIBUTION METHOD FOR US STATES?

Under our system of government, the US Constitution reflects that certain powers have been delegated to the federal legislature, Congress. The remainders – all those powers that are not explicitly delegated – are reserved to the states or to the people.[128] With that power comes responsibility, and states rely on their sovereign taxing authority to raise the revenue necessary to carry out those governmental responsibilities. Although there are certain exceptions, in general, Congressional proceedings and a very long line of US Supreme Court decisions 'have shown an aversion to federal interference with state tax administration'.[129]

With states' sovereign taxing authority a priority, no states have entered multilateral agreements that would require surrender of any aspect of that authority regarding corporate income or franchise taxes. Sixteen states have enacted the MTC Compact. But the MTC Compact is not a 'binding compact' subject to enforcement by a governing body. As a technical matter, it is an 'advisory compact' that may be modified unilaterally by a member state, consistent with the purposes of the Compact.[130] The MTC is the administrative agency for the Compact and charged with several responsibilities, including staffing members' development of model rules and regulations.[131] But the Commission has no regulatory authority over its members. The Commission's powers are limited to advisory and informational roles.

Nonetheless, in this environment of carefully guarded tax sovereignty, states have gravitated towards a single method, formulary apportionment, for attribution of the corporate income tax base. And states work to maintain some reasonable degree of uniformity with respect to that method. Why? While the answer to that question cannot be known for certain, some observations can be made.

---

126. Tex. Tax Code Ann. § 171.001(a); Tex. Admin. Code § 3.586.
127. CCH Smart Charts, State Tax Smart Charts, ¶14-030, Nexus (Ohio Commercial Activity Tax); CCH Smart Charts, State Tax Smart Charts, ¶60-025, Nexus-Doing Business in the State (Washington Business & Occupation Tax).
128. US Constitution amendment X.
129. *Nat'l Private Truck Council v. Oklahoma Tax Comm'n*, 515 US 582, 586 (1995). *See also, e.g.*, Tax Injunction Act 28 USC §1341; *Dows v. Chicago*, 78 US 108 (1870); *Matthews v. Rodgers*, 284 US 521 (1932); *Fair Assessment in Real Estate Association, Inc., et al., v. McNary, et al.*, 454 US 100 (1981); *Great Lakes Dredge & Dock Co. v. Huffman*, 319 US 293 (1943).
130. *The Gillette Company, et al. v. Franchise Tax Board*, 363 P.3d 94 (2015).
131. Model Multistate Tax Compact Arts. VI and VII.

[A] Relative Simplicity

No corporate income attribution method would ever be described as 'simple'. But one could arguably say that formulary apportionment is *relatively* simple compared to other income attribution methods. Simplicity was a goal of the original UDITPA drafters and was also a goal of the MTC in forging its amendments to the version of UDITPA in Article IV of the MTC model Compact. The US Supreme Court itself noted that formulary apportionment is only a 'rough approximation' of the income attributable to a state.[132] The thought of the states and the US Supreme Court is that an income attribution method does not really need to be anything more than that. The US Supreme Court has gone so far as to suggest that it would be 'misleading to characterize the income of [a] business as having a single identifiable "source"'.[133] In the view of the Court, '[t]he principal virtue of the unitary business principle of taxation is that it does a better job of accounting for "the many subtle and largely unquantifiable transfers of value that take place among the components of a single enterprise" than, for example, geographical or transactional accounting'.[134]

[B] Inherent Parameters and Incentives for Uniformity

Of course, there are innumerable details around a system of formulary apportionment that each state legislature and administrative agency must consider. Lack of uniformity with respect to important details creates problems, most notably the potential for multiple taxation. But there are some inherent limitations that states must take into account, and some uniformity incentives that states tend to take into account, when considering their options. These 'guardrails' help maintain some degree of uniformity.

The main limitation is that a state's formulary apportionment structure must fall within the parameters of the US Constitution. There is a great deal of room for diversity within these parameters, but they do set some outer boundaries. And, within these boundaries, there are incentives and common objectives that lead states to lean in the direction of uniformity. Examples are the revenue-sharing objectives that led to the development of the UDITPA three-factor formula in the 1950s, the desire to avoid Congressional pre-emption that led to the enactments of UDITPA in the 1960s, and the economic development objectives driving the movement towards a single sales factor and market-based sourcing in recent years. The national movement towards combined reporting and expanded definition of business income addresses concerns several states have raised regarding income shifting across affiliates, among other things.

States may also recognize uniformity as an objective in itself. The use of formulary apportionment, scope of the unitary business it applies to, definition of business income, choice of factors, definition of factors, and sourcing of factor numerators are the main components of formulary apportionment. Common understandings and applications of these components, even if not entirely uniform, can

132. *Moorman Mfg. Co. v. Bair*, 437 US 267, 273 (1978).
133. *Mobil*, 445 US at 438.
134. *Allied-Signal*, 504 US at 783.

reduce compliance costs for taxpayers, and reduced compliance cost for taxpayers can lead to increased compliance for states. Uniformity also reduces administrative costs for states that can then piggyback on each other's regulations, case law experiences, and administrative experiences and leads to more productive information exchanges between the states. States with similar laws are more likely to speak with one voice in Congress and support each other at the US Supreme Court. If lack of uniformity were to become extreme, Congress may be prompted to step in and pre-empt states by setting some apportionment boundaries of its own, as nearly occurred half a century ago – something no state would welcome.

[C] Forums for Promoting Model Laws and Uniform Administrative Practices

States have created forums that may assist with promoting uniformity in tax laws. The Federation of Tax Administrators (FTA) and the MTC are two of the main forums. The FTA is an association of fifty state tax agencies and some local government tax agencies; it tends to focus on administrative and operational issues. The MTC is an intergovernmental agency whose membership includes forty-nine states and the District of Columbia. Each member state is represented at the MTC by its tax agency Director or Commissioner and other tax agency staff. The MTC develops model business tax laws which states may consider for adoption. The MTC's procedure for developing model laws fosters inclusivity by giving each state a voice and a vote. Even non-Compact member states participate and vote on most MTC committees. Likewise, taxpayers and the general public may participate in workgroups, address the committees, and testify during public hearings on proposed model laws. There is no requirement that member states adopt the MTC model laws once they have been developed. But the models are a resource for states and are often used, in whole or part, by states when drafting their own laws on those topics.[135]

[D] Flexibility

[1] Flexibility to Modify the Formula on a Case-by-Case Basis

Formulary apportionment, as adopted by the US states, has built-in safety valves to deal with extreme results. The US Constitution requires a state to offer an alternative apportionment formula for any particular taxpayer if the state's statutory regime, though it might otherwise be constitutional, nonetheless results in attribution of that taxpayer's income to the state that is 'out of all appropriate proportion' to the taxpayer's business conducted there.[136] As a result, virtually every state's statute includes tax agency authority to require or, at the request of the taxpayer, to permit use

135. *E.g.*, every state combined reporting statute that has been enacted since 2006 has been based in whole or part on the MTC model.
136. *Hans Rees' Sons, Inc. v. North Carolina*, 283 US 123, 135 (1931).

of an alternative formula. In fact most states have adopted the UDITPA language which authorizes the agency to provide relief at a lower threshold: if the general formula does not 'fairly reflect' the taxpayer's business activities in the state.

Sometimes there can be multiple taxation of a taxpayer's income by two or more states even though none of the states' formulas is necessarily distortive for that taxpayer under either the US Constitutional or state statutory standards. The MTC created a forum to address these circumstances. Under the MTC Alternative Dispute Resolution Program, multiple states may engage in alternative dispute resolution – non-binding mediation or non-binding arbitration – at a taxpayer's request. In addition, the MTC has adopted model regulatory language under which a state would commit to engage in this Program if the taxpayer requests it when faced with multiple taxation arising from different state sales factor numerator sourcing provisions for services.[137] The MTC Program has not been used extensively. But now that almost all states have moved to single sales factor sourcing, the potential for significant multiple taxation due to numerator sourcing differences has increased and these types of 'relief valves' may become increasingly important.

[2] Flexibility to Modify the Formula Generally

While the premium placed on state sovereignty and lack of multilateral agreements creates a potential for multiple taxation, the fact that states have not tied themselves down to particular agreements means that their legislatures have more scope to adapt and adjust their apportionment structures to meet changing economic conditions and tax policy objectives. Model laws that help states achieve their new objectives while maintaining some reasonable degree of uniformity can be useful during these times of transition. And in a multi-jurisdictional arrangement that allows such a high degree of unilateral decision-making, it is important that taxpayers have forums and mechanisms available to address instances of multiple taxation, especially during times of transition.

137. 2017 MTC Regs. IV.17.(h).

Map 2.1 US State Combined Reporting – January 2019

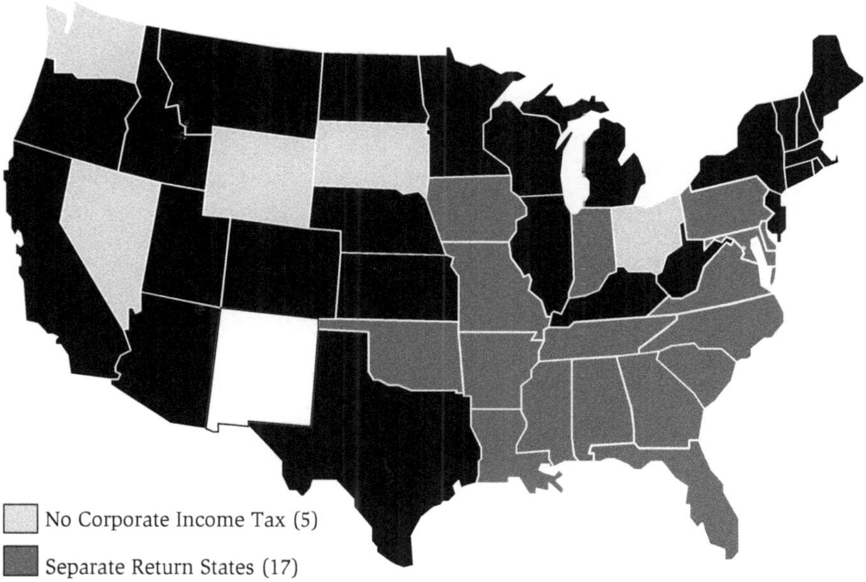

No Corporate Income Tax (5)

Separate Return States (17)

Mandatory Unitary Combined Reporting (AK, HI, DC)(28)

Combined reporting for certain retailers until 2020 when combined or consolidated reporting is required (1)

AK: Alaska
HI: Hawaii
DC: District of Columbia.

Map 2.2 US State Apportionment Formulas – January 2019

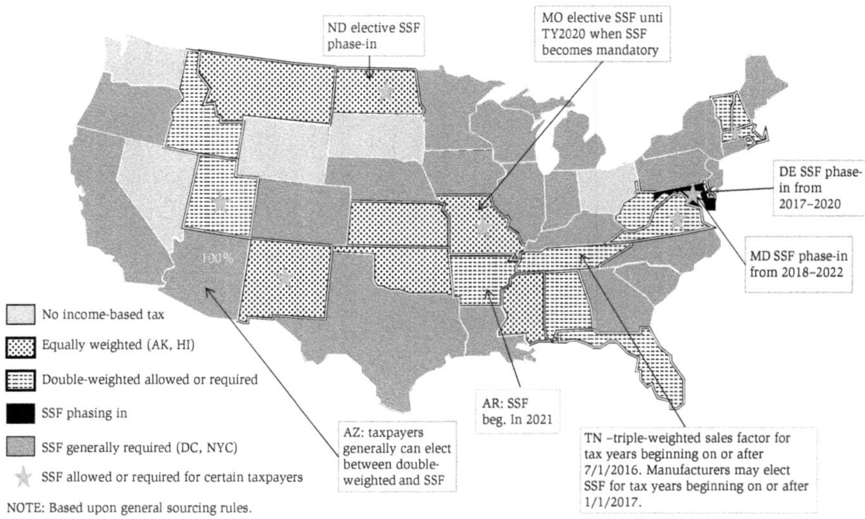

Note: Based upon general sourcing rules.
ND: North Dakota
MO: Missouri
DE: Delaware
AK: Alaska
HI: Hawaii
DC: District of Columbia
NYC: New York City
AZ: Arizona
AR: Arkansas
TN: Tennessee
TY: Tax Year
SSF: Single Sales Factor.

Table 2.2 Sales Factor Numerator Sourcing for Services – January 2019

Market Based Sourcing Customer Activity	Market Based Sourcing Taxpayer Activity	Cost of Performance
Benefit Received • Arizona (elective)* • California* • Georgia* • Iowa* • Indiana* (beg. 2019) • Michigan* • Missouri* (if SSF elected and if ultimate beneficiary is in MO; mandatory beg. in 2020) • New Jersey* (beg. 2019) • New York* • Ohio (CAT) • Rhode Island* • Utah* (SSF phase in) • Washington (B&O) • Wisconsin* ***Service Received*** • Illinois* • Maine* • Minnesota* ***Service Used*** • Connecticut • Hawaii (beg. 2020) ***Customer Located*** • Maryland* (SSF phase in) • Nebraska* • Oklahoma	***Service Delivered*** • Alabama • Colorado (beg. 2019)* • District of Columbia* • Kentucky* (beg. 2018) • Louisiana* • Massachusetts • Montana (beg. 2018) • New Hampshire (beg. 2021) • New Mexico (beg. 2020) • Oregon (beg. 2018)* • Pennsylvania* • Tennessee • Vermont (beg. 2020) ***Service Performed*** • New Jersey • South Carolina • Texas*	• Alaska • Arkansas • Delaware • Florida • Idaho • Kansas • Mississippi • North Carolina* • North Dakota • Virginia • West Virginia

* Single Sales Factor Apportionment

* Single Sales Factor Apportionment.

SSF: Single Sales Factor

CAT: Commercial Activity Tax

MO: Missouri

B&O: Business and Occupation Tax.

Table 2.3 Sales Factor Numerator Sourcing for Intangibles – January 2019

Market/ Use	Cost of Performance	Other
• Alabama	• Alaska	***Commercial Domicile***
• California	• Arizona (elective)	• Texas
• Connecticut	• Arkansas	• Oklahoma
• District of Columbia	• Delaware	
• Georgia	• Florida	***Other***
• Hawaii	• Idaho	• Colorado (as TPP)
• Illinois	• Kansas	• Maryland (no guidance)
• Indiana	• Mississippi	• Wisconsin (use, commercial domicile, or billing)
• Iowa	• Missouri (elective)	
• Kentucky	• North Dakota	
• Louisiana	• Pennsylvania	
• Maine	• Virginia	
• Massachusetts	• West Virginia	
• Michigan		
• Minnesota		
• Montana		
• Nebraska		
• New Hampshire		
• New Jersey		
• New Mexico		
• New York		
• North Carolina		
• Oregon		
• Rhode Island		
• South Carolina		
• Tennessee		
• Utah		
• Vermont		

TPP: tangible personal property.

CHAPTER 3

Formulary Apportionment in Canada and Taxation of Corporate Income in 2019: Current Practice, Origins and Evaluation

*Michael Smart & François Vaillancourt**

§3.01 INTRODUCTION

The purpose of this chapter is to present the Canadian approach to apportioning taxable income, commonly referred to as profits, between provinces for income taxation purposes. This can be of interest for jurisdictions considering implementing such a formula, as it has been in use in Canada for over seventy years. The chapter is set out as follows. Section 3.02 presents details on Canadian provincial corporate income taxation (CIT) and data on the importance of multi-provincial firms in Canada and then turns to an analysis of the formulas used to allocate profits in 2019. Section 3.03 examines the history of how these formulas came about in the context of changes in the role of the Canadian federal and provincial governments in corporate income taxation. Section 3.04 turns to a consideration of the general purpose of formulary apportionment and then examines the specific issues of tax shifting between provinces and the interaction of formulary apportionment and Canada's provincial fiscal equalization scheme.

* The authors thank participants in the Formulary Apportionment workshop held at the Centre for Interuniversity Research and Analysis of Organizations (CIRANO), Montréal, 25-26 April 2019 for their useful comments.

§3.02 FORMULARY APPORTIONMENT IN CANADA: WHY AND HOW

This section presents the context in which formulary apportionment operates in Canada and then turns to an analysis of the formulas used.

[A] Provincial Taxation of Corporate Income in Canada and Multi-Provincial Firms

The need for formulary apportionment comes from the interaction in a given economic space (usually a country) of: (i) jurisdictions such as subnational governments (SNGs) that tax corporate profits and (ii) taxable entities (in this chapter, termed multi-jurisdictional enterprises – MJEs) with activities in more than one such jurisdiction. In such cases, application of the source and arm's-length principles may be difficult, creating risks of double taxation or non-taxation of MJE profits. We first discuss SNG taxation and then examine the importance and characteristics of MJEs in Canada.

[1] Provincial Taxation in Canada

In Canada, the corporate income tax base has long been vertically shared between federal and provincial governments, with both orders of government exercising independent tax powers in the field and with all ten Canadian provinces levying their own corporate taxes at significant levels.

There is therefore considerable decentralization of legal tax powers in the Canadian system. In particular, provincial governments have constitutional powers to design the corporate tax base as they choose and freedom in the choice of statutory tax rates. General corporate tax rates levied by the provinces currently range from 11% to 16%, compared to a federal rate of 15%. Like the federal government, most provinces levy a low rate on small private companies, and a few provinces levy a reduced rate on manufacturing and processing activities as well.

Provincial governments currently receive about one-third of combined federal and provincial revenues from corporate income taxes.[1] It is important to emphasize, however, that this subnational revenue share represents decentralization with a high degree of tax autonomy for the provinces, including discretion over tax rates as well as certain aspects of the tax base. This is in contrast to other federal countries, where corporate income tax revenues may be earmarked in part for SNGs, but tax powers

1. For 2016: (1) federal CIT was CAD 53.408 billion; (2) Québec CIT was CAD 8.559 billion; and (3) other provinces' CIT was CAD 18.804 billion. Sources: (1) Canada Revenue Agency, *Corporate Statistical Tables (2012 to 2016 Tax Years)* Table 10: Federal Tax Payable by Jurisdiction, 2012 to 2016 (2019), https://www.canada.ca/content/dam/cra-arc/prog-policy/stats/t2-corp-stats/2012-2016/t2-crp-sttstcs-tbl10-e.pdf (accessed 1 July 2019); (2) Revenu Québec, *Rapport Annuel de Gestion 2017-2018* 21, Table 2 (2018), https://www.revenuquebec.ca/documents/fr/publications/adm/ADM-500%282018-12%29.pdf; (3) Canada Revenue Agency, *Corporate Statistical Tables (2012 to 2016 Tax Years)* Table 11: Provincial or Territorial Tax Payable by Jurisdiction, 2012 to 2016, https://www.canada.ca/content/dam/cra-arc/prog-policy/stats/t2-corp-stats/2012-2016/t2-crp-sttstcs-tbl11-e.pdf.

remain the purview of the central government; this is the case for Austria or Germany, for example.

Notwithstanding the decentralization of tax powers, there is considerable coordination of tax policy and tax collection among federal and provincial governments. Eight (all but Alberta and Québec) of the ten provinces (and three territories) have entered into Tax Collection Agreements (TCAs)[2] with the federal government, whereby provincial corporate income taxes are legislated provincially but administered and collected by the federal Canada Revenue Agency (CRA).[3] This implies 'one-stop shopping' for taxpayers in the eight acceding provinces (i.e., those with TCAs). Provincial own-source corporate tax revenues are remitted by the CRA to provincial governments - nominally on a derivation basis, although this is modified through apportionment arrangements described in §3.02[B] below. Under the TCAs, costs of administering the system are borne by the CRA, provided that the provincial government abides by the federal definition of the tax base and uses similar measures to those of the federal government. Where a province chooses to deviate from the federal tax base, for example by introducing different tax credits, a system of incremental cost pricing is applied to allocate the cost of administering this deviation to the relevant provincial treasury.[4] For example, the TCA with Ontario implemented in 2008 states that:

> Clause 3.6 of the Model TCA ... sets out the rules with respect to the administrative fees payable for a year by Ontario to Canada for the administration of corporation income tax. Consistent with this costing approach, specific elements of the provincial corporation income tax system not covered by the general provisions of the Model TCA, such as a provincial corporate minimum tax, will be costed on an incremental basis by CRA.[5]

Two large provinces, Alberta and Québec, have not acceded to the TCA system for CIT, and so these provincial governments administer their own CIT systems. CIT taxpayers in those provinces therefore file separate returns at the federal and provincial levels. Nevertheless, these non-acceding provinces coordinate closely on tax policy with the federal government, and deviations from the federal tax base definitions are rare in practice. Moreover, Alberta appears to rely largely on federal audit and enforcement activities to administer its CIT, while Québec spends substantially on tax

2. For general if somewhat dated information on TCAs in Canada, see Finance Canada, *Federal Administration of Provincial Taxes*, http://www.collectionscanada.gc.ca/eppp-archive/100/200/301/finance/other_pubs/both/fapt-ef/fapt1e.html (accessed 1 July 2019).
3. In the case of the personal income tax, only Québec has not entered into a TCA.
4. CRA collects fees for 'non-harmonized measures', i.e., provincial measures that differ from the federal ones. In 2017 CRA collected CAD 112 million in fees from provinces and CAD 113 billion of provincial tax revenues. Thus fees account for 0.1% of provincial collected revenues: Canada Revenue Agency, *2017-18 Departmental Results Report, Financial Statements* 26 and 30 (2018), https://www.canada.ca/en/revenue-agency/corporate/about-canada-revenue-agency-cra/departmental-performance-reports/2017-18-departmental-results-report.html.
5. Memorandum of Agreement Concerning a Single Administration of Ontario Corporate Tax, Annex a, item 2.2, https://www.fin.gov.on.ca/en/agreements/moa_ctao.html.

administration.[6] This differentiated spending is most likely explained by the fact that Alberta only administers CIT, while Québec administers provincial CIT, personal income tax and provincial value added tax, as well as the federal goods and services tax (GST) for its province.

Table 3.1 presents evidence on general provincial corporate income tax rates for three years; they have been slowly converging; this is confirmed when annual data for the four largest provinces and the other six together are examined in Figure 3.1.

Table 3.1 General Corporate Income Tax Rate by Provinces, Canada, 2000, 2010 and 2018, %

	2000	*2010*	*2018*
NFL	14	14	15
PEI	16	16	16
NS	16	16	16
NB	17	11	14
Qc	9	11.9	11.7
Ont	14.5	14	11.5
Man	17	12	12
Sask	17	12	12
Alt	15.5	10	12
BC	16.5	10.5	12
Range	8	5.5	4.5

Sources: 2000 and 2010: Department of Finance, Canada, Interprovincial Tax Planning by Corporate Groups in Canada: A Review of the Evidence, in Tax Expenditures and Evaluations 2014 71, 88, Table A1 (2015); 2018: BDO, 2018 Corporate Income Tax Rates (21 Jun. 2018), http://www.bdo.ca/BDO/media/Misc-Documents/2018-Corporate-Income-Tax-Rates_v2018-06-21.pdf.

6. In Alberta, the provincial Tax and Revenue Administration department had an annual budget of CAD 22 million in 2017-18, or about CAD 5.50 per provincial resident: Alberta Treasury Board and Finance, *Annual Report 2017-18* 107 (2018). In comparison, aggregate spending by the federal Canada Revenue Agency was CAD 3.87 billion, or about CAD 110 per national resident. In Québec the budget of the Agence Revenu Québec was CAD 1.11 billion in 2017 or CAD 132 per Québec resident. Core provincial spending was CAD 827 million or CAD 100 per resident, while core Québec + GST cost reimbursement from the federal government was CAD 973 million or CAD 117 per resident: Revenu Québec, *Rapport Annuel de Gestion 2016-2017* 134 (2017), https://www.revenuquebec.ca/documents/fr/publications/adm/ADM-500%282017-12%29.pdf.

Figure 3.1 Provincial Statutory Corporate Tax Rates, 1995-2016

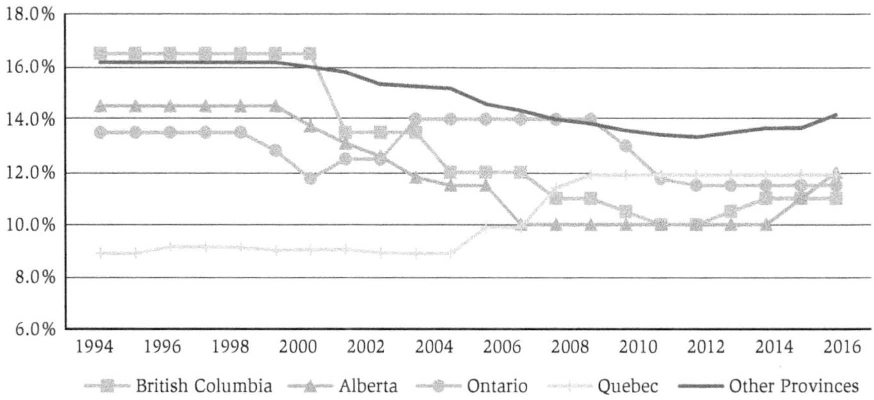

Source: Canadian Tax Foundation, *Finances of the Nation* database, http://financesofthenation .ca/.

[2] Multi-Provincial Firms in Canada

How important are multi-provincial businesses? The Mintz Committee reported that 'at present, about 45 percent of corporate taxable income is earned by corporations operating in more than one jurisdiction'.[7] Using taxation statistics for the period 2011-2015, we find that multi-jurisdiction firms account for an average share of total revenue of 43%[8] and net income of 37%,[9] with much greater variability between years for the second (30%-42%) than the first indicator (41%-44%). Using different data, Rollin finds that the 23,810 multi-provincial businesses account in Canada for 2.3% of businesses and 43.4% of employees.[10] Their importance varies according to the following factors:[11]

- size: 80% of businesses with more than 500 employees are multi-provincial compared to only 8.5% of those with 10-199 employees;

7. Technical Committee on Business Taxation (Jack M. Mintz, chair), *Report of the Technical Committee on Business Taxation* 11.9-11.10 (Department of Finance, Canada 1997) (Mintz Committee).
8. Our calculations using Canada Revenue Agency, *Corporate Statistical Tables (2011 to 2015 Tax Years)* Table 3: Total Revenue by Jurisdiction, 2011 to 2015 (2018), https://www.canada.ca/content/dam/cra-arc/prog-policy/stats/t2-corp-stats/2011-2015/tbl03-en.pdf (accessed 2 July 2019).
9. Our calculations using *ibid.*, Table 4: Net Income (or Loss) for Income Tax Purposes by Jurisdiction, 2011 to 2015, https://www.canada.ca/content/dam/cra-arc/prog-policy/stats/t2-corp-stats/2011-2015/tbl04-en.pdf.
10. Anne-Marie Rollin, *Enterprises with Employees in Many Provinces or Territories*, Statistics Canada Economic Insights Analytical Paper 1 (2014), https://www150.statcan.gc.ca/n1/en/pub/11-626-x/11-626-x2014037-eng.pdf?st=vh4D002j (accessed 2 July 2019).
11. *Ibid.*, various tables.

- sector: only 21.8% of employees work for construction businesses present in more than one province, while 75.2% of employees in information and cultural industries do so;
- number of provinces/pairing: 68.8 % of multi-provincial businesses are present in only two provinces. Most common pairings are Prairie provinces (Alberta, Saskatchewan and Manitoba) and British Columbia, Ontario and Québec, and Ontario and Prairie provinces;
- ownership: foreign-owned enterprises tend to be present in more than one province more often than Canadian-owned enterprises.

[B] The Formula

The existing formula is specified in section 400 of the Income Tax Regulations, entitled Taxable Income Earned in a Province by a Corporation. It relies on the presence of a permanent establishment to identify provinces entitled or not to levy a tax on a share of taxable income. More precisely:

> 402 (1) Where, in a taxation year, a corporation had a permanent establishment in a particular province and had no permanent establishment outside that province, the whole of its taxable income for the year shall be deemed to have been earned therein.
>
> 402 (2) Where, in a taxation year, a corporation had no permanent establishment in a particular province, no part of its taxable income for the year shall be deemed to have been earned therein.

The presence of a permanent establishment relies on factors set out in section 400(2) such as the presence of 'substantial machinery' or the ownership of land in a particular jurisdiction. How is the income allocated between eligible provinces? The general rule is as follows: 50% according to the share of gross revenue and 50% according to the share of salaries and wages associated with a province. If one of these is nil, the other is used with a 100% weight. Establishing the place where revenue is earned, addressed in section 402(4), is based on the destination of a shipment in the case of the sale of goods and the corporation having a permanent establishment in that destination. The attribution of gross revenue from services is based on the location where services are rendered, as prescribed in paragraphs 402(4) (g) to (h).

Nine sectors have specific rules. They are (as ordered in the regulation):

> *Insurance corporations*: 100% according to the distribution of net premiums based on the location of the insured property or the place of residence of the insured person;
> *Banks*: one-third according to the share of salaries and wages and two-thirds according to the proportion between provinces of the total amount of loans and deposits;
> *Trust and loan corporations*: 100% according to the share of gross income;

Railways: 50% according to the share of equated track miles[12] and 50% according to the share of gross ton miles;
Airlines: 25% according to the share of capital cost of all fixed assets except aircraft and 75% according to the share of revenue plane miles[13] flown in each province;
Grain elevator operators: 50% according to the share of the number of bushels received and 50% according to the share of salaries and wages;
Bus and truck operators: 50% according to the share of kilometres and 50% according to the share of salaries and wages;
Ship operators: for its allocable income, the share of port-call-tonnage,[14] and for excess income, the share of salaries and wages;
Pipeline operators: 50% according to the share of pipeline miles and 50% according to the share of salaries and wages.

Finally, the tax regulations are supplemented by four Provincial income allocation newsletters,[15] while CIT statistics are found in a series of tables produced by the Canada Revenue Agency.[16]

Figure 3.2 presents the outcome for 2015 of the application of these income allocation rules and the taxation of single-province taxpayers.

12. Equated track miles is made up of: (a) the number of miles of first main track; (b) 80% of the number of miles of other main tracks; and (c) 50% of the number of miles of yard tracks and sidings.
13. Revenue plane miles are weighted according to take-off weight of the aircraft defined when feasible as the maximum permissible take-off weight according to Transport Canada.
14. Port-call-tonnage in a province is the number of calls made in the year multiplied by the registered net tonnage of that ship.
15. Canada Revenue Agency, Gross Revenue – Exclusion of Interest, Provincial Income Allocation Newsletter No. 1 (February 2010); Canada Revenue Agency, Permanent Establishment – Substantial Machinery or Equipment, Provincial Income Allocation Newsletter No. 2 (February 2010); Canada Revenue Agency, Gross Revenue – Leasing Revenue, Provincial Income Allocation Newsletter No. 3 (February 2010); Canada Revenue Agency, Salaries and Wages – Inclusion of Taxable Benefits, Provincial Income Allocation Newsletter No. 4 (March 2013). *See* https://www.canada.ca/en/revenue-agency/services/tax/technical-information/technical-information-provincial-income-allocation-newsletters.html.
16. *See* https://www.canada.ca/en/revenue-agency/programs/about-canada-revenue-agency-cra/income-statistics-gst-hst-statistics/t2-corporate-statistics.html.

Figure 3.2 Share of Taxable Income, All Corporations, Canada, Ten Provinces, 2015

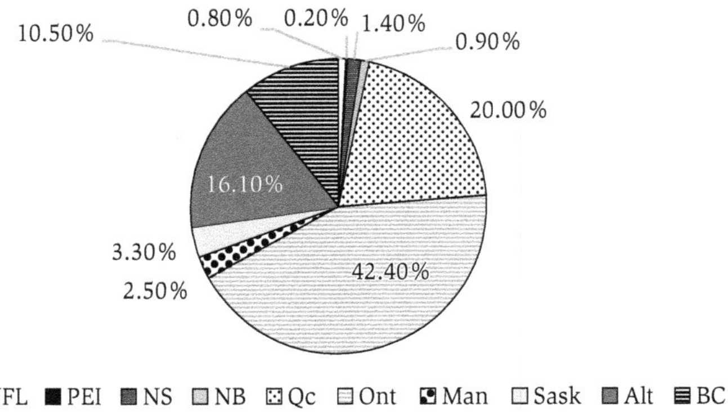

Source: Calculations by authors using Canada Revenue Agency, *Corporate Statistical Tables (2011 to 2015 Tax Years)* Table 5: Taxable Income by Jurisdiction, 2011 to 2015 (2018), https://www.canada.ca/content/dam/cra-arc/prog-policy/stats/t2-corp-stats/2011-2015/tbl05-en.pdf.

What is the importance of the sector-specific rules? Data from CRA indicate that for the 2015-2017 period, firms using the general formula accounted for 88% of revenue of multi-jurisdiction firms in Canada, so we focus our discussion on this formula.

What is the impact of the choice of one or another indicator to allocate profits between provinces? Table 3.2 examines this for the general formula for the average 2015-2017 and shows that the largest absolute differences are for British Columbia and Québec; the first would benefit from a shift to a single factor formula using wages and salaries, while the second would benefit from a shift to a single factor formula using total revenue (leaving aside the impact of equalization raised in the next part of the chapter). Net income (loss) categorized as 'multi-jurisdiction' for income tax purposes for Canada for 2011 was CAD 188 billion,[17] so a one percentage point shift is worth CAD 1.8 billion of taxable income and, given provincial corporate income tax rates (*see* Table 3.1), between CAD 180 and 250 million of tax revenue (2010 rates).

In the ongoing debate on the proper formula as discussed, for example, by Weiner in this volume, it has been suggested that a three-factor - assets, labour and sales - formula could be used. It has also been suggested that labour should be broken down into the wage bill and the number of workers. Table 3.3 presents information on the interprovincial allocation of these various indicators for 2011. These data are for all businesses, not only MJEs, and thus yield provincial shares different than those that could have been obtained from CRA data. There can be important differences between formulas in terms of provincial shares. For example, Alberta and Ontario both *see* a 4%

17. Canada Revenue Agency, *Corporate Statistical Tables (2011 to 2015 Tax Years)*, *supra* n. 8, Table 4: Net Income (or Loss) for Income Tax Purposes by Jurisdiction, 2011 to 2015.

point shift when one compares the simulations of the two and three factors formulas (columns (5) and (6)).

Table 3.2 General FA, Wages and Salaries (W&S) and Revenues (Rev) Statistics, % by Province, Canada, Average 2015-2017

	Average 2015-2017 of Annual %s		*Average of Two Factors*	*W&S% – Rev% = Diff % Points*	*Diff/W&S*
	W&S	Rev	(W&S + Rev)/2		
	(1)	(2)	(3) = ((1) + (2)/2	(4) = (1)-(2)	(5) = (4)/(1)
Newfoundland and Labrador	1.10	1.05	1.08%	0.05	4.5%
Newfoundland and Labrador Offshore	0.06	0.19	0.13%	-0.13	-216.7%
Prince Edward Island	0.26	0.23	0.24%	0.03	11.7%
Nova Scotia	1.86	1.94	1.90%	-0.08	-4.3%
Nova Scotia Offshore		0.01	0.01%	-0.01	
New Brunswick	1.28	1.56	1.42%	-0.28	-21.8%
Quebec	15.25	17.58	16.42%	-2.33	-15.3%
Ontario	40.31	39.90	40.11%	0.41	1.0%
Manitoba	3.21	3.16	3.19%	0.04	1.4%
Saskatchewan	3.36	4.24	3.80%	-0.88	-26.2%
Alberta	20.56	18.94	19.75%	1.62	7.9%
British Columbia	12.02	10.35	11.18%	1.67	13.9%

Source: calculations by the authors using data obtained from the Canada Revenue Agency.

Table 3.3 Simulation of Various Allocation Formulas, All Firms, Canada, Provinces, 2011

Allocators\ Provinces	*Gross Revenue (1)*	*Wages (2)*	*Employment (3)*	*Assets (4)*	*Two-Factors Formula (5)*	*Three-Factors Formula (6)*	*Two Factors with Two Labour Indicators (7)*	*Population Share (8)*	*GDP Share (9)*
NFL	1.6%	1.3%	1.3%	2.0%	1.5%	1.6%	1.5%	1.5%	1.9%
PEI	0.3%	0.3%	0.4%	0.2%	0.3%	0.3%	0.3%	0.4%	0.3%
NS	2.0%	2.2%	2.6%	2.0%	2.1%	2.1%	2.2%	2.8%	2.1%
NB	2.1%	1.8%	2.0%	1.8%	1.9%	1.9%	2.0%	2.2%	1.8%
Qc	19.4%	20.0%	22.5%	15.9%	19.7%	18.5%	20.3%	23.6%	19.8%
Ont	38.2%	39.4%	38.7%	27.1%	38.8%	34.9%	38.6%	38.4%	38.2%
Man	3.2%	3.2%	3.7%	3.0%	3.2%	3.1%	3.3%	3.6%	3.3%
Sask	4.1%	3.1%	3.2%	5.3%	3.6%	4.2%	3.6%	3.1%	4.4%
Alt	17.0%	15.9%	12.4%	29.6%	16.5%	20.8%	15.6%	10.9%	17.7%
BC	11.4%	12.1%	12.8%	11.7%	11.7%	11.7%	11.9%	13.1%	12.3%

Source: calculations by authors with data from Statistics Canada: CANSIM (1): Table 36-10-0419-01: Provincial Input-Output Tables, Inputs and Outputs, Summary Level, Basic Prices (2007-2011); (2): Table 36-10-0221-01: Gross Domestic Product, Income-Based, Provincial and Territorial (annual series); (3): Table 36-10-0096-01 Flows and stocks of fixed non-residential capital, by industry and type of asset, Canada, provinces and territories (× 1,000,000); (4): Table 36-10-0489-01 Labour statistics consistent with the System of National Accounts (SNA), by job category and industry; (5) = ((1) + (2))/2; (6) = ((1) + (2) + (4))/3; (7) = (((2) + (3)/2) + (1))/2 (8): https://www12.statcan.gc.ca/census-recensement/2011/dp-pd/hlt-fst/pd-pl/Table-Tableau.cfm?LANG = Eng&T = 101&S = 50&O = A; (9): Statistics Canada. Table 36-10-0402-01 Gross domestic product (GDP) at basic prices, by industry, provinces and territories (× 1,000,000)

Note: Columns may not sum to 100% due to rounding and omission of territories

While formulary apportionment applies to multi-province taxpayers, there is no group consolidation in the Canadian corporate tax system, so that these rules apply only at the affiliate level within groups of related companies. Each affiliate of the group uses separate accounting to report income for tax purposes, and formulary apportionment applies only to income earned by corporations through branches rather than separately incorporated affiliates. Thus a taxpayer may in principle avoid the effects of formulary apportionment by incorporating a separate affiliate in any province in which it does business. While incorporation as such is not costly, cross-border flows of goods and services - which were previously internal movements within a company - would become transactions between separate entities; this would require, for example, setting transfer prices and may be costly in terms of administrative resources. That said, formulary apportionment in the Canadian case might properly be regarded as elective for taxpayers. This evidently has implications for the role of formulary apportionment in influencing interprovincial tax planning and tax loss shifting across provinces, a subject which we take up in §3.04.

§3.03 HISTORY[18]

Taxation of corporate income was first introduced in Canada by Prince Edward Island in 1894. It was followed at the provincial level by British Columbia in 1901; then Manitoba in 1931; and Québec, Ontario, Saskatchewan and Alberta in 1932; and finally New Brunswick in 1938 and Nova Scotia in 1939.[19] The federal government introduced corporate income taxation in 1916. According to Panel A,[20] these provincial legislations allocated profits according to sales except for British Columbia; Smith provides some specific examples of provincial policies.[21] The federal Royal Commission on Dominion-Provincial Relations established in 1937 (known as the Rowell-Sirois Commission) recommended that the corporate income tax become solely federal since 'only by such a step can we hope to achieve reasonable uniformity in impositions on business'.[22] This recommendation was not implemented as such, but during part of World War II and for two years afterwards (1942-1947) corporate income taxation (CIT) along with succession duties and personal income taxation were 'rented out' by provinces to the federal

18. This section was prepared using both Internet searches and a systematic examination of the annual Conference reports of the Canadian Tax Foundation; they can be seen as reasonable indicators of issues relevant for tax professionals at a given point in time. We thank the Montreal office of the Canadian Tax Foundation for its help in carrying out this task.
19. A. Milton Moore, J. Harvey Perry & Donald I. Beach, *The Financing of the Canadian Federation: The First Hundred Years* 114, Table 26 (Canadian Tax Foundation 1966). Newfoundland became a province of Canada in 1949.
20. Panel A, *Allocation of Corporate Profits: Federal-Quebec Overlapping*, in *Report of the Proceedings of the Tax Conference Convened by the Canadian Tax Foundation, 1955*, 103, 104 and 122 (Canadian Tax Foundation 1956). We use the term panel to refer to panel discussions reported in the annual proceedings of the Canadian Tax Foundation.
21. Ernest H. Smith, *Allocating to Provinces the Taxable Income of Corporations: How the Federal-Provincial Allocation Rules Evolved*, 24(5) Can. Tax J. 545, 548 (1976).
22. Royal Commission on Dominion-Provincial Relations (Chief Justice Newton Rowell; Dr Joseph Sirois, chair), *Report of the Royal Commission on Dominion-Provincial Relations, Bk II: Recommendations* 113 (King's Printer 1940) (Rowell-Sirois Commission).

government, and these taxes were thus suspended in exchange for federal rental (transfers) payments. Since then, the provinces have reactivated their tax powers in the field, through a combination of unilateral actions and coordinated reforms to federal-provincial fiscal arrangements, leading to provincial governments gaining own-source corporate tax revenues together with various changes in federal transfer arrangements. We examine this process in further detail in the remainder of this section.

After World War II, a first set of federal-provincial tax arrangements was put in place for the 1947-1952 period. The federal government reduced its CIT rate from 40% to 30%[23] and required provinces that wanted to remain a party to the tax rental agreements to introduce a provincial CIT at a rate of 5%. Indeed the federal government drafted a model provincial CIT law for their adoption. This yielded no extra income for these provinces as their transfer or rental payments were reduced accordingly.[24] Seven of the then nine provinces agreed to this; the allocation of taxable profits between these seven provinces was done through the introduction of Formulary Apportionment (known as 'Appendix C' then) developed by the federal government with inputs from the provinces.[25] Two points should be noted: first Appendix C was an appendix to the model provincial law and thus to the provincial CIT laws and, second, most of the content of the rules in place in 2019 can be found in the 1947 rules and, in particular, the two-factor formula: payroll and sales with equal weight. These compulsory provincial taxes were administered by the federal government.[26]

Ontario and Québec did not agree to the federal request. Both reintroduced a CIT at a rate of 7%, above the 5% rate set by the federal government for the other provinces. Moore, Perry and Beach observed that 'the two central provinces also employed their own principles for attributing the income of interprovincial corporations to individual provinces'.[27] Thus there were three formulary apportionment formulas used in the 1947-1952 period in Canada.

A second set of arrangements was put in place for the 1952-1957 period. Québec kept its own CIT, while Ontario abandoned its own CIT and rejoined the federal tax rental agreement, so nine out of ten provinces were covered by this new tax agreement. It did not require, nor allow, agreeing provinces to levy a CIT, contrary to the 1947-1952 agreement;[28] at the same time the federal CIT rate was increased by 5 percentage points. However a 5% abatement against the federal CIT was introduced;[29] this accommodated firms operating in a non-agreeing province, in this case Québec.[30] The term 'abatement' is used since it was federal taxable income that was reduced by 5% irrespective of the amount of CIT paid to Québec. The calculation of the tax rental payments could be done using: (1) a historical amount indexed to gross national

23. It was increased in 1951 to finance the Korean War.
24. Ronald M. Burns, *The Acceptable Mean: The Tax Rental Agreements, 1941-1962*, 79 (Canadian Tax Foundation 1980).
25. Smith, *supra* n. 21, at 550. Newfoundland became the eight agreeing province in 1949.
26. Moore, Perry & Beach, *supra* n. 19, at 29.
27. *Ibid.*, 32.
28. Burns, *supra* n. 24, at 98.
29. *Ibid.*, 102.
30. Moore, Perry & Beach, *supra* n. 19, at 43.

product and population or (2) a sum of potential tax yields including that of a CIT set at an 8.5% rate on 1948 taxable income.[31] Note that the calculation of the federal abatement required the creation of federal allocation rules since Québec was not renting out this tax field. These rules became Part IV of the federal income tax regulations.[32] This credit (strictly speaking an abatement as it was allowed even in the absence of paid taxes, but the writings at the time tend to use credit) was increased to 7% in 1953, fully offsetting the then Québec rate. Thus there were two formulary apportionment formulas used in Canada in the 1952-1957 period. These arrangements were the object of a panel discussion at the 1955 Canadian Tax Association annual meeting,[33] the first such discussion in an expert forum apparently. One participant (from the federal government) indicated a fear that this would become a recurring theme as in the annual National Tax Association meeting in the United States.

The final set of arrangements involving a hybrid form of tax rental was for the 1957-1962 period. The federal abatement increased to 9%,[34] a tax rate adopted by all provinces except Ontario, which re-enacted its provincial CIT and set its own rate at 11%. Thus, in Ontario the rate diverged from that of other provinces; however, it enacted income allocation rules corresponding to the federal ones. In Québec, the tax rate was the same as in the other provinces, but the allocation rules put in place by Québec diverged from those in place in the other nine provinces.[35] There were thus two formulary apportionment systems in place then. The 1957 federal changes were part of a broader reform in which Ottawa transferred tax powers back to the provinces, including also personal income tax and succession duties. The revenues from these taxes were to be allocated on a derivation basis, i.e., that received by the provinces in which the relevant taxpayers resided, which raised an issue of interregional equity[36] compared to the previous, more centralized, regime. As part of the 1957 reform, therefore, Ottawa introduced the first formal version of its fiscal capacity grants known simply as Equalization. Under the 1957 formula, grants were paid from federal revenues to bring each province's per capita tax yield from these three taxes up to the average of the two highest-yielding provinces. This implied that nine provinces (all but the richest) at the time received equalization grants.

Figure 3.3 shows the occupation of the CIT field by the provinces over the 1937-2016 period. The dip to zero in the 1942-1947 period corresponds to the tax rental agreement and the dip in the 1952-1957 period to the fact that, under the tax rental agreement for that period, no agreeing province levied a CIT; thus collections are for Québec and reflect the withdrawal of Ontario from this tax field. The generally increasing share reflects both increases in the provincial rates and decreases in the federal rate.

31. Smith, *supra* n. 21, at 555.
32. *Ibid.*
33. Panel A, *Allocation of Corporate Profits*, *supra* n. 20.
34. The federal abatement was increased to 10% in 1960 for provinces not accepting federal per capita university grants which was the case of Québec only.
35. Moore, Perry & Beach, *supra* n. 19, at 56.
36. Due to differences in economic activity, income levels and thus taxable income between provinces.

Figure 3.3 Provincial Share of Corporate Income Tax Revenue, 1934-2016

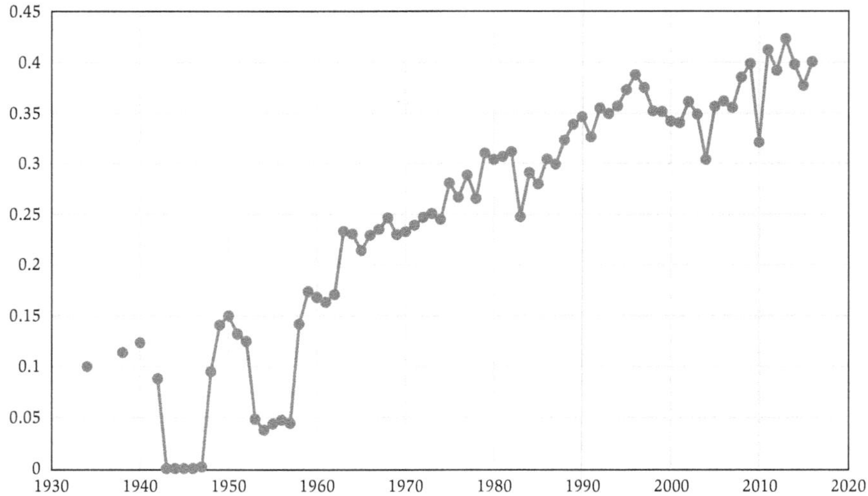

Source: Canadian Tax Foundation, *Finances of the Nation* database, http://financesofthenation.ca/.

The Ontario policy and the resulting interprovincial tax differentials led to a greater interest in the apportionment of profits between provinces, as evidenced by discussions at the 1957 Canadian Tax Association conference[37] – in particular as the higher rate in that province was seen as leading to double taxation. Changes were first made to the federal and Ontario formulary apportionment rules and, as of 1 January 1961, Québec adopted the federal two-factor formula.[38] From then on only one formulary apportionment formula was used in Canada. This harmonization reduced the interest of policymakers and practitioners. Neither the Carter Commission nor the Ontario Committee on Taxation addressed formulary apportionment in the late 1960s,[39] nor do the conferences of the Canadian Tax Foundation that examined these reports. This may reflect the finding of Panel C that '[t]he problem of allocation is much less acute since the province of Quebec has decided to follow the federal policy'.[40] Similarly, Lees writes that:

> there is not much evidence that the Québec and Ontario tax administrations are selecting 'allocation' determination as an area for administrative conflicts. Such

37. Panel B, *Provincial Profit Allocation Rules*, in *Report of the Proceedings of the Tax Conference Convened by the Canadian Tax Foundation, 1957*, 28 (Canadian Tax Foundation 1958).
38. Smith, *supra* n. 21, at 562 and 564.
39. Royal Commission on Taxation (Kenneth Le M. Carter, chair), *Report of the Royal Commission on Taxation* (Queen's Printer 1966) (Carter Commission); Ontario Committee on Taxation (Lancelot J. Smith, chair), *Report of the Ontario Committee on Taxation* (Frank Fogg 1967).
40. Panel C, *Quebec Tax Developments*, in *Report of the Proceedings of the Tax Conference Convened by the Canadian Tax Foundation, 1973*, 556 (Canadian Tax Foundation 1974).

> conflicts do arise from time to time, but it is significant that such issues have not been even a minor point of litigation or professional inquiry to this point.[41]

From the mid-1970s onwards, we found only four mentions of the public policy issues associated with the allocation formula. The first three are quite brief: (1) Thirsk summarized the issues,[42] noting that the formula used does not find its roots in either the ability to pay principle or the benefits principle of taxation but rather aims for minimizing conflicts between provinces and ensuring simplicity in administration; (2) LePan examines its interaction with introducing loss consolidation for corporate groups;[43] and (3) Bossons notes the significant administrative advantages that follow from using the federal definition to allocate profits between provinces.[44]

There was a more detailed discussion in the report of the Technical Committee on Business Taxation (Mintz Committee) of 1997. It notes that in the mid-1990s:

> disputes arise with respect to the allocation of taxable income among the provinces. The resolution mechanisms available to a business in the case of a dispute between Canada and its tax treaty partners, although cumbersome, are often more complete and adequate than measures in place for similar issues between the provinces.[45]

The Mintz Committee put forward the observations set out in Box 3.1.

Box 3.1: Mintz Committee Observations on Formula Allocation

In the view of the Committee, there are a number of specific trends that will require attention in the future given the ongoing evolution of the Canadian economy:

- Changes to the Canadian economy and their impact in determining income allocated to provinces: Under the corporate allocation formula, revenues are apportioned across provinces according to two criteria: the relative sales volume of the corporation in the jurisdictions in which it has permanent establishments (except for exports); and the relative payroll in such jurisdictions. When the formula was first developed, it was considered appropriate to use the destination of sales as a factor in allocating revenues. More corporate tax revenues were thereby allocated to those provinces that

41. John Lees, *Problems in the Allocation of Business Income among Different Jurisdictions in Canada*, in *Proceedings of the Annual Conference on Taxation Held under the Auspices of the National Tax Association-Tax Institute of America Vol. 66*, 410, 415 (National Tax Association 1973).
42. Wayne Thirsk, *Tax Harmonization and its Importance in the Canadian Federation*, in *Fiscal Dimensions of Canadian Federalism* 118, 136 (Richard M. Bird ed., Canadian Tax Foundation 1980).
43. Nicolas Lepan, *Federal and Provincial Issues in the Corporate Loss Transfer Proposal*, in *Report of the Proceedings of the Tax Conference Convened by the Canadian Tax Foundation, 1985*, 13.1-13.11 (Canadian Tax Foundation 1986).
44. John Bossons, *Provincial Taxes on Corporations*, in *Provincial Public Finances, Vol. 2: Plaudits, Problems and Prospects* 301, 306 (Melville L. McMillan ed., Canadian Tax Foundation 1991).
45. Mintz Committee, *supra* n. 7, at 10.5.

imported manufactured goods from Ontario and Quebec industries. However, provinces with non-protected industries would also receive less corporate income allocated to them, to the extent that shipments were destined to other provinces. Forty years later, the Canadian economy is different. New methods of selling and distributing goods and services mean that businesses may often have no need for permanent establishments in some provinces. Moreover, Canadian businesses have been rationalizing production processes by consolidating plants and other infrastructure, reducing the number of provinces in which they have a permanent establishment. As a result, the corporate allocation formula should be updated to reflect new business practices, with particular attention to investment income, investment companies and services.

- Evolving international trends: As we noted earlier, the development of electronic commerce and the growth of new forms of financial transactions will challenge governments, at the international level, to develop rules for the determination of the location of income earned and sales made. Such trends will also affect the provincial allocation of corporate income, such as determining the place of permanent establishment, the point of sale or origin and the source of financial income.
- Administration of the corporate allocation formula in an increasingly complex world: Even though the interprovincial allocations do not affect federal revenues, Revenue Canada plays an important role in administering the corporate allocation formula to ensure that provinces party to the tax collection agreements receive their fair share of corporate income. Given the increased complexity of many corporate transactions, additional resources need to be devoted by Revenue Canada.

Technical Committee on Business Taxation (Jack M. Mintz, chair), *Report of the Technical Committee on Business Taxation* 11.10 (Department of Finance, Canada 1997) (Mintz Committee).

By 1979, public policy discussions were replaced by examinations of the tax planning opportunities that may result from differences between Ontario and Québec in the definition of permanent establishment and other aspects of their income allocation formulas.[46] This tax planning theme was taken up again in the early 1990s: Thivierge,[47] Lewin[48] and Reid[49] address various possibilities. Reid focuses on the

46. Elinore J. Richardson, *Planning for Corporations in light of Differences in Federal and Provincial Income Tax Legislation*, in *Report of the Proceedings of the Tax Conference Convened by the Canadian Tax Foundation, 1979*, 766 (Canadian Tax Foundation 1980).
47. Manon Thivierge, *Tax Planning for corporations in the Light of Québec and Ontario Tax Legislation other than Income Tax*, in *Report of the Proceedings of the Tax Conference Convened by the Canadian Tax Foundation, 1990*, 12.1 (Canadian Tax Foundation 1991).
48. Richard M. Lewin, *Interprovincial Tax Planning for Businesses*, in *Report of the Proceedings of the Tax Conference Convened by the Canadian Tax Foundation, 1991*, 28.1 (Canadian Tax Foundation 1992).

differences in the definitions of permanent establishments in a five-page appendix, while Lewin notes that creating permanent establishments in lower tax provinces is one possible tax planning technique.

Auger and Bélanger present in detail the federal and provincial rules (including relevant case law) of interprovincial allocation of corporate profits but do not discuss their appropriateness or use.[50] Boehmer and Landau write that:

> [o]ther interprovincial income tax and capital tax planning techniques have been used to allocate income among a corporation's provincial permanent establishments, by reallocating gross revenues, salaries, and wages in order to take advantage of differences in the provincial corporate income and capital taxes rates.[51]

Chan and Taylor discuss the 'Québec shuffle' and 'Québec truffle' as tax planning techniques;[52] this is the last example of tax planning analysis related to formulary apportionment we found, but one can expect this to be taken up anew.

§3.04 ISSUES AND ANALYSIS

We begin this section with a general discussion of the role of formulary apportionment. We then turn to two specific issues: tax competition, and the interaction of formulary apportionment and equalization.

In order to provide an assessment of Canada's system, it is useful to start with some discussion of what the objectives of formulary apportionment are more broadly. Indeed, proponents of formulary apportionment as a reform of international tax regimes have a number of different objectives in mind. If possible, it would be desirable to design a system that: (i) simplifies tax compliance for taxpayers operating in multiple jurisdictions; (ii) eliminates 'double non-taxation' of income due to transfer pricing and other profit shifting strategies available to multi-jurisdiction taxpayers; (iii) results in an equitable or appropriate allocation of tax revenues among jurisdictions, and, in the process; (iv) reduces fiscal externalities among jurisdictions, alleviating tax competition pressures. That is a long list of *desiderata*, and it is clear from the literature

49. Robert J. Reid, *Provincial Tax Planning*, in *Report of the Proceedings of the Tax Conference Convened by the Canadian Tax Foundation, 1992*, 24.1 (Canadian Tax Foundation 1993).
50. Claude Auger & Marc-André Bélanger, *Interprovincial Allocation of Income*, in *Report of the Proceedings of the Tax Conference Convened by the Canadian Tax Foundation, 1999*, 10.1 (Canadian Tax Foundation 2000).
51. Greg Boehmer & Stephen Landau, *Update on Capital Tax and Interprovincial Tax Planning*, in *Report of the Proceedings of the Tax Conference Convened by the Canadian Tax Foundation, 2002*, 24.1, 24.15 (Canadian Tax Foundation 2003).
52. Michelle Chan & Charles Taylor, *Provincial General Anti Avoidance Rules and Government's Response to Interprovincial tax Planning*, in *Report of the Proceedings of the Tax Conference Convened by the Canadian Tax Foundation, 2008*, 7.1 (Canadian Tax Foundation 2009). Both involve moving income between provinces often using trusts. For details, *see* Michael N. Kandev, *Québec Putting the Screws on Aggressive Tax Planning*, CCH Tax Topics 1927, notes 5 and 6 (12 February 2009), http://www.finances.gouv.qc.ca/documents/Autres/en/AUTEN_PFA-14-MichaelNKandev.pdf (accessed 2 July 2019); or Finances Québec, *Aggressive Tax Planning*, Working Paper (January 2009), http://www.finances.gouv.qc.ca/documents/Autres/en/AUTEN_DocCons_PFA.pdf (accessed 2 July 2019).

discussed in this section that formulary apportionment is not a panacea that can solve all these problems or satisfy all proponents in the debate.

The fundamental problem with separate accounting is the difficulty in defining and implementing the source principle for income in the presence of cross-border transactions. Multi-jurisdictional enterprises use a variety of tax planning strategies to exploit tax rate differences between countries, shifting profits from high-tax to low-tax jurisdictions. Corporations may, for example, manipulate transfer prices for cross-border trade between affiliates; they may lend to affiliates in high-tax jurisdictions to generate tax-deductible interest payments, and they may locate intellectual property and other intangible assets in low-tax jurisdictions to reduce worldwide total tax payments.

Formulary apportionment attempts to solve these problems by allocating a taxpayer's total income to jurisdictions based on other factors - in the Canadian case, provincial shares of payroll and sales, for the most part. This eliminates the potential for taxpayers to reduce global taxes by shifting profits among jurisdictions through accounting transactions. However, formulary apportionment does not eliminate the fiscal externalities among jurisdictions. McLure first observed that formulary apportionment converts the corporate income tax into an excise tax (in high-tax jurisdictions) or subsidy (in low-tax jurisdictions) on the underlying factors.[53] Thus a corporation would be induced to locate more employment or sales in low-tax jurisdictions in order to reduce its average tax rate, and so on. Gordon and Wilson showed that tax competition among jurisdictions might be more intense under formulary apportionment than separate accounting, because of those additional fiscal externalities related to the apportionment factors.[54] A related issue is that application of formulary apportionment depends on the entity's nexus in different jurisdictions, which is also a potential source of tax avoidance, particularly for entities that can rely on remote sales of goods or delivery of services. (A similar point was made about new business models by the Mintz Committee.[55])

However, these results are obtained in a model with no excess profits earned by capital, and no potential for taxpayers to shift profit except by changing real economic choices about the location of capital, employment and sales. This perspective, of course, ignores one of the main arguments against separate accounting, which is profit shifting incentives per se. Subsequent research has offered a new perspective on this comparison. Mintz and Smart examined an extended version of the Gordon-Wilson

53. Charles E. McLure, Jr., *The State Corporate Income Tax: Lambs in Wolves' Clothing*, in *The Economics of Taxation* 327 (Henry J. Aaron & Michael J. Boskin eds., Brookings Institution 1980).
54. Roger Gordon & John D. Wilson, *An Examination of Multijurisdictional Corporate Income Taxation Under Formula Apportionment*, 54(6) Econometrica 1357 (1986). *See also* the elegant simplification of this framework and associated discussion in Michael Keen & Kai A. Konrad, *The Theory of International Tax Competition and Coordination*, in *Handbook of Public Economics, Vol. 5*, 257 (Alan J. Auerbach, Raj Chetty, Martin Feldstein & Emmanuel Saez eds., Elsevier 2013).
55. Mintz Committee, *supra* n. 7, at 11.10.

model,[56] incorporating profit shifting through the strategic use of inter-affiliate borrowing between high-tax and low-tax jurisdictions, as well as the potential for relocating real assets as in Gordon and Wilson.[57] Mintz and Smart show how profit shifting under separate accounting can reduce tax competition among jurisdictions around the location of real assets while nevertheless exacerbating revenue losses in high-tax jurisdictions. Nielsen, Raimondos-Moeller and Schjelderup provide a fuller treatment of the issue,[58] establishing conditions on profitability and profit shifting technologies under which formulary apportionment is more effective than separate accounting as a means of controlling tax competition.

Of course, in this discussion we have taken formula weights as fixed and focused on tax competition through tax rate changes. But weights themselves are a choice. Goolsbee and Maydew provide evidence of how payroll weights in US state-level corporate tax apportionment distort firms' employment location decisions,[59] and how this creates incentives for states to increase weights on the sales factor.[60] While this literature emphasizes tax competition incentives, there is potential for fiscal externalities that cause tax exporting as well. Anand and Sansing emphasize that states will not generally agree on formula weights,[61] with net exporters preferring higher weights on payroll, and net importers on sales. However, in recent years, many US states, even net exporters, have moved towards double-weighting sales or even a single factor based on sales. This suggests that tax competition pressures remain strong within formulary apportionment systems, at least when revenue capacity equalization is not present, and they tend to trump the tax incentives related to exporting highlighted by Anand and Sansing. Regardless, there is arguably some inherent instability in formula weights, which reflects both the distortions the formula creates for business location and issues of interregion equity.

[A] The Effectiveness of Formulary Apportionment: Evidence from Canada on Tax Shifting

Nevertheless, we argue that the Canadian experience suggests that it is possible to design a system of formulary apportionment that attains at least some of these objectives to a reasonable degree. In particular, the stability in the Canadian formula weights, and the lack of strong apparent tax competition among provinces, suggests

56. Jack Mintz & Michael Smart, *Income Shifting, Investment, and Tax Competition: Theory and Evidence from Provincial Taxation in Canada*, 88(6) J. Pub. Econ. 1149 (2004).
57. Gordon & Wilson, *supra* n. 54.
58. Søren Bo Nielsen, Pascalis Raimondos-Møller & Guttorm Schjelderup, *Company Taxation and Tax Spillovers: Separate Accounting versus Formula Apportionment*, 54(1) Eur. Econ. Rev. 121 (2010).
59. Austan Goolsbee & Edward L. Maydew, *Coveting Thy Neighbor's Manufacturing: The Dilemma of State Income Apportionment*, 75(1) J. Pub. Econ. 125 (2000).
60. For related evidence on distortions in Germany's apportionment of local business income tax base, *see* Nadine Riedel, *The Downside of Formula Apportionment: Evidence on Factor Demand Distortions*, 17(3) Int'l Tax & Pub. Fin. 236 (2010).
61. Bharat N. Anand & Richard Sansing, *The Weighting Game: Formula Apportionment as an Instrument of Public Policy*, 53(2) Nat'l Tax J. 183 (2000).

that provincial governments at least think that the system works from their perspectives. So why is that? We offer some thoughts on the key design features of Canadian formulary apportionment from this perspective.

First, recall the provincial general statutory corporate tax rates for the largest four provinces, and an average of the other six, shown in Figure 3.1 (§3.02[A][1]). While there were substantial tax rate differentials among provinces in the 1980s and 1990s, they have since been converging - but apparently to substantial positive levels, not to zero. In this sense, there is little evidence of a 'race to the bottom' in subnational corporate tax rates, and with the convergence in rates, there is little incentive for profit shifting or other locational distortions in the behaviour of taxpayers. Moreover, given the near convergence in tax rates, the potential for the formulary apportionment weights themselves to distort business location decisions is rather minimal. That said, three studies have examined whether differences in provincial corporate income tax rates had an impact on the allocation of taxable profits between provinces.[62] They all use multivariate analysis to ascertain this impact.

In the first study, Lachance and Plante used data for sixteen manufacturing sectors for the period 1975-1987;[63] they pair Québec with three other provinces (Alberta, British Columbia and Ontario). They use a pooling methodology and conclude that:

> this empirical study shows that manufacturing enterprises do use planning since we find a relation between the interprovincial gap in corporate income tax rates and the share of taxable income reported in Quebec between 1975 and 1987. The gap between Ontario and Québec for large businesses is the one with the largest impact on the share of taxable income reported in Québec.[64]

They also note that this shifting of tax bases does not fully compensate the loss of revenue resulting from a lower tax rate.

Mintz and Smart carried out the second study.[65] They used administrative data from the 1980s and 1990s (when interprovincial CIT rate differences were larger than now - *see* Figure 3.1) aggregated as follows: six provinces multiplied by seven industries multiplied by fourteen years multiplied by six types of firms, for a theoretical *N* of 3528 and a real *N* of 3509. The six types are two small firms and four large firm groups. Of particular interest is their capacity to distinguish between single- and multi-jurisdictional firms and those using formulary apportionment or not. They compare the response of corporate taxable income to tax rate changes[66] for single-province subsidiaries of corporate groups, which declare income under separate

62. A study by Joan Weiner, *Estimates of How the Unitary Tax Affects Business Investments*, Allied Social Science meetings, 1996, San Francisco, mimeo, examines the impact of these tax differences on manufacturing investment; it shows an impact of CIT rates on the location of said investment.
63. Renaud Lachance & Lucie Plante, *Fiscalité et Mobilité Interprovinciale des Bénéfices: Qui Gagne Perd*, 42(3) Can. Tax J. 843 (1994).
64. *Ibid.*, 858-859 (our translation).
65. Mintz & Smart, *supra* n. 56.
66. Thus estimates come from a difference-in-difference specification, controlling for industry, province and year-fixed effects.

accounting, to other large firms operating in multiple provinces, which declare income under formulary apportionment. Firms in the first group have greater access to profit shifting opportunities, and so, according to predictions of the theory, their income should be more responsive to tax rates. Consistent with this prediction, the estimated elasticity of taxable income (with respect to 1 minus the tax rate) is 4.6 for single-province 'shifters' compared to 2.3 for multi-province firms. They thus wrote that:

> taxable income of corporate subsidiaries that do not allocate income is significantly more elastic with respect to tax rates than income of other comparable firms that do allocate income by formula and those who are not corporate subsidiaries.[67]

They also showed that the elasticity of the corporate tax base with respect to local tax rates was generally higher under separate accounting than formulary apportionment, as long as tax rates do not differ too much among jurisdictions. So, with profit shifting activities, the Gordon-Wilson result noted in §3.04[A] above may be reversed, and a move from separate accounting to formulary apportionment reduces fiscal externalities and alleviates tax competition.

The third study by Finance Canada begins by noting that not all businesses carry out activities in more than one province.[68] It uses data for the 2005-2012 period, finding that 41% of corporations and 27% of corporate groups are potential shifters since they are present in more than one province; these shares and the characteristics of potential shifters are similar to those reported in §3.02 of this chapter above. Potential shifters are larger (capital, income, wages) and more likely to have a foreign connection.[69] Box 3.2 summarizes the possibilities for tax planning. The econometric work in the study uses corporate-level data. It finds that potential shifters react more strongly to differences in provincial corporate income tax rates when they do not have unused non-capital losses and, of course, more strongly than non-potential shifters.[70]

Box 3.2 Tax Planning Transactions

A business conducting income-earning activities in more than one province may do so under two broad corporate structures: it may operate as a single corporation with permanent establishments in more than one province ('multi-jurisdictional corporation'), or it may operate via a group of commonly-controlled corporations, each having a permanent establishment in one or more province ('corporate groups').

Multi-jurisdictional corporations in Canada must allocate taxable income to each province where the corporation has a permanent establishment using a general allocation formula or, for corporations in certain specific sectors, using a formula that applies exclusively to those sectors. The general formula allocates

67. Mintz & Smart, *supra* n. 56, at 1166.
68. Department of Finance, Canada, *Interprovincial Tax Planning by Corporate Groups in Canada: A Review of the Evidence*, in *Tax Expenditures and Evaluations 2014* 71 (2015).
69. *Ibid.*, 83, Table 1.
70. *Ibid.*, 85.

income based on the proportions of salaries and wages paid and gross revenue earned in each province where the corporation has a permanent establishment. Under this regime, a multi-jurisdictional corporation would allocate a greater share of its taxable income to a province if either the share of salaries and wages paid to employees that report to permanent establishments located in that province increases, the share of gross revenue attributable to that province increases, or a corporation that previously had no permanent establishment in that province decides to establish one. Therefore, corporations subject to the allocation formula have limited flexibility to undertake interprovincial tax planning without a concurrent shift in business activity.

Corporations that are members of a corporate group are taxed on a stand-alone basis. Although there is no formal rule for transferring income, losses or other tax attributes among members of a corporate group, corporations could use related-party transactions and various provisions of the Income Tax Act to shift income among group members. For example, a loan from one group member to another would reduce the taxable income of the borrowing corporation, as interest payments on this loan would represent a tax-deductible expense, and would increase the taxable income of the lender, as the interest revenue would be included in the taxable income of that corporation. Similarly, transfers of property with an accrued gain between group members on a tax-deferred basis may result in the gain being realized on the final disposition of the property by another group member. These transactions may be undertaken for genuine business reasons and the end result on income allocation may well be reflective of where the substantive activities take place, but when such transactions coincide with an increase in taxable income allocated to low-tax rate jurisdictions and a decrease in taxable income allocated to high-tax rate jurisdictions, it remains that the corporate group as a whole would pay a lower amount of provincial taxes than it would in the absence of these transactions.

Department of Finance, Canada, *Interprovincial Tax Planning by Corporate Groups in Canada: A Review of the Evidence, in Tax Expenditures and Evaluations 2014* 71, 75 (2015).

[B] The Interaction of Formulary Apportionment and Equalization

The stability and harmonization in subnational corporate tax systems may reflect the influence of other fiscal arrangements, in addition to the effect of federal leadership on formulary apportionment. Certainly, the strong federal presence in the corporate tax field in terms of coordination plays a role. Given the small number of jurisdictions, the gains to harmonization and coordination may be more equally distributed, and defection of a province from the harmonized standard easier to control. As well, the federal government offers two kinds of financial incentives to induce provinces to sign Tax Collection Agreements. The first offered in all cases is ongoing free or low-cost administration of provincial tax rules;[71] the second offered in some cases are large one-time 'transitional' payments to acceding provinces to sweeten the deal,[72] be it for Canada Revenue Agency collection of the CIT, having provinces replace their retail sales taxes by the CRA-administered Harmonised Sales Tax (HST) or to Québec for harmonizing its QST with the federal GST. Indeed, it seems quite appropriate to use fiscal transfers as a way to redistribute the gains of coordination among provinces and ensure a Pareto improvement.

One key aspect is that while tax base is allocated to provinces on a derivation basis according to these rules, Canada also operates a system of fiscal capacity equalization (known simply as Equalization) that interacts with the apportionment rules in important ways. The federal government pays equalization grants to provinces with own-source fiscal capacity that is below a target level of capacity. (In 2019-2020, five of ten provinces will receive equalization grants; all have received it at some time since the programme's inception in 1957.) The result is that an equalization-receiving province that receives more (or less) of the tax base under the apportionment formula also receives less (or more) transfers under the equalization formula – and the transfers offset the effects of apportionment very nearly dollar-for-dollar in most cases. As we discuss in detail in the remainder of this section below, this changes provincial incentives under the apportionment regime markedly. Thus, Equalization interacts with the apportionment formula in important ways, and it exerts direct effects on fiscal externalities and provincial incentives to engage in tax competition.

A more detailed (and yet still simplified) description of the equalization formula and its implications for corporate tax apportionment follows.[73] For each provincial tax base, including corporate income taxes, a receiving province's equalization grant is equal to the difference between its share of national population and its share of the tax base, multiplied by the aggregate of all provincial revenues accruing from the base. In algebraic terms, let X be the aggregate provincial base, and let $a_{i)}$ and $b_{i)}$ represent the shares of province i in national population and in the tax base, respectively. The province's statutory corporate tax rate is $t_{i)}$, and the base-weighted average of all provincial rates is T. After operation of the formulary apportionment system, the province's tax base is $B_i = b_i X$, and its own-source revenues are $R_i = t_i b_i X$. Its equalization grant in respect of the corporate tax base is as follows.

$$E_i = (a_i - b_i) T X$$

71. The lowering of administrative costs when Ontario transferred the administration of the CIT to the Canadian Revenue Agency was accompanied by a fall in compliance costs incurred by firms: PricewaterhouseCoopers LLP for Canada Revenue Agency, *Corporate Tax Administration for Ontario (CTAO): Study of Compliance Cost Savings* (2011), https://www.canada.ca/en/revenue-agency/news/whats-new/corporate-tax-administration-ontario-ctao-study-compliance-cost-savings.html#_Toc309979729 (accessed 2 July 2019).
72. Ontario received a CAD 400 million payment in exchange for agreeing to have CRA collect its CIT for free and presumably for incurring lower tax administration expenses.
73. For more detail on the current formula, *see* Jim Feehan, *Canada's Equalization Formula: Peering Inside the Black Box ... and Beyond*, University of Calgary School of Public Policy SPP Research Paper 7(24) (2014).

so that net revenues, after equalization grants, are as follows.

$$R^n_i = R_i + E_i = [a_i T + (t_i - T) b_i] X$$

Thus, after Equalization, the revenue allocation departs from a pure derivation basis, becoming a formula that in effect pays each province its per capita share of national total revenues, plus an adjustment that is proportional to its formulary share of the base (b_i) and to the difference ($t_i - T$) between its own tax rate and the national average rate. Evidently, then, Equalization reduces the sensitivity of a province's revenues to its apportioned share of the weights in the allocation formula (b_i), as changes in own-source revenues are approximately offset by compensatory changes in equalization transfers. Indeed, when a province's tax rate equals the national average rate, the offset is complete, and equalized revenues reduce to equal per capita shares of the national base:

$$R^{n^*}_i = a_i T X$$

In this sense, formulary apportionment is of only secondary importance within Canadian fiscal arrangements, at least for equalization-receiving provinces. Provincial governments have only minimal incentives to change formula weights, either to increase their share of revenues or to induce changes in business location decisions.

Indeed, Equalization has an influence not just on how provinces interact under formulary apportionment, but on the incentives for interprovincial tax rate competition in general. Because federal equalization grants compensate provinces for revenues lost when tax base shifts to another province (the horizontal fiscal externality), it follows that capacity equalization reduces tax competition incentives, and it may lead provinces to impose higher tax rates. In a theoretical model, Bucovetsky and Smart showed that equalization grants can be designed to decentralize the national optimal tax system as a Nash equilibrium of a tax competition game among provinces.[74] In other words, tax competition incentives can be eliminated entirely by an appropriately designed equalization formula. That said, the optimal rate of capacity equalization in this sense depends on the extent to which tax competition is present between provinces in the federation (which can be controlled through the equalization formula), or between countries (which cannot). This distinction is analysed further by Smart.[75]

Moreover, these effects seem quantitatively important. Analysing the expansion of equalization grants in Canada over the 1970s and 1980s, Smart[76] compared the resulting changes in tax rates of equalization-receiving provinces, relative to other provinces, in order to estimate the causal effect of Equalization on provincial tax rates. The estimates suggest that cutting grants in half (and so reducing the marginal incentive effects of equalization) would cause tax rates to fall by about 30% in

74. Sam Bucovetsky & Michael Smart, *The Efficiency Consequences of Local Revenue Equalization: Tax Competition and Tax Distortions*, 8(1) J. Pub. Econ. Theory 119 (2006).
75. Michael Smart, *Raising Taxes Through Equalization*, 40(4) Can. J. Econ./Rev. Can. Écon. 1188 (2007).
76. *Ibid.*

equalization-receiving provinces. Similar effects have been found for the capacity equalization grants of other countries.[77] Some direct, albeit merely suggestive, evidence for the effect can be seen in the trends in statutory tax rates for receiving and non-receiving provinces, as shown in Figure 3.4. Since 1995, tax rates have fallen in the four provinces that do not traditionally receive Equalization, perhaps evidence of an increase in tax competition among provinces. Over the same period, however, tax rates have remained fairly stable among equalization-receiving provinces, where the fiscal incentives for tax competition are attenuated by the effects of the grant.

Figure 3.4 Statutory Tax Rates and Equalization, 1995-2016

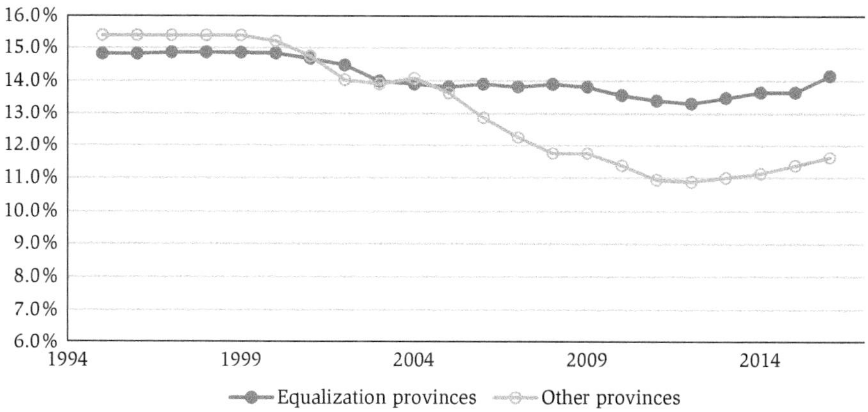

Source: Canadian Tax Foundation, *Finances of the Nation* database, http://financesofthenation.ca/.

§3.05 CONCLUDING REMARKS

First, recall as noted by Thirsk that there is no evidence as to: (1) why the various allocators used in the Canadian formulary apportionment formulas should be used and (2) what their weight should be.[78] The results in Table 3.3 illustrate how changes can affect one province or another. Thus it makes sense to follow up on the queries raised in the Mintz Committee report (Box 3.1, §3.03 of this chapter above), especially as digital commerce has become more important since that report was produced in 1997.

77. *See also* Hayashi & Boadway for Canada, Dahlby & Warren for Australia, and Buettner as well as Egger, Koethenbuerger & Smart for Germany: Masayoshi Hayashi & Robin Boadway, *An Empirical Analysis of Intergovernmental Tax Interaction: The Case of Business Income Taxes in Canada*, 34(2) Can. J. Econ./Rev. Can. Écon. 481 (2001); Bev Dahlby & Neil Warren, *Fiscal Incentive Effects of the Australian Equalisation System*, 79(247) Econ. R. 434 (2003); Thiess Buettner, *The Incentive Effect of Fiscal Equalization Transfers on Tax Policy*, 90(3) J. Pub. Econ. 477 (2006); Peter Egger, Marko Koethenbuerger & Michael Smart, *Do Fiscal Transfers Alleviate Business Tax Competition? Evidence from Germany*, 94(3-4) J. Pub. Econ. 235 (2010).

78. Thirsk, *supra* n. 42.

That said, the lack of discussion on the allocators and their weight may indicate that they are still seen by provinces as providing a correct, or at least an acceptable, allocation of taxable income between provinces for CIT purposes, particularly since equalization compensates implicitly for errors in said allocation.

Second, formulary apportionment does not exist in a vacuum; it is part of a set of intergovernmental financial arrangements that can be almost non-existent as in the European Union or fairly complex as in Canada. In the case of Canada, Equalization changes the formula, and it changes incentives as well. We are not sure any of this would work without Equalization. Nor perhaps should we expect to. The use of formulary apportionment by Canadian policymakers most likely reduces tax competition. But formulary apportionment will create winners and losers - the latter perhaps especially among low-income and low-tax jurisdictions. It is in a sense natural that we should expect to support these policies with net transfers towards these regions if we do not want them to become tax havens. The lesson for the rest of the world seems to be that if there are perceived global gains from formulary apportionment, then rich high-tax countries should expect to have to pay other states in order to prevent defections from a voluntary formulary apportionment scheme.

CHAPTER 4

The Dream Is Alive: EU Tax Policy with a Common Consolidated Corporate Tax Base and Formulary Apportionment

Joann Martens Weiner[*]

§4.01 INTRODUCTION

In December 2001, while living in Brussels and continuing my research on issues related to implementing formulary apportionment in the European Union, I presented a paper in Mons, Belgium, titled 'Formula Apportionment in the European Union: A Dream Come True or the EU's Worst Nightmare?'.[1]

That paper received a warm reception as it seemed to capture the strong views surrounding the European Commission's efforts to bring coherence to the ways the then fifteen EU Member States taxed companies doing business across the European economic bloc. The strength of those views had been reinforced on 23 October 2001, which was the day the European Commission presented formulary apportionment as a feasible element of its comprehensive company tax reform for the European Union.[2]

---

* The views in this chapter do not necessarily reflect the views of any organization with which the author is or has been affiliated. I would like to thank Richard Krever and François Vaillancourt for inviting me to participate in the Montreal workshop on formulary apportionment on which this volume is based. I thank Jack Mintz for helpful insights on the text.

1. Joann M. Weiner, *Would Introducing Formula Apportionment in the European Union Be a Dream Come True or the EU's Worst Nightmare?* (2002) 48(4) *Ifo Studien* 519 (paper presented at the CESifo/ARPEGE conference *Corporate and Capital Income Taxation in the European Union: The EU Commission Report on Companies' Taxation and Beyond*, Catholic University of Mons,7-8 December 2001). A report on the roundtable discussion and two additional papers on the topic are available in 3(1) *CESifo Forum*, Spring 2002.
2. The Commission Services released both the Communication from the Commission to the Council, the European Parliament, and the Economic and Social Committee, *Towards an Internal Market without Tax Obstacles: A Strategy for Providing Companies with a Consolidated Corporate Tax*

Until then, the Commission had never even considered formulary apportionment as a possibility, much less as a viable option, for an EU company tax system. Those days were in the past, as the Commission now believed that it was not only time to take concrete steps to remove the tax-induced distortions in the Single Market but also that formulary apportionment might be the best way to remove those distortions.

The study pointed out that many EU multinational enterprises operated in one economic zone but faced up to fifteen different company tax systems when computing their tax liabilities. These overlapping systems created compliance and administrative nightmares for taxpayers and tax authorities alike. Multinational enterprises wanted to simplify the process of paying taxes across the EU while avoiding excessive compliance costs simply because they did business in more than one Member State. Likewise, EU governments wanted to reduce administrative complexity while maintaining the ability to collect an appropriate level of taxes from multinational enterprises. Hence, the dilemma: could formulary apportionment make the dream of company tax reform in the EU come true? Or, would it make company taxation in the EU a nightmare?

Many tax experts were surprised that the EU was even considering a method of taxing multinational corporations that used a formula to distribute profits across national borders for taxation.[3] After all, since the early years of the twentieth century, the international community had endorsed the separate entity, arm's length transfer pricing method for allocating profits across jurisdictions.[4] The US Treasury Department,[5] the Organisation for Economic Co-operation and Development (OECD), and the international tax policy community viewed methods that allocated a multinational enterprise's income using a predetermined formula as contradictory to the separate entity method that allocated such income according to specific transactions. The OECD's Transfer Pricing Guidelines, for example, noted that a correct application of the separate entity approach requires using the arm's length principle to evaluate the transfer prices that enterprises use to price internal transfers of physical goods,

Base for their EU-wide Activities COM(2001) 582 final and the Staff Working Paper *Company Taxation in the Internal Market,* SEC(2001) 1681 final on 23 October 2001.

3. Retired Deputy Assistant Treasury Secretary Joseph Guttentag noted in the foreword to my 2006 book that '[h]aving spent almost fifty years of my life defending the separate accounting, arm's length pricing method, I have to admit that I was somewhat surprised to be asked to contribute to a book suggesting that the European Union might do well to consider adopting a formulary approach to deal with the taxation of inter- and intra-company transactions': in Joann Martens-Weiner, *Company Tax Reform in the European Union: Guidance from the United States and Canada on Implementing Formulary Apportionment in the EU* xi (Springer 2006). In between the time I started writing on the subject and now, the European Community has become the European Union and formula apportionment is now referred to as formulary apportionment.
4. For details on this history of separate entity and formulary apportionment taxation and empirical estimates of how apportionment affects business investment with a view to its implementation in the European Community, see Joann Martens Weiner, *Company Taxation for the European Community: How Sub-National Tax Variation Affects Business Investment in the United States and Canada* (unpublished PhD dissertation, Harvard University, 1994). I presented the empirical results in *Estimates of How the Unitary Tax Affects Business Investment* at the Allied Social Sciences Association meetings in San Francisco in 1996.
5. *See* US Department of the Treasury, *Conference on Formula Apportionment* (Office of Tax Policy, 12 December 1996). Among others, Onno Ruding, the chair of the Ruding Committee that had recently evaluated the company taxation systems in the European Community, raised the international concerns in adopting formulary apportionment.

intangible property and services.[6] Formulary apportionment was viewed as being inconsistent with that separate entity approach.

That is one reason why European experts were shocked by the Commission's position. As German tax attorney and law professor Albert Rädler recalled, on the most recent occasion that the EU had evaluated the taxation of European multinational enterprises, in the Ruding Report of 1992, the Ruding Committee had considered formulary apportionment to be the 'devil's work'.[7]

Yet, the consensus in favour of the separate entity method was weakening as the twentieth century ended. The Commission was blunt in its October 2001 analysis of why this was happening:

> The underlying cause of those additional tax and compliance burdens is the existence within the Internal Market of 15 separate tax systems.... In particular, companies are obliged to allocate profits to each jurisdiction on arm's length basis by separate accounting, i.e., on a transaction by transaction basis.[8]

Formulary apportionment was a well-known concept to the Commission, as it had already been identified as an appropriate way to tax multinational enterprises in the integrated European economy.[9] Economists in the United States had concluded that formulary apportionment could be a good system for an economically integrated area[10] while economists analysing company taxation in the European Community were finding that formulary apportionment could better reflect the cross-border nature of European multinational operations than the current system.[11]

The increased level of economic integration in the EU motivated the European Commission to question whether the separate entity approach, which required treating internal transfers among related parties as if they had happened at 'arm's length'

---

6. For the latest statement, see OECD *Transfer Pricing Guidelines for Multinational Enterprises and Tax Administrations 2017*, 15 (OECD Publishing 2017).
7. Rädler made this comment during an electronic forum where participants debated the Commission's recently released *Company Taxation in the Internal Market*, *supra* n. 2. *See Tax Analysts e-Forum: Company Taxation in the European Union*, 25 Tax Notes Int'l 153, 153-174 (2002).
8. European Commission, *Company Taxation in the Internal Market*, *supra* n. 2, at 8.
9. My dissertation evaluates the US and Canadian experience with formulary apportionment as guidance for the European Community. *Company Taxation for the European Community*, *supra* n. 4.
10. Lawrence H. Summers, *Taxation in a Small World*, in *Tax Policy in the Twenty-First Century* 64 (Herbert Stein ed., John Wiley 1988); Alicia H. Munnell, *Taxation of Capital Income in a Global Economy: An Overview*, New Eng. Econ. Rev. 33 (September/October 1992).
11. *See* Peggy B. Musgrave, *Interjurisdictional Coordination of Taxes on Capital Income*, in *Tax Coordination in the European Community* 197 (Sijbren Cnossen ed., Kluwer 1987); Charles E. McLure, Jr., *Economic Integration and European Taxation of Corporate Income at Source: Some Lessons from the US Experience*, 29 Eur. Tax'n 243 (1989); Sijbren Cnossen, *How Much Tax Harmonisation in the EC?*, Institute for Fiscal Studies, Proceedings of the Fourth IFS Residential Conference: Beyond 1992: A European Tax System (IFS Commentary No. 13, Oxford, 1989); Mervyn King, *Harmonization of Taxes on Income from Capital in the EEC* (Special Paper No. 18, LSE Financial Markets Group, 1990); George Kopits (ed.), *Tax Harmonization in the European Community: Policy Issues and Analysis*, IMF Occasional Papers No. 94 (International Monetary Fund 1992); Charles E. McLure, Jr. & Joann M. Weiner, *Deciding Whether the European Union Should Adopt Formula Apportionment of Company Income*, in *Taxing Capital Income in the European Union: Issues and Options for Reform* 243 (Sijbren Cnossen ed., Oxford University Press 2000).

between independent enterprises, was still appropriate for taxing multinational enterprises in the Single Market.[12] The Commission realized that not only is transfer pricing an 'international company tax problem' but also, as shown by the US and Canadian experience, formulary apportionment is a method that, despite complications, 'in practice ... works'.[13]

The Commission presented a two-step procedure for reforming EU company taxation. First, the EU should create a consolidated corporate tax base. As the Commission noted:

> By definition, an essential element of all the solutions is that there should be group consolidation on an EU-wide basis.[14]

Then, the EU should distribute that consolidated base for taxation according to a predetermined sharing rule. In the Commission's words:

> A further key element of all the comprehensive approaches is a mechanism for allocating the common consolidated tax base to the various Member States.[15]

By 2011, these ideas evolved into the Common Consolidated Corporate Tax Base (CCCTB) with formulary apportionment that the Commission proposed in March that year.

This proposal to share the company's tax base using a specific formula was novel. Previous studies, which started just after the creation of the European Economic Community, had persisted with the separate entity, arm's length transfer pricing method. These studies called for various degrees of tax system, tax base, and tax rate harmonization, but the European economic bloc had never adopted any comprehensive measures not even one that proposed formulary apportionment. Measures that eliminated specific taxes were the greatest company tax harmonization that Member States had been able to achieve at the turn of the twenty-first century.[16]

12. *See* European Commission, *Company Taxation in the Internal Market, supra* n. 2, at 6. The Commission's study suggested creating an 'EU Joint Transfer Pricing Forum' to deal with transfer pricing tax problems as an Internal Market issue.
13. European Commission, *Company Taxation in the Internal Market, supra* n. 2, at 411.
14. *Ibid.*, 15.
15. *Ibid.*, 15. Under all options, Member States retain the right to set tax rates at the local level.
16. These measures are the Merger Directive, the Parent-Subsidiary Directive, and the Arbitration Convention. *See* European Commission, *Company Taxation in the Internal Market, supra* n. 2, at 8. For a history of these measures, see Philippe Cattoir, *A History of the 'Tax Package.' The Principles and Issues Underlying the Community Approach* (European Commission Taxation Paper No. 10, December 2006). The earlier reports included the Neumark Report in 1962, the Tempel Report in 1970, and the Commission's Proposal for a Directive of 1975. Commission of the European Communities, Fiscal and Financial Committee (Fritz Neumark, chair), *Report of the Fiscal and Financial Committee on Tax Harmonization in the Common Market* (1962) (Neumark Report); A. J. van den Tempel, *Corporation Tax and Individual Income Tax in the European Communities* (Commission of the European Communities 1970) (van den Tempel Report); European Commission, *Proposal for a Council Directive concerning the harmonization of systems of company taxation and of withholding taxes on dividends* COM(75) 392 final, 23 July 1975; on 23 July 1990 the Council adopted Directive 90/434/EEC on a common system of taxation applicable to mergers, divisions, transfers of assets, and exchanges of shares concerning companies of different Member States (the Merger Directive); Directive 90/435/EEC on the common system of taxation applicable in the case of parent companies and subsidiaries of

Given the glacial pace of tax reform, the rapid shift from rejection to acceptance of formulary apportionment is historic. How and why did this happen and what are the implications of this shift? Drawing from decades of experience, this chapter will analyse the evolution of formulary apportionment on the European stage, discuss the implications of the shift, and gauge the possibility that the European Union will move to a company tax system that uses formulary apportionment.[17]

§4.02 THE EUROPEAN UNION'S PATH TOWARDS FORMULARY APPORTIONMENT

There are three key phases in the move to an EU company tax system with formulary apportionment.

The first phase started in 1992 with the report by the Committee of Independent Experts on Company Taxation (Ruding Committee).[18] The report rejected formulary apportionment.

different Member States (the Parent-Subsidiary Directive); and *Convention on the elimination of double taxation in connection with the adjustment of profits of associated enterprises* (the Arbitration Convention) (90/463/EEC).

17. My experience analysing formulary apportionment in the EU began in 1989 when I was a graduate student and my academic advisor, Lawrence Summers, suggested that I read his paper, *supra* n. 10, that advocated considering the formulary method for taxation in the European Community, because I was moving to Brussels. I moved there in 1990 and worked at the Université Libre de Bruxelles (ULB) until 1992. Thanks to US tax attorney Howard Liebman, I had the good fortune to become friends with Albert Rädler who introduced me to Onno Ruding, who was then beginning his work on evaluating EC company tax systems. I contributed *Tax Coordination and Competition in the United States of America*, Annex 9C to Ruding's report. While at the ULB, I organized a conference in 1991 titled *Company Taxation in Europe 1992: Design and Implementation of Company Tax Reform* and published my first paper on the system, titled *A New Direction in Company Taxation*, which evaluated issues in using formulary apportionment in the European Community. My work on using apportionment in the European Community led to my dissertation *Company Taxation for the European Community, supra* n. 4. My book *Company Tax Reform in the European Union, supra* n. 3, summarizes the research and history presented in my dissertation. I was an economist in the US Treasury Department and presented a paper at Treasury's conference on formulary apportionment in December 1996. The Treasury subsequently published that conference paper *Using the Experience in the US States to Evaluate Issues in Implementing Formula Apportionment at the International Level* (US Treasury Department Office of Tax Analysis Paper 83, April 1999). Finally, I returned to Brussels from 1999 to 2006 and was hired by the Commission's tax and customs unit as an independent contractor to help analyse formulary apportionment in the EU. During this period, I was the EU correspondent for Tax Analysts, an American publisher of tax news, and I wrote extensively about developments in company taxation in the EU. For example, see Joann M. Weiner, *EU Commission, Member States Commit to EU-Wide Company Taxation, Formulary Apportionment*, 26 Tax Notes Int'l 515 (2002) and *Approaching an EU Common Consolidated Tax Base*, 46 Tax Notes Int'l 647 (2007).
18. That report is known as the Ruding Report, after its chairman, Onno Ruding, former finance minister in the Netherlands. The Committee's other members were Donal de Buitléir, Jean-Louis Descours, Lorenzo Gascon, Carlo Gatto, Ken Messere, Albert Rädler, and Frans Vanistendael. *See Report of the Committee of Independent Experts on Company Taxation* (Office for Official Publications of the European Communities 1992) (Ruding Report).

The second phase started in 2001 when the Commission officially put formulary apportionment on the table.[19]

The third phase started in 2011 when the Commission formally proposed a company tax system that adopted a predetermined formula for sharing the tax base.[20]

This chapter evaluates these three phases in the context of how each one has helped keep the formulary apportionment dream alive.

§4.03 PHASE 1: 1992 – THE RUDING COMMITTEE REPORT

The long road to formulary apportionment began in 1990 with the creation of an independent committee of tax experts (the Ruding Committee) that examined whether differences in corporation tax caused distortions in the Internal Market and, if so, how to remove them. The Ruding Committee met eleven times between January 1991 and February 1992 and, at the end of this process, found that cross-border investment faced higher hurdle rates of return than did domestic investment.[21] The Committee's report cited empirical evidence that taxes affect multinational companies' location and financing decisions.[22]

It also found that, although company tax practices had converged to some extent, neither market forces nor independent action by the Member States had been able to eliminate these distortions. Yet, the Committee stopped short of calling for a specific company tax system to address these problems. Instead, it advocated a soft tax harmonization that would create a level playing field within the European Union by setting basic standards for taxation.[23]

The Ruding Committee endorsed the Commission's efforts to eliminate withholding taxes on cross-border inter-corporate dividend, interest, and royalty payments; it recommended a minimum statutory corporate tax rate of 30% and a maximum rate of 40%; and it called for common rules concerning a minimum tax base. For the corporate tax system, it encouraged Member States, in the short-term, to extend on a reciprocal basis any shareholder relief and, in the long term, to consider a fully harmonized corporation tax system. As stated in the Report:

> Adoption by all Member States of a common non-discriminatory corporation tax system is clearly desirable in principle, because it would foster the establishment

19. European Commission, *Company Taxation in the Internal Market*, *supra* n. 2.
20. Commission of the European Communities, *Proposal for a Council Directive on a Common Consolidated Corporate Tax Base (CCCTB)*, COM(2011) 121/4, 16 March 2011. The Commission updated an annex to the document on 3 October 2011 to reflect the reference to Cyprus. See COM(2011) 121 final/2.
21. Ruding Report, *supra* n. 18. For a summary of the report, see Michael Daly & Joann Weiner, *Corporate Tax Harmonization and Competition in Federal Countries: Some Lessons for the European Community?*, 46(4) Nat'l Tax J. 441 (1993).
22. Peter Birch Sørensen, *The Effects of Taxation on International Investment and Economic Efficiency*, Annex 5A of the Ruding Report, *supra* n. 18.
23. For an analysis of the report by one of the committee's members, see Frans Vanistendael, *The Ruding Committee Report: A Personal View*, 13(2) Fiscal Stud. 85 (1992). *See Conclusions and Recommendations of the Committee of Independent Experts on Company Taxation* (Office for Official Publications of the European Communities 1992).

of a single European capital market. It is by no means clear, however, which system is most desirable from the standpoint of the efficient allocation of new investment.[24]

The Ruding Committee focused on the need to preserve Member State sovereignty and noted that maintaining sovereignty required taking only the minimum steps necessary to remove discrimination and major distortions. The Ruding Committee reached this conclusion while highlighting the fact that eliminating obstacles to economic integration and creating an internal market are fundamental objectives of the Treaty of Rome.[25]

Furthermore, although the Ruding Report discussed the formulary methods used in the Canadian provinces, the Swiss cantons, and the US states, it firmly rejected the notion that formulary apportionment could eliminate these distortions. Since Onno Ruding had relatively recently registered his opposition to the method when he was the Dutch finance minister, it was no surprise that the Ruding Report also took that position.

This position was understandable. Several high-profile controversies involving the US states had tarnished formulary apportionment's reputation outside the United States. Although the US states had used formulary apportionment since the early twentieth century, the international controversy did not erupt until 1976 when the US Senate rejected the US-UK double tax treaty over a restriction on the US states' use of worldwide formulary apportionment.[26] The controversy widened as some states extended the reach of their tax systems to the worldwide operations of both US and foreign multinational companies.

The international community took notice in 1983 when the US Supreme Court validated the global formulary apportionment method.[27] However, as that decision

24. *See* Ruding Report, *supra* n. 18, ch. 10.
25. The Treaty of Rome that established the European Economic Community, one of the three European Communities, was signed in 1957 and came into force on 1 January 1958.
26. The system is often referred to as worldwide unitary taxation, or worldwide combined reporting, reflecting the concept that the company prepares a combined report on its worldwide combined unitary operations and is taxed on its combined unitary operations around the world. The idea of a unitary tax developed from the states' application of the corporate income tax to the unitary business of the transcontinental railroad. *See* Weiner, *Company Taxation for the European Community*, *supra* n. 4, and the papers collected in *The State Corporation Income Tax: Issues in Worldwide Unitary Combination* (Charles E. McLure, Jr. ed., Hoover Institution Press 1984). A combined report is not the same thing as a consolidated tax return. A consolidated return treats related entities as a single taxpayer whereas a combined report includes only the income and activities of a single unitary business. California tax authorities developed the combined reporting approach in the 1930s to address practices by the motion picture industry of producing films in California and then transferring them to low-tax states for distribution and, thus, reporting profits out of state. Moreover, taxpayers would include foreign operations in their unitary report if doing so would reduce their tax liability. The growth of worldwide trade and taxpayers' use of worldwide combination to reduce their tax liabilities led California to adopt worldwide combination as a rule in the 1970s. *See* Benjamin F. Miller, *Worldwide Unitary Combination: The California Practice*, in *The State Corporation Income Tax: Issues in Worldwide Unitary Combination* 132.
27. *See Container Corp. v. Franchise Tax Board*, 63 US 159 (1983) upholding application to a US company.

concerned a US-based multinational company, it was not seen as a major issue for European entities.

That perception changed when the tax affected a foreign-based multinational company. In 1994, the US Supreme Court heard arguments from British bank Barclays that the Californian system inappropriately taxed profits that it claimed had no connection to the US state.[28] European governments had made their opposition to this tax system loud and clear, as the Supreme Court recognized when it noted that a 'battalion of foreign governments' had 'marched to Barclays' aid, deploring worldwide combined reporting in diplomatic notes, amicus briefs, and even retaliatory legislation'.[29] The Court reported that it had 'received diplomatic notes complaining about state use of the worldwide unitary method of taxation from virtually every developed country in the world'. These countries condemned the method as being 'contradictory to, and incompatible with, accepted international principles of corporate tax assessment and the purpose of double taxation and/or friendship, commerce and navigation treaties to which the United States is a part; and is an impediment to investment and trade with the US'.[30]

However, as the *Barclay's Bank* case was making its way through the US court system when the Committee was writing its report, the Ruding Committee was not in a position to look favourably upon, much less endorse the method.[31] European companies and governments were convinced that worldwide combined reporting with formulary apportionment was a nightmare. These views were reinforced when the Court upheld the California tax.

Years later, things had changed. A few days after the Commission released its 2001 company tax study, Ruding spoke about the state of company tax reform in the EU.[32] He recognized that significant economic integration had taken place since the Ruding Report, and the creation of the internal market and the Economic and Monetary Union had stimulated a substantial increase in cross-border activity within Europe. In his speech, Ruding seemed to support the Commission's proposal for an optional EU-wide company tax system that was likely to require using some sort of formula to share profits across the Member States.

By the end of the 1990s, economic integration in Europe was a reality. The newly named European Union was working to create a single market that would no longer have obstacles to the freedom of movement of goods, people, services, and capital

28. For details on this controversy, *see* Martens-Weiner, *Company Tax Reform in the European Union, supra* n. 3, ch. 1.
29. *See Barclays Bank, plc v. Franchise Tax Board of California*, 512 US, 129 L.Ed.2d 244 (1994) upholding application to a foreign company.
30. *Ibid.*
31. *Barclays Bank Int'l v. Franchise Tax Bd.*, 275 Cal. Rptr. 626, 225 Cal. App. 3d 1342 (30 November 1990); *Barclay's Bank Int'l, Ltd v. Franchise Tax Bd.*, 2 Cal. 4th 708 (11 May 1992), 829 P. 2d 279, *cert. denied*, 506 US 870 (1992).
32. Onno Ruding, *The Long Way to Removing Obstacles in Company Taxation in Europe*, speech to the International Bureau of Fiscal Documentation, Amsterdam (26 October 2001).

across borders. Yet, despite these economic changes, EU politicians had failed to take the steps necessary to eliminate these obstacles.[33]

This failure at the political level spurred the European Court of Justice (ECJ) to take the lead in establishing a non-discriminatory environment for cross-border investment across the EU.[34] In general, the ECJ had ruled against a Member State when its tax policy levied higher tax rates on non-residents than on residents and if it failed to give non-residents the same tax benefits given to residents. The impact of these decisions was far-reaching, as they applied not only to the Member State whose tax policy the ECJ had rejected but also to all Member States applying the same type of policy.[35]

On the tax front, experts from the European Union and the OECD were working simultaneously in the late 1990s on ways to combat harmful tax practices and harmful tax competition in their respective jurisdictions.[36] The OECD's 1998 report led to the creation of the Forum on Harmful Tax Practices whose mandate included, among other things, identifying and curbing harmful tax practices in the OECD member countries,[37] while the EU had simultaneously adopted a tax package that called on EU Member States to eliminate and refrain from introducing harmful tax measures.[38] In 1998, EU finance ministers established the Code of Conduct group under the direction of UK Paymaster General Dawn Primarolo to evaluate Member State tax measures that may fall afoul of the Code of Conduct.[39] The ministers also called for a comprehensive study on company taxation in the European Community.

§4.04 PHASE 2: 23 OCTOBER 2001 – COMPANY TAXATION IN THE INTERNAL MARKET

Three years later, the European Commission took one small step towards formulary apportionment when it released its Communication *Towards an Internal Market without Tax Obstacles*[40] and the accompanying Study *Company Taxation in the*

33. The requirement that Member States unanimously approve direct tax legislation created a barrier. For details on EU tax law, see Ruth Mason, *Primer on Direct Taxation in the European Union* (Thomson 2005).
34. The 1986 *Avoir Fiscal* case, where the Court ruled that France's dividend imputation system violated the Treaty, was the ECJ's first major decision in the company tax area. *See Commission v. France*, C-270/83, ECLI:EU:C:1986:37 (28 January 1986).
35. For a comprehensive analysis of the ECJ's decisions, see Ruth Mason, *Made in America for European Tax: The Internal Consistency Test*, 49(5) B.C. L. Rev. 1277 (2008).
36. At that time, all fifteen members of the EC were also members of the OECD.
37. *See* OECD, *Harmful Tax Competition: An Emerging Global Issue* (OECD 1998).
38. The EU's Council of Economics and Finance Ministers adopted the Tax Package at its 1 December 1997 meeting. The Commission had proposed *A Package to Handle Harmful Tax Competition* on 5 November 1997. The package was designed, among other things, to tackle harmful tax competition. *See* Council of the European Union, *Conclusions of the Ecofin Council Meeting on 1 December 1997 Concerning Taxation Policy*, OJ C2, 6 January 1998, 1.
39. For details on the Code of Conduct and the Primarolo Group, see European Commission, *Harmful Tax Competition: Code of Conduct*, https://ec.europa.eu/taxation_customs/business/company-tax/harmful-tax-competition_en (accessed 20 June 2019).
40. *See* European Commission, *Towards an Internal Market without Tax Obstacles*, *supra* n. 2.

Internal Market.[41] The study identified numerous tax provisions - the use of arm's length pricing, failure to provide cross-border loss compensation, unrelieved double taxation - that distorted cross-border trade, investment, and establishment. Those tax obstacles misallocate EU resources and prevent EU companies from operating efficiently. The Commission viewed the existence of a different tax system in each of the fifteen Member States as the main cause of the distortions.

To eliminate these distortions, the Commission sought a new direction in company taxation that would allow EU companies to use one set of rules to calculate their EU-wide tax base and then share that tax base among the Member States for taxation at local rates.[42] Specifically, the Commission said it was necessary to give companies a consolidated corporate tax base for their EU operations, develop and agree on an apportionment mechanism, and allow Member States to set their own tax rates.[43]

The study examined four approaches that would allow (or require) companies to consolidate their activities on an EU-wide basis and share the group income using a formula.[44] For the first time in its history, the Commission had formally supported using a formula instead of transfer prices to distribute profits across EU Member States. Given the preliminary stage of the analysis, the Commission stopped short of recommending a specific sharing mechanism and, instead, launched a process to define a mechanism to share the company tax base among the Member States.[45]

It was not easy for the European Commission to convince the tax community that the benefits of an EU-wide company tax system using an apportionment mechanism outweighed the drawbacks. Formulary methods were not acceptable when the Commission set out to fulfil its mandate, and opposition to any formula-based method to allocate the tax base across national borders was widespread.

As an example, when the OECD updated its transfer pricing guidelines in the mid-1990s, the allegation that a transfer pricing method 'involved a formulary method was considered in itself by some to be a sufficient criticism of the merits of the method'.[46] To some extent, the United States had sparked this controversy when it

41. The Directorate-General for Taxation and Customs Union (TAXUD) prepared the study under the chairmanship of Michel Aujean, the Director of TAXUD. *See* European Commission, *Company Taxation in the Internal Market, supra* n. 2. The Commission published the study as a book in 2002 under the same title.
42. For a summary of the study, see Joann M. Weiner, *EU Commission Study on Company Taxation, Internal Market Considers Comprehensive Tax Reform*, 24 Tax Notes Int'l 511 (23 October 2001).
43. *See* European Commission, *Towards an Internal Market without Tax Obstacles, supra* n. 2, at 16.
44. The methods were Home State Taxation, a common (consolidated) tax base, a European Union company income tax (EUCIT), and a single compulsory harmonized tax base.
45. Reflecting the still present scepticism about apportionment, the Commission referred to an allocation key rather than to formulary apportionment. Two expert panels advised the Commission, one from the business community and social partners and the other from the academic community.
46. *See* Michael C. Durst & Robert E. Culbertson, *Clearing Away the Sand: Retrospective Methods and Prospective Documentation in Transfer Pricing Today*, 57(1) Tax L. Rev. 37 (2003).

introduced new transfer price approaches in 1988.[47] Innovative profit-based approaches to transfer pricing had no chance of being accepted internationally once they had been accused of having formulary characteristics.

The OECD's *Transfer Pricing Guidelines* did accept certain formulary or transactional profit-split methods, as long as they reflected the company's particular facts and circumstances. They rejected a global formulary apportionment method that applied what it called a pre-determined and mechanistic formula because, according to the OECD, the method was arbitrary and disregarded market conditions.[48]

By the time the Commission was conducting its analysis, the tide was turning away from a system that considered multinational companies as independent entities applying transfer prices for each individual transaction towards one that looked at the multijurisdictional enterprise as a whole and looked to where the enterprise conducted its business. To justify an EU-level tax system, the Commission noted that European companies were increasingly defining their home as the European Union, not as a single Member State. If the common tax base treated companies as if they were a single European-wide entity, they would be able to operate much more efficiently. 'Our businesses look at things on a pan-European basis, not as a series of separate markets', said the tax head at a UK chemicals firm.[49] With an EU-level home, it made sense to have a tax system that was designed to be seamless when a group did business across national borders.

[A] Key Elements

The study identified two essential elements of any EU company tax system.

First, it required group consolidation on an EU-wide basis. This element led to the Common Consolidated Corporate Tax Base (CCCTB).

Second, it required a mechanism to allocate the tax base. This requirement eventually led to formulary apportionment.

The Commission took an inclusive approach towards the second issue. The study had discussed the option of using separate accounting with transfer pricing to share the consolidated tax base. Yet, even though it would be possible to do so, the Commission described such an approach as 'rather self-defeating' as it would negate many of the advantages of moving to a single tax base.[50] Thus, although separate accounting was still an acceptable method, the Commission set that approach aside and turned towards various sharing mechanisms. These mechanisms included the innovative macro-based and industry-based formulas as well as the traditional firm-specific formulas.

While advocating US-style formulary apportionment, the Commission also acknowledged the relative 'chaos' that existed in the US states due to their multiple tax

47. US Department of the Treasury and the Internal Revenue Service, *A Study of Intercompany Pricing Under Section 482 of the Code*, Notice 88-123, 1988-2 C.B. 458 (1988).
48. OECD, *Transfer Pricing Guidelines for Multinational Enterprises and Tax Administrations* (OECD 1995).
49. Ben McLannahan, *Never Say Never*, CFO Europe.Com, November 2004, quoting Philip Gillett of ICI.
50. *See* European Commission, *Company Taxation in the Internal Market*, *supra* n. 2, at 408.

base definitions, formulas, and factor definitions. Yet, even with these flaws, it still concluded that '[d]espite complications, in practice it works'.[51]

To bring the debate in the open, the Commission held a conference in early 2002 where participants debated the implications of the 2001 study.[52] At that conference, EU Tax Commissioner Frits Bolkestein stressed that a comprehensive company tax reform was essential for the European Union to meet its self-imposed objective of becoming the 'most competitive and dynamic knowledge-based economy in the world'.[53] European Parliament member Benedetto Della Vedova, Rapporteur of the Economic and Monetary Affairs Committee, highlighted the Parliament's resolution that a CCCTB with formulary apportionment was the ultimate goal for EU company tax policy. By contrast, Onno Ruding, the former Dutch finance minister, noted that his cautious support for formulary apportionment reflected practical realities rather than an 'expression of love' for formulary apportionment.[54]

Given the variety of options available, the Commission set out to analyse all aspects of the proposed system. As part of this process, it set up a CCCTB Working Group made up of technical experts from Member State tax administrations, led by a chair from the Directorate-General for Taxation and Customs Union (TAXUD) and, on an ad hoc basis, experts from business and academia. The working group held thirteen formal meetings and numerous informal meetings.[55] The group also met with academic experts on the allocation mechanism,[56] commissioned a study by an outside expert,[57] performed its own study,[58] and held an open meeting with invited experts to evaluate the formula.[59]

The Commission noted that the European Parliament, which had considered the communication and study immediately following their release, supported the project. In a motion for a resolution on the communication, the Parliament recognized that EU companies with community-wide operations should be able to have a consolidated

51. *See* European Commission, *Company Taxation in the Internal Market, supra* n. 2, at 411.
52. *See* European Commission *EU Company Tax Conference*, Brussels, 29-30 April 2002.
53. *See* European Commission, *Conference on Company Taxation Supports Further Work on an EU-Wide Consolidated Company Tax Base*, MEMO/02/84, Brussels (30 April 2002).
54. For a report on the conference, see Weiner, *EU Commission, Member States Commit to EU-Wide Company Taxation, Formulary Apportionment, supra* n. 17.
55. *See* European Commission, *Progress To Date and Future Plans for the CCCTB*, CCCTB\WP\020\doc\en (15 November 2005). For a summary of these meetings, see https://ec.europa.eu/taxation_customs/business/company-tax/common-consolidated-corporate-tax-base-ccctb/preparation-2011-ccctb-proposal_en [accessed 19 September 2019.]
56. *See* European Commission, *Summary Report of the Workshop on the Allocation Mechanism Held in Brussels on 4 March 2004*, TAXUD/C/1/AAG/equD(2004)16172 (6 April 2004). The Directorate-General for Taxation and Customs Union prepared the summary.
57. *See* Joann M. Weiner, *Formulary Apportionment and Group Taxation in the European Union: Insights from the United States and Canada*, European Commission Taxation Paper No. 8 (March 2005).
58. *See* Ana Agúndez-García, *The Delineation and Apportionment of an EU Consolidated Tax Base for Multi-jurisdictional Corporate Income Taxation: A Review of Issues and Options*, European Commission Taxation Paper No. 9 (October 2006).
59. *See* European Commission, *Twelfth Meeting of the CCCTB Working Group*, 10-12 December 2007, https://ec.europa.eu/taxation_customs/business/company-tax/common-consolidated-corporate-tax-base-ccctb/twelfth-meeting-ccctb-wg-december-101112-2007_en (accessed 21 June 2019).

corporate tax base and a mechanism to distribute that base across the Member States. It adopted this resolution on 20 February 2002.[60] It also voted in favour of the CCCTB in 2005.[61]

[B] How the Commission Came Up with Its Formula

This section discusses the process the Commission followed as it sought to devise a way to share the tax base across the Member States.[62] Although it did not prejudge any alternative, it took a close look at the suitability of the formulary apportionment system used in the US states and Canadian provinces.

[1] First, Ask the Experts

An early step in this process involved holding a workshop on the allocation mechanism with European, Canadian, and US tax experts in March 2004. The Commission held this one-day workshop to verify the accuracy of its analysis of the various sharing options and to obtain advice from experts on how to design the key features of the CCCTB, especially on the benefits and drawbacks of the sharing mechanisms under consideration.[63]

The Commission was especially concerned about how the formula approach used in the United States and Canada might distort cross-border investment decisions. As economist Charles McLure, Jr., had identified, allocating income according to the shares of firm-specific capital and labour in a location effectively transforms a tax on income into a tax on the factors included in the formula.[64] The incidence, or burden, of the tax would be borne in the same manner as taxes applied directly to the factor.

This incidence happens in two ways, as formulary apportionment has both a direct effect through the tax rate and an indirect effect through the formula.[65] The direct

60. *See* European Parliament, *Report on the Commission Communication to the Council, the European Parliament and the Economic and Social Committee on Tax Policy in the European Union – Priorities for the Years Ahead* (COM(2001) 260 – C5-0597/2001/2248(COS)), Final A5-0048/2002 (22 February 2002).
61. The Parliament adopted a report 392 in favour, 121 against, and 89 abstentions backing the idea of a CCCTB in the EU. *See* European Parliament, *Resolution on Taxation of Undertakings in the European Union: A Common Consolidated Corporate Tax Base*, 2005/2120(INI), 13 December 2005; European Parliament, Committee on Economic and Monetary Affairs, *Report on Taxation of Undertakings in the European Union: A Common Consolidated Corporate Tax Base*, A6-0386/2005, 1 December 2005.
62. The Commission documented its meetings and provides details on its website. See https://ec.europa.eu/taxation_customs/business/company-tax/common-consolidated-corporate-tax-base-ccctb/preparation-2011-ccctb-proposal_en (accessed 7 January 2020).
63. European Commission, *Summary Report of the Workshop on the Allocation Mechanism*, *supra* n. 56.
64. Charles E. McLure, Jr., *The Elusive Incidence of the Corporate Income Tax: The State Case*, 9(4) Pub. Fin. Q. 395 (1981); *The State Corporate Income Tax: Lambs in Wolves' Clothing*, in *The Economics of Taxation* 327 (Henry Aaron & Michael Boskin eds., The Brookings Institution 1980).
65. Roger Gordon & John Wilson, *An Examination of Multijurisdictional Corporate Income Taxation Under Formula Apportionment*, 54(6) Econometrica 1357 (1986). For an analysis in the

effect happens in the same way as if the tax were levied directly on the factor. Reducing the statutory tax rate, all else equal, makes investment in a location relatively more attractive than otherwise.

The indirect effect happens through the formula. If the formula distributes income according to the location of capital, then when a company invests additional capital in a location, the share of income apportioned to that location increases. Normally, the marginal tax rate would be expected to increase. However, that is not necessarily the case with apportionment since the marginal tax burden under apportionment depends on whether the tax rate applied at that location is above or below the firm's average tax rate. As a result, a low-tax location is a relatively attractive place for investment since high-tax locations effectively encourage investment in those low-tax locations.[66]

Likewise, a jurisdiction may keep its statutory tax rate unchanged yet reduce the marginal effective tax rate by reducing the weight on the capital (property) factor.[67] This policy acts as an investment incentive, as shown by many empirical studies. US states that reduced the weight on the property factor stimulated additional investment in their state.[68] This result explains why nearly all US states have abandoned the equally weighted three-factor Massachusetts formula[69] in favour of one that overly weights the destination-based sales factor.[70]

In the EU, however, exerts were split about whether to use a traditional firm-specific factor-based formula or to use a novel value-added formula. Supporters of using value added to allocate income noted that it skips the difficulties in valuing intangibles, it is a widely used system, and the existing consumption-based value-added accounts could form the basis for moving to an income-based value added tax. Because it includes labour costs and the return on all capital, its base is broader than profits and thus faces fewer transfer pricing problems than the current system.

European context, see Wolfgang Eggert & Andreas Haufler, *Company-Tax Coordination cum Tax-Rate Competition in the European Union*, 62(4) FinanzArchiv 579 (2006).

66. Under apportionment, effective marginal tax rates are firm specific. For evidence on how state corporate income taxes affect business investment, see Joann Weiner, *Company Taxation for the European Community, supra* n. 4. For a summary of these results, see Joann Weiner, *Formulary Apportionment and the Future of Company Taxation in the European Union*, 3(1) CESIfo Forum 10 (2002).
67. Martens-Weiner, *Company Tax Reform in the European Union, supra* n. 3, at 16. For an analysis of the strategic choice of factor weights in the US states, see Bharat N. Anand & Richard Sansing, *The Weighting Game: Formula Apportionment as an Instrument of Public Policy*, 53(2) Nat'l Tax J. 183 (2000).
68. The states did this by increasing the weight on the sales factor. *See* Weiner, *Company Taxation for the European Community, supra* n. 4, and the references cited in Martens-Weiner, *Company Tax Reform in the European Union, supra* n. 3.
69. This formula is known as the Massachusetts formula for the first state to use the equally weighted three-factor property, payroll, and sales formula when it adopted the corporate income tax in 1919. In 1963, two-thirds of the states that had a corporate income tax used the Massachusetts formula. That uniformity soon broke down. By 1996, twenty-six states used the double-weighted sales formula.
70. Iowa was the first state to tax entirely on the basis of sales, while Florida became the first state to adopt a double-weighted sales factor, which it did when it adopted the corporate income tax in 1971. As of 2019, twenty-five states including the District of Columbia use a sales-only formula, and most other states use a super-weighted sales formula.

Opponents viewed the system as difficult to implement due to complications involved in converting the current system to an origin-based one used to apportion income.

At the end of the workshop, there was a preference for traditional formulary apportionment over allocation according to value added, largely due to perceived intractable problems with the value-added approach.[71] The experts considered that it was more important to get agreement on the formula than on exactly which factors were included in the formula, subject to the constraint that the factors have an economic basis for allocating income. The Commission used this analysis, among other things, to prepare its presentation to the full CCCTB Working Group.

[2] Second, Identify Potential Sharing Factors

The Commission focused its efforts on the traditional formulary apportionment method that allocates income according to firm-specific factors representing the contributions of labour, capital, and sales to income. It first worked on identifying which of these traditional factors to include in the formula and then on how to define the factors.[72]

Under formulary apportionment, payroll represents labour's contribution in generating income. Most jurisdictions use employee compensation to measure labour's contribution to income.

Although labour productivity tends to equalize across jurisdictions over time, the Commission noted that using compensation without adjusting for differences in labour costs across jurisdictions could allocate the tax base in an unacceptable way. For example, compensation might differ across locations for reasons unrelated to productivity. Moreover, companies might choose to move their operations to a low-cost area to take advantage of labour cost savings, but the formula would still allocate the tax base to the high-wage jurisdiction.[73]

One way to deal with differences in wage levels across the EU would be to include the number of employees in the labour factor. This issue was deemed particularly important for the newer Member States, where wages tend to be lower than in the older Member States. However, using the number of employees could be distortionary since employees might have different levels of productivity in different locations, but those locations would receive the same share of the tax base based on the number of employees.[74]

Assets represent capital's contribution to income and are a logical element of the apportionment formula from a theoretical point of view since capital generates income. Yet, including assets in the formula creates some concerns. One concern is that it is difficult to value assets, which is one reason why the Canadian provinces exclude

71. The macro- and industry-based approaches are discussed later in this chapter, §4.04[C].
72. This chapter only briefly discusses the definitions of the factors. For a comprehensive analysis of US state taxes, see Jerome R. Hellerstein, Walter Hellerstein & John A. Swain, *State Taxation* (Thomson Reuters 3d ed. 2019 rev.).
73. *See* Charles E. McLure, Jr., *Replacing Separate Entity Accounting and the Arm's Length Principle with Formulary Apportionment*, 56(12) Bull. Int'l Tax'n 586, 594 (2002).
74. *See* Agúndez-García, *The Delineation and Apportionment of an EU Consolidated Tax Base*, *supra* n. 58, at 48.

assets from the apportionment formula.[75] Another concern is that the assets factor generally includes tangible assets but excludes intangible assets. Many experts recommend leaving intangible assets out of the formula due to problems in valuing them and identifying their location. Finally, the factor should include rented or leased assets since the value-generating aspects of an asset do not depend on whether the company owns them or not.

Sales, or gross receipts, reflect the role of demand and are viewed as an important element of the formula since companies would not have income if they did not have sales. Moreover, the location of sales is less mobile than capital so that using the sales factor reduces the distortionary impact of the formula on a company's location decision. Concerns with sales generally centred on whether they should be measured at origin, i.e., from their shipping location, or at destination, i.e., the location of consumption. No consensus arose on the sales factor.

[3] Third, Evaluate the Alternatives to Share the CCCTB

The most important documents in the debate over formulary apportionment are the Commission's Working Documents that evaluate the sharing mechanism and the issues in favour of and against the numerous options. These documents highlight that, as the EU becomes more and more economically integrated, the existing tax systems become less and less appropriate for taxing EU multinational enterprises.

The Commission issued its first report on the sharing mechanism in November 2006.[76] The ninth meeting of the CCCTB Working Group discussed that report on 13 December 2006 and highlighted two aspects of the sharing mechanism. The first aspect evaluates the factors that should be included in the formula and the related issue of how each factor should be weighted, while the second aspect considers the definitions of the factors.

As background, the Commission referred to papers written by Ana Agúndez-García for guidance on the general apportionment method and me on the experience in the US states and Canadian provinces.[77] Agúndez-García's paper discussed the broad issues of achieving equity and efficiency, where efficiency covers such issues as neutrality, enforceability, simplicity, and cost-effectiveness, with the sharing mechanism. My paper examined how the experience in the states and provinces could help the EU design its sharing mechanism.

The Commission first evaluated the traditional formulary apportionment method for sharing the tax base. That method would use a predetermined formula with elements that represent the factors that generate income. Locations with a relatively

75. *See* Weiner, *Formulary Apportionment and Group Taxation in the European Union, supra* n. 57, at 15; Ernest H. Smith, *Allocating to Provinces the Taxable Income of Corporations: How the Federal-Provincial Allocation Rules Evolved*, 24(5) Can. Tax J. 545 (1976).

76. *See* European Commission, *The Mechanism for Sharing the CCCTB*, CCCTB\WP\047\doc (17 November 2006).

77. *See* Agúndez-García, *The Delineation and Apportionment of an EU Consolidated Tax Base, supra* n. 58; Weiner, *Formulary Apportionment and Group Taxation in the European Union, supra* n. 57.

large presence of income-generating factors would be allocated a relatively large share of the group's consolidated profits. Thus, the mechanism would link profits to the location where they are earned.

Perhaps the most significant factor in favour of the traditional formulary apportionment method is that the United States and Canada have used it for many decades and, thus, provide actual experience with implementing that system.[78] The Commission noted that the basic principle of formulary apportionment is that it should be based on factors that reflect the source of income as closely as possible.[79] The US states[80] and Canadian provinces[81] use a combination of payroll/compensation, assets/property, and sales/gross receipts to share the tax base across subnational jurisdictions. With some industry-specific exceptions, the provinces have never used property as an allocation factor.

The Canadian experience is instructive for another reason. When designing their system from the start, the provinces chose a two-factor payroll and sales formula, and they have largely retained that common formula for more than fifty years. As a Canadian economist noted, although the factors in the formula might have seemed arbitrary when introduced, the fact that the provinces have applied them for so many years makes it difficult for any province to deviate from the uniform rules.[82]

The Commission considered sharing the tax base using value added. That approach was appealing because it is a familiar concept for EU taxpayers and tax administrators and is an innovative, firm-specific way to allocate income that was not associated with the still controversial formulary apportionment method used in the US states.

Moving from the consumption-type value added measured at destination to an income-type value added measured at origin would not be insurmountable. Value added at origin would contain a profit element that would partially attribute the taxable base to the location where the group earned profits. However, using value added had some problems. First, because firms must use arm's length pricing for intra-group transactions to calculate value added, it reintroduces transfer pricing obligations and

78. *See* Martens-Weiner, *Company Tax Reform in the European Union, supra* n. 3.
79. European Commission, *The Mechanism for Sharing the CCCTB, supra* n. 76, at 5.
80. *See* Joann M. Weiner, *Using the Experience in the US States to Evaluate Issues in Implementing Formula Apportionment, supra* n. 17.
81. As part of the Tax Rental Agreements with the federal government, the Canadian provinces agreed to use a common payroll and gross revenue formula. When the provinces regained the corporate income tax after World War II, they dropped the separate accounts rule because few companies used it and it was an 'administrative nightmare'. *See* Ernest H. Smith, *Allocating to Provinces the Taxable Income of Corporations, supra* n. 75; Weiner, *Company Taxation for the European Community, supra* n. 4.
82. *See* J. Harvey Perry, *A Fiscal History of Canada – The Postwar Years,* 85 Can. Tax Paper (Canadian Tax Foundation 1989). Some provinces have made minor changes to the formula and tax base and that provinces do set their own investment tax credits and tax rates. *See* Jack Mintz, *Corporate Tax Harmonization in Europe: It's All About Compliance,* 11(2) Int'l Tax & Pub. Fin. 221 (2004).

profit shifting opportunities. Second, because labour makes up about two-thirds of value added, the formula places a heavy tax burden on labour.[83]

Since the firm-specific traditional and value-added based formulas potentially distort the location of activity, the Commission considered options that were not dependent on the firm's choices. Using macroeconomic factors, such as gross domestic product or national VAT bases, would avoid distorting the location of economic activity.[84] However, the Commission did not support these approaches because they could not guarantee a match between the taxpayer's value added or income in a location and its tax liability in that location. The Commission also rejected using an industry-average formula for similar reasons.

[4] Ask the Member States

After its preliminary discussion on the sharing mechanism in December 2006, the Commission sent a note on it to the Commission's subgroup for further analysis. Experts from seventeen Member States attended the group's meeting in February 2007.[85]

To set the stage for the discussion, the Commission emphasized that the approaches to sharing the tax base had three features. First, apportionment is a necessary consequence of consolidation; second, the tax base should be distributed to companies and not to the Member States; and, third, the sharing should be fair, not prone to manipulation, enforceable, simple, and cost-efficient.[86]

The experts in the subgroup requested additional details from the Commission on why it seemed to have rejected the macro-based and value-added approaches to sharing the tax base. Concerning the macro-based approach, they appreciated the fact that it was straightforward, cost-efficient, simple, and easy to manage for both companies and tax administrations. However, it had the drawback that it did not connect economic activity with the tax liability and some members thought that the approach might lead to a race-to-the-top with tax rates because Member States would get a fixed share of any consolidated group's income. In the end, the Member States agreed that while the macro-based method was simple, its disadvantages outweighed its benefits, and they decided to set it aside and focus on other sharing mechanisms.

They also examined using a company's value added to share the tax base. Unlike the macro-based approach, value added links the company's economic activity with its tax liability in a country, and the Member States saw it as an attractive economic

---

83. *See* European Commission, *Summary Record by the Chair of the Meeting of the Common Consolidated Corporate Tax Base Working Group, Held in Brussels on 12 December 2006*, CCCTB\WP\050, 9 (13 February 2007).
84. Belgian economist Marcel Gérard analysed using macroeconomic weights to eliminate the incentives to shift capital and labour for tax purposes. Marcel Gérard, *Multijurisdictional Firms and Governments' Strategies under Alternative Tax Designs* (CESifo Working Paper 1527, 2005).
85. Austria, Belgium, Cyprus, Czech Republic, Denmark, Finland, France, Germany, Hungary, Italy, Latvia, Luxembourg, Netherlands, Poland, Slovenia, Spain, and Sweden.
86. *See* European Commission, *An Overview of the Main Issues That Emerged During the Discussion on the Mechanism for Sharing the CCCTB*, CCCTB/WP/052, 2 (27 February 2007).

concept. However, the approach had drawbacks in that, although the value added tax base could be used as a starting point for the calculation, in principle the company would have to recalculate value added under the income method instead of the consumption method used for VAT purposes. This practice would introduce complexities that the CCCTB is designed to reduce. As noted in §4.04[B][3] above, the most serious drawback was that the method would reintroduce the need for transfer pricing, thus negating one of the benefits of using a sharing mechanism. As with the macro-based method, the experts recommended setting aside the value-added method for the time being. (The Commission did not return to either of these two methods.)

The Commission indicated that formulary apportionment was its preferred method. It was, therefore, time to choose the factors.

The experts generally agreed that the formula should include labour and it should be measured by compensation, but they wished to adjust the labour factor to account for differences in price and wage levels across countries. The Commission suggested that the formula could include the number of employees to offset these wage and price differences.

They agreed that tangible assets (property or capital) are a critical element of generating profits and should be included in the formula, even though it is difficult to establish a market value for assets. The Commission discussed measuring value either as a flow of services that the capital provides each year or as a stock of capital, ideally measured at market value. For matters of simplicity, however, the Member States agreed to use the same value for tangible property that the company used for tax purposes in the CCCTB.

Most experts preferred to exclude financial assets from the formula because of their high mobility, but they reached different conclusions regarding intangible assets. Most felt that the formula should consider intangible assets, such as intellectual property, goodwill and patents, etc., but recognized that there are significant problems both with valuing and with locating intangible assets. In the end, they agreed to undertake additional research into how to reflect intangible assets in the formula.

The question of whether to include a sales factor (sales of goods and services, or gross receipts) created major divisions. From a theoretical viewpoint, sales are not an income-generating factor of production in the same way the capital and labour are. (In all cases, intra-group sales should be excluded.) In addition, when measured at origin, sales duplicated the property and payroll factors and, when measured at destination, their location is too easily manipulated. Moreover, sales might occur in a state where the company had no taxable presence, thus creating so-called no-where income that is not identified with a specific location. Furthermore, marketing countries already receive revenue from the value added tax, so there is no need to apportion income based on sales. For all these reasons, sales should not be included in an income-allocation formula.

Others felt that sales are the most important factor for a company since it would not have any income without sales. Furthermore, the sales factor ensures that the marketing states receive a share of total income. A formula that includes a sales factor creates a balance between the location of demand (sales) and the location of supply (capital and labour).

The Commission presented the subgroup's report to the full CCCTB Working Group on 13 March 2007.[87]

Most members did not want to adjust the payroll factor, noting that payroll is a simple approach, that wages would converge across countries over time, that all factors might need adjusting so there was no need to adjust only the labour factor, and that different wage levels often correspond to higher productivity that should be remunerated. Other experts gave reasons to modify the payroll factor. It could take years for wage levels across the EU to converge and using unadjusted payroll rewards high-wage economies and could have implications for international competitiveness. Adding the number of employees to the formula would be a simple way to adjust the payroll factor.[88]

The experts generally agreed to measure property at its tax value and to exclude financial assets from the formula. It postponed a decision on whether to include intangible and leased assets.

The experts debated the sales factor at length. All the experts wanted to include sales by origin, possibly making an adjustment using macro-stabilizing factors. No experts favoured measuring sales at destination.[89] The Commission, itself, favoured a destination-based sales factor. Support for including sales was based, in part, on the experiences in the places that currently use formulary apportionment. The US states and the Canadian provinces include sales in their formulas. Nearly all US states use a formula that apportions largely on destination-based sales.[90]

In the face of these conflicting views, the Commission faced a formidable task in finding a common apportionment formula.[91] It continued to work to resolve those differences.

[5] Presenting the CCCTB and Formulary Apportionment

In November 2007, after having held numerous meetings with experts and with the subgroup that evaluated the sharing mechanism, the Commission was ready to present a specific formula for sharing the tax base among the various entities of consolidated groups.[92]

This document formed the background for the joint meeting with business and academics on 10-11 December 2007. This document made it clear that the purpose of the Commission's work on the CCCTB was to introduce EU-wide profit consolidation

87. European Commission, *Summary Record of the Meeting of the Common Consolidated Corporate Tax Base Working Group, Held in Brussels on 13 March 2007*, CCCTB\WP\055 (28 June 2007).
88. *Ibid.*, 2.
89. *Ibid.*, 3.
90. *See* Federation of Tax Administrators, *Tax Rates/Surveys – Tax Rates*, https://www.taxadmin.org/current-tax-rates (accessed 21 June 2019).
91. Joann M. Weiner, *Formula One: The Race to Find a Common Formula to Apportion the EU Tax Base*, 17(3) EC Tax Rev. 100 (2008).
92. *See* European Commission, *CCCTB: Possible Elements of the Sharing Mechanism*, CCCTB\WP\060 (13 November 2007).

and that a sharing mechanism was a 'necessary and unavoidable consequence of the consolidation'.[93]

The Commission then defended how apportionment works. It explained that the formulary apportionment approach distributes the tax base using a formula with multiple, firm-specific factors. A multiple-factor formula avoids placing too much weight on a single factor and is likely to capture the variety of elements that generate profit. The formula considers both the supply and the demand side of generating income. The property and payroll factors represent supply and sales factor measures demand.

In a divergence from the approach used in the US states, the EU formula would apportion the tax base to each individual entity within the group, rather than directly to the Member State. This process allows the formula to assign income to several entities within a single Member State and, as a result, allows each entity to calculate its own tax liability, taking into account any pre-existing losses, possible tax credits, etc.[94]

The December 2007 meeting in Brussels included experts from the United States. These experts noted that formulary apportionment is reasonable and preferable to a separate entity approach in unified economies such as those in the United States and Canada and as the EU hopes to become.[95] As EU integration proceeds, maintaining a separate entity approach is less appropriate than a unified approach.

Although the US experts had different views about the elements of the sharing mechanism, they unanimously agreed that 'the principle of formulary apportionment is essential as transfer pricing cannot be done correctly in highly integrated economies'.[96] As the Commission's record of the meeting noted, the result of this situation is that 'formulary apportionment is therefore inexorable'.[97]

Experts from the US and from the business sector at the December workshop agreed on several key elements of the EU's CCCTB and the sharing mechanism:

(1) it should be uniform and identically applied by all Member States to avoid the problems of double taxation and double non-taxation;
(2) one threshold for consolidating entities is preferable;
(3) the formula should allocate all income and not draw a distinction between business and passive, non-business income to avoid creating complexity and triggering economic distortions.[98]

The US experts, who included tax administrators and academics, made additional points. They agreed that, although it is conceptually a good idea to include intangibles

93. *Ibid.*, 5.
94. *Ibid.*, 7.
95. European Commission, *Summary Record by the Chair of the Meeting of the Common Consolidated Corporate Tax Base Working Group Held in Brussels on 10-11 December 2007*, CCCTB/WP/064, 10 (4 March 2008).
96. *Ibid.*, 10.
97. *Ibid.*, 10.
98. The US states distinguish between business and non-business income. They apportion business income using a formula and assign non-business income according to specific source rules. *See* Uniform Division of Income for Tax Purposes Act, s. 1(a), 7A U.L.A. 336 (2015).

in the property factor, they should be excluded for practical reasons. Special formulas should be developed for certain industries. These points were not particularly controversial.

The issue of sales, however, continued to be problematic.

US experts agreed that, if the formula includes sales, there are good reasons to measure them by destination. It is difficult to manipulate the market location. It brings about 'fairness' by apportioning income to the marketing states. Because companies value their customers, they would not be likely to turn sales over to independent contractors just to avoid taxes. Including a sales factor also increases the number of factors in the formula, thus reducing the impact of any single factor. Most importantly, they felt that businesses do not base their business activities primarily on tax considerations.

By contrast, business experts were sceptical about including sales measured at destination, pointing out that this approach would be inconsistent with how EU tax treaties allocate taxing rights. Firms might allocate sales to locations where they did not have a taxable presence and thus escape taxation. On this point, there was a recognition that the traditional approach of requiring a physical presence (or permanent establishment) for taxation might be outdated in the twenty-first century. Yet, Member States are not yet ready to abandon the permanent establishment approach, which is enshrined in double tax treaties and the OECD Model Tax Convention.

Business experts also explained that, because corporate tax rates are much higher in the EU than in the US states, any distortions to economic activity caused by apportionment would be magnified.[99] Table 4.1 shows that in 2019 the average tax rate in the twenty-eight EU Member States is just under 22% (which is significantly lower than the 35% average in 2000, when the Commission commenced its work).

Table 4.1 Top Statutory Corporate Income Tax Rates (Including Surcharges), %

	1995	*2000*	*2005*	*2010*	*2015*	*2019*
Austria	34.0	34.0	25.0	25.0	25.0	25.0
Belgium	40.2	40.2	34.0	34.0	34.0	29.6
Bulgaria	40.0	32.5	15.0	10.0	10.0	10.0
Croatia	25.0	35.0	20.0	20.0	20.0	18.0
Czech Republic	41.0	31.0	26.0	19.0	19.0	19.0
Cyprus	25.0	29.0	10.0	10.0	12.5	12.5
Denmark	34.0	32.0	28.0	25.0	23.5	22.0
Estonia	26.0	26.0	24.0	21.0	20.0	20.0
Finland	25.0	29.0	26.0	26.0	20.0	20.0

99. Apportionment, however, narrows these differences. *See* Martens-Weiner, *Company Tax Reform in the European Union, supra* n. 3, at 94, Table 13, for an example of how apportionment leads to a convergence of tax rates due to the way the formula distributes the tax base. Apportionment that is not based entirely on the property factor reduces the effective tax rate on capital and the potential distortions to the location of investment.

	1995	*2000*	*2005*	*2010*	*2015*	*2019*
France	36.7	37.8	35.0	30.0	28.0	25.0
Germany	56.8	51.6	38.4	29.5	29.8	29.9
Greece	40.0	40.0	32.0	24.0	29.0	28.0
Hungary	19.6	19.6	17.5	20.6	20.6	10.8
Ireland	40.0	24.0	12.5	12.5	12.5	12.5
Italy	52.2	41.3	37.3	31.4	31.3	27.8
Latvia	25.0	25.0	15.0	15.0	15.0	20.0
Lithuania	29.0	24.0	15.0	15.0	15.0	15.0
Luxembourg	40.9	37.5	30.4	28.6	29.2	24.9
Malta	35.0	35.0	35.0	35.0	35.0	35.0
The Netherlands	35.0	35.0	31.5	25.5	25.0	25.0
Poland	40.0	30.0	19.0	19.0	19.0	19.0
Portugal	39.6	35.2	27.5	29.0	29.5	31.5
Romania	38.0	25.0	16.0	16.0	16.0	16.0
Slovenia	25.0	25.0	25.0	20.0	17.0	19.0
Slovakia	40.0	29.0	19.0	19.0	22.0	21.0
Spain	35.0	35.0	35.0	30.0	28.0	25.0
Sweden	28.0	28.0	28.0	26.3	22.0	21.4
United Kingdom	33.0	30.0	30.0	28.0	20.0	19.0
Simple Averages						
EU-28	35.0	32.0	25.2	23.2	22.8	21.7

Source: European Commission, Taxation and Customs Union, *Taxation Trends in the European Union: Data for the EU Member States, Iceland and Norway, 2019 Edition* 40 (Publications Office of the European Union, 2019) (and earlier editions). The data are available online at https://ec.europa.eu/taxation_customs/business/economic-analysis-taxation/data-taxation_en.

By contrast, Table 4.2 shows that the average US state corporate income tax rate in 2019 is about 7%. A few states do not have a corporate income tax. Other states have a graduated tax rate structure. Due to these variations, some experts expressed concern about applying the US state experience to the EU without considering these differences in statutory tax rates.

Table 4.2 US State Corporate Income Tax Rates (Tax Year 2019, as of 1 January 2019)

State	*Tax Rate, %*	*Tax Brackets (Lowest–Highest), USD*	*State*	*Tax Rate, %*	*Tax Brackets (Lowest–Highest), USD*
Alabama	6.5	Flat Rate	Missouri	6.25	Flat Rate
Alaska	0 – 9.4	25,000 -- 222,000	Montana	6.75	Flat Rate
Arizona	4.9	Flat Rate	Nebraska	5.58 – 7.81	100,000
Arkansas	1.0 – 6.5	3,000 – 100,001	Nevada	No Corporate Income Tax	
California	8.84	Flat Rate	New Hampshire	7.7	Flat Rate
Colorado	4.63	Flat Rate	New Jersey	9.0	Flat Rate
Connecticut	7.5	Flat Rate	New Mexico	4.8 – 5.9	500,000
Delaware	8.7	Flat Rate	New York	6.5	Flat Rate
District of Columbia	8.25	Flat Rate	North Carolina	2.5	Flat Rate
Florida	5.5	Flat Rate	North Dakota	1.41 – 4.31	25,000 – 50,001
Georgia	5.75	Flat Rate	Ohio	Ohio Imposes a Commercial Activity Tax	
Hawaii	4.4 – 6.4	25,000 – 100.001	Oklahoma	6.0	Flat Rate
Idaho	6.925	Flat Rate	Oregon	6.6 – 7.6	1,000,000
Illinois	9.5	Flat Rate	Pennsylvania	9.99	Flat Rate
Indiana	5.75	Flat Rate	Rhode Island	7.0	Flat Rate
Iowa	6.0 – 12.0	25,000 – 250,001	South Carolina	5.0	Flat Rate
Kansas	4.0	Flat Rate	South Dakota	No Corporate Income Tax	
Kentucky	5.0	Flat Rate	Tennessee	6.5	Flat Rate
Louisiana	4.0 – 8.0	25,000 – 200,001	Texas	Texas Imposes a Franchise Tax	
Maine	3.5 – 8.93	350,000 – 3,500,000	Utah	4.95	Flat Rate
Maryland	8.25	Flat Rate	Vermont	6.0 – 8.5	10,000 – 25,000
Massachusetts	8.0	Flat Rate	Virginia	6.0	Flat Rate

State	*Tax Rate, %*	*Tax Brackets (Lowest–Highest), USD*	*State*	*Tax Rate, %*	*Tax Brackets (Lowest–Highest), USD*
Michigan	6.0	Flat Rate	Washington	No Corporate Income Tax	
Minnesota	9.8	Flat Rate	West Virginia	6.5	Flat Rate
Mississippi	0 – 5.0	2,000 – 10,001	Wisconsin	7.9	Flat Rate
			Wyoming	No Corporate Income Tax	

Source: Compiled by Federation of Tax Administrators from various sources. https://www.taxadmin.org/current-tax-rates.

The US experts responded that, because the EU Member States would use the same formula, they would have a clear advantage over the US states, where the various state formulas create tax planning opportunities. Table 4.3 shows the variety of US state formulas for 2019. The Canadian provinces do not have this problem because they use the same formula. However, tax planning opportunities in Canada arise from the lack of consolidation for legally independent subsidiaries of firms doing business in more than one province.[100]

Table 4.3 US State Apportionment of Corporate Income (Tax Year 2019, as of 1 January 2019)

State	*Formula/Alternate Formula*	*State*	*Formula/Alternate Formula*
Alabama	Double wtd Sales	Missouri	3 Factor
Alaska	3 Factor	Montana	3 Factor
Arizona	Sales/Double wtd Sales	Nebraska	Sales
Arkansas	Sales	Nevada	No State Income Tax
California	Sales	New Hampshire	Double wtd Sales
Colorado	Sales	New Jersey	Sales
Connecticut	Sales	New Mexico	Sales
Delaware	75% Sales, 12.5% Property & Payroll	New York	Sales
District of Columbia	Sales	North Carolina	Sales
Florida	Double wtd Sales	North Dakota	3 Factor
Georgia	Sales	Ohio	Ohio Tax Department Publishes Specific Rules for Situs of Receipts under the CAT Tax
Hawaii	3 Factor	Oklahoma	3 Factor
Idaho	Double wtd Sales	Oregon	Sales
Illinois	Sales	Pennsylvania	Sales
Indiana	Sales	Rhode Island	Sales
Iowa	Sales	South Carolina	Sales
Kansas	3 Factor	South Dakota	No State Income Tax
Kentucky	Sales	Tennessee	Triple wtd Sales

100. The separate entity system allows companies to shift profits across provinces through strategic lending and borrowing: Jack Mintz & Michael Smart, *Income Shifting, Investment, and Tax Competition: Theory and Evidence from Provincial Taxation in Canada*, 88(6) J. Pub. Econ. 1149 (2004). Weiner, *Company Taxation for the European Community, supra* n. 4, finds that reductions in either the provincial cost of capital or in the provincial statutory tax rate increase provincial investment.

State	*Formula/Alternate Formula*	*State*	*Formula/Alternate Formula*
Louisiana	Sales	Texas	Sales
Maine	Sales	Utah	Sales
Maryland	66 2/3 Sales, 16 2/3 Property and Payroll	Vermont	Double wtd Sales
Massachusetts	Sales/Double wtd Sales	Virginia	Double wtd Sales/ Sales
Michigan	Sales	Washington	No State Income Tax
Minnesota	Sales	West Virginia	Double wtd Sales
Mississippi	Sales	Wisconsin	Sales
		Wyoming	No State Income Tax

Source: Compiled by Federation of Tax Administrators from various sources. https://www.taxadmin.org/current-tax-rates.

The formulas are for general manufacturing businesses. Some industries have a special formula that differs from the one shown.

Note that 3 factor is sales, property, and payroll, equally weighted (1/3 each). Double wtd Sales is 2 factors with sales double-weighted (50%) and property and payroll weighted 25% each. Sales is a single-factor sales formula.

A basic point that repeatedly arose was that there is no single, correct formula.[101] The Canadian provinces have used a common formula for half a century, and, apart from interest in certain provinces that wish to deviate at times, there is little interest in changing that formula. The US states, which have no restrictions on choosing their formula, are increasingly moving towards a single-factor destination-based sales formula, regardless of the economic arguments against using such a formula.[102] For purposes of apportioning income across jurisdictions, the experts agreed that the main point is to agree on a formula and adhere to it.

[C] How Did the European Business and Political Community React?

The European business community generally supported the idea of creating one company tax system for the European Union. As an example, a telephone survey by the

101. European Commission, *Summary Record by the Chair of the Meeting of the Common Consolidated Corporate Tax Base Working Group Held in Brussels on 10-11 December 2007*, *supra* n. 95, at 14.
102. In 2019, twenty-five states and the District of Columbia used a sales-only formula and another four states made the formula available. By contrast, just one state (Iowa) used a single-factor sales formula in 1980. A Supreme Court decision in 1978 holding that sales-only apportionment was permissible led additional states to move to that formula. For current data, see the Federation of Tax Administrators, https://www.taxadmin.org/current-tax-rates (accessed 14 August 2019).

accountancy firm KPMG taken in mid-2007 found that nearly 80% of the 403 large companies from each of the then twenty-seven EU Member States plus Switzerland supported a common tax base, whether consolidated or not, for the EU.[103] It was only in Ireland and Slovakia that a majority of companies were against the proposal. In terms of the formula, nearly half of the respondents preferred a mixture of sales, non-financial assets, and the size of the labour force, while one-third preferred a sales-only formula. Simplifying tax compliance and allowing them to be more confident in making their business plans were the main reasons these companies supported the Commission's plans.

In addition to supporting a common formula, the BusinessEurope Task Force, led by Swedish businessman Krister Andersson, recommended an allocation key that minimized the tax-induced incentives to shift factors.[104] The Task Force argued against including sales in the formula since it would be rather easy to manipulate and favoured a two-factor formula based on assets and labour instead.[105] The US-based Tax Executives Institute supported the Commission's principal objectives of introducing a CCCTB that would be distributed across the Member States using a uniform formula.[106] Both groups insisted that the system be optional for companies, at least initially.

An editorial in a business magazine focused on how the Commission's proposal would help combat profit shifting. It noted that is 'easier to reshuffle a firm's profits on paper than it is to restructure a firm's activities in reality'.[107]

The Commission summarized these views to mean that, even with the differences in tax rates and tax laws, it could use the US system as a starting point to design the EU sharing mechanism, but it could not import it as is.[108] Regarding the specific formula, the Commission asked national tax administrations for their input.[109] As part of this request, the Commission sought an evaluation of six different formulas, two of which included a factor based on number of employees, in addition to employee compensation.[110]

This variety of views reflects the basic conundrum of formulary apportionment. If the formula contains factors, such as labour and capital, that represent where the

103. Charles Gnaedinger & Joann Weiner, *EU Businesses Want Common Tax Base*, 48 Tax Notes Int'l 7 (2007).
104. BusinessEurope Task Force, *Comments on Document CCCTB\WP\060, Possible Elements of the Sharing Mechanism* (7 December 2007).
105. The Willis Committee of the US Congress had also recommended a two-factor, property, and payroll formula in 1963. The states ignored that advice and used the three-factor, property, payroll, and sales formula that had already been recommended in 1957 in the Uniform Division of Income for Tax Purposes Act (UDITPA), *supra* n. 98.
106. Letter from Tax Executives Institute to Mr. Paul Farmer (17 May 2007).
107. *Discord Over Harmony: One Market, One Profit, 25 Taxmen*, The Economist (10 November 2005).
108. European Commission, *Summary Record of the Meeting of the Common Consolidated Corporate Tax Base Working Group Held in Brussels on 12 December 2007*, CCCTB/WP/063 (4 March 2008).
109. European Commission, *Input from National Tax Administrations for the Impact Assessment of the Reforms at the EU Level of Corporate Tax Systems*, CCCTB\WP\058 (11 September 2007).
110. European Commission, *Report and Overview of the Main Issues That Emerged during the Discussion of the Sharing Mechanism*, CCCTB\WP\056\doc (20 August 2007).

company generates income, then the formula acts as a tax on the factors.[111] If the formula includes a sales factor, then it recognizes that the interaction of supply and demand creates income even if, theoretically, a firm actually generates income through the use of inputs, such as capital and labour. Sales are not an input to the production process and technically do not generate income. As many have noted, however, a firm would not have any income if it did not sell any of its output.[112]

European politicians reflected several views on the Commission's company tax reforms.

In the European Parliament, Christa Randzio-Plath, the President of the Economic and Monetary Affairs Committee, was a reliable supporter of the Commission's efforts to do something about the problems faced by European companies conducting business in the European Union.[113] As she noted at the European Commission's tax conference held in Rome in December 2003, the Commission had released numerous reports, including the Neumark, van den Tempel, and Ruding Reports, and yet, '[d]espite the consistent support of the European Parliament, as we know, little became of them'.[114] She blamed the Council of Ministers for blocking efforts to improve the tax treatment of individuals and companies.

Randzio-Plath warned that, in the absence of action at the EU level, the European Court of Justice would ultimately be the European body that set company tax rules as it worked to preserve non-discrimination and proportionality in the application of individual Member State tax laws.[115] The requirement that all policies be approved unanimously would become even more difficult to achieve once the EU expanded from fifteen states to twenty-five Member States.[116] Despite this outlook, she concluded with

111. Charles E. McLure, Jr., *Defining a Unitary Business: An Economist's View*, in *The State Corporation Income Tax: Issues in Worldwide Unitary Combination* 89 (Charles E. McLure, Jr. ed., Hoover Institution Press 1984).
112. Peggy B. Musgrave, *Principles for Dividing the State Corporate Tax Base*, in *The State Corporation Income Tax: Issues in Worldwide Unitary Combination* 228 (Charles E. McLure, Jr. ed., Hoover Institution Press 1984).
113. Her statement that 'Tax coordination policy and common systems in corporate taxation are part of the reforms Europe needs so badly' reflects this view. *See* Christa Randzio-Plath, *Tax Coordination in the Enlarged European Union*, 13(4) EC Tax Rev. 162 (2004).
114. Christa Randzio-Plath, *Speech to the European Commission Conference on Company Taxation, EU Corporate Tax Reform: Progress and New Challenges*, Rome, 6 December 2003. On 19 April 2012, the European Parliament approved the Commission's 2011 proposal as amended. The Parliament noted that the CCCTB would improve growth and lead to more jobs in the Union and should be adopted by as many states as possible and as soon as possible: European Parliament, Legislative Resolution of 19 April 2012 on the Proposal for a Council Directive on a Common Consolidated Corporate Tax Base (CCCTB) COM(2011) 0121 – C7-0092/2011 – 2011/0058(CNS), http://www.europarl.europa.eu/sides/getDoc.do?type=TA&language=EN&reference=P7-TA-2012-135 (accessed 9 August 2019).
115. For an analysis of ECJ rulings in the company tax area, see Mason, *Made in America for European Tax*, *supra* n. 35.
116. After having fifteen members since 1995, the EU added ten members in 2004, two in 2007, and one in 2013 and has twenty-eight Member States as of 2019. (The United Kingdom has voted to leave the European Union but is still a member as of the end of 2019.)

an optimistic quote from Plato: 'never discourage anyone ... who continually makes progress, no matter how slow'.[117]

Although twenty of the Member States supported the CCCTB initiative, a handful opposed the Commission's efforts. For example, Ireland has long viewed company tax reform from the European Commission with scepticism. As an example, although the Commission explicitly ruled out tax rate harmonization when it released its study, an Irish economist who had been a member of the Ruding Committee wrote that 'a proposal to impose minimum rates can be expected at some time in the future'.[118] He said that a move to greater tax harmonization is not in the interests of core economies and 'should be resisted'.[119]

Some Member States opposed the Commission's idea because they feared that it might lead to a common EU tax rate, would eliminate generous tax depreciation rules, or would complicate the flat tax system.[120] In early 2007, shortly after the Commission released a Communication touting the importance of the CCCTB,[121] the Irish Department of Finance issued a statement that re-emphasized its opposition to the Commission's efforts.[122] Irish Internal Market Commissioner Charlie McCreevy was vocal in his opposition to the Commission's efforts. In a November 2005 speech, he said he was 'emphatically opposed to tax harmonization – be it by the front door or the back'[123] and in February 2007 he charged that the European Commission's effort to create a consolidated tax base was a 'condition precedent to consolidating the rate'.[124]

117. Randzio-Plath, *Speech to the European Commission Conference on Company Taxation, supra* n. 114.
118. *See* Donal de Buitléir, *Tax Harmonisation: Ireland's Position*, in *One Size Fits All?* EU Taxation Policy 55 (Institute of European Affairs and the Institute of Taxation in Ireland, 2002).
119. *Ibid.*, 68.
120. *See* William Echikson, *EU Bid to Unify Tax Code May Overcome Objections: Nations Aim to Set Common Rules, Not Single Levy*, The Wall Street Journal 2 (6 April 2006).
121. European Commission, *CCCTB: Possible Elements of a Technical Outline*, CCCTB\WP\057 (26 July 2007) provided details about the tax base, the consolidated group, and other technical issues.
122. For details on this issue, see Joann Weiner, *An Economist's View of Income Allocation Under the Arm's Length Standard and Under Formulary Apportionment*, St. & Local Tax Lawyer: Symposium Edition 25 (2009/10).
123. Charlie McCreevy, *Tax harmonization- No thanks*, speech to the European Business Initiative on Taxation, 10 November 2005.
124. *See* Charlie McCreevy, *Higher Taxes Feed Fatter Government*, speech to the Irish Tax Institute/Revenue Commissioners Joint Conference, Kilkenny 3 (9 February 2007), https://ec.europa.eu/archives/commission_2004-2009/index_en.htm. Former Irish Minister McCreevy was then European Commissioner for Internal Market and Services. For a report on the views of the CCCTB in the Member States, see Weiner *Approaching an EU Common Consolidated Tax Base, supra* n. 17.

§4.05 PHASE 3: MARCH 2011 – THE COMMISSION PROPOSES FORMULARY APPORTIONMENT

On 16 March 2011, just short of a decade after launching its project, the Commission took a giant leap towards company tax reform when it proposed that Member States adopt a company tax system with formulary apportionment.[125]

The Commission's formal proposal for a Common Consolidated Corporate Tax Base (CCCTB) with formulary apportionment was a historic achievement.[126] Specifically, the Commission proposed that the Member States adopt a tax policy designed to eliminate overtaxation and under-taxation of EU multinational enterprises and reduce the administrative burdens and high compliance costs that affect companies doing business across the EU's internal borders.

Under the proposal, each Member State would allow EU multinational corporations the option to consolidate their EU tax base using a common set of rules and then use a formula to share the consolidated EU tax base among the group members in the various Member States. The Member States would tax the group's apportioned share of total income at their own tax rates. Multinational companies would have the option to use the current system instead of the proposed CCCTB.

Companies would share the CCCTB across group members in each tax year using a formula with the traditional three factors – sales, labour and capital.[127] The formula allocates one-third of income according to sales at destination, one-third of income according to assets and one-third of income to labour, with the labour factor divided equally between payroll and number of employees to reflect the variation in employee compensation across the EU. There is a key difference between the Commission's proposed apportionment method and the method used in the US states. Whereas the states assign income according to the geographic location of the apportionment factors, the Commission's proposed formula assigns income to members of the group.[128]

The proposal defines each apportionment factor. For example, the definition of an employee is based on the national law of the Member State where the employment is exercised. The assets factor consists of the average value of all fixed owned or rented tangible assets. Assets are included in the asset factor of its economic owner.

The sales factor consists of sales of goods and supplies of services, excluding value added tax and other taxes and duties. Sales of goods are included in the sales factor of the group member located in the Member State where the transport of the

---

125. *See* European Commission, *Proposal for a Council Directive on a Common Consolidated Corporate Tax Base (CCCTB)*, COM(2011) 121/4, 16 March 2011, *supra* n. 20.
126. The proposal includes a complete set of rules for the new system and an impact assessment. For detailed documents, see European Commission, *Preparation of the 2011 CCCTB Proposal*, https://ec.europa.eu/taxation_customs/business/company-tax/common-consolidated-corporate-tax-base-ccctb/preparation-2011-ccctb-proposal_en.
127. *See* European Commission, *Proposal for a Council Directive on a Common Consolidated Corporate Tax Base (CCCTB)*, COM(2011) 121/4, 16 March 2011, *supra* n. 20, ch. XVI, Apportionment of the Consolidated Tax Base.
128. For a detailed explanation of this process, see Walter Hellerstein, *Tax Planning under the CCCTB's Formulary Apportionment Provisions: The Good, the Bad and the Ugly*, in *CCCTB: Selected Issues* 221 (Dennis Weber ed., Kluwer Law International 2012).

goods ends, i.e., on a destination basis. If that location cannot be determined, then sales are assigned to the last identifiable location of the goods. Supplies of services are included in the sales factor of the group member where the services are physically carried out.

The Commission has a unique way of assigning sales in cases where there is no group member in the Member State where the goods are delivered or the services are carried out. In these cases, sales are included in the sales factor of all group members in proportion to their labour and asset factors. The Commission calls this rule the spread throw-back rule. If there is more than one group member in the Member State, then the sales are included in the sales factor of all group members in proportion to their labour and asset factors.

[A] Reactions

On 19 April 2012, the European Parliament's Monetary and Economic Affairs Committee called on the Council to adopt the CCCTB as soon as possible to as many companies as possible. The European Parliament agreed with the Commission's proposal, as amended.[129] Among the amendments, it suggested modifying the formula to increase the weights on the assets and labour factors to 45% each and decrease the weight on sales to 10%. It also said that the CCCTB should be mandatory after a transition period, rather than optional as proposed by the Commission.

For many reasons, the European Council did not act on the proposal, with a frequent objection being that it violated the principle of subsidiarity, which provides that the Commission should act only if the individual states cannot achieve the results individually. In terms of the specific elements of the CCCTB, some business opposition centred on the requirement that companies must calculate the tax base on a consolidated basis, believing that the consolidation rules were not well defined. Governments objected to the provision that the new rules would be optional for EU multinational enterprises, believing that optionality would leave the door open for gaming the tax system.

To address these issues, the Commission issued a public request for comments on two features of the CCCTB: first, whether the Commission should offer a non-consolidated tax base instead of a consolidated tax base and, second, whether the proposal should be mandatory instead of elective for businesses.

---

129. *See* European Parliament, *Legislative Resolution of 19 April 2012 on the Proposal for a Council Directive on a Common Consolidated Corporate Tax Base* (CCCTB), COM(2011) 0121 – C7-0092/2011 – 2011/0058(CNS), *supra* n. 114. The Parliament approved the resolution with 452 votes in favour, 172 against, and 36 abstentions. The Parliament indicated that if not all Member States wished to participate, those that did could proceed using the EU's enhanced cooperation procedure.

[B] Revised Proposal

Following this request, the European Commission issued a revised proposal on 25 October 2016 that made two major changes to the 2011 proposal.[130] First, consolidation is no longer required at the outset.[131] Second, the system is mandatory for groups with global consolidated revenues above EUR 750 million.

The CCCTB will be implemented in two steps. Member States will first adopt a common corporate tax base, the CCTB, and later move to consolidation, the CCCTB, with formulary apportionment.[132] The Commission's revised proposal keeps the apportionment formula from the 2011 proposal. Although the CCCTB (Common *Consolidated* Corporate Tax Base) technically becomes the CCTB (Common Corporate Tax Base) for now, because the proposal envisions consolidation as the result, the Commission continues to refer to the proposal as the CCCTB. The European Parliament held a public hearing on the revised proposal in May 2017 where business representatives and stakeholders representing trade unions and an advocacy group presented their ideas on the proposal.[133] Parliament adopted its opinion on 15 March 2018.

[C] Digital Taxation

A change to the Commission's company tax reform efforts occurred in March 2018 when the European Commission set forth a two-pronged package for taxing digital companies in the EU.[134] Pierre Moscovici, the Commissioner for Economic and Financial Affairs, Taxation and Customs said that:

---

130. European Commission, *Proposal for a Council Directive on a Common Corporate Tax Base,* 25 October 2016 COM(2016) 685 final 2016/0337(CNS), https://ec.europa.eu/taxation_customs/sites/taxation/files/com_2016_685_en.pdf (accessed 16 August 2019); European Commission, *Proposal for a Council Directive on a Common Consolidated Corporate Tax Base (CCCTB),* 25 October 2016, COM(2016) 683 final, 2016/0336 (CNS).
131. One business group, BusinessEurope, that has been active in the process, noted that a proposal without consolidation would raise costs without providing competitiveness benefits, the allocation key should take into account intangible investment, and that many companies would like the proposal to be optional. *See* BusinessEurope, *Common Corporate Tax Base (CCTB) and Common Consolidated Corporate Tax Base (CCCTB)*, position paper (22 February 2017). The paper stressed that consolidation is essential, especially because the CCTB would keep the complications of transfer pricing and no cross-border loss relief.
132. The revised proposal also includes efforts to combat tax avoidance and new anti-abuse measures designed to limit harmful tax competition.
133. *See* European Parliament, Economic and Monetary Affairs Committee, *Hearings*, http://www.europarl.europa.eu/committees/en/econ/events-hearings.html?id=20170427CHE01521.
134. Digital Tax Package, 21 March 2018: European Commission, *Communication from the Commission to the European Parliament and Council, Time to Establish a Modern, Fair and Efficient Taxation Standard for the Digital Economy*, COM(2018) 0146; European Commission, *Proposal for a Council Directive on the Common System of a Digital Services Tax on Revenues Resulting from the Provision of Certain Digital Services*, COM(2018) 0148; European Commission, *Commission Recommendation of 21 March 2018 Relating to the Corporate Taxation of a Significant Digital Presence*, COM(2018) 1650. For the press release, *see* European Commission, *Digital Taxation: Commission Proposes New Measures to Ensure that All Companies Pay Fair Tax in the EU*, press release (21 March 2018), https://europa.eu/rapid/press-release_IP-18-2041_en.htm (accessed 16 August 2019).

> The digital economy is a major opportunity for Europe and Europe is a huge source of revenues for digital firms. But this win-win situation raises legal and fiscal concerns. Our pre-Internet rules do not allow our Member States to tax digital companies operating in Europe when they have little or no physical presence here. This represents an ever-bigger black hole for Member States, because the tax base is being eroded. That's why we're bringing forward a new legal standard as well an interim tax for digital activities.

To illustrate the importance of the digital economy, the Commission noted that every day, people send 20 billion emails, make 150 million social media posts, and conduct 650 million online searches in the EU.[135] In justifying the tax, the Commission showed that, on average, digitalized companies pay an effective tax rate of just 9.5%, compared with a 23.2% effective tax rate for traditional business models.[136]

The Commission proposed a phased-in approach to deal with the difficulties with the digital economy. Member States should begin with an interim measure to tackle the immediate problems and then, as the ultimate goal, they should adopt a common set of rules for taxing digital activities. The European Commission views the CCCTB package as the best way to establish a modern, fair, and efficient taxation standard for the digital economy.

The digital tax plan incorporates the idea of a digital presence so that a company would be taxed where its users are located even if it does not have a physical presence in that state. Thus, it would link the locations where digital profits are earned to the locations where they are taxed.

The profit allocation rules would follow the conventional approach by attributing profits as if the entities had operated as independent enterprises with the modification that the rules reflect the ways that digital activities create value through criteria such as data and users. Profit would consider the market values of profits from user data, services connecting users, and other digital services. Examples include the placement of advertising, online marketplace platforms for the so-called sharing economy, and subscriptions to streaming services. These values consider the location of the user rather than the location of the multinational enterprise. Taxpayers should use the profit-split method to attribute profits using items such as research and development expenses, marketing expenses, and the number of users and data collected per jurisdiction.

In addition to following the traditional notions of a permanent establishment, a company would establish a taxable threshold and pay tax in each Member State where it had a significant digital presence, or a virtual permanent establishment. This standard differs from the traditional physical presence that identifies a permanent establishment. A significant digital presence would be considered to exist in a Member State if the business consisted of the supply of digital services through a digital interface and that digital presence exceeded EUR 7 million per year in revenues from digital services, or had more than 100,000 users who accessed its digital services, or created

135. The data come from the website http://www.internetlivestats.com/.
136. *See* European Commission, *Questions and Answers on a Fair and Efficient Tax System in the EU for the Digital Single Market*, Fact Sheet (21 March 2018), https://europa.eu/rapid/press-release_MEMO-18-2141_en.htm (accessed 16 August 2019).

more than 3,000 business contracts for digital services in a taxable year in that Member State. The new rules would allocate profits to Member States in a way that reflects better 'how companies can create value online: for example, depending on where the user is based at the time of consumption'.[137]

As an interim measure, the Commission proposed levying a 3% tax on revenue from the digital activities of certain entities to help generate tax revenue from activities that currently are not effectively taxed. These activities include selling online advertising space, supplying platforms that connect users with suppliers of goods and services, selling data generated from user-provided information, etc. The tax would apply only to companies with at least EUR 750 million annual revenue worldwide and EUR 50 million annual revenue in the EU and the tax will be collected by the Member States where users are located.

§4.06 CONCLUSION

The European Commission has stressed that the full benefits of the company tax reform arise only when companies use a consolidated tax base. The lack of consolidation in the latest proposal is a setback for EU companies because, without consolidation, EU multinational enterprises will not be able to benefit from cross-border loss offset or from being able to file a single tax return through the one-stop shop tax administrative system.

The Commission continues to promote its comprehensive tax proposal through, for example, a series of online videos highlighting the benefits of the CCCTB.[138] The European Parliament steadfastly supports the Commission's proposal on digital taxation and the Common Consolidated Corporate Tax Base, voting on 15 March 2018, 438 in favour, 145 against, with 69 abstentions.[139]

Since releasing its proposal, economic developments in the European Union have pushed comprehensive company tax reform off the Union's list of priorities. Even so, the Commission continues to promote a coordinated company tax system within the European Union. It has incorporated its recent proposals in the area of digital taxation, for example, within the broad CCCTB effort.

Moreover, in a shock that echoes the one expressed when the EU formally proposed formulary apportionment, the OECD is considering formulary apportionment in the area of digital taxation.[140] The OECD's work programme dealing with taxation in

---

137. Digital Tax Package, *supra* n. 134. This approach may or may not lead to a formulary approach.
138. European Commission, *Common Consolidated Corporate Tax Base (CCCTB)*, https://ec.europa.eu/taxation_customs/business/company-tax/common-consolidated-corporate-tax-base-ccctb_en.
139. *See* European Parliament, *MEPs Approve New EU Corporate Tax Plan Which Embraces 'Digital Presence'*, press release (15 March 2018). The Parliament also supported the scaled-back version of the proposal to create a Common Corporate Tax Base by 451 votes in favour, 141 against, with 59 abstentions.
140. *See* Alexander Hartley, *OECD to Consider Worldwide Fractional Apportionment*, Int'l Tax Rev (31 May 2019), https://www.internationaltaxreview.com/article/b1fn11dyl8mz6d/oecd-to-consider-worldwide-fractional-apportionment (accessed 16 August 2019).

the digital economy refers to using a fractional apportionment method using factors, such as employees, assets, sales, and users, to apportion profit.[141]

On 9 October 2019, the OECD issued its base erosion and profit shifting (BEPS) report for public consultation that addressed issues dealing with digital taxation. It noted that it aimed to create a new, stable international corporate tax system because 'the current rules dating back to the 1920s are no longer sufficient to ensure a fair allocation of taxing rights in an increasingly globalised world'.[142] The report later stressed that 'there are increasing doubts that the arm's length principle can be relied on to give an appropriate result in all cases' thus justifying the introduction of 'formula-based solutions'.[143] This move at the OECD is remarkable.

While encountering inevitable setbacks, the prospect of implementing formulary apportionment in the European Union is no longer a nightmare. Given the international community's growing acceptance of formulary methods and after considering all the evidence, the dream of formulary apportionment may come true after all.

141. *See* OECD, *Programme of Work to Develop a Consensus Solution to the Tax Challenges Arising from the Digitalisation of the Economy* (OECD, May 2019). The 'fractional apportionment method' involves first determining profit, then selecting an allocation key, and finally applying the formula to allocate a fraction of the profit to the market locations.
142. *See* OECD Secretariat *Proposal for a 'Unified Approach' under Pillar One* 6 (9 October 2019), http://www.oecd.org/tax/oecd-leading-multilateral-efforts-to-address-tax-challenges-from-digitalisation-of-the-economy.htm (accessed 14 Oct. 2019). These proposals may have shifted.
143. *Ibid.*, 6.

CHAPTER 5

The Application of Formulary Apportionment to Related Entities: Lessons from the US Experience

Walter Hellerstein

§5.01 INTRODUCTION

If formulary apportionment is embraced as the accepted method of dividing the taxable income of a single corporation that conducts a unitary business in more than one state, which is the prevailing standard for application of formulary apportionment in the United States,[1] there is no justification, in principle at least, for failing to apply formulary apportionment to the income of a group of related corporations that conduct a unitary business in more than one state.[2] The only difference between the two cases

1. As the US Supreme Court famously declared in *Mobil Oil Corp. v. Commissioner of Taxes*, 445 US 425, 439 (1980), 'the linchpin of apportionability in the field of state income taxation is the unitary business principle'. *See generally* Jerome R. Hellerstein, Walter Hellerstein & John A. Swain, *State Taxation*, ch. 8 (3rd ed., Thomson Reuters 2019 rev.) (describing history of formulary apportionment in the US subnational corporate income tax context and the development and implementation of the unitary business principle). The ensuing discussion draws freely from my previous work in this area including *State Taxation* and other sources cited in the balance of this chapter.
2. Walter Hellerstein, *The Case for Formulary Apportionment* (in Symposium: Income Allocation in the 21st Century: The End of Transfer Pricing?), 12(3) Int'l Transfer Pricing J. 103, 107 (2005). The leading speakers for American corporate business have also recognized that 'consolidation based upon the unitary relationship of the consolidated corporations ... has the same degree of theoretical justification that applies to the taxation of a corporation with unitary divisions – it differs principally in the legal concept of "piercing the corporate veil"'. *See* Industry Statement on Proposed Interstate Tax Legislation, in US Senate, *State Taxation of Interstate Commerce: Hearings Before the Subcommittee on State Taxation of Interstate Commerce of the Committee on Finance*, 93rd Cong., 1st Sess. 260, 282 (1973). The opposition of the Industry Statement to combined reporting was based instead on various asserted 'practical' considerations. James F. Buresh & Marc S. Weinstein, *Combined Reporting: The Approach and Its Problems*, 1(1) J. St. Tax'n 5 (1982).

lies in the form of business organization, that is, the organization of a business enterprise through subsidiaries, as distinguished from branches, a factor that should not affect the allocation of income among states. Indeed, it is a fundamental tenet of tax policy that substance, not form, should determine matters of taxation. Consequently, if the nature of the taxpayer's activity – be it horse-trading or securities trading – warrants the use of formulary apportionment when the activity is carried on by a single entity because the entity is engaged in a unitary business conducted across state lines, it likewise warrants the use of formulary apportionment when such activity is carried on by a group of formally separate legal entities.

As the California Supreme Court observed in the seminal case sustaining the application of formulary apportionment to a group of commonly controlled corporations, after formulary apportionment had been sustained in *Butler Bros. v. McColgan*[3] and other cases involving a single corporation:

> The business of the parent and all of its subsidiaries is owned and managed under one centralized system, to the same extent as in the *Butler Brothers* case ... Thus the business is unitary regardless of the fact that in the *Butler Brothers* case there was but one corporation involved, owning as parts of the unitary system seven different branches in as many states, and that in the present case there is a parent corporation owning and controlling as units of one system fifteen different branches organized in corporations in as many states. No difference in principle is discernible. If the crux of the matter is to ascertain the portion of the business which is done within this state, the same considerations justify the use of the formula allocation method in the one case as in the other.[4]

If formulary apportionment is accepted as the method of income allocation for a group of commonly controlled corporations, then, as a theoretical and practical matter, consolidated or combined reporting[5] should be employed as the method for determining the tax base to which the formula should be applied. The justification for formulary apportionment of the income of a single corporation or a group of commonly controlled corporations is that they are engaged in integrated cross-border economic activity (a 'unitary business') that cannot meaningfully be unbundled on an arm's length/separate geographic accounting basis.[6] These same considerations justify consolidation or combination of the income of the separate legal entities, because the

3. 315 US 501 (1942), *aff'g Butler Bros. v. McColgan*, 17 Cal. 2d 664, 111 P.2d 334 (1942).
4. *Edison California Stores, Inc. v. McColgan*, 30 Cal. 2d 472, 480, 183 P.2d 16, 21 (1947).
5. Although the terms 'consolidated' and 'combined' reporting generically refer to the same concept, namely the filing of a single return or report reflecting the income of a group of related entities, there are significant differences in subnational US tax parlance between 'consolidated' and 'combined' filings, and these differences are considered below, §5.02 *infra*.
6. At least that is the justification from a US subnational perspective, which is the perspective from which this chapter is written, except when otherwise specified. The use in the text of the somewhat awkward phrase 'arm's length/separate geographic accounting basis', which is repeated elsewhere in this chapter, is designed to emphasize the distinction between (1) *separate geographic accounting* and (2) *separate entity reporting*. Separate geographic accounting, like formulary apportionment, is an approach to allocating income among jurisdictions, and each approach may apply either to a single legal entity or to a group of related entities. Separate entity reporting, by contrast and by definition, applies only to a single entity just as *consolidated* or *combined reporting*, by definition, applies to a group of entities. In short, *separate geographic*

transactions between them often will lack economic significance, will be difficult and expensive to disaggregate, and will be subject to manipulation to minimize tax liabilities.[7]

In fact, the case for formulary apportionment of the income of a group of commonly controlled entities often goes hand in hand with the case for reporting the income of those entities on a consolidated or combined basis. For example, the European Commission's proposal for a company tax strategy designed to further the goal of creating an internal market without tax obstacles declared that '[c]onsolidation is an essential element of such a system' and '[c]onsolidation necessarily entails rules for apportionment of the results between the Member States in which group members are established'.[8] Moreover, the underlying reasons advanced for consolidation or combination and formulary apportionment are overlapping and reinforcing. They include avoiding complex, costly, and theoretically questionable transfer pricing enquiries; preventing the use of tax minimization strategies that rely on the respect for transactions between commonly controlled entities; and administrative simplification, for both taxpayers and taxing authorities.

If this were all there was to say about the 'lessons from the US experience' regarding the 'application of formulary apportionment to related entities', this chapter would be mercifully short. The lesson would be simply that the underlying principles justifying the application of formulary apportionment to a single corporate entity conducting a unitary business across state lines likewise justify the application of formulary apportionment to a group of related entities conducting a unitary business across state lines, and these principles should be implemented through consolidated or combined reporting. As the ensuing discussion reveals, however, the US experience regarding the application of formulary apportionment to related entities is considerably more complex and the lessons that might be learned from that experience correspondingly more nuanced than might appear at first glance.

---

accounting and *separate entity reporting* are discrete concepts, but they are frequently confused. These concepts are considered in more detail below.

7. Although allocation of the income of a group of affiliated corporations on a formulary basis suggests that the group's income should be consolidated or combined, the converse of this proposition (like the converse of many propositions) is not necessarily true: the consolidation of the income of a group of affiliated corporations does not necessarily imply that the group's income should be allocated on a formulary basis, For example, one could adopt an arm's length/separate geographic accounting approach for allocating the consolidated income of a group of affiliated corporations analogous to the preferred method for allocating profits of a single corporation attributable to permanent establishments in different states set out in the Model Tax Convention of the Organisation for Economic Co-operation and Development (OECD): OECD, *Model Tax Convention on Income and on Capital*, art. 7(7) (2017).
8. European Commission, *Proposal for a Council Directive on Common Consolidated Corporate Tax Base (CCCTB)*, COM(2011) 121 final/2, 3 October 2011. In 2016, the Commission 're-launched' its proposal, postponing work on its recommendation for consolidation and formulary apportionment, until work on the common tax base had been completed, but the definition of the consolidated group and the proposal for formulary apportionment were unchanged from the 2011 proposal. European Commission, *Proposal for a Council Directive on a Common Consolidated Corporate Tax Base (CCCTB)*, COM(2016) 683 final, 25 October 2016.

§5.02 FEDERAL CONFORMITY AND CONSTITUTIONAL CONSIDERATIONS INFORMING THE US EXPERIENCE IN THE APPLICATION OF FORMULARY APPORTIONMENT TO RELATED ENTITIES

Any effort to discover 'lessons' from the US subnational tax experience for other cross-border tax regimes, be they international or subnational, must begin with the recognition that US subnational tax rules are informed, in significant respects, both by federal statutory rules governing the treatment of related entities and by federal constitutional restraints governing the exercise of state tax power over cross-border economic activity. These federal rules and constitutional limitations must be identified and explored to avoid 'lost in translation' problems in drawing lessons from the US subnational experience.[9]

[A] Federal Conformity Informing the US Experience in the Application of Formulary Apportionment to Related Entities

Subject to federal constitutional restraints on their taxing power,[10] the US states generally conform to the federal statutory rules governing corporate income taxation.[11] Under the federal corporate income tax, a group of affiliated corporations may elect to file a consolidated return in lieu of separate returns. The affiliated group is defined by reference to share ownership, namely, one or more chains of includible corporations connected through share ownership with a common parent.[12] Shares conferring at least 80% of the total voting power and at least 80% of the total value of each of the includible corporations (other than the common parent) must be owned directly by one or more of the other includible corporations. In addition, the common parent must possess 80% of the voting power and 80% of the value of at least one of the includible corporations.[13] The Internal Revenue Code prohibits certain corporations from joining in the consolidated return, most significantly *foreign* corporations.[14] As a consequence, *every* corporation joining in consolidated return is *taxable on all of its income on a residence basis*, and the filing of consolidated return for federal income purposes can be viewed as essentially a matter of administrative convenience without any implications regarding the taxability of income or taxpayers.

9. *See* Walter Hellerstein & Charles E. McLure, Jr., *Lost in Translation: Contextual Considerations in Evaluating the Relevance of the US Experience for the European Commission's Company Taxation Proposals*, 58(3) Bull. Int'l Tax'n 86 (2004).
10. The implications of those restraints for the US application of formulary apportionment to related entities are addressed in the next section, §5.02[B] *infra*.
11. Hellerstein, Hellerstein & Swain, *State Taxation*, *supra* n. 1, para. 7.02 ('[t]he outstanding characteristic of state corporate net income taxes is their broad conformity to the federal corporate income tax').
12. Internal Revenue Code § 1504.
13. *Ibid.*
14. *Ibid.*, § 1504(b).

Many states provide corporations that elect to file a consolidated return at the federal level with the option of filing a consolidated return at the state level.[15] However, because of federal constitutional restraints on the states' power to tax an affiliated group of corporations on a consolidated or combined basis predicated solely on common ownership,[16] no state may *require* that a group filing a consolidated return at the federal level likewise file a consolidated return at the state level, unless the group also meets constitutional requirements for mandatory consolidated or combined filing. Accordingly, the federal consolidated model for consolidated filing, unlike the federal model for delineation of the taxable base, has a more limited impact on the states' delineation of the consolidated group.

State corporate taxpayers naturally elect to file on a consolidated basis at the state level only when it is in their economic interest to do so, although once having elected to file on a consolidated basis they often are required to continue to file on such a basis unless they receive permission from the state tax administrator to change their method of filing. With respect to the implications for the other tax regimes of the US experience with filing elective consolidated returns at the state level, it is worth observing that there generally is no requirement that a taxpayer electing to file on a consolidated basis in one state must also do so in other states, even though it is eligible for filing on a consolidated basis in both states. Hence, state taxpayers are able to 'cherry-pick' among states in determining whether to file on a consolidated basis, depending on whether it will produce a better tax result. It should be emphasized, however, that the foregoing comments pertain *only* to the elective filing at the state level of consolidated returns based on the federal 'affiliated group' definition of corporations linked by common ownership; they do not apply to the mandatory 'combined' filing that many states require with respect to 'unitary' corporate affiliates (described immediately below).

[B] Federal Constitutional Rules Informing the US State Experience in the Application of Formulary Apportionment to Related Entities

The federal constitutional restraints on state tax power have a much more significant impact on the delineation of the group of related entities whose income may be subjected to formulary apportionment and consolidated or combined reporting than do the federal rules governing consolidated filing. These restraints in substance are the same as those that apply to the determination of the apportionable tax base of a single corporate entity,[17] but they are applied to circumscribe the states' ability to apportion the income from a group of related entities and to require that a group of related corporations file on a consolidated or combined basis.

15. *See* Hellerstein, Hellerstein & Swain, *State Taxation, supra* n. 1, para 8.11[3]; William Goldman, Kenneth Brown & Laura Farrell-Legrand, *Income Taxes: Consolidated Returns and Combined Reporting*, BNA Tax Management Tax Portfolios 1130 TM-2nd (2016 rev.).
16. *See* the discussion immediately below, §5.02[B] *infra*.
17. *See* Hellerstein, Hellerstein & Swain, *State Taxation, supra* n. 1, ch. 8 (describing and analysing these restraints in detail).

[1] *The Distinction Between Consolidated and Combined Returns or Reports*

Before this chapter explores the US Supreme Court's constitutional jurisprudence controlling the application of formulary apportionment and consolidated or combined reporting to related corporations, it may be appropriate briefly to elaborate upon what may appear to be the semantic distinction between 'consolidated' and 'combined' returns or reports, to which the chapter has frequently alluded in the preceding discussion without distinguishing between them (up to this point), in order to avoid confusion over this distinction, at least for those who have not spent most of their waking hours labouring in the weeds of the state tax terrain.

Consolidated returns and combined reports have much in common, but there are important differences between them. Consolidated state returns usually are confined to affiliates each of which is taxable in the state: '[i]t seems entirely clear that a state may not ordinarily require the inclusion in a consolidated return of the income of an affiliated group member over which the state has no jurisdiction'.[18] Moreover, as noted above,[19] state consolidated returns, which typically mirror federal consolidated return filings, are generally elective and often do not require that members of the consolidated group be engaged in a unitary business.[20] The return is that of all the affiliates, and each may be made liable for the consolidated tax, at least in cases in which the group has made an election to file on a consolidated basis, as is normally the case.

Combined reports, however, or the determination of a taxpayer's liability on a combined basis, may include corporate affiliates that are not taxable by the state. Combined reporting is not designed to tax the income or other tax base of the non-taxable affiliates, although taxpayers sometimes assert that the combined method has that effect. The purpose of combined reporting is to determine the income or other tax base of the in-state taxpayer or taxpayers by viewing the taxpayer or taxpayers as part of the unitary business and applying the apportionment factors of the entire unitary business to the taxable net income of the unitary business.[21] The apportioned income thus determined is then attributed to the in-state taxpayer or taxpayers, either

---

18. E. George Rudolph, *State Taxation of Interstate Business: The Unitary Business Concept and Affiliated Corporate Groups*, 25(2) Tax L. Rev. 171, 198 (1970) (citing *Bay Cities Transp. Co. v. Johnson*, 8 Cal. 2d 706, 68 P.2d 710 (1937)).
19. *See* §5.02[A] *supra*.
20. As one court has observed, 'a consolidated return is based solely on the degree of ownership of a common parent, I.R.C. §§ 1501, 1504 ..., whereas a combined return is based on the unitary nature of the affiliated group': *Williams Cos. v. Director of Revenue*, 799 S.W.2d 602, 606 (Mo. 1990) (citations omitted), *cert. denied*, 501 US 1260 (1991). For this reason, no state may constitutionally require a consolidated filing, at least when the income is purportedly subject to formulary apportionment that includes corporations without nexus with the state or that are not members of a unitary group. To do so would include income in the apportionable tax base that lacked the minimum connection required by the Constitution. *See* Hellerstein, Hellerstein & Swain, *State Taxation*, *supra* n. 1, para. 8.07[1]. The elective character of consolidated reporting, however, or its limitation to corporations with nexus with the state, generally avoids this issue.
21. Rudolph, *supra* n. 18, at 198.

individually, based on their respective proportion of in-state factors,[22] or by designating one of the in-state taxpayers responsible for paying the aggregate in-state tax liability of the taxable members of the group.[23] The computation of net income and the factors is essentially the same in both consolidation and combination. Inter-company transactions, such as purchases and sales of inventory and interest payments, automatically offset each other, and other inter-company items, such as dividends and gains or losses on the sale of capital assets between affiliates, are eliminated. In contrast to consolidated return filing, combined reporting is often mandatory if the affiliated group of corporations is engaged in a unitary business.[24]

Finally, it is worth emphasizing the distinction between the filing of consolidated *returns* and the filing of combined *reports*. Thus it has been observed that '[t]he combined report reflects a method of computing state taxable income. It is not merely a type of tax return'.[25] Specifically:

> On a combined report, the members of a unitary, multicorporate group that have nexus with the state determine their state taxable incomes by apportioning the group's combined [apportionable] income to the taxing state on the basis of the combined apportionment factors. California is illustrative. [The instructions] set forth the following steps in computing California income using a combined report. First, the combined [apportionable] income of the unitary group is determined. The group's combined [apportionable] income is then apportioned to California on the basis of [the] ... apportionment formula. ... Any [non-apportionable] income that is specifically allocated[[26]] to California is then added to the amount of unitary business income apportioned to California. The total apportioned ... income and allocated ... income becomes the base for imposition of the California franchise tax.[27]

22. This has sometimes been referred to as 'second stage apportionment of unitary income'. *See* Jerome R. Hellerstein & Walter Hellerstein, *The* Finnigan *Case: A Reply to Vogelenzang's 'Second Stage Apportionment of Unitary Income'*, 51 Tax Notes 891 (1991).
23. *See* Goldman, Brown & Farrell-Legrand, *supra* n. 15.
24. For further explication of the nature of (and the distinctions between) consolidated and combined returns or reports, see *ibid.*; Frank Keesling, *A Current Look at the Combined Report and Uniformity in Allocation Practices*, 42(2) J. Tax'n 106 (1975); *Caterpillar Tractor Co. v. Department of Revenue*, 289 Or. 895, 618 P.2d 1261 (1980).
25. Goldman, Brown & Farrell-Legrand, *supra* n. 15, at 1130.01.A.2.b.
26. 'Allocated' income is income that does not arise out of the taxpayer's unitary business and is not apportioned by formula but is instead assigned to specific states based on the location (or deemed location) of the income-producing property or activity. For example, rental income from real property that is not part of the unitary business would be assigned to the property's location and interest and dividend income that was not derived from the corporation's unitary business would be assigned to the state of the corporation's commercial domicile.
27. Goldman, Brown & Farrell-Legrand, *supra* n. 15, at 1130.01.A.2.b (citations omitted). California's 'franchise' tax is its corporate net income tax.

[2] Constitutional Restraints on the Apportionability of the Income of a Group of Related Corporations

[a] General Principles Applicable to Corporations Reporting on a 'Separate Company' (as Distinguished from a 'Combined') Basis

The US Supreme Court has made it clear that the constitutional restraints on the states' power to require a taxpayer, or a group of related taxpayers, to apportion their income are to be decided on the basis of substance, not form. Thus, the Court has declared that '[o]ne must look principally at the underlying activity, not the form of investment, to determine the propriety of apportionability'.[28] Consequently, in implementing its view that 'the linchpin of apportionability in the field of state income taxation is the unitary business principle',[29] the Court has held that the same criteria it has employed to determine whether an individual corporation's income is subject to apportionment likewise determines whether the income generated by a group of related corporations' income is subject to apportionment. However – and here is where the US subnational experience becomes more complex (and, perhaps more to the point, untidy) from a theoretical and practical standpoint – the Court first articulated the constitutional restraints on the apportionability of income generated by a group of related corporations in the context of *separate company* reporting rather than *combined* reporting.[30] Indeed, despite the strong theoretical case for applying combined reporting to the income of a group of related corporations whose income is being apportioned because they are engaged in a unitary business,[31] largely as a result of historical accident, the piecemeal adoption of apportionment before the growth of large interstate enterprises, and corporate opposition, twenty of the forty-four states with corporate income taxes, all of which attribute taxable income of corporations and groups of related corporations by formulary apportionment, nevertheless apply separate company reporting rather than combined reporting to determine the income of a group of related corporations that is apportioned to (and therefore taxable by) the state.[32]

The seminal case articulating the restraints on states' power to tax an apportioned share of the income of a group of related corporations engaged in a unitary business was *Mobil Oil Corp. v. Commissioner of Taxes*.[33] The *Mobil* case involved the question

28. *Mobil Oil Corp. v. Commissioner of Taxes*, 445 US 425, 440 (1980).
29. *Ibid.*, 439.
30. *See supra* n. 6.
31. *See* §5.01 *supra*.
32. *See* CCH, *Combined Reporting Requirements*, Multistate Quick Answer Charts, http://smartcharts.cch.com (accessed 25 Jun. 2019). For an overview of the history and development of combined reporting in the United States, see Hellerstein, Hellerstein & Swain, *State Taxation*, *supra* n. 1, para. 8.11.
33. 445 US 425, 439 (1980). The case is explored in detail in Walter Hellerstein, *State Income Taxation of Multijurisdictional Corporations: Reflections on* Mobil, Exxon, *and H.R. 5076*, 79(1) Mich. L. Rev. 113 (1980); *see also* Hellerstein, Hellerstein & Swain, *State Taxation*, *supra* n. 1, paras. 8.08[2][a], 9.15[2].

of whether a state (Vermont) could tax the dividends that a non-domiciliary corporation (Mobil) earned from its investments in its subsidiaries.[34] Mobil's worldwide activities included the production, refining, and marketing of petroleum and petroleum products. In Vermont, Mobil's activities were limited to marketing. Since Mobil was plainly conducting a unitary petroleum business from well head to gas pump as one of the world's largest integrated oil companies, there could have been no serious question about Vermont's constitutional power to include all of the income generated by such business in Mobil's apportionable tax base and to tax a fairly apportioned share of such income.

The wrinkle in the case, however, was that Mobil was conducting much of that business - particularly in foreign countries - through wholly and partly owned subsidiaries and affiliates.[35] Consequently, the disputed income that Vermont sought to include in Mobil's apportionable tax base was dividend income that Mobil received from its subsidiaries and affiliates. Indeed, there was no controversy in the case over Vermont's power to include in Mobil's apportionable tax base the operating income that Mobil derived from the unitary petroleum business that Mobil itself carried on directly in Vermont and other states. Moreover, presumably there would have been no controversy over Vermont's power to include in Mobil's apportionable tax base the operating income that it derived from its worldwide petroleum business if Mobil's business had been carried on directly through divisions rather than through separately incorporated subsidiaries.

Mobil contended, however, that the requisite link between its activities in Vermont and the intangible income that Vermont sought to include in its apportionable tax base was missing because all of its activities relating to its shareholdings in these corporations, including the receipt and management of the dividends themselves, occurred outside of Vermont at its commercial domicile in New York.[36] In essence, Mobil argued that the form in which Vermont sought to tax the income Mobil earned

---

34. In fact, some of the dividends that Vermont included in Mobil's apportionable tax base were from minority interests in other companies, many of which plainly had no relationship to Mobil's petroleum business. *Mobil*, 445 US at 455-457 (Stevens, J., dissenting). Nevertheless, the Court assumed, in the absence of evidence to the contrary, that all of the dividends at issue arose from subsidiaries and affiliates engaged in activities related to Mobil's petroleum business: *ibid.*, 442. Accordingly, the development of the Court's doctrine in this area should be analysed on the basis of the same assumption. Subsequent developments make it clear, however, that Mobil's income from non-unitary corporations would be apportionable only if the investments served an 'operational function' in its business. *See* Hellerstein, Hellerstein & Swain, *State Taxation*, *supra* n. 1, paras. 8.07[3][a][v], 8.08[2][e][v].
35. For purposes of the enquiry into the apportionability, it makes no difference, as the Court ultimately concluded in *Mobil*, 445 US at 446-449, whether the subsidiaries or affiliates were conducting their business in foreign countries or in the United States. The significant point for present purposes is simply that the income at issue was formally income from intangibles (i.e., dividends from investments in stock).
36. It was also true that Mobil's subsidiary and affiliate corporations, which paid the dividends, conducted none of their business in Vermont. This fact, however, was relevant neither to the theory on which Vermont sought to include the dividends in Mobil's apportionable tax base - that the income was derived from Mobil's unitary business carried on in Vermont - nor to the theory on which Mobil resisted such inclusion - that the dividend income had to be viewed separately from the income from its operations and, so viewed, such income had no connection with Vermont.

dictated the constitutional analysis of Vermont's power to tax that income. Because Vermont treated Mobil as a separate company, earning operating income from its own operations and dividend income from its investments in subsidiaries, Mobil contended that Vermont had to demonstrate a connection between the state and Mobil's activities as an investor to warrant inclusion of the income from such investments in Mobil's Vermont apportionable tax base. If Vermont wanted to rely on the unitary relationship between Mobil and its subsidiaries as a basis for including the income generated by such subsidiaries in Mobil's apportionable tax base, then, according to Mobil, Vermont should have treated Mobil and its subsidiaries as a single unitary enterprise by filing on a combined basis, combining the operating income of Mobil and its subsidiaries and apportioning this income on the basis of the combined apportionment factors of the unitary corporate group.[37]

The Supreme Court was unimpressed by Mobil's argument, in part because it had not been raised in a timely manner,[38] in part because it was addressed to the fairness of the apportionment rather than to the apportionability of the income,[39] but principally because it emphasized form over substance - rarely a winning card in a tax case. As the Court approached the case, the question of whether Mobil's dividend income was apportionable by Vermont turned simply on whether the income arose from a unitary business that Mobil was conducting in Vermont. Since an integrated oil company is the quintessential unitary business, the answer to that question was easy, especially in light of Mobil's failure seriously to contest the issue. As the Court declared:

> [T]he form of business organization may have nothing to do with the underlying unity or diversity of business enterprise. Had [Mobil] chosen to operate its foreign subsidiaries as separate divisions of a legally as well as a functionally integrated enterprise, there is little doubt that the income derived from those divisions would meet due process requirements for apportionability. Transforming the same income into dividends from legally separate entities works no change in the underlying economic realities of a unitary business, and accordingly it ought not to affect the apportionability of income the parent receives.[40]

Mobil is typically cited for its classic observation that 'the linchpin of apportionability in the field of state income taxation is the unitary business principle'[41] and for the general guidance it offered in delineating that principle. But the case has special significance for the US experience in applying formulary apportionment to related entities and for the lessons of that experience for other jurisdictions that are contemplating the adoption of a formulary apportionment for attributing corporate income among taxing states.

First, the Court made it clear (in language already quoted) that the income generated by a group of related corporations conducting a unitary business in the state

37. *See* §5.02[B][1] *supra*.
38. *Mobil*, 445 US at 441 n. 15.
39. *Ibid.*
40. *Ibid.*, 440-441 (citation omitted).
41. *See supra* n. 1.

is subject to taxation on a formulary basis regardless of the form in which the income arises (whether as operating income of the group or as income from 'ownership' of related corporations derived from unitary activities):

> So long as dividends from subsidiaries and affiliates reflect profits derived from a functionally integrated enterprise, those dividends are income to the parent earned in a unitary business. One must look principally at the underlying activity, not at the form of investment, to determine the propriety of apportionability.[42]

Second, the Court explicitly declined to address Mobil's contention that Vermont was constitutionally required to determine the income of a group of related corporations engaged in a unitary business on a combined basis if it sought to attribute the group's income to the state by formulary apportionment. As the Court observed:

> 'combined apportionment' ..., while including the income of subsidiaries and affiliates as part of appellant's net income, would eliminate intercorporate transfers, such as appellant's dividend income, from that calculation. A necessary concomitant of this would be inclusion of the subsidiaries' and affiliates' sales, payroll, and property in the calculation of the apportionment formula.[43]

The Court further noted that 'the result, presumably, would be advantageous' to Mobil, because 'virtually nothing would be added to the "Vermont" numerators of the apportionment factors, while there would be substantial increases in the "everywhere" denominators, resulting in a diminution of the apportionment fraction'.[44] However, because the Court viewed the argument as an 'afterthought', and '[t]he evidence in the record surely is inadequate to evaluate the effect of the proposal ... or its potential implications', the Court concluded: '[a]t this juncture and on these facts, we need not, and do not, decide whether combined apportionment of this type is constitutionally required'.[45]

[b] *Constitutional Approval of Combined Apportionment of the Income of a Group of Related Corporations*

Although in *Mobil* the US Supreme Court declined, as a constitutional matter, to *require* a state to employ combined reporting if it wished to tax the apportioned share of the income of a group of related corporations engaged in a unitary business in the state, the Court subsequently approved combined reporting as a constitutionally acceptable approach to taxation of such income. In *Container Corp. of America v. Franchise Tax Board*,[46] the Court looked to the factors it had identified in *Mobil* as reflecting a unitary business – 'functional integration, centralized management, and economies of scale'[47] – in addressing the question of whether California possessed the constitutional power

42. *Mobil*, 445 US at 440.
43. *Ibid.*, 441 n. 15.
44. *Ibid.*
45. *Ibid.*
46. 463 US 159 (1983).
47. *Mobil*, 445 US at 438.

to require a multinational corporation engaged in business in the state to file on a combined basis. Because the existence of these factors persuaded the Court that there was a 'flow of value'[48] among the commonly controlled companies and that they were engaged in a unitary business, the Court concluded that the state could properly require that the corporations file on a combined basis. In *Barclays Bank plc v. Franchise Tax Board*,[49] the Court extended its approval of combined reporting to a group of multinational corporations with a foreign parent.

In approving the application of combined reporting to a group of related corporations in both *Container* and *Barclays*, the Court laid to rest any doubt as to the constitutionality of applying formulary apportionment to the apportioned tax base of a unitary group of corporations, some of whose members were not taxable by the state, as a means of ascertaining the income of the corporations that were taxable by the state. As the Court declared in *Barclays*:

> [T]he theory underlying unitary taxation is that 'certain intangible "flows of value" within the unitary group serve to link the various members together as if they were essentially a single entity'. Formulary apportionment of the income of a multijurisdictional (but unitary) business enterprise, if fairly done, taxes only the 'income generated within a State'. *Quill* held that the Commerce Clause requires a *taxpayer's* physical presence within the taxing jurisdiction before that jurisdiction can constitutionally impose a use tax. The California presence of the taxpayers before us is undisputed, and we find nothing in *Quill* to suggest that California may not reference the income of corporations worldwide with whom those taxpayers are closely intertwined in order to approximate the taxpayers' California income.[50]

In this connection, it may be worth keeping in mind that the combined group defined in terms of a 'unitary business' may be both broader and narrower than the consolidated group defined in terms of the federal consolidated return requirements.[51] The combined group may be broader than the federal consolidated group because it may include foreign corporations as well as corporations that are linked by the typical state common ownership standard of 50% rather than the 80% federal standard.[52] Indeed, in both *Container* and *Barclays*, the Court sustained the states' power to require combined reporting with respect to related companies, including *foreign* corporations. The 'combined' group may also be narrower than the federal consolidated group, because a related corporation linked by the requisite 80% share-and-value ownership threshold may nevertheless fall outside the unitary business because there is no

48. *Container*, 463 US at 178 n. 17.
49. 512 US 298 (1994).
50. *Ibid.*, 312 n. 10 (emphasis in original, citations omitted). Although the US Supreme Court subsequently overruled *Quill* in *South Dakota v. Wayfair, Inc.*, 138 S. Ct. 2080 (2018), with respect to the requirement of that out-of-state vendors have a physical presence in the state before a state may impose tax collection obligations upon such vendors, that has no impact on the key principle that the Court articulated, to wit, that there is no constitutional infirmity with the inclusion in the apportionable tax base of the income of corporations that are not taxable in the state for purposes of determining the apportioned income of corporations that are taxable in the state and engaged in a unitary business with the non-taxable corporations.
51. *See* §5.02[B][1] *supra*.
52. *See* Hellerstein, Hellerstein & Swain, *State Taxation*, *supra* n. 1, para. 8.11[3][a].

functional integration, centralized management, or economies of scale tying it to its affiliates.

Finally, it is important to understand that the states' constitutional authority to require combined filing (including foreign affiliates) is not the final word on state practice. Under political pressure from the federal government and its foreign trading partners, and, perhaps more importantly from multinational corporations, the states have uniformly adopted legislation voluntarily restricting the scope of the combined group to the 'water's edge', thereby excluding most foreign corporations from mandatory combined reporting.[53] This change is discussed in some detail in the last section of this chapter.

§5.03 THE RELATIONSHIP BETWEEN THE APPORTIONMENT FACTORS AND THE APPORTIONABLE TAX BASE: FACTOR REPRESENTATION

[A] Overview

The factors that are employed to apportion income among the states should reflect the factors that produce the income being apportioned. This virtually axiomatic proposition is also a principle of constitutional law. In describing the characteristics of a constitutionally 'fair' apportionment formula required by the Due Process and Commerce Clauses of the US Constitution, the US Supreme Court has said that the 'factor or factors used in the apportionment formula must actually reflect a reasonable sense of how income is generated'.[54]

The requirement that the 'factor or factors used in the apportionment formula must actually reflect a reasonable sense of how income is generated' has two dimensions. At the more general level, it means that the factors employed to apportion income should correspond in a generic sense to our general understanding of the factors that produce income. Courts and commentators have recognized that property, payroll, and sales, at least when used together - satisfy this standard.[55] As the US Supreme Court has observed, 'payroll, property, and sales appear in combination to reflect a very large share of the activities by which value is generated'.[56] Nevertheless, the Court declined to constitutionalize the three-factor formula,[57] even though at the time it refused to do so, forty-four of the forty-five states that taxed corporate income employed the three-factor formula.[58]

53. *Ibid.*, para 8.18.
54. *Container Corp. of America v. Franchise Tax Board*, 463 US 159, 169 (1983).
55. *See* Hellerstein, Hellerstein & Swain, *State Taxation, supra* n. 1, paras. 8.06, 8.15.
56. *Container*, 463 US at 183.
57. *See Moorman Mfg. Co. v. Bair*, 437 US 267 (1978) (sustaining application of single-factor sales formula to apportion corporate income among the states), discussed in Hellerstein, Hellerstein & Swain, *State Taxation, supra* n. 1, para 8.14[2][b][ii].
58. *Moorman*, 437 US at 282 (Powell, J., dissenting) (observing that forty-four of the forty-five states with corporate income taxes employed the equally weighted three-factor formula). Since *Moorman* was decided in 1978, the states have dramatically abandoned the equally weighted

There is also a more specific dimension to the principle that the 'factor or factors used in the apportionment formula must actually reflect a reasonable sense of how income is generated', namely, that there should be a correspondence between the particular sources of income that are included in the apportionable tax base and the factors that are used to apportion such income. For example, if real or tangible personal property is employed in the taxpayer's unitary business and therefore contributes to the production of apportionable income, such property should be included in the property factor of the apportionment formula.[59] By the same token, if real or tangible personal property is not employed in the taxpayer's unitary business and therefore does not contribute to the production of the taxpayer's apportionable income, such property should not be included in the property factor of the formula employed to apportion the income arising out of the taxpayer's unitary business.[60]

While there is widespread recognition and acceptance of this principle with regard to income generated by tangible property and labour, its application to income from intangibles has given rise to considerable controversy. The controversy stems in large part from the fact that the standard income tax apportionment statutes, which were designed to attribute income from manufacturing and mercantile operations,[61] generally take no explicit account of income from intangibles, including in particular dividends from related corporations that are apportionable under *Mobil* because the dividends reflect income from the conduct of a unitary business in the state.[62]

The heart of the controversy, then, is the extent, if any, to which the property, payroll, or receipts associated with income from intangible assets (and the underlying enterprises they may represent) should or must be reflected in the factors of the apportionment formula (however defined) when income attributable to such assets is included in the apportionable tax base. This so-called factor representation issue raises statutory, constitutional, and policy questions whose proper analysis depends in part on the underlying theory on which the apportionability of the intangible income rests.

[B] Intangible Income Apportionable on the Basis of Payor-Payee Unity

If the theoretical foundation for apportioning income from intangibles is that the corporate payor of the intangible income is a subsidiary or other related corporation engaged in a unitary business with the corporate payee, it follows as a matter of

three-factor formula in favour of formulas based more heavily, if not exclusively, on sales, so that today only five of the forty-four states with corporate income tax employ the equally weighted three-factor formula. *See* Walter Hellerstein, *The Transformation of the State Corporate Income Tax into a Market-Based Levy*, 130(5) J. Tax'n 4 (2019).

59. *See* Uniform Division of Income for Tax Purposes Act (1957), s 10 (comment), https://www.uniformlaws.org/committees/community-home/librarydocuments?communitykey = f2ef73d2-2e5b-488e-a525-51be29fbee47&tab = librarydocuments (accessed 4 Jul. 2019).
60. *Ibid.*
61. *See* Hellerstein, Hellerstein & Swain, *State Taxation*, *supra* n. 1, ¶ 9.04; William Pierce, *The Uniform Division of Income for State Tax Purposes*, 35(10) Taxes 747, 749 (1957).
62. *See* §5.02[B][2] *supra*.

principle that the payor's factors should be included in the formula employed to apportion such income.[63]

The rationale for holding intangible income apportionable when the payor and payee are engaged in a unitary business is that such income is in substance the operating income of the unitary enterprise even though it takes the form of intangible income paid by one related corporation to another.[64] *Mobil*,[65] which rested the case for the apportionability of intangible income squarely on payor-payee unity, makes this clear. The dividend income derived from a unitary enterprise was apportionable unless Mobil could 'demonstrate something about the nature of this income that distinguishes it from operating income, a proper portion of which the State concededly may tax'.[66] Because Mobil failed in this regard - with the Court concluding that 'the underlying activity'[67] rather than 'the form of investment'[68] should determine apportionability - the Court found no constitutional bar to Vermont's treating the dividend income like operating income.[69]

Once it has been determined that dividends and other intangible income are apportionable like operating income,[70] the next logical step - apart from combining the unitary group and eliminating the intangible income as such[71] - is to apportion the intangible income like operating income. Although the Court has yet to address the

63. *See* Rudolph, *supra* n. 18, at 205.
64. This is not to suggest that intangible income is in fact identical to the operating income it is assumed to represent. Obviously, dividends, which reflect payments from the earnings and profits of the payor corporation, will at best imperfectly reflect the current income derived from the unitary business. *See Mobil Oil Corp. v. Commissioner of Taxes*, 445 US 425, 460 n. 18 (1980) (Stevens, J., dissenting). The fit between other forms of intangible income (e.g., interest and capital gains) and the current income derived from the unitary business may be even looser. The equation of intangible income and operating income nonetheless remains the theoretical foundation for apportioning intangible income based on payor-payee unity.
65. The *Mobil* case is discussed generally in §5.02[B][2] *supra*.
66. *Mobil*, 445 US at 437-438; *see also ibid.*, 459 (Stevens, J., dissenting).
67. *Ibid.*, 440.
68. *Ibid.*
69. *Ibid.*, 441.
70. In its opinions dealing with the apportionability of intangible income, the Court has not drawn any distinction between the various types of intangible income - dividends, interest, and capital gains - whose treatment was at issue. Indeed, in *ASARCO, Inc. v. Idaho State Tax Comm'n*, 458 US 307 (1982), discussed in Walter Hellerstein, *State Income Taxation of Multijurisdictional Corporations, Part II: Reflections on* ASARCO *and* Woolworth, 81(1) Mich. L. Rev. 157 (1982) and in Hellerstein, Hellerstein & Swain, *State Taxation*, *supra* n. 1, para. 8.08[2][b], the Court joined Idaho and ASARCO in agreeing 'that interest and capital gains derived from these companies should be treated in the same manner as dividend income': *ASARCO*, 458 US at 330. In *Allied-Signal, Inc. v. Director, Division of Tax'n*, 504 US 768 (1992), the Court accorded this agreement constitutional stature, declaring that 'we have held that for constitutional purposes capital gains should be treated as no different from dividends': *ibid.*, 780. For purposes of the ensuing discussion of factor representation, it will likewise be assumed that there is no constitutionally significant distinction between different types of intangible income. In fact, however, there are differences between various types of intangible income that arguably should inform their proper treatment under different theories of apportionability. *See generally* Walter Hellerstein, *State Taxation of Corporate Income From Intangibles:* Allied-Signal *and Beyond*, 48(4) Tax L. Rev. 739, 858-876 (1993).
71. *See* §5.02[B] *supra*. As noted above (*see* text accompanying *supra* nn. 31-32), despite the strong theoretical case for applying combined reporting to the income of a group of related corporations whose income is being apportioned because they are engaged in a unitary business, twenty of

question of whether this logical step is constitutionally compelled, Justice Stevens has explained why it should be. Observing in *Mobil* that the Court had sanctioned Vermont's inclusion of 'huge quantities'[72] of intangible income in Mobil's apportionable tax base on the theory that it represented the operating income of a unitary enterprise,[73] Justice Stevens pointed out that Vermont nevertheless had made no attempt to include in the apportionment formula the property, payroll, or sales of the subsidiaries that had generated the income. Because the subsidiaries did no business in Vermont, it followed that '[u]nless the sales, payroll, and property values connected with the production of income by the payor corporations are added to the denominator of the apportionment formula, the inclusion of earnings attributable to those corporations in the apportionable tax base will inevitably cause Mobil's Vermont income to be overstated'.[74]

More generally, Justice Stevens noted that Mobil's worldwide petroleum business was either part of one unitary business or it was not: '[i]f it is, Vermont must evaluate the entire enterprise in a consistent manner'.[75] This meant that if Vermont wished to include the intangible income in Mobil's apportionable tax base on the theory that the income derived from its unitary business, it would have to 'tak[e] the payroll, sales and property of the payor corporations into account'.[76] As noted above,[77] the Court has reinforced the essential position taken by Justice Stevens in *Mobil* by subsequently observing that 'fairness in an apportionment formula' requires that 'the factor or factors used in the ... formula must actually reflect a reasonable sense of how income is generated'.[78]

The requirement of factor representation in the context of payor-payee unity, and indeed, in other contexts as well, ultimately rests on the broad constitutional foundation that 'income attributed to the State for tax purposes must be rationally related to "values connected with the taxing State"'.[79] The Court has warmly endorsed the once-familiar[80] three-factor formula 'precisely because payroll, property, and sales appear in combination to reflect a very large share of the activities by which value is generated'.[81] When, however, the formula gives no recognition to the factors of the

the forty-four states with corporate income taxes nevertheless apply separate company reporting rather than combined reporting to determine the income of a group of related corporations that is apportioned to the state.

72. *Mobil*, 445 US at 459 (Stevens, J., dissenting).
73. *Ibid.*
74. *Ibid.*, 461 (Stevens, J., dissenting).
75. *Ibid.*
76. *Ibid.*, 462 (Stevens, J., dissenting).
77. *See* §5.03[A] *supra*.
78. *Container Corp. of America v. Franchise Tax Bd.*, 463 US 159, 169 (1983).
79. *Moorman Mfg. Co. v. Bair*, 437 US 267, 273 (1978).
80. As observed above (*see supra* n. 58), the states in recent years have dramatically abandoned the equally weighted three-factor formula in favour of formulas based more heavily, if not exclusively, on sales.
81. *Container*, 463 US at 170; *see also General Motors Corp. v. District of Columbia*, 380 US 553, 561 (1965) (approving three-factor formula 'as a rough approximation of the distribution of either a corporation's sources of income or the social costs it generates'); *Butler Bros. v. McColgan*, 315 US 501, 509 (1942) (approving three-factor formula as reflecting 'the relative contribution of the activities in the various states to the production of total unitary income').

entities that helped generate the apportionable income, and whose unitary relationship to the payor provides the foundation for apportionability, there ceases to be a rational relationship between the income being taxed and the activities that gave rise to the income. In short, a state should not be able to have it both ways: i.e., including income of the corporate subsidiaries or other related corporate payors in the corporate payee's apportionable tax base on the theory that the payee and the payor are engaged in a unitary business but then apportioning such income by factors reflecting only the payee's own operations on a separate company basis.

[1] Implementing Factor Representation Based on Payor-Payee Unity

[a] Dividends

Determining that policy and constitutional considerations mandate factor representation when payor-payee unity establishes the basis for the apportionability of intangible income is easier than determining the appropriate means for implementing that mandate. In the analysis of this question, it makes sense to start with the paradigmatic case where the appropriate adjustment to the taxpayer's apportionment factors seems clear. If a parent owns 100% of the shares of a unitary subsidiary, and if the only transfers of intangible (investment) income from the subsidiary to the parent are dividends equal to the subsidiary's earnings and profits for the taxable year, the argument for inclusion of the subsidiary's factors in the parent's apportionment formula is at its strongest. Since the theory for apportioning the dividend income is that it is indistinguishable in substance from the operating income of the unitary enterprise, and since the subsidiary's operating income will largely be reflected in the subsidiary's dividends paid to the parent, if the value of the subsidiary's factors is added to the value of the factors in the parent's apportionment formula, the fit between the income being apportioned and the factors being used to apportion it will be as close as it is ever likely to be.[82]

Even on these utopian assumptions, however, the fit is less than perfect. First, the subsidiary's operating income will not be identical to its current earnings and profits. For example, any federal income taxes paid by the subsidiary will reduce its current earnings and profits and hence its dividends.[83] Consequently, inclusion of 100% of the

82. Conceivably, the fit would be even closer if one assumed that the subsidiary paid dividends equal to its current operating income rather than to its current earnings and profits. Since dividends are in fact paid out of earnings and profits, however, the latter assumption seemed more realistic. In any event, most of the issues discussed below would arise in one form or another whether one assumed that the subsidiary's dividends equalled its current earnings and profits or its current operating income.
83. This follows from the assumed equivalence between the subsidiary's current earnings and profits and its dividend payments.

subsidiary's factors in the parent's apportionment formula will overstate the subsidiary's contribution to the parent's income if each dollar of the factor or factors is presumed to bear the same relationship to the apportionable income it produces.[84]

Second, the subsidiary's operating income, which has thus far been left undefined except insofar as the analysis has assumed a constitutionally acceptable correlation between such income and the subsidiary's factors, may in fact represent only a portion of the subsidiary's earnings and profits and, derivatively, its dividend payments. For example, if the subsidiary has intangible income from its own unitary subsidiary, the subsidiary's factors may not fairly reflect the dividend income it pays to its parent.[85]

The point is not that it is impossible to make adjustments to tighten the fit between the income being apportioned and the factors being employed to apportion it. As suggested in the preceding notes,[86] such adjustments might well be feasible. Rather the point is that even on the strictest of assumptions concerning the correlation between the parent's intangible income derived from its subsidiary and the subsidiary's operating income, there are complicated issues bearing on the proper adjustment of the parent's factors to reflect fairly the subsidiary's contribution to the apportionable tax base that tend to be overlooked in the broad endorsements of the *principle* of factor representation.

Moreover, when the strict assumptions concerning the correlation between the parent's intangible income derived from its subsidiary and the subsidiary's operating income are relaxed, the proper adjustment in the parent's factors becomes more complex. If a parent owns less than 100% of its subsidiary's shares or if the subsidiary pays out less than its current earnings and profits in dividends, clearly only a pro rata portion of the subsidiary's factors should be reflected in the parent's apportionment formula.[87] If a subsidiary's dividends exceed its current earnings and profits, or if it has

84. Put differently, the subsidiary's factors would relate to after-tax apportionable income whereas the parent's factors would relate to pre-tax apportionable income. If one had assumed that the subsidiary's dividends were equal to its operating income rather than to its earnings and profits, this problem would disappear. But that would ignore the essential relationship between dividends and earnings and profits. Internal Revenue Code § 316. One could, however, include in the parent's apportionment formula only that percentage of the subsidiary's factors as its dividends bear to its operating income in order to adjust for the disparity between its earnings and profits and its operating income.
85. With respect to the income from the subsidiary's own subsidiary, one should in principle provide for the same type of factor representation that is made for the parent and flow these adjustments through to the parent's factors. Compare the treatment of tiers of controlled foreign corporations under Subpart F of the Internal Revenue Code. Internal Revenue Code §§ 951-964. It is also important to keep in mind that only dividends representing income from the unitary business conducted by the payor and the payee are properly apportionable. For example, if the payor and payee are engaged in a unitary automotive parts business, but the subsidiary also carries on a wholly unrelated hula hoop manufacturing operation, only the dividends representing the income from the automotive parts business would be apportionable and only the factors associated with such business would be entitled to representation in the parent's formula. Dividends representing earnings from the hula hoop operation would presumably be allocated to the parent's commercial domicile.
86. *See supra* nn. 82-85.
87. For example, if a corporation owns 75% of a subsidiary's stock, then 75% of its factors should be included in parent's apportionment formula. Similarly, if a subsidiary pays out only 50% of

no earnings and profits in a year that it pays dividends, the analytically correct solution to factor representation is less clear.[88]

---

its current earnings and profits as dividends, only 50% of its factors should be included in the parent's apportionment formula. And if a 75% owned subsidiary paid out 50% of its current earnings and profits as dividends, only 37.5% of its factors should be included in the parent's apportionment formula. *See* Frank Keesling, *The Impact of the* Mobil *Case on Apportionment of Income*, 1981(1) B.Y.U. L. Rev. 87, 102 (pro rata inclusion 'preferable' to complete exclusion or inclusion, but 'far from a satisfactory solution').

These principles are embodied in the 'Detroit formula' for apportioning dividends from foreign subsidiaries. The Detroit formula was developed under the Detroit income tax. It was set forth in a letter dated 12 July 1979, written by A.L. Warren, Director, Income Tax Division, City of Detroit, to Burns Stanley, Ford Motor Company, and is reproduced in Hellerstein, Hellerstein & Swain, *State Taxation*, *supra* n. 1, para. 9.15[2][a], which reads in part as follows:

> Dividends from foreign subsidiaries received by a corporation subject to the Detroit income tax are considered taxable pursuant to section 14 of the ordinance, and are subject to apportionment as part of the entire net profits pursuant to section 24. However, we propose a modification to the apportionment formula, as authorized by Section 25 of the ordinance, by including in the denominators of the property, payroll and sales factors the property, payroll and sales of the taxpayer's controlled foreign subsidiaries, in the same ratio that the net dividends received from such subsidiaries bears to each subsidiary's entire net profits, but not to exceed 100% thereof. For example: if the taxpaying corporation owns 50% of Corporation A, a foreign subsidiary, and Corporation A pays 50% of its profits in dividends, the taxpaying corporation would then include 25% of the subsidiary's property, payroll and sales in the denominators [sic] its property, payroll and sales factors respectively. By net dividends from foreign subsidiaries we mean foreign dividends reported on the taxpayer's federal income tax return less gross up for foreign taxes deemed to have been paid. By controlled foreign subsidiaries we mean foreign corporations in which the taxpayer owns 10% or more of the voting stock. By entire net profits we mean the subsidiaries' net profits after taxes.
>
> The apportionment percentage as then determined shall then be applied to the entire net profits of the taxpaying corporation including net dividends from foreign corporations. The inclusion of the foreign corporation's property, payroll and sales factor shall not reduce the parent company's income subject to the Detroit tax by an amount in excess of the net foreign dividend portion of the parent company's taxable income. Should a controlled foreign subsidiary having no net profits (loss year) in which year a dividend is paid to the taxpaying parent, the ratio to be used to determine the amount of that foreign subsidiary's property, payroll and sales to be included in the denominator of the modified apportionment formula shall be the net dividends received from such foreign subsidiaries divided by its retained earnings at the beginning of the taxable year.
>
> Please note that our proposal requires you to include all dividends from foreign sources, but that the denominator of the apportionment formula is to include property, payroll and sales from only those foreign subsidiaries which are controlled by you. Further, as provided in section 25 of the ordinance, when a special or modified formula has been approved by the City it shall continue to be used by the taxpayer until a written request is made and approved for further modification or for reverting to the formula provided in the ordinance.

See Lynn Gandhi, *Rev Your Engines – The Detroit Formula, Time for a Revival?*, 91 St. Tax Notes 467 (2019).

88. There are two discrete problems here. The first is to determine the appropriate percentage of the subsidiary's factors that should be included in the parent's formula. The second is to determine the appropriate factors of the subsidiary to use for this purpose. If, for example, in 2018 a subsidiary had $100 of earnings and profits but paid no dividends, and in 2019 had $100 of earnings and profits and paid $200 of dividends, it would make sense to include 100% of the

[b] Intangible Income Other than Dividends

The quest for a theoretically sound methodology of factor representation becomes truly daunting, however, when one focuses on intangible income other than dividends, especially if a corporate payee receives more than one type of intangible income from its related corporate payor. Take capital gains from the sale of a unitary subsidiary, for example. While the Court may believe that 'for constitutional purposes capital gains should be treated as no different from dividends',[89] there are in fact differences between dividends and capital gains that have implications for factor representation.[90]

The assumption that the corporate parent's intangible income is in substance equivalent to the unitary corporate subsidiary's operating income – an assumption that shows strains even in the context of dividends – is considerably more problematic in the context of capital gains. To be sure, part of the parent's gain upon disposition of a unitary subsidiary will reflect the subsidiary's current and past earnings and profits, and, to this extent, the factor representation principles applicable to dividends ought to apply equally to capital gains. But the capital gain may also reflect unrealized appreciation in the subsidiary's assets, future earning capacity, or goodwill, and other factors that may not be accurately represented in the subsidiary's property, payroll, and sales in the state for the tax year at issue. Any attempt to account for these considerations, which bear no direct relation to the subsidiary's past or current earnings, by adjusting the proportion of the subsidiary's apportionment factors that are included in the parent's apportionment formula, would involve considerable guess-work.

Interest, which the Court in *ASARCO*[91] agreed 'should be treated in the same manner as dividend income'[92] raises even thornier issues of factor representation. In contrast to dividends and capital gains, which can be viewed as reflecting the underlying earnings of the subsidiary, interest does not constitute, even in the loosest

subsidiary's factors for 2018 as well as 100% of its factors for 2019 in the parent's apportionment formula. A single year's factors are generally viewed as producing a single year's apportionable income, and there is no reason to abandon that view when apportioning prior years' income. *See* Keesling, *The Impact of the* Mobil *Case, supra* n. 87, at 102 n. 37. Under the Detroit formula, discussed in the preceding note, if a subsidiary with no current earnings and profits pays dividends, the ratio used to determine the percentage of the subsidiary's factors includible in the parent's formula is the dividends divided by the retained earnings at the beginning of the year. Although this may be an acceptable practical solution to what may be an administratively insuperable problem, it is theoretically flawed on two counts. First, it employs current factors to apportion a prior year's income; second, it spreads the factors for a single year over income that may have been earned in the course of many years. The theoretically correct, if administratively impractical, approach would include in the parent's apportionment formula a percentage of each year's factors determined by the ratio of the earnings and profits from that year that were paid out as dividends to the total earnings and profits for the year in which they were earned.

89. *Allied-Signal, Inc. v. Director, Division. of Tax'n*, 504 US 768, 780 (1992).

90. In fairness to the Court, it was focusing on the question of apportionability, not factor representation.

91. *ASARCO, Inc. v. Idaho State Tax Comm'n*, 458 US 307 (1982).

92. *Ibid.*, 330.

sense, a proxy for the subsidiary's operating income.[93] Rather it is an expense that *reduces* the subsidiary's operating income, although it constitutes apportionable interest income to the parent. Nevertheless, since the foundation for including the interest in the parent's apportionable tax base is that it is income derived from a unitary business carried on by the payor and the payee, and since the form in which the income is received 'works no change in the underlying realities of a unitary business',[94] one could address the problem of factor representation by treating the interest income as the operating income of the unitary business.

Assume, for example, that a corporation makes a $100 loan to a related unitary corporation at a 10% annual interest rate; the corporate borrower uses the loan proceeds to purchase inventory, which it sells for $120; the corporate borrower then repays the loan, along with the $10 interest, to the corporate lender, retaining $10 in profit. If this enterprise had been structured as a single corporation, with the borrower operated as a division, then the transaction described above would presumably have involved the intra-company transfer of funds to the division, and the subsequent purchase and sale of the inventory, resulting in $20 of operating income from the sale of goods. There would be no interest income because there was no loan, and the $10 of interest income that was received by the parent when the enterprise was organized along separate corporate lines would take the form of operating income when the enterprise was organized as a single corporation.

To be sure, this effectively combines the income of the corporate lender and the corporate borrower for purposes of the factor representation analysis,[95] thereby eliminating the very interest income that is being apportioned. It does, however, permit one to pursue the factor representation issue consistently with the underlying theory on which the apportionability of the intangible income is based. Under this approach, then, the interest income would be treated as a portion of the unitary enterprise's operating income. The ratio of such interest income to the unitary enterprise's overall operating income[96] would provide the percentage of the subsidiary's factors to be included in the parent's apportionment formula. Admittedly, this approach is analytically awkward at best. It applies an *enterprise-wide* ratio to the *corporate borrower's* factors for purposes of apportioning the *corporate lender's* income. Nevertheless, rather than provoking muffled laughter, it might well elicit Dr Johnson's reaction to the sight

93. In the context of payor-payee unity, however, one could simply assume that the debt-equity distinction is without substance and recharacterize the interest payment as a dividend payment. One would then have to recompute the income of the payor without any deduction for the recharacterized interest payments and implement the factor representation along the lines suggested above with respect to dividends.

94. *Mobil Oil Corp. v. Commissioner of Taxes*, 445 US 425, 441 (1980).

95. It is not, however, a true combined report. *See* §§5.02[B][1], 5.02[B][2] *supra*. Indeed, the resort to what is effectively combined reporting analysis to deal with the factor representation issue arising out of the apportionment of intangible income based on payor-payee unity reinforces the case for combined reporting in this context.

96. Ideally, this income would be determined on a combined basis. If determined on a separate company basis, it would presumably include intangible income whose apportionability was based on payor-payee unity.

of a dog walking on its hind legs: '[i]t is not done well; but you are surprized [sic] to find it done at all'.[97]

Other common forms of intangible income, such as patent and copyright royalties and licence and franchise fees, would appear to raise the same factor representation issues as interest when the income is apportionable on the basis of payor-payee unity. These income items are expenses to the corporate payor. They would appear as operating income to the enterprise if it were organized as a single corporate entity.[98] Under the analysis set forth above with regard to interest income, the factor representation question would be resolved by determining the relationship of the royalty or licence fee to the enterprise's operating income and including an *aliquot* portion of subsidiary's apportionment factors in the parent's apportionment formula.[99]

Wholly apart from the difficulties of determining the appropriate approach to factor representation for different types of intangible income, there is also the problem of coordinating these various approaches. Clearly, there could be serious overcounting of the subsidiary's factors in the parent's apportionment formula if one simply summed the results of the various enquiries. For example, if a subsidiary paid out all of its earnings and profits in dividends, but also made substantial interest and royalty payments to its parent, a mechanical application of the rules suggested above would lead to inclusion of well over 100% of the subsidiary's factors in the parent's

97. James Boswell, *Life of Samuel Johnson LL.D., Great Books of the Western World: Vol. 44*, 132 (R. Hutchins ed., 1952 [1791]). An alternative approach to the factor representation issue in this context might focus on the relationship between the corporate borrower's interest expense and its operating income. If one could correlate a given amount of the borrower's interest expense with a given amount of its operating income, the resulting figure could be compared with its total operating income, yielding the percentage of its factors that should be included in the corporate lender's apportionment formula. For example, if $10 of interest expense was attributable to a loan of $100 the use of which yielded $115 of revenue and thus $5 of net operating income, a corporate borrower could determine the operating income attributable to its interest expense by taking 50% of its interest expense. Thus if the corporate borrower had $10 of interest expense and $100 of operating income, the operating income attributable to the interest expense ($5) would amount to 5% of its operating income. Five per cent of its factors would then be included in the corporate lender's apportionment formula to reflect the contribution that the related borrower's operations made to the production of the lender's interest income. The approach suggested in the text seems more defensible than the suggested alternative because it views the interest as income derived from the unitary business rather than as a separate expense item of the borrower and is therefore more consistent with the theory on which the interest is being apportioned.

98. Assume, for example, that a parent licenses a patent to a subsidiary for $100 per year; the subsidiary exploits the patent to generate $120 of revenues attributable directly to the patent; the subsidiary pays the royalty of $100, leaving it with $20 in profit from the use of the patent. If this enterprise had been structured as a single corporation, with the subsidiary operated as a division, then the transaction described above would presumably have involved the intra-company transfer of the patent licence to the division, and its subsequent exploitation resulting in $120 of operating income attributable directly to the patent. There would be no royalty income because there was no licensing agreement, and the $100 of royalty income that was received by the parent when the enterprise was organized along separate corporate lines would take the form of operating income when the enterprise was organized as a single corporation.

99. As noted above with respect to interest, *supra* n. 97, one could look alternatively at the relationship between the subsidiary's operating income attributable to the royalty or licence expense and take the appropriate percentage of the subsidiary's operating income as a measure of the contribution of the subsidiary's factors to the parent's royalty or licence income.

apportionment formula. While inclusion of more than 100% of the subsidiary's factors in the parent's apportionment formula may be justified in cases in which the intangible income reflects several years of the subsidiary's income, no more than 100% of the subsidiary's factors should be included in the parent's apportionment formula when income from only one tax year is involved.[100] It might also be appropriate to limit the tax benefit provided by factor representation to the benefit that would be provided by eliminating the intangible income altogether from the apportionable tax base.

[c] State Court Decisions Addressed to Factor Representation

State court decisions addressed to the question of whether a taxpayer is entitled to factor representation and, if so, how such factor representation is to be implemented have been decidedly mixed. This state of the law is understandable. After all, the Supreme Court has yet to consider the former question,[101] and the solution to the latter is mired in the complexities considered above. Although detailed consideration of these decisions lies outside the scope of this chapter, such discussion can be found elsewhere.[102]

It may nevertheless be appropriate to conclude with a 'heads up' regarding what may be the focus of the next wave of litigation over factor representation in the state courts. As is now widely known, in late 2017, the US Congress enacted sweeping tax reform legislation (commonly referred to as 'The Tax Cuts and Jobs Act of 2017') with significant implications for states whose corporate income tax bases conform to the federal income tax base,[103] as they generally do.[104] The Tax Cuts and Jobs Act included several key provisions taxing foreign source income to which the states have conformed (and, at this writing, are still considering the extent to which they will conform).[105] After reviewing these provisions, two seasoned representatives of the business sector concluded:

> Shockingly, virtually none of the states conforming to the new foreign-source income provisions have adopted the traditional factor representation used for decades in state corporate income taxation – the inclusion in the denominator of each factor of the sales (and when appropriate, property and payroll) that produced the income subject to tax.
>
> This outcome ... both is bad public policy and likely constitutes unconstitutional discrimination against foreign commerce.[106]

---

100. The Detroit formula, described in *supra* n. 87, includes such a ceiling in its factor representation method.
101. *See* text accompanying *supra* nn. 70-74.
102. *See* Hellerstein, Hellerstein & Swain, *State Taxation*, *supra* n. 1, para. 9.15[4].
103. Pub. L. No. 115-97, 131 Stat. 2054 (22 Dec. 2017).
104. *See* §5.02[A] and *supra* n. 11.
105. *See* Walter Hellerstein & Jon Sedon, *State Corporate Income Tax Consequences of Federal Tax Reform*, 88 St. Tax Notes 187 (2018); Hellerstein, Hellerstein & Swain, *State Taxation*, *supra* n. 1, para. 7.16A.
106. Karl A. Frieden & Joseph Donovan, *Where in the World Is Factor Representation for Foreign-Source Income?*, 92 St. Tax Notes 199 (2019).

Whatever uncertainty there may be over the right to factor representation, and its appropriate implementation, one thing that may be said with a high degree of certainty is that litigation over these issues will continue.

[C] Continuing Uncertainty

Nearly four decades after the Court's decision in *Mobil*, the federal constitutional principles informing the application of formulary apportionment to state corporate income taxation of related entities remain essentially where *Mobil* left them: the unitary business principle is the 'linchpin of apportionability' and the question of whether 'combined apportionment ... is constitutionally required' has never been resolved.[107] To be sure, the Court has held that states *may* employ combined reporting to a group of related corporations engaged in a unitary business,[108] and twenty-four of the forty-four states with corporate income taxes currently apply combined reporting to such unitary groups to determine the group's apportionable tax base that is subject to the state's apportionment formula.[109] Nevertheless, despite the strong case for the application of combined reporting for determining the income of a group of related corporations whose income is allocated to states by formulary apportionment,[110] the states remain roughly divided as to their application of combined or separate company reporting to related corporations engaged in a unitary business. This adds considerable complexity to US state taxation of corporate income, particularly with respect to the question of factor representation, whose constitutional stature and proper implementation remain mired in uncertainty, as the preceding discussion reveals.

§5.04 LESSONS

The preceding analysis has laid the groundwork for fulfilling the basic purpose of this chapter, namely, identifying lessons from the US experience for other jurisdictions that are contemplating the adoption of formulary apportionment as the method for attributing income to a taxing state, particularly as that experience bears on the application of formulary apportionment to related entities. In contrast to the preceding discussion, this portion of the chapter *is* 'mercifully short'.[111] Perhaps the overarching message is simply 'don't do what we do', or, perhaps more charitably put, 'insofar as you are going to do what we do, do it selectively and carefully'.

Before the chapter turns to specific 'lessons' from the US experience, it is critically important to reiterate the point, which was stressed at the outset, that the US experience with the application of formulary apportionment to related entities in large

107. *See* §5.03[C] *infra* for further discussion of this issue.
108. *See* §5.03[B][2] *supra*.
109. *See* CCH, *Combined Reporting Requirements*, Multistate Quick Answer Charts, *supra* n. 32.
110. *See* §5.01 *supra*.
111. *See* §5.01 *supra* (observing, after brief summary of theoretical issues informing the enquiry into the application of FA to related entities in the state corporate income tax context, that if this were all there were to the enquiry the chapter would be 'mercifully short').

part simply reflects the context in which the US states exercise their taxing powers. Under the US constitutional scheme, the states, particularly with respect to taxation, enjoy broad authority to exercise their taxing power. Indeed, as Justice Brandeis famously observed, '[i]t is one of the happy incidents of the federal system that a single courageous State may, if its citizens choose, serve as a laboratory; and try novel social and economic experiments without risk to the rest of the country'.[112] To be sure, Congress has the power to limit state taxing authority and state authority is also subject to broad constitutional restraints. However, Congress has rarely acted to limit state taxing authority except in targeted contexts,[113] and it has never sought to impose uniform division of income rules upon the states. Moreover, as the foregoing discussion makes clear, the broad federal constitutional restraints on state taxing authority have not been construed to impose uniform sourcing rules on the states.[114]

There are two fundamental lessons that those contemplating the adoption of corporate tax regimes employing formulary apportionment can learn from the US experience with regard to the application of formulary apportionment to a group of related entities. The first concerns the question of how to define the group to which formulary apportionment is applied. The second concerns the question of whether the group should be required to file on a combined or consolidated basis.

[A] Legal Versus Economic Unity

Perhaps the most fundamental question confronting the designers of a formulary regime as applied to a group of related entities is whether to define the group to which formulary apportionment applies in terms of legal or economic relationships. It is worth keeping in mind that the US states had no choice about the answer to this question. They simply had to play the hand they were dealt by the US Constitution as construed by the US Supreme Court, namely, that 'the linchpin of apportionability in the field of state income taxation is the unitary business principle'.[115] The unitary business principle, as further explicated by the US Supreme Court, is a quintessentially economic concept, defined in terms of such factors as 'functional integration, centralization of management, and economies of scale'.[116] But if a jurisdiction (or group of taxing jurisdictions) is free to choose its own definition of the group of related entities to which the formulary regime should be applied, it might alternatively adopt a definition based on the 'legal' as distinguished from 'economic' unity of the related entities. For example, the group could be defined as all corporations linked by a specified degree of ownership (e.g., more than 50% direct or indirect ownership).

This brings the analysis back to the essential design question: which approach to delineating the group to which the formulary regime should be applied – one based on

112. *New State Ice Co. v. Liebmann*, 285 US 262, 311 (1932) (Brandeis, J., dissenting).
113. *See* Hellerstein, Hellerstein & Swain, *State Taxation*, *supra* n. 1, paras. 4.25, 4.26.
114. *See Barclays Bank plc v. Franchise Tax Board*, 512 US 298 (1994); *Container Corp. of America v. Franchise Tax Board*, 463 US 159 (1983); *Moorman Mfg. Co. v. Bair*, 437 US 267 (1978).
115. *Mobil Oil Corp. v. Commissioner of Taxes*, 445 US 425, 439 (1980).
116. *Ibid.*, 438. *See generally* Hellerstein, Hellerstein & Swain, *State Taxation*, *supra* n. 1, paras. 8.07 et seq. (delineating the contours of the unitary business principle).

legal or economic relationships – recommends itself from a normative and a practical standpoint?

At first blush, the economic or 'unitary'[117] approach to the delineation of the consolidated or combined group may appear to be superior to the legal or 'ownership' approach. After all, the underlying rationale, at least historically, for the use of formulary apportionment for determining the source of income is that economic interrelationships involving cross-border activities make it impossible to determine the source of income from such activities on the basis of separate geographic accounting. If one could determine where income was earned with precision and at reasonable costs by separate geographic accounting, there would be no justification for resorting to a 'necessarily imperfect'[118] 'mathematical generalization'[119] for making that determination. Consequently, because it is the immeasurable economic 'flows of value'[120] between various components of a single economic enterprise that justify the use of formulary apportionment in the first place, such economic interrelationships should lay the foundation for determining the delineation of the group of entities whose income is to be assigned to taxing jurisdictions by formula. If two commonly owned entities have no underlying economic ties with one another (apart from their ownership by a common parent), there does not appear to be any compelling public policy reason why their incomes should be lumped together and apportioned according to a formula reflecting (presumably[121]) the combined factors of the two unrelated businesses.

Despite the theoretical strength of the case for an economic approach to the delineation of the consolidated group, it raises a number of problems from the standpoint of practical administration. As US Supreme Court Justice Oliver Wendell Holmes once wisely observed, 'a page of history is worth a volume of logic'.[122] If history in the form of the American states' experience with the 'unitary business' principle is any guide, the use of economic criteria to define the consolidated group is a recipe for uncertainty and inconsistency in the determination of the consolidated group. Although the US Supreme Court has attempted to delineate the unitary business principle in broad strokes over the course of the past century, the Court, recognizing that states have great latitude in the tax area, itself has acknowledged that 'the unitary business concept … is not, so to speak, unitary: there are variations on the theme, and

117. At least in US subnational tax parlance. Although it is a little late in the day from the standpoint of this chapter to make this point, the term 'unitary' is sometimes used generically in discussions of cross-border taxation (particularly in the international tax context) to describe the formulary approach to assigning taxing rights under corporate income taxes and is not limited to economically integrated activity. Throughout this chapter (and, specifically, in the instant discussion of legal versus economic unity), the term 'unitary' is employed as understood in the US subnational context (economic unity) and not as embracing formulary apportionment as applied to any 'unit' of activity, however that unit may be defined.
118. *Container Corp. of America v. Franchise Tax Board*, 463 US 159, 183 (1983).
119. *Ibid.*, 188.
120. *Ibid.*, 178.
121. *But see* §5.02[B][2] and text accompanying *supra* nn. 70-74 (indicating that, at least in the US subnational context, the right to combined reporting or factor representation has never been established as a matter of constitutional law).
122. *New York Trust v. Eisner*, 256 US 345, 349 (1921).

any number of them are logically consistent with the underlying principles motivating the approach'.[123] As a consequence, the decisions of the US Supreme Court - not to mention the scores of decisions emanating from state courts - 'leave much room for controversy and confusion and little in the way of precise guides'[124] to taxpayers and taxing authorities as to the scope of the consolidated or combined group. To be sure, any jurisdiction or group of jurisdictions that is 'bound by a common legal framework'[125] could reduce the uncertainty and inconsistency by formulating a single statutory standard defining the concept of economic unity. Even so, the concept of a unitary business, while compelling in principle, may be difficult to codify and implement successfully.

The difficulties of defining a consolidated group on the basis of economic interrelationships lead to the conclusion that the determination of the group that is subject to formulary apportionment should be based on legal rather than economic unity.[126] Such a test for consolidation would be relatively certain and thus easy to comply with and administer, and it would avoid the problematic fact-sensitive enquiries required by definition of a group based on economic criteria.[127] There are two principal weaknesses in such an approach, however. First, as in the analogous case of apportioning what is arguably income that does not arise from the unitary business, it could lead to misattribution of income, because the income from affiliated - but economically unrelated - enterprises would (presumably[128]) be sourced by reference to consolidated or combined apportionment factors that would not have contributed to the production of the income in question. Second, a definition of the consolidated or combined apportionable tax base predicated solely on legal control could lead to manipulation by the careful adjustment of ownership interests in other corporations to minimize tax burdens, depending on whether consolidation or separate company reporting was more advantageous or disadvantageous from a tax standpoint.

123. *Container*, 463 US at 167.
124. *Northwestern States Portland Cement Co. v. Minnesota*, 358 US 450, 458 (1959).
125. To use the OECD vernacular to refer to the EU: OECD, *Taxation and Electronic Commerce: Implementing the Ottawa Taxation Framework Conditions* 45 n. 6 (OECD 2001) ('In accordance with the Ottawa Framework Conditions, specific measures adopted in relation to the place of taxation by a group of countries that is bound by a common legal framework for their consumption tax systems may, of course, apply to transactions between those countries').
126. I am not alone in reaching this conclusion - *see* Michael Aikins, *Common Control and the Delineation of the Taxable Entity*, 121(3) Yale L.J. 624 (2011) - nor is it the first time that I have reached it: *see* Walter Hellerstein & Charles E. McLure, Jr., *The European Commission's Report on Company Income Taxation: What the EU Can Learn from the Experience of the US States*, 11(2) Int'l Tax & Pub. Fin. 199 (2004). As Aikins observes, after summarizing the US subnational experience with the unitary business principle, 'the unitary business test is fact-intensive and costly to administer'; 'the unitary business test is arbitrary'; and 'the states differ in their application of the unitary business test': *see* Aikins, in this footnote, at 640-650.
127. *See also* Aikins, *supra* n. 126, advocating and delineating a 'legal' common control test based in Internal Revenue Code § 1563.
128. This assumes, contrary to the US experience documented in this chapter, that any jurisdiction (or group of jurisdictions) adopting formulary apportionment for a group of related entities (whether defined by economic or legal unity) would likewise adopt consolidated or combined reporting, as suggested at the outset of this chapter and briefly reiterated below, §5.04[B] *infra*

If the consolidated group includes affiliates that are less than 100% owned, one may raise the question of whether all the income of such affiliates should be included in the apportionable tax base or only the proportionate share of income reflecting the consolidated group's ownership percentage in the affiliate. Under US state practice, once it is determined that an affiliate is includible in the combined group, all of its income (and all of its factors) typically are included in the base and the apportionment formula.[129] One might well argue, however, that it would be more appropriate to include only the pro rata share of the affiliate's income and factors in the base and formula, as reflected in the 'Detroit formula' described above[130] and as is typically done with corporate investments in pass-through entities, such as partnerships and limited liability companies.[131] Although there is a plausible case for adopting either approach, the former approach appears preferable because of its greater administrative simplicity and because it is not likely to lead to distortion in the sourcing of income if the factors are properly constructed.

There is no magic wand to resolve the tension between a group definition that is conceptually attractive, but administratively cumbersome, and one that is administratively attractive but could lead to manipulation of ownership interests to minimize tax liability. One could, however, introduce anti-tax abuse safeguards into a group definition based on legal ownership that might mitigate this issue. For example, the constructive share ownership rules embodied in the Internal Revenue Code for purposes of denying losses among related parties[132] and in connection with various corporate transactions[133] would restrain the ability of economically related parties to manipulate their ownership interests to achieve tax benefits. In addition, one might impose certain objective and easily administrable indicia of economic integration as a condition of consolidated filing (e.g., a percentage of revenues derived from related party transactions).

[B] Consolidated/Combined Versus Separate Company Reporting

As was noted at the outset of this chapter, if formulary apportionment is accepted as the method of income allocation for a group of commonly controlled corporations, then, as a theoretical and practical matter, consolidated or combined reporting should be employed as the method for determining the tax base to which the formula should be applied. Moreover, the same principle should apply whether the criterion for determining the application of formulary apportionment to the group of related entities is economic or legal unity. Although the case for consolidated or combined reporting may be more compelling when economic rather than legal unity is the touchstone of apportionability, in both circumstances, there is likely to be integrated cross-border

129. *See* §5.02[B][1] *supra*; Hellerstein, Hellerstein & Swain, *State Taxation*, *supra* n. 1, para. 8.11.
130. *See supra* n. 87.
131. *See* Hellerstein, Hellerstein & Swain, *State Taxation*, *supra* n. 1, para. 9.15[6].
132. Internal Revenue Code § 267.
133. Internal Revenue Code § 318.

activity between the related entities and the administrative advantages of consolidated or combined filing may also be significant.

Indeed, if there is any 'lesson' for other jurisdictions from the US experience with the application of formulary apportionment to a group of related entities, it is that the failure generally to require combined reporting for apportioning the group's income has been a nightmare from the standpoint of tax policy and administration. With the states roughly divided in half over the determination of whether to require combined reporting, with separate company reporting states relegated to the treatment of apportionable income from other group members as 'intangible' income (which may or may not receive 'factor representation'), and with the factor representation question triggering another layer of complex enquiries that may lead to outcomes that perplexing at best, the case for mandatory combined or consolidated reporting for the group of related entities whose income is determined (by whatever standard) to be subject to formulary apportionment is unassailable.

[C] State Legislation Restricting Worldwide Combined Reporting

It may be appropriate to end this chapter with another 'lesson' from the US experience regarding the application of formulary apportionment that reflects yet another 'page of history' that is worth 'a volume of logic'.[134] In one of history's ironic twists, California's victory in *Container*[135] sustaining the constitutionality of worldwide combined reporting actually led to its demise in some states and to its restriction in many others. The ink was hardly dry on the *Container* decision in 1983 when President Ronald Reagan responded to the pressure of multinational enterprises, supported by foreign governments, by convening a Worldwide Unitary Taxation Working Group to review worldwide combined reporting.[136] In its 1984 report, the Working Group recommended that the states adopt legislation or administrative action that would limit combined apportionment of both US and foreign-based multinationals to a US water's edge combined group. In the event 'there are not sufficient signs of appreciable progress by the states' in adopting the agreed principles, Secretary of the Treasury Donald Regan stated that he would recommend 'federal legislation that would give effect to a water's edge limitation'.[137]

Responding to the threat of federal legislation and to political pressure from multinational corporations, the states acted with unusual legislative speed. Although Florida had adopted worldwide combined reporting in 1983, within a few weeks after the Court's decision in *Container*, a little more than a year later Florida reversed course

134. *See supra* n. 122 and accompanying text.
135. *See* §5.02[B][2] *supra*.
136. Office of the Secretary, Department of the Treasury, *Final Report of the Worldwide Unitary Taxation Working Group: Chairman's Report and Supplemental Views* (1984). The following discussion draws freely from Hellerstein, Hellerstein & Swain, *State Taxation*, *supra* n. 1, para. 8.18, which treats this issue in more detail and with additional citation to relevant authority (e.g., state legislation limiting worldwide combination).
137. Office of the Secretary, Department of the Treasury, *supra* n. 136, at iii (transmittal letter of Secretary of the Treasury Donald T. Regan to the President).

and repealed its combined reporting provisions that permitted worldwide unitary apportionment. In 1984, Oregon, one of the first states to employ worldwide combined reporting, and characterized by one observer as 'an unlikely candidate to repeal worldwide combination ... [as] a stronghold of the ... [Multistate Tax Commission]',[138] responded to strong pressure brought particularly by Japanese business by replacing its combined reporting regime with a state consolidated reporting regime based on the federal consolidated group,[139] thus eliminating foreign corporations from the state filing group. The result of the Oregon legislation was to exclude the income of non-US corporations from the Oregon apportionable income base.

In 1985, Arizona and Colorado limited combined reporting to water's edge income. Idaho, Indiana, Montana, New Hampshire, North Dakota, and Utah also followed suit. The actions of other states were too much for California, the once-feared 'tiger' of worldwide apportionment. In 1986, California enacted legislation that granted taxpayers an option to limit apportionment to the US water's edge. In 1987, Minnesota likewise limited its unitary approach to domestic corporations, excluding both '[t]he net income and apportionment factors ... of foreign corporations ... which are part of a unitary business'.[140] And in 1991, Alaska adopted water's edge legislation. As a result, no state currently applies worldwide combination without an elective or mandatory water's edge or domestic corporation limitation, with the exception of Alaska's continuing application of mandatory worldwide combined reporting to taxpayers engaged in the production or transportation of oil and gas. There are, however, considerable variations from state to state as to the composition of the water's edge group, the definition of 80/20 corporations,[141] and the definition of tax havens.

As suggested above, the states' headlong rush to discard or restrict worldwide combined reporting did not grow out of the states' philosophical conversion from formulary apportionment to separate accounting as the appropriate methodology of taxing a worldwide multicorporate unitary enterprise. Rather, the states yielded to economic and political pressures and the threats of multinationals, particularly foreign-based enterprises, that they would not locate new plants in states that applied the unitary method to the apportionment of their incomes,[142] and the political threat of federal legislation that would restrict the use of worldwide apportionment by the states. While the state's 'logic' was informed largely by political concerns rather than concerns of tax policy, it may nevertheless contain a useful lesson for jurisdictions contemplating the adoption of formulary apportionment with respect to the income of related entities when some of those entities are likely to be foreign corporations.

138. Fred Ferguson, *Worldwide Unitary Taxation: The End Appears Near*, 4(4) J. St. Tax'n 241, 245 (1986).
139. *See* §5.02[A] *supra*.
140. Hellerstein, Hellerstein & Swain, *State Taxation*, *supra* n. 1, para. 8.18.
141. The term '80/20 corporation' generally refers to a US corporation with at least 80% of its payroll and property outside the United States. Broadly speaking, the problem of the 80/20 corporation is the problem of how the states should tax corporations whose operations are principally foreign.
142. *See* Ferguson, *supra* n. 138, at 245.

PART II Future Possibilities: Variations on the Formulary Apportionment Theme

CHAPTER 6

Is Unilateral Formulary Apportionment Better than the Status Quo?*

*J. Clifton Fleming, Jr., Robert J. Peroni*** *& Stephen E. Shay*

§6.01 INTRODUCTION

Some advocates of a formulary approach to international income taxation seem to hope for a multilateral arrangement in which all the world's countries, or at least those with large economies, agree on a common formula to allocate international income among themselves for taxing purposes.[1] But what if a critical mass of countries cannot agree on an allocation formula, and conditions do not exist for a unilateral move to formulary apportionment by a large economy that would lead others to follow,[2] as seems likely

* The views expressed in this chapter are those of the authors and do not reflect those of their universities, any organization for which any of the authors serves as an officer or renders pro bono services, or, in the case of Mr Shay, any client.

** Professor Peroni dedicates this chapter to his loving parents, Emil Peroni, his late father, and Betty Peroni, his late mother, for their tremendous support and inspiration over the years. Professor Peroni thanks Dean Ward Farnsworth for his generous research support.

1. *See, e.g.*, Reuven S. Avi-Yonah, Kimberly A. Clausing & Michael C. Durst, *Allocating Business Profits for Tax Purposes: A Proposal to Adopt a Formulary Profit Split*, 9(5) Fla. Tax Rev. 497, 509-510, 519-520 (2009); Tommaso Faccio & Valpy Fitzgerald, *Sharing the Corporate Tax Base: Equitable Taxing of Multinationals and the Choice of Formulary Apportionment*, 25(2) Transnat'l Corp. 67, 70-71 (2018); *see also* Joann M. Weiner, *Using the Experience in the US States to Evaluate Issues in Implementing Formula Apportionment at the International Level*, 13 Tax Notes Int'l 2113 (1996). This multilateral approach, although unrealistic at the present time, would have the benefit of reducing the problems of double taxation and double non-taxation that arise with unilateral formulary apportionment. Moreover, multilateral formulary apportionment could be implemented in a way that would not abrogate most bilateral income tax treaties of the adopting country.
2. *See, e.g.*, Tsilly Dagan, *International Tax Policy: Between Competition and Cooperation* 23-35, 68-71 (Cambridge University Press 2018) (arguing that because of international tax competition, a cooperative multinational income tax regime is unlikely to emerge and may be undesirable); Nigel Chalk, Michael Keen & Victoria Perry, *The Tax Cuts and Jobs Act: An Appraisal* 35-40

for the foreseeable future? The objective of this chapter is to provide a framework for analysing the consequences and desirability of countries adopting formulary apportionment by unilateral, uncoordinated action. It will be helpful to begin with an example.

Example 1

Assume that Parentco, a Country A corporate resident, manufactures electronic widgets in Country A and sells them to its wholly owned Country B subsidiary, Subco, for resale by Subco to customers in Country B. Parentco also licenses to Subco the Country B patent, logo, and brand name rights that Subco needs to execute the resale activity. Because Parentco and Subco are a single economic unit, i.e., a multinational enterprise (MNE), the total pre-tax profits of the Parentco-Subco MNE (eliminating intercompany items) will be the same regardless of the widget prices and licence royalties that Parentco charges to Subco. If, however, there are significant differences between corporate tax rates in Countries A and B, the product prices and royalties charged by Parentco will significantly affect the Parentco-Subco MNE's after-tax profits because low product prices and royalty rates will shift the total MNE profit towards Country B and high product prices and royalty rates will tilt total profit towards Country A.

If Parentco and Subco were unrelated, the product prices and royalties charged by Parentco (collectively referred to as transfer prices) would be determined by arm's length bargaining and the profit allocation between Countries A and B would reflect market supply and demand dynamics rather than tax planning.[3] Parentco and Subco are, however, a single economic unit. Therefore, arm's length bargaining will not exist, and in the absence of legal constraints, the transfer prices charged by Parentco may be set to maximize after-tax returns by allocating profit between Countries A and B to minimize their overall tax burden.

If Countries A and B follow the globally accepted arm's length standard, they will adopt transfer pricing rules that authorize adjustments to achieve (or prescribe) arm's length product prices and royalties that supersede any non-arm's length charges provided in contracts and licences between Parentco and Subco.[4] These arm's length charges, together with appropriate source or income attribution rules, are designed to allocate the MNE profits between Country A and Country B to achieve the same pre-tax allocation as would be the result of transactions agreed upon between unrelated parties in the same circumstances.

The arm's length approach has, however, been the target of much highly critical literature.[5] The criticisms can be distilled to the following points:

(International Monetary Fund Working Paper WP/18/185, August 2018) (assessing possible foreign responses to the 2017 US tax legislation, including the possibility of the United States being a Stackelberg leader).

3. The evidence that earnings of publicly traded US companies consist of a high percentage of infra-marginal returns strongly suggests that markets in which MNEs operate are not perfectly competitive. For a review of the estimates of infra-marginal returns, see Hayley Reynolds & Thomas Neubig, *Distinguishing Between 'Normal' and 'Excess' Returns for Tax Policy* (Organisation for Economic Co-operation and Development (OECD) Taxation Working Paper No. 28, 2016).
4. *See* OECD, *Model Tax Convention on Income and on Capital* Art. 9 (21 November 2017); Hugh J. Ault & Brian J. Arnold, *Comparative Income Taxation: A Structural Analysis* 529 (3rd ed., Kluwer Law International 2010).
5. *See, e.g.*, Joe Andrus & Paul Oosterhuis, *Transfer Pricing After BEPS: Where Are and Where Should We Be Going*, 95(3) Taxes: The Tax Mag. 89, 90-96 (2017); Avi-Yonah, Clausing & Durst,

(1) The arm's length approach is so dependent on the particular facts and context of each case that it cannot be effectively administered by tax authorities or complied with by taxpayers.[6]
(2) The arm's length approach creates system-gaming scenarios in which the greater information and professional resources available to MNEs allow them to overwhelm tax administrations.[7]
(3) The complexity and imprecision of the arm's length approach produces controversies that are expensive and time-consuming for both taxpayers and tax administrators to resolve.[8]

Allocating Business Profits for Tax Purposes, *supra* n. 1, at 501-507, 510-513; Lorence L. Bravenec, *Connecting the Dots in US International Taxation*, 27 Tax Notes Int'l 845 (2002); Michael C. Durst, *A Statutory Proposal for US Transfer Pricing Reform*, 115 Tax Notes 1047, 1050 (2007); Julie Roin, *Can the Income Tax Be Saved? The Promise and Pitfalls of Adopting Worldwide Formulary Apportionment*, 61(3) Tax L. Rev. 169, 172-173 (2008); Faccio & Fitzgerald, *supra* n. 1, at 69-70; *see also* US General Accounting Office (GAO), *IRS Could Better Protect US Tax Interests in Determining the Income of Multinational Corporations* (1981); GAO, *International Taxation: Problems Persist in Determining Tax Effects of Intercompany Prices* (1992); Reuven S. Avi-Yonah, *The Rise and Fall of Arm's Length: A Study in the Evolution of US International Taxation*, 15(1) Va. Tax Rev. 89 (1995); Michael C. Durst, *The President's International Tax Proposals in Historical and Economic Perspective*, 54 Tax Notes Int'l 747 (2009); Jerome R. Hellerstein, *Federal Income Taxation of Multinationals: Replacement of Separate Accounting With Formulary Apportionment*, 60 Tax Notes 1131 (1993); Louis M. Kauder, *Intercompany Pricing and Section 482: A Proposal to Shift From Uncontrolled Comparables to Formulary Apportionment Now*, 58 Tax Notes 485 (1993); Stanley I. Langbein, *The Unitary Method and the Myth of Arm's Length*, 30 Tax Notes 625 (1986); Stanley I. Langbein, *A Modified Fractional Apportionment Proposal for Tax Transfer Pricing*, 54 Tax Notes 719 (1992); Brian Lebowitz, *Profit Sharing as a New World Order in International Taxation*, 52 Tax Notes Int'l 585 (2008); Sol Picciotto, *Problems of Transfer Pricing and Possibilities for Simplification* 14-16 (International Centre for Tax and Development Working Paper No. 86, 2018); Dale W. Wickham & Charles J. Kerester, *New Directions Needed for Solution of the International Transfer Pricing Tax Puzzle: Internationally Agreed Rules or Tax Warfare?*, 56 Tax Notes 339 (1992). However, for a generally positive assessment of the arm's length approach, see Jefferson VanderWolk, *The Arm's-Length Standard Enters Its Second Century*, 93 Tax Notes Int'l 962 (2019).

6. *See* Reuven S. Avi-Yonah & Ilan Benshalom, *Formulary Apportionment – Myths and Prospects: Promoting Better International Tax Policies by Utilizing the Misunderstood and Under-Theorized Formulary Alternative*, 3(3)World Tax J. 371, 376-377 (2011); Yariv Brauner, *Value in the Eye of the Beholder: The Valuation of Intangibles for Transfer Pricing Purposes*, 28(1) Va. Tax Rev. 79, 169 (2008); Michael C. Durst, *Congress: Fix Transfer Pricing and Protect US Competitiveness*, 128 Tax Notes 401, 402-403 (2010); Lebowitz, *supra* n. 5, at 587-588; Lee A. Sheppard, *The Twilight of the International Consensus*, 141 Tax Notes 7, 12 (2013) ('[T]he United States cuts deals with multinationals approving their transfer prices. These deals, called advance pricing agreements, are an admission that transfer pricing cannot be enforced'); *see also* Richard T. Ainsworth & Andrew B. Shact, *Transfer Pricing: Data Dumps and Comparability – Studies from the US, UK, Canada, and Australia*, 65 Tax Notes Int'l 299 (2012).
7. *See* Avi-Yonah & Benshalom, *Formulary Apportionment – Myths and Prospects*, *supra* n. 6, at 377, 379; Durst, *Fix Transfer Pricing*, *supra* n. 6, at 403; Charles I. Kingson, *Can a Piece of Paper Earn Billions?*, 71 Tax Notes Int'l 243-244 (2013). Stated differently, there are substantial information and professional resource asymmetries between the government and taxpayers with respect to transfer pricing issues. *See* Ilan Benshalom, *Sourcing the 'Unsourceable': The Cost Sharing Regulations and the Sourcing of Affiliated Intangible-Related Transactions*, 26(3) Va. Tax Rev. 631, 647 (2007).
8. *See* GAO, *IRS Could Better Protect US Tax Interests*, *supra* n. 5, at 44-45, 52-53; Charles H. Gustafson, Robert J. Peroni & Richard Crawford Pugh, *Taxation of International Transactions:*

(4) The arm's length approach does not adequately recognize that MNEs have internal efficiencies that cannot be reproduced by independent parties dealing at arm's length.[9]
(5) The arm's length approach relies materially on comparable transaction data that may be unavailable because the data belongs to competitors or relates to materially different intangibles.[10]
(6) The arm's length approach has not prevented taxpayers from shifting substantial amounts of profits out of high-tax countries.[11]

Critics argue that these deficiencies create significant systemic costs that can be eliminated from an international income tax system by replacing the source/income attribution and transfer pricing rules of the arm's length approach with a global formulary system that uses a mathematical, factor-based formula, to allocate the aggregate worldwide income of an MNE among the various countries in which the MNE carries on activities. Some of these critics of the arm's length method harbour the additional hope that the nations of the world (or at least the major economic powers) will agree to jointly employ a uniform allocation formula that will apportion the worldwide business income tax base among themselves in a way that they all find acceptable and that avoids both double taxation and partial or full non-taxation.[12]

Materials, Text and Problems 718 n. 1 (4th ed., West 2011); Avi-Yonah & Benshalom, *Formulary Apportionment – Myths and Prospects*, *supra* n. 6, at 377; Picciotto, *supra* n. 5, at 15; Roin, *supra* n. 5, at 183-184.

9. *See* Avi-Yonah & Benshalom, *Formulary Apportionment – Myths and Prospects*, *supra* n. 6, at 378-379; Avi-Yonah, Clausing & Durst, *Allocating Business Profits for Tax Purposes*, *supra* n. 1, at 501; Ilan Benshalom, *Rethinking the Source of the Arm's-Length Transfer Pricing Problem*, 32(3) Va. Tax Rev. 425, 431 (2013); Brauner, *supra* n. 6, at 168-169; Langbein, *The Unitary Method and the Myth of Arm's Length*, *supra* n. 5; Susan C. Morse, *Revisiting Global Formulary Apportionment*, 29(4) Va. Tax Rev. 593, 598-599 (2010); Picciotto, *supra* n. 5, at 15; Roin, *supra* n. 5, at 185; H. David Rosenbloom, *Angels on a Pin: Arm's Length in the World*, 38 Tax Notes Int'l 523, 526 (2005); Lee A. Sheppard, *Is Transfer Pricing Worth Salvaging?*, 136 Tax Notes 467, 471 (2012).
10. *See* Staff of the Joint Committee on Taxation, *Present Law and Background Related to Possible Income Shifting and Transfer Pricing* 110 (JCX-37-10, 2010); Avi-Yonah & Benshalom, *Formulary Apportionment – Myths and Prospects*, *supra* n. 6, at 377; Avi-Yonah, Clausing & Durst, *Allocating Business Profits for Tax Purposes*, *supra* n. 1, at 500; Brauner, *supra* n. 6, at 169; Edward D. Kleinbard, *Stateless Income*, 11(9) Fla. Tax Rev. 699, 734 (2011); Lebowitz, *supra* n. 5, at 587; Roin, *supra* n. 5, at 183; Rosenbloom, *supra* n. 9, at 525. In certain cases, the arm's length standard permits use of internal methods of allocation that do not rely on third-party comparable data. *See, e.g.*, *Altera Corporation v. Comm'r*, 2019-1 USTC (CCH) ¶ 50,231, at 83,553 (9th Cir. 2019).
11. *See* Kimberly A. Clausing, *Profit Shifting Before and After the Tax Cuts and Jobs Act* (2018), https://ssrn.com/abstract=3274827; Kimberly A. Clausing, *Competitiveness, Tax Base Erosion, and the Essential Dilemma of Corporate Tax Reform*, 2016(6) BYU L. Rev. 1649, 1665-1671 (2016); Picciotto, *supra* n. 5, at 15.
12. *See, e.g.*, Avi-Yonah, Clausing & Durst, *Allocating Business Profits for Tax Purposes*, *supra* n. 1, at 507-515; Bravenec, *supra* n. 5, at 848-850; Faccio & Fitzgerald, *supra* n. 1, at 70-71; Sheppard, *Is Transfer Pricing Worth Salvaging?*, *supra* n. 9, at 472.

In our view, this hope was dashed in 1648 when the Peace of Westphalia gave rise to today's sovereign nation states[13] that recognize few external restraints on their unilateral taxing powers and that mostly prefer it to remain that way.[14] The United Kingdom and Australian-diverted profits taxes;[15] proposals by the Czech Republic, France, the United Kingdom, and Spain to unilaterally enact a tax on digital services or transactions;[16] the unilateral approach taken by the United States in enacting the Foreign Account Tax Compliance Act (FATCA),[17] the Foreign-Derived Intangible Income (FDII),[18] and the Base Erosion and Anti-Abuse Tax (BEAT)[19] regimes; and the painfully slow progress of European Union countries towards adopting a common consolidated corporate tax base (CCCTB),[20] even though the EU treaties bind those countries to cooperative efforts,[21] all are evidence that the political will to support a uniform, multilateral approach to formulary apportionment will not be forthcoming until a far-distant time, if at all.

If our political economy assessment is correct, tax systems must be designed to anticipate that, absent agreement by treaty, nation states will act unilaterally and not in coordination (or may defect from coordination) when it serves national interests. Accordingly, countries should analyse formulary apportionment as a regime potentially tailored to each country's differing circumstances, rather than a regime adopted by a large number of cooperating countries who all follow the same apportionment rules and ancillary provisions. From that standpoint, the question is not whether formulary apportionment in a multilateral, cooperative system would be better than the present combination of the arm's length principle and source or income attribution rules. Instead, the question for each country is whether its present system for taxing international income will be improved by replacing the arm's length principle and the source or income attribution rules with a formulary approach that will likely be inconsistent with approaches adopted by trading partners that defect from a consensus.

---

13. *See* Sean D. Murphy, *Principles of International Law* 24 (3rd ed., West 2018).
14. *See generally* Diane M. Ring, *What's at Stake in the Sovereignty Debate?: International Tax and the Nation-State*, 49(1) Va. J. Int'l L. 155 (2008).
15. *See* Arthur J. Cockfield, *Tax Wars: The Battle Over Taxing Global Digital Commerce*, 161 Tax Notes 1331, 1337 (2018).
16. *See* Congressional Research Service, *Digital Services Taxes (DSTs): Policy and Economic Analysis* 7-8 (R45532; 25 February 2019); Cockfield, *supra* n. 15, at 1334-1335; Stephanie Soong Johnston, *Czech Republic Going It Alone with Digital Tax*, 94 Tax Notes Int'l 358 (2019).
17. *See* IRC §§ 1471, 1473-1474.
18. *See* J. Clifton Fleming, Jr., Robert J. Peroni & Stephen E. Shay, *Expanded Worldwide Versus Territorial Taxation After the TCJA*, 161 Tax Notes 1173, 1178 (2018).
19. *See* Jasper L. Cummings, Jr., *Selective Analysis: The BEAT*, 158 Tax Notes 1757 (2018). *But see* Susan C. Morse, *International Cooperation and the 2017 Tax Act*, 128 Yale L.J. F. 362, 374-375, 379-380 (2018) (evaluating potential of the BEAT as a cooperative international tax measure that protects and preserves the corporate income tax).
20. *See* Marie Sapirie, *Hope Springs Eternal for the CCCTB*, 152 Tax Notes 1765 (2016).
21. *See Treaty on European Union* Art. 3.3 ('[The Union] shall promote economic, social and territorial cohesion, and solidarity among Member States').

We recognize that no country has either a pure territorial or pure worldwide system for taxing international income.[22] Nevertheless, the analysis necessary to answer the preceding question will be clearer and simpler if we address the question in terms of those two paradigm approaches. In addition, we will separately evaluate unilateral formulary apportionment when it is limited to allocating one particular type of income – income from intangibles.

§6.02 DOES FORMULARY APPORTIONMENT REQUIRE TERRITORIALITY?

It is well known that the international law right of each country to tax non-residents on income earned within its borders[23] overlaps with the international law right of each country to tax its own residents on their worldwide income.[24] It is equally well known that the network of more than 3,000 bilateral tax treaties that covers most international transactions generally requires residence countries to mitigate the resulting double taxation[25] and that they do so principally in one of two ways. They either employ a worldwide system that taxes both domestic-source and foreign-source income, while allowing a credit for the foreign income tax paid by residents on foreign-source

---

22. *See* Rosanne Altshuler, Stephen E. Shay & Eric Toder, *Lessons the United States Can Learn From Other Countries' Territorial Systems for Taxing Income of Multinational Corporations* 1 (Urban Institute & Brookings Institution Tax Policy Center 2015).
23. *See* Restatement (Third) of the Foreign Relations Law of the United States §§ 411-412 (American Law Institute 1986); Reuven S. Avi-Yonah, *International Tax as International Law: An Analysis of the International Tax Regime* 27 (Cambridge University Press 2007); Ilan Benshalom, *The New Poor at Our Gates: Global Justice Implications for International Trade and Tax Law*, 85(1) N.Y.U. L. Rev. 1, 75 (2010); Allison Christians, *Sovereignty, Taxation and Social Contract*, 18(1) Minn. J. Int'l L. 99, 104, 110-111 (2009); Manal S. Corwin, *Sense and Sensibility: The Policy and Politics of BEPS*, 145 Tax Notes 133, 138 (2014); Jinyan Li, *Improving Inter-nation Equity through Territorial Taxation and Tax Sparing*, in *Globalization and Its Tax Discontents: Tax Policy and International Investments, Essays in Honour of Alex Easson* 117, 120 (Arthur J. Cockfield ed., University of Toronto Press 2010); Wolfgang Schön, *International Tax Coordination for a Second-Best World (Part I)*, 1(1) World Tax J. 67, 67, 72-73 (2009). For normative justifications of this rule, see Roy Rohatgi, *Basic International Taxation* 12 (Kluwer Law International 2002); Stephen E. Shay, J. Clifton Fleming, Jr. & Robert J. Peroni, The David R. Tillinghast Lecture, *'What's Source Got to Do with It?' Source Rules and US International Taxation*, 56(1) Tax L. Rev. 81, 88-106 (2002).
24. *See* Restatement (Third) of the Foreign Relations Law of the United States § 412 (1)(a) (American Law Institute 1986); Avi-Yonah, *International Tax as International Law*, *supra* n. 23, at 22-27; Benshalom, *The New Poor at Our Gates*, *supra* n. 23, at 75; Christians, *supra* n. 23, at 104, 110-111; Corwin, *supra* n. 23, at 138; Schön, *supra* n. 23, at 90-91. For a normative justification for this rule, see Rohatgi, *supra* n. 23, at 12; J. Clifton Fleming, Jr., Robert J. Peroni & Stephen E. Shay, *Fairness in International Taxation: The Ability-to-Pay Case for Taxing Worldwide Income*, 5(4) Fla. Tax Rev. 299 (2001).
25. *See* OECD, *Model Tax Convention*, *supra* n. 4, arts. 23A, 23B (prescribing methods countries may use to eliminate double taxation); United Nations, *Model Double Taxation Convention Between Developed and Developing Countries*, arts. 23A, 23B (2017); Yariv Brauner, *An International Tax Regime in Crystallization*, 56(2) Tax L. Rev. 259, 265-266, 284 (2003).

income,[26] or they utilize a territorial or exemption system that exempts foreign-source active business income from residence country taxation.[27]

A prevalent and logical assumption is that the formulary approach and territoriality are linked.[28] In most instances, formulary apportionment is used to delineate what portion of net income is taxed and what portion is not. This is the approach taken by most US states though that is in part attributable to apparent constitutional limitations on state taxation. It is also used by Canadian provinces.[29] For this reason, adoption of the formulary approach is perceived as rejecting a worldwide system and embracing a territorial regime. Consequently, our earlier work on formulary apportionment focused on the utilization of the formulary approach in a territorial system.[30] But there is no necessary linkage between formulary apportionment and territoriality. Territorial regimes and worldwide regimes both require a system for distinguishing foreign-source income from domestic-source income. The distinction is necessary for a territorial system so that the foreign-source income that qualifies for exemption can be identified. And, the same distinction is required in a worldwide system so that the credit for payments of foreign income taxes can be limited to foreign taxes imposed on foreign-source income. At the present time, the nations of the world generally use the arm's length method, together with source or income attribution rules, to make this distinction regardless of whether a country's international income tax regime is territorial or worldwide. Clearly, a formulary system could replace the arm's length *cum* source/income attribution rules approach in a worldwide regime as readily as it could in a territorial system.[31] The difference would be that in a worldwide regime, the primary function of the formulary approach would be limited to identifying foreign-source income that would be involved in the foreign tax credit computation,[32] whereas in a territorial system, the purpose of the formulary approach would be to identify exempt income. Accordingly, adoption of the formulary approach does not require a

26. *See* Gustafson, Peroni & Pugh, *Taxation of International Transactions*, *supra* n. 8, at 23. A country can tax its residents on their worldwide incomes without a credit for foreign taxes and, instead, allow its residents to treat foreign tax payments as deductible expenses in calculating their residence country tax liability. This approach is largely ineffective in alleviating international double taxation and is little used. *See* Staff of the Joint Committee on Taxation, *The Impact of International Tax Reform: Background and Selected Issues Relating to US International Tax Rules and the Competitiveness of US Business* 60 (JCX-22-06, 2006); Gustafson, Peroni & Pugh, *Taxation of International Transactions*, *supra* n. 8, at 23-24.
27. *See* Congressional Budget Office, *Options for Taxing US Multinational Corporations* 3 (Pub. No. 4150, 2013); J. Clifton Fleming, Jr., Robert J. Peroni & Stephen E. Shay, *Formulary Apportionment in the US International Income Tax System: Putting Lipstick on a Pig?*, 36(1) Mich. J. Int'l L. 1, 16-18 (2014).
28. *See, e.g.*, Congressional Budget Office, *Options for Taxing US Multinational Corporations*, *supra* n. 27, at 22; Avi-Yonah, Clausing & Durst, *Allocating Business Profits for Tax Purposes*, *supra* n. 1, at 508; Bravenec, *supra* n. 5, at 849; Edward D. Kleinbard, *The Lessons of Stateless Income*, 65(1) Tax L. Rev. 99, 149 (2011).
29. *See* Brian J. Arnold, *International Tax Primer* 112 (4th ed., Wolters Kluwer 2019).
30. *See* Fleming, Peroni & Shay, *Formulary Apportionment in the US International Income Tax System*, *supra* n. 27.
31. *See* Robert J. Peroni, *Back to the Future: A Path to Progressive Reform of the US International Income Tax Rules*, 51(4) U. Miami L. Rev. 975, 1002-1003 n. 78 (1997).
32. *See ibid.*

territorial system and the formulary approach can be inserted into a worldwide system with no greater, or less, difficulty than within a territorial regime.

The significance of these observations is that answering the question of whether adoption of formulary apportionment would be better than the status quo seems to require specification of the context. Would the proposed adoption involve inserting the formulary apportionment approach into a territorial regime or into a worldwide system?

§6.03 UNILATERAL FORMULARY APPORTIONMENT IN A TERRITORIAL SYSTEM

In earlier work, we made an extensive examination of the problematic consequences produced by a territorial system that uses formulary apportionment.[33] This chapter, however, has a narrower focus – the specific issues arising from unilateral action. We recommend that researchers go to the earlier work if they have broader interests.

A country with a territorial system that employs the arm's length principle with source or income attribution rules and that exempts business income earned by its residents in low-tax foreign countries effectively gives those residents an incentive to shift both business operations and profits to low-tax countries. This is because the residence country exemption permits avoidance of the higher residence country tax and makes the lesser foreign tax the only relevant levy. If the country in question replaces its arm's length and source/income attribution rules system by unilaterally adopting formulary apportionment, the operations-shifting and the profit-shifting incentives of territoriality might be increased if more income is allocated abroad to the source country (and decreased if more income is allocated to the residence country). To understand why, consider the facts of Example 1 above, involving an MNE consisting of Parentco, a Country A corporation, and Subco, its wholly owned Country B subsidiary. Parentco makes electronic widgets in Country A and sells them to Subco for resale to customers in Country B. The original formulary systems employed by US states used an equally weighted, three-factor formula (assets, payroll, and sales) that would apply to the Parentco-Subco MNE as follows.

$$\frac{\text{Country A assets of Parentco and Subco}}{\text{Total worldwide assets of Parentco and Subco}} \times \text{Worldwide profits of Parentco and Subco} = \text{Worldwide profits allocated to Country A per assets factor}$$

$$\frac{\text{Country A payroll of Parentco and Subco}}{\text{Total worldwide payroll of Parentco and Subco}} \times \text{Worldwide profits of Parentco and Subco} = \text{Worldwide profits allocated to Country A per payroll factor}$$

33. *See* Fleming, Peroni & Shay, *Formulary Apportionment in the US International Income Tax System*, *supra* n. 27.

$$\frac{\text{Country A sales of Parentco and Subco}}{\text{Total worldwide sales of Parentco and Subco}} \times \text{Worldwide profits of Parentco and Subco} = \text{Worldwide profits allocated to Country A per sales factor}$$

The sum of the items in the worldwide profits allocation column, divided by three, is the equally weighted average of the individual allocations derived with respect to each of the three factors. More importantly, it is the portion of worldwide Parentco-Subco profits allocable to Country A under the three-factor formula. The remaining profits of the Parentco-Subco MNE are allocable to Country B. The two-thirds weight given to the production factors (assets and payroll) in this three-factor formula likely would increase the inherent bias of Country A's territorial system in favour of locating the new factory in Country B if Country B is a low-tax location.[34]

Over time some jurisdictions have given,[35] and some commentators have suggested giving,[36] greater weight to one or two of the original three allocation factors. The effects of these variations on the formulary apportionment theme in a territorial system can be illustrated by Example 2, which is a variation of Example 1.

Example 2

Parentco, a Country A corporate resident with no foreign affiliates, manufactures electronic widgets in Country A for sale in Country A. Parentco is presently deciding between building a new Country A factory to expand its Country A sales or building a Country B factory to expand its sales into Country B, which has a lower corporate tax rate than Country A. Country A employs a unilateral formulary apportionment system in a territorial regime but has decided to modify the equal factor weights of standard formulary apportionment.

To the extent that the modified formula weights either or both of the production factors (assets and payroll) more heavily than sales, the incentive to build the new factory in Country B is increased. Conversely, if the modified formula weights sales more heavily than the production factors, the incentive to build the new factory in Country B will be lessened (and totally eliminated if the formula relies exclusively on sales), but there will be a strong incentive to shift profits to low-tax Country B by expanding sales in that market (or trying to route sales through that market if formal sales dictate routing results for tax purposes), instead of in Country A.

34. *See* John Mutti & Eric Ohrn, *Taxes and the Location of US Business Activity Abroad*, 72(1) Nat'l Tax J. 165, 186 (2019) ('[o]ur estimates confirm that taxes have a significant effect on the location of affiliate capital, employment, employee compensation, and assets . . . Alternatively stated, MNEs cannot so easily shift profits to avoid taxation that taxes have become irrelevant in the location of real activity').

35. *See* Jerome R. Hellerstein, Walter Hellerstein & John A. Swain, *State Taxation* 8-64 to 8-67 (3rd ed., Thomson Reuters 2019 rev.); Kimberly A. Clausing, *The US State Experience Under Formulary Apportionment: Are There Lessons for International Reform?*, 69(2) Nat'l Tax J. 353, 381 (2016).

36. *See* Avi-Yonah, Clausing & Durst, *Allocating Business Profits for Tax Purposes*, *supra* n. 1, at 508-509; Michael J. Graetz & Rachael Doud, *Technological Innovation, International Competition, and the Challenges of International Income Taxation*, 113(2) Colum. L. Rev. 347, 418-419 (2013); Morse, *supra* n. 9, at 603-606.

The necessary analysis does not end with Example 2, however, because consideration must also be given to the effects of double taxation and double non-taxation. This issue arises because a country that unilaterally adopts formulary apportionment will likely find that its formula will not mesh with the systems of trading partners and that there will be incentive consequences. Thus, assume that in Example 2, Country B employs a territorial regime with either a formulary system or an arm's length system that uses source or income attribution rules. If this regime allocates to Country B a smaller portion of the Country B sales profits than are allocated to Country B by Country A's formulary system, the allocation difference will not be taxed by either country.[37] Foreign-source income that is not taxed by either the residence country or the foreign-source country receives an obvious preference that encourages residents to forgo domestic activities and investments in favour of activities and investments in the foreign country. Thus, Country A has a legitimate interest in preventing this result.

Some US states address the double non-taxation issue with a so-called throw-back rule. Under this approach, income from sales of goods out of State A that is allocated by State A's formula to State B, but not taxed by State B, would be reallocated to State A.[38] The US throw-back rule generally would not apply where State B's non-taxation was a discretionary decision made in pursuit of some policy or economic goal, but a concept of equitable apportionment may be used to cover cases where the general rule does not yield appropriate results. Thus, the throw-back approach, as employed in the United States, may have to be modified in the international context so that it clearly reached the situation where Country B's non-taxation was a discretionary tax competition measure. Moreover, the throw-back approach would have to be further modified to apply where Country B's tax rate was greater than zero but, nevertheless, sufficiently low to distort decisions by Country A residents in choosing between Country A and Country B business and investment locations. In other words, in the international sphere, the throw-back approach would need to function as a minimum tax requirement. Income allocated by Country A's formula to Country B and taxed by the latter at a rate greater than zero, but nevertheless 'too low', would be reallocated to Country A's tax base. Country A should, however, allow a credit for any tax charged on the reallocated income by Country B. This credit would cut against the alleged 'simplicity' of formulary apportionment but seems unavoidable from the standpoint of adopting sound international tax policy.

Returning to Example 2, if lack of coordination between Country A's formulary system and Country B's regime results in a portion of Parentco's Country B sales profits being taxed by both countries,[39] this double taxation will somewhat mitigate the bias

37. Assume, for example, that the MNE consisting of Parentco and its wholly owned Country B subsidiary, Subco, earns USD 1 million in profits from Country B sales, that Country A's formula allocates USD 400,000 of these profits to Country A, that Country B's formula likewise allocates USD 400,000 of these profits to Country B, and that both countries use a territorial regime. On these facts, USD 200,000 of the USD 1 million of profits will not be taxed in either Country A or Country B.
38. *See* Hellerstein, Hellerstein & Swain, *State Taxation, supra* n. 35, at 9-258 to 9-260.
39. Change the hypothetical in n. 37, *supra*, to assume that Country A's formula allocates $600,000 of profits to Country A and Country B's formula allocates $600,000 of profits to Country B. Now $200,000 of the $1 million in profits will be taxed by both countries.

inherent in Country A's territorial system for shifting profits to low-tax Country B. However, the extent of the mitigation will be contingent on the amount of double taxation, and, thus, neutralization of the profit-shifting bias may be under- or over-accomplished. To the extent that a measure of double taxation exists after the location bias has been neutralized, a barrier to trade and investment will exist between Countries A and B. This suggests the need for a foreign tax credit. As Parentco's residence country, Country A would under current practice ordinarily have the obligation of granting the credit but the conflict between the allocation and sourcing rules of the two countries may result in an inadequate credit.[40] A bilateral agreement between Countries A and B will likely be necessary to achieve a more complete solution.

The distortive effects outlined above suggest that a territorial country that is considering unilateral adoption of formulary apportionment must do a careful cost-benefit analysis. The focus of the analysis should be on the degree to which unilateral adoption is likely to: (1) increase or decrease tax-induced distortions regarding the location of real business and investment activities; (2) increase or decrease tax-induced profit-shifting; (3) create a simpler or more complex system; (4) increase or decrease administrative and compliance difficulties; and (5) increase or decrease revenue yield.[41] Moreover, this analysis should take into consideration the fact that formulary apportionment in a cross-border context requires worldwide consolidation of the income of all units of an MNE (or all the units comprising a unitary business) and that these incomes may have been calculated under different timing and base-defining

40. The formulary apportionment experience of the US states does not provide useful guidance for resolving this international double taxation issue. This is because the Commerce Clause of the US Constitution imposes the relevant limits on the power of US states to tax interstate and foreign commerce and the US Supreme Court has created a body of Commerce Clause case law that dictates the extent to which the states can engage in double taxation. *See* Hellerstein, Hellerstein & Swain, *State Taxation, supra* n. 35, at 4-54, 8-13 to 8-16. There is no analogue to this case law in the international tax sphere. The potential for allocation of income to a market country under the Unified Framework proposed by the OECD Secretariat to the G20/OECD Inclusive Framework would raise a similar issue. *See* OECD, *Secretariat Proposal for a 'Unified Approach' under Pillar One*, OECD/G20 Base Erosion and Profit Shifting Project (OECD Publishing, Oct. 2019). The proposal does not specify from which countries profits allocated to the market country derive nor how double taxation would be relieved.

41. *See generally* Harry Grubert & Rosanne Altshuler, *Fixing the System: An Analysis of Alternative Proposals for the Reform of International Tax*, 66(3) Nat'l Tax J. 671, 682 (2013). Our suggested approach to cost-benefit analysis does not make direct use of the observation by economists that formulary apportionment effectively imposes a tax on factors included in the apportionment formula (and ultimately on individuals who might bear the incidence of that tax). *See* Kimberly A. Clausing & Reuven S. Avi-Yonah, *Reforming Corporate Taxation in a Global Economy: A Proposal To Adopt Formulary Apportionment* 12 (The Hamilton Project June 2007); Charles E. McLure, Jr., *The State Corporate Income Tax: Lambs in Wolves' Clothing*, in *The Economics of Taxation* 327 (Henry J. Aaron & Michael J. Boskin eds., Brookings Institution 1980); Martin A. Sullivan, *Tax Avoidance Under Residual Profit Splits*, 163 Tax Notes 513, 514 (2019). That point is not helpful in isolation. It is illuminating to the extent that it improves our understanding of the extent to which formulary apportionment might increase or decrease behavioural distortions (relating to such factors), render the system more or less administrable, increase or decrease revenue yield, etc.

rules, thus requiring that they be normalized.[42] This approach to cost-benefit analysis will allow policymakers to determine whether the gains from avoiding the systemic costs of the arm's length approach by moving to a formulary system are greater than the inefficiency costs arising from the formulary regime's locational and profit-shifting distortions plus the costs of transitioning to a new legal order.[43]

We recognize that international income tax systems that employ the arm's length principle with source or income attribution rules may also fail to mesh with each other and that the incongruities may create undesirable location-shifting and profit-shifting incentives as well as distortive double non-taxation and double taxation problems. Countries address these issues to some extent through bilateral treaty negotiations and the problems discussed above can also be addressed in this way. However, this point highlights another significant cost of unilateral adoption of formulary apportionment – the need for the adopting country to revisit and revise its bilateral income tax treaty network.

To be specific, unilateral adoption of a formulary system would create at least two serious treaty issues. First, the bilateral treaties of an adopting country will almost certainly include Article 9 of the OECD Model, which requires treaty partners to deal with transfer pricing by using the arm's length approach and limits the obligation to provide a corresponding adjustment to a treaty partner's adjustment to arm's length allocations of income or deductions.[44] Thus, an adopting country would, at a minimum, have to renegotiate Article 9 with each of its treaty partners to achieve coordination between the formulary approach of the adopting country and the arm's length approach of the partner. How this could be done is not clear. Moreover, renegotiating Article 9 would likely give the partner country an opening to demand renegotiation of other parts of the treaty.

---

42. This analysis should not include a debate over the relative merits of capital export neutrality, capital import neutrality, and capital ownership neutrality and an examination of the degree to which unilaterally adopted formulary apportionment is consistent, or inconsistent, with any of these three norms. We agree with commentators who have argued that these neutrality norms are not very helpful in resolving difficult policy questions. *See* IMF, *Spillovers in International Corporate Taxation* 72-73 (IMF Policy Paper, 9 May 2014) (stating that capital export neutrality and other neutrality standards 'provide only limited guidance . . . and indeed are rarely invoked in policy discussions'); Grubert & Altshuler, *supra* n. 41, at 674 ('[T]he usual evaluation of reforms relative to these norms is not very helpful because each proposed standard is based on very special assumptions. Furthermore, none of the standards address the most important issues in designing an international income tax system…'). We have registered our agreement with this observation for sometime. *See, e.g.*, J. Clifton Fleming, Jr., Robert J. Peroni & Stephen E. Shay, *Two Cheers for the Foreign Tax Credit, Even in the BEPS Era*, 91(1) Tul. L. Rev. 1, 10-16 (2016); Fleming, Peroni & Shay, *Formulary Apportionment in the US International Income Tax System*, *supra* n. 27, at 7-8; J. Clifton Fleming, Jr., Robert J. Peroni & Stephen E. Shay, *Perspectives on the Worldwide vs. Territorial Taxation Debate*, 125 Tax Notes 1079, 1083-1091 (2009).
43. For an econometric analysis of the benefits of formulary apportionment relative to the then-current US international tax system, see Rosanne Altshuler & Harry Grubert, *Formulary Apportionment: Is It Better Than the Current System and Are There Better Alternatives?*, 63(4) Nat'l Tax J. 1145 (2010). The authors concluded that the then-current US international tax system caused fewer capital distortions than formulary apportionment under capital-based formulas.
44. *See* OECD Model Tax Convention, *supra* n. 4, Arts. 9(1), 9(2).

The second and narrower problem created by unilateral adoption of formulary apportionment arises under the mutual agreement procedure specified in Article 25 of the OECD Model.[45] Where both partner countries use the arm's length approach, they can use Article 25 to negotiate a resolution of inconsistent transfer pricing positions by referring to principles accepted by both. However, it is not clear whether this process can be made to work where one partner's position is based on the location of factors of production and the weights assigned thereto (formulary apportionment) and the other partner's position is based on an assessment of prices that would be charged by independent parties (arm's length). Successful resolution of this conundrum is an uncertain matter.[46]

§6.04 UNILATERAL FORMULARY APPORTIONMENT IN A WORLDWIDE SYSTEM

In earlier work,[47] we have explained how a worldwide system that taxes residents on both domestic-source and foreign-source income, with a credit for foreign tax payments on foreign-source income, mimics territoriality if the system allows both deferral of residence country tax until repatriation[48] and cross-crediting with inappropriate source/income attribution and foreign tax credit limitation rules.[49] If this were the baseline, the discussion in §6.03 would be fully applicable to the insertion of a formulary system into a worldwide regime that permits deferral and cross-crediting.

However, deferral and cross-crediting are not necessary elements of a properly designed worldwide system. Previously, we have explained how deferral can, and should, be eliminated from worldwide systems through immediate imposition of residence country tax[50] and how cross-crediting can, and should, be very substantially curtailed by employing a per-country limitation on the foreign tax credit.[51] In earlier

45. *Ibid.*, Art 25.
46. *See generally* William J. Wilkins & Kenneth W. Gideon, *Memorandum to Congress: You Wouldn't Like Worldwide Formula Apportionment*, 135 Tax Notes 1351, 1352-1353 (2012).
47. *See* J. Clifton Fleming, Jr., Robert J. Peroni & Stephen E. Shay, *Worse than Exemption*, 59(1) Emory L.J. 79, 96-104 (2009).
48. Deferral is a feature of most worldwide systems that allows residence country taxation of a foreign subsidiary corporation's income to be deferred until the income is repatriated to the residence country. *See* Gustafson, Peroni & Pugh, *Taxation of International Transactions*, *supra* n. 8, at 24-26.
49. Cross-crediting in a worldwide system occurs when the portion of a high-tax foreign country's tax that exceeds a residence country's foreign tax credit limitation is allowed to be credited against the tax that the residence country would otherwise collect on income earned in a different foreign country that imposes a lower tax rate than the residence country. *See ibid.*, 409-410.
50. *See, e.g.*, Robert J. Peroni, J. Clifton Fleming, Jr. & Stephen E. Shay, *Getting Serious About Curtailing Deferral of US Tax on Foreign Source Income*, 52(2) SMU L. Rev. 455 (1999); Peroni, *Back to the Future*, *supra* n. 31, at 986-994.
51. *See, e.g.*, Robert J. Peroni, J. Clifton Fleming, Jr. & Stephen E. Shay, *Reform and Simplification of the US Foreign Tax Credit Rules*, 101 Tax Notes 103 (2003); Peroni, *Back to the Future*, *supra* n. 31, at 995-996.

work, we have called this approach 'real worldwide taxation'[52] but most recently we have referred to it as 'expanded worldwide taxation'.[53]

Because expanded worldwide taxation imposes an immediate residence country tax on foreign-source income earned in low-tax countries and because a per-country foreign tax credit limitation significantly prevents that tax from being curtailed or eliminated by claiming excess foreign tax credits on income earned in high-tax foreign countries, the incentive for residents to shift business operations and profits to low-tax foreign countries is largely eliminated. More importantly for purposes of this chapter, there is no point in residents shifting profits to low-tax countries by using non-market prices for sales of goods and non-market-rate payments for interest, royalties, and services. Under expanded worldwide taxation, the shift is ineffective because there is an immediate residence country tax on the affected income items. Thus, there is far less need to have rules that police income shifting to low-tax foreign countries and the contest between the arm's length *cum* source/income attribution rules approach and the formulary approach is irrelevant to this issue.

Of course, income earned by residents in foreign countries would still have to be characterized as foreign-source or domestic-source for purposes of applying the foreign tax credit limitation. As noted in §6.02, either an arm's length system with source or income attribution rules or a formulary system can be used for this purpose. The differences described in §6.03 between income allocations under arm's length and formulary approaches also would apply in an expanded worldwide system with an analogous risk of double non-taxation and double taxation. There is a potential additional treaty issue for a country employing a credit version of Article 23.[54] If the treaty article follows US practice and expands its credit limitation to include income that is permitted to be taxed under the treaty by the source country, there would need to be agreement on whether to retain, or how to modify, this rule in cases of inconsistent income allocation. This would have to be included as one of the issues to be addressed in a treaty renegotiation to harmonize the two approaches for purposes of applying the treaty.

Since no country presently has an expanded worldwide system and virtually all countries use the arm's length approach with source/income attribution rules, adoption of an expanded worldwide system would realistically involve moving from a conventional worldwide regime with arm's length and source/income attribution rules or from a territorial system with arm's length and source or income attribution rules. A country making that move would need to do a cost-benefit calculation regarding the simplification benefits to be gained from the formulary approach versus the cost of transitioning to an unfamiliar formulary regime. But with the rewards for over-characterizing income as foreign-source being greatly constrained by an expanded

52. *See, e.g.*, Fleming, Peroni & Shay, *Formulary Apportionment in the US International Income Tax System*, *supra* n. 27, at 18-19; Fleming, Peroni & Shay, *Two Cheers for the Foreign Tax Credit*, *supra* n. 42, at 6.

53. *See* Fleming, Peroni & Shay, *Expanded Worldwide Versus Territorial Taxation*, *supra* n. 18, at 1174.

54. *See, e.g.*, US Department of the Treasury, *US Model Income Tax Convention*, Art. 23(3) (17 February 2016).

worldwide system, it might be possible to utilize carefully constructed source/income attribution rules without coupling them with either a formulary system or an arm's length system.

Non-residents would not be subject to the extraterritorial effect of a residence country's expanded worldwide system. Thus, adoption of expanded worldwide taxation would not diminish the importance of transfer pricing with respect to domestic-source income earned by non-residents. If the residence country is a comparatively high-tax jurisdiction, there will be an incentive for non-residents to extract profits through deductible payments from residence country subsidiaries for interest, royalties, and services fees that exceed market rates. This suggests a role for transfer pricing rules and indicates that the controversy over arm's length versus formulary apportionment would continue in this area even with an expanded worldwide system. Nevertheless, countries have been policing this area both directly and indirectly with deduction limitations.

Thus, when constructing an expanded worldwide taxation system, a country must make a cost-benefit comparison between regulating this specific area with: (1) an arm's length *cum* source/income attribution rule system or a formulary system, with the chosen approach being backed up by a deduction-limitation regime; or (2) a deduction-limitation regime that is not complemented by either an arm's length system or a formulary system.

§6.05 PROFIT SPLITS AND SIMILAR LIMITED FORMULARY APPROACHES

Even if a country does not adopt formulary apportionment as an overall feature of its international income tax regime, it should consider limited formulary approaches to intangible income transfer price regulation. We believe that when the arm's length approach is properly understood as a way to achieve outcomes that reflect what would occur in transactions between independent parties, an arm's length system can include objective criteria formulas to divide specific types of profits. For example, the United States employs a residual profit split transfer pricing method[55] with respect to intangible income that uses a formulary approach rather than comparable transaction data. There is an expanding acceptance of the role that profit split methods may play under current international tax rules as well as in possible future reworking of income allocations to market countries.[56]

55. *See* Treas. Reg. § 1. 482-6(c)(3); Gustafson, Peroni & Pugh, *Taxation of International Transactions*, *supra* n. 8, at 1046.

56. *See* OECD, *Revised Guidance on the Application of the Transactional Profit Split Method, Inclusive Framework on BEPS: Action 10*, OECD/G20 Base Erosion and Profit Shifting Project (OECD 2018); OECD, *Programme of Work to Develop a Consensus Solution to the Tax Challenges Arising from the Digitalisation of the Economy*, OECD/G20 Inclusive Framework on BEPS 12-15 (31 May 2019) (proposing a modified residual profit split method and fractional apportionment method of income allocation).

§6.06 CONCLUSIONS

The arm's length system with source rules has been vigorously criticized on numerous grounds and formulary apportionment has been advanced as a replacement that will improve international income taxation regimes. Although some formulary advocates hope that replacement can take the form of a uniform, multilateral system agreed upon among the world's economically developed countries, that hope seems unrealistic. Thus, the merits of formulary apportionment as a replacement for the arm's length approach with source rules must be analysed under the assumption that, if replacement occurs, it will happen through unilateral action by independently acting countries.

Discussions of formulary apportionment typically assume that adoption of a formulary system means that the adopting country either already has a territorial system or is moving to one. This assumption is too restrictive. Formulary apportionment can also be used in a worldwide system in order to identify foreign-source income for foreign tax credit purposes. Thus, analysis of the desirability of moving to formulary apportionment must include a consideration of the possible role of formulary apportionment in worldwide systems.

This chapter has shown that unilateral substitution of formulary apportionment in a territorial regime involves transaction costs, locational and profit-shifting incentives, and double non-taxation and double taxation risks. Moreover, simplification gains may not be great. Any territorial country contemplating such a move must do a cost/benefit analysis that fully reflects the realities of its particular situation. There is no rule of thumb that can be used to avoid this difficult analysis.

Substitution of formulary apportionment in a conventional worldwide regime that allows deferral and cross-crediting raises the same issues as substitution in a territorial system. In contrast, if the worldwide system is of the expanded variety that eliminates or very substantially restricts deferral and cross-crediting, transfer pricing issues largely disappear, and so the debate over arm's length with source rules versus formulary apportionment largely becomes relevant only to inbound taxation. Again, rigorous cost-benefit analysis informed by the subject country's particular situation is required before an appropriate choice can be made.

CHAPTER 7

A Framework for Assessing Business Sector Formulary Apportionment

Kerrie Sadiq

§7.01 INTRODUCTION

The adoption of formulary apportionment is viewed as a key potential paradigm shift in the international tax regime. Traditionally international tax policy has followed a deliberate and evolutionary path as is well illustrated by the recent Base Erosion and Profit Shifting (BEPS) reform programme of the Organisation for Economic Co-operation and Development (OECD) and G20. Neither proponents nor supporters of formulary apportionment regard the system as a step only on the traditional path. Proponents of the traditional transfer pricing regime view formulary apportionment as an outlier that threatens to undermine a well-settled regime that has existed for almost a century, while proponents of formulary apportionment generally view such a model as an alternative to the arm's length standard rather than a complementary option. Where there is any suggestion of the two models working together, it is in the form of using formulary apportionment as a model for residual or hard to allocate profit.[1] In this chapter, formulary apportionment is proposed as a complementary parallel approach to the allocation of profits in situations where the traditional arm's length approach fails to provide a satisfactory result. It argues that, while formulary apportionment is ultimately a theoretically superior model, the technical and political

1. Reuven S. Avi-Yonah & Ilan Benshalom, *Formulary Apportionment – Myths and Prospects: Promoting Better International Tax Policies by Utilizing the Misunderstood and Under-Theorized Formulary Alternative*, 3(3) World Tax J. 371 (2011). More recently, the OECD suggested this approach may be used in the digital economy: OECD, *Public Consultation Document: Secretariat Proposal for a 'Unified Approach' under Pillar One, Public Consultation Document, 9 October 2019 – 12 November 2019* (OECD 2019), https://www.oecd.org/tax/beps/public-consultation-document-secretariat-proposal-unified-approach-pillar-one.pdf.

challenges that implementation inevitably entail may currently be too great to overcome in business sectors where an arm's length price has been used to some success. Consequently, a more appropriate approach may be to consider formulary apportionment as a viable alternative for certain business sectors only.

A formulary apportionment approach can potentially provide economic certainty to business sectors which are notoriously difficult to price from a transfer pricing perspective. Business sectors which are unique in nature and can be distinguished from more traditional sectors include financial institutions, the extractives industry, and e-commerce businesses. The unique features of these business sectors can be divided into two core categories: the unique nature of the services and consequent products supplied, and the non-traditional organizational structure adopted. It is these unique features which also result in difficulties applying the traditional transfer pricing regime.

Formulary apportionment is currently used to allocate business profits for subnational business income taxes in the United States and Canada and for the subnational allocation of a portion of national tax revenues in Switzerland and a trade tax in Germany. Subnational formulary apportionment systems follow a number of different models and are either standardized across business sectors or varied according to different weighted factors or a special formula. As noted elsewhere in this volume,[2] the Canadian system is an often-cited example of a standard two-factor formula of payroll and sales, with modifications for the sectors of insurance corporations, banks, trust and loan corporations, railway corporations, airline corporations, grain elevator operations, bus and truck operators, ship operators, and pipeline operators. Those modifications range from altering the weighting of the factors to special definitions for factor determination with the approach demonstrating the potential need to take into account industry-specific dynamics.

The adoption of a complementary parallel approach to the arm's length system would not be without its challenges. In particular, challenges around the taxable unit, nexus, tax base, and appropriate formula are compounded when an industry-specific approach is considered. This chapter looks at how those challenges may be addressed and what such an approach could look like. It ultimately proposes that a practical transition to formulary apportionment could be achieved via industry-specific adoption and the two models of arm's length pricing and formulary apportionment could work in tandem, with traditional business sectors continuing to use the traditional methods, and more modern and/or difficult-to-price business sectors, such as e-commerce, using an industry-specific formulary apportionment method. Ultimately, the chapter argues that formulary apportionment on an industry basis is a viable approach to industries where technical and political challenges in the current regime are becoming too great.

The chapter is set out as follows. Section 7.02 considers a possible framework for assessing the viability of an industry-specific approach to the adoption of formulary apportionment. It does so by noting the challenges of defining the taxable unit, determining jurisdiction to tax, ascertaining the tax base, and considerations around an

2. *See further* Michael Smart & François Vaillancourt, *Formulary Apportionment in Canada and Taxation of Corporate Income in 2019: Current Practice, Origins and Evaluation* (this volume).

appropriate formula. Sections 7.03 to 7.06 then investigate in depth these issues that would need to be considered in each of the steps of the proposed framework. They do so from a theoretical as well as pragmatic perspective. Further, where relevant, two particular business types are discussed as potential specific industries where formulary apportionment may be a viable alternative: e-commerce and the extractives industry. First, the e-commerce industry is discussed on the basis that it is a 'new' type of international business and therefore the traditional system fails in many respects to deal with its distinct features. The second industry analysed is the extractives industry which, while dating back to the beginning of civilization, is one that has historically (and increasingly in recent times) proved difficult to tax when undertaken by MNEs. Section 7.07 concludes.

§7.02 AN OVERVIEW OF A PROPOSED FRAMEWORK

Obstacles facing the introduction of formulary apportionment are many and varied. Perhaps the greatest challenge in determining whether such a model should be adopted, as either a holistic approach or industry-specific solution, is determining the questions that need to be considered and answered and ensuring a logical debate ensues. In an attempt to ensure a value-neutral discussion of any required decisions, judgments, and preferences, this section establishes a decision framework for ascertaining whether formulary apportionment could and should be adopted for a specific industry.

Moving to a formulary apportionment model for specific industries requires a framework to be developed to determine the scope and application of the model. At the outset, a change from the current regime to a formulary apportionment model requires an in-principle agreement, with the technicalities to be dealt with as a secondary issue. By far, the greatest challenge to an in-principle agreement would be resistance due to path dependency by international organizations, particularly the OECD, and regulatory capture by business and the profession. However, given the difficulties various industries face in applying the traditional model, this may be a simpler approach than one which requires a paradigm shift. This is particularly the case where there is a great deal of uncertainty in an industry and where, for example, advance pricing agreements between taxpayers and tax authorities setting out the transfer prices that will be acceptable to the authorities are more common.

The developed framework starts with the overarching question as to whether a particular business sector has related party transactions that are particularly difficult to price from a transfer pricing perspective. Business sectors that are unique in nature and can be distinguished from more traditional business sectors include financial institutions and e-commerce businesses. The unique features of these business sectors can be divided into two core categories: the unique nature of the services and consequent products supplied, and the non-traditional organizational structure adopted. For example, e-commerce provides digital goods and services, often through a two-sided market structure, where the e-commerce business connects or facilitates transactions rather than being the provider of the goods and services. The finance industry takes on a similar role in facilitating borrowing and lending between customers and does so in a highly integrated international business model. Once this overarching question is answered, in-principle agreement can be reached as to whether formulary apportionment offers a viable alternative. At this stage, the taxable unit, jurisdiction to tax, the tax base, and the selection of an appropriate formula all become technical issues then to be resolved.

Those who oppose formulary apportionment generally do so on two grounds, which tend not to be value-neutral but rather grounded in sociopolitical rationales. The first is that international consensus on an acceptable formula would be impossible to achieve. The second is that such a method for allocating profits would reduce neither aggressive tax planning (base erosion and profit shifting) nor tax competition between jurisdictions. Each of these challenges would need to be overcome at the initial stage of justifying a move to formulary apportionment.

As to the first criticism that international consensus could not be reached, it is simply a case of pointing to the current transfer pricing regime which is a fiction that was devised and agreed to after political debate around a system of best practice. Once regulatory capture and path dependency are recognized and accounted for, the process of determining a best practice model for a twenty-first-century tax system is no different, with many arguing that formulary apportionment would prevail. Jurisdictional fear as to the redistributive consequences, that is, allocating profits to one jurisdiction over another, is perhaps a more accurate descriptor of this first hurdle in introducing formulary apportionment. There is no simple answer to the redistributive effects, with economic studies offering conflicting results and second-line effects difficult to take into account. As to the second criticism, a suitable formula takes into account 'real' factors with jurisdictions having to consider the interaction between tax revenue and foreign direct investment.[3] Unlike the current system which takes into account book or paper transactions that allow corporate income to be reduced in a jurisdiction, multinational enterprise (MNE) manipulation of formulary apportionment requires actual movement of the two factors, if used, of labour or property. Each of these criticisms, along with other areas of dispute, are discussed below in the context of the devised framework.

Literature on formulary apportionment highlights four key areas of dispute: (1) whether a move to formulary apportionment can be justified; (2) whether the 'business' can be identified; (3) whether the current 'jurisdiction to tax' rules allow for the suitable allocation to locations where economic activity takes place; and (4) whether a suitable formula can be designed and agreed upon. Seldom, however, are the issues discussed using a framework for assessment. Figure 7.1 is suggested as one possible approach to doing so with the ensuing discussion based on the four key steps.

---

3. Sol Picciotto, *Unitary Alternatives and Formulary Apportionment*, in *Taxing Multinational Enterprises as Unitary Firms* 27, 34 (Sol Picciotto ed., Institute of Development Studies 2017).

Figure 7.1 A Framework for Assessing Business Sector Formula Apportionment

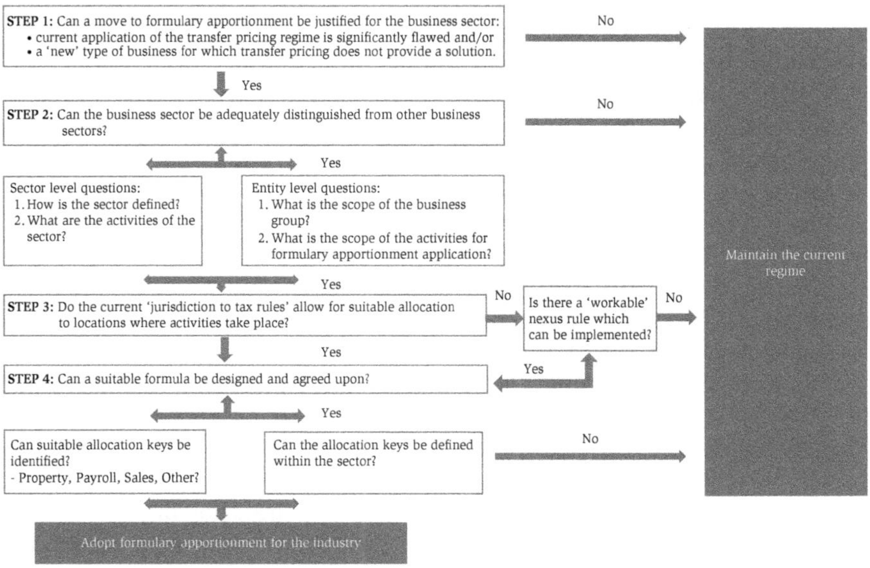

§7.03 STEP 1: JUSTIFICATION FOR A BUSINESS SECTOR FORMULARY APPORTIONMENT APPROACH

A move to a business sector formulary apportionment method for allocating business profits necessarily requires justification of such an approach. This requires an investigation of the current application of the transfer pricing regime to determine whether it is significantly flawed and/or an assessment of the type of business being considered. With respect to the latter, it is necessary to determine whether the business type is a traditional one where transfer pricing is found to be significantly flawed (for example, the extractives industry) or a 'new' type of business (for example, e-commerce). Alternative models beyond transfer pricing and formulary apportionment may also be considered at this stage.

[A] Investigating the Current Model and Alternatives

Alternative models to taxing MNEs and related party transactions are several, including minimum tax schemes such as a minimum tax on outbound investment, inbound investment, or minimum taxes for low-income countries, border adjustment taxes such as a destination-based cash flow tax, and presumptive models such as a flat percentage of gross revenue in a jurisdiction as were used historically for long periods in many countries, such as the Australian States in the late nineteenth and early twentieth century. In addition, models for sharing residual profit have been designed, most notably using a profit split approach which closely resembles on many occasions a formulary apportionment model. A comprehensive discussion of these different approaches is outside the scope of this chapter but should not be dismissed in a broader assessment of options to taxing the profits of MNEs.

Further, many of the alternatives to traditional transfer pricing methodologies recognize the difficulties in addressing profit shifting. However, formulary apportionment is generally ruled out as a viable approach. The OECD/G20 BEPS programme for international reform is perhaps the strongest example of such opposition. While it has made improvements to the transfer pricing regime and the arm's length pricing model, it specifically ruled out a consideration of alternative approaches such as formulary apportionment for two reasons. First, formulary apportionment would require an international consensus on a number of key issues which the OECD believes would not be attainable in the short or medium term. Second, formulary apportionment 'would not be immune from manipulation and could not ensure that profits are truly aligned with value'.[4] A shift to an industry approach would not remove the obstacles to adoption of formulary apportionment. However, these objections may be less valid in particular circumstances. Further, the move towards the profit split method as acceptable for transfer pricing purposes highlights the need for more flexible approaches to difficult-to-price business sectors. The OECD continues to maintain the stance that profit splits must be determined on a case-by-case basis. It has, however, more recently canvassed the possibility of a formula-based approach where there is residual profit. The implementation of an approach which maintains the arm's length principle with a complementary formula-based solution is set out in a recent OECD consultation paper on the taxation of the digital economy.[5] Such an approach, which combines both traditional and formulary apportionment methods, maintains a large element of subjectivity. However, a sectoral approach arguably removes that subjectivity, along with the complexity of combining methods, and provides certainty to notoriously difficult-to-price business sectors.

There are three main advantages of formulary apportionment for specific sectors. First, through a specifically developed formula, many of the incentives to shift income are removed; second, the underlying economic substance of the business is better reflected than under the arm's length standard; and third, certainty and potentially simplicity are provided. These advantages are reflected in the adoption of formulary apportionment for all industries but are particularly highlighted in difficult-to-price sectors and for MNEs in more modern industries due to the even greater difficulties in those cases in applying the traditional model. The first two advantages provide the benefits of an increase in tax revenues globally as transfer price and internal debt financing manipulations are no longer possible. There is also a more equitable allocation of income between jurisdictions based on key factors or allocation keys. The

4. OECD, *BEPS – Frequently Asked Questions*, http://www.oecd.org/ctp/beps-frequentlyaskedquestions.htm.
5. OECD, *Secretariat Proposal for a 'Unified Approach' under Pillar One*, *supra* n. 1.

first benefit stems from the fact that formulary apportionment relies on consolidated global income. This means that internal transactions, their locations, and their prices are no longer relevant as they are ignored in the determination of consolidated global income. It is the consolidated global income that is then allocated to jurisdictions according to a predetermined formula.

The predetermined formula, with its allocation keys, needs to reflect the relevant activities carried out in a taxing jurisdiction. Critics of formulary apportionment argue that the allocation keys can be manipulated by MNEs, but these keys, while potentially mobile, represent real activity. It is at this stage that an industry-specific formula provides significant benefits over a traditional transfer pricing approach as the unique characteristics of that particular industry are recognized and accounted for. Further, where there is an industry with hard to tax transactions, such as e-commerce, a major advantage of formulary apportionment is that all profits of an MNE are allocated to a jurisdiction rendering certain tax avoidance measures ineffective. Allocating income to low- or no-tax countries using paper transactions is meaningless as there will be little or no activity of any substance recognized by the allocation keys and therefore no profits allocated under the formulary apportionment approach.

Despite theoretical and practical advantages to an industry-specific formulary apportionment approach, the challenges to its introduction are significant. There is no doubt that both regulatory capture and path dependency are two significant factors in the maintaining of the current arm's length approach. Regulatory capture stems from those who have significant investment in the current model, most notably the profession, and particularly the 'Big 4' accounting firms which have a significant investment in intellectual capital as well as a fiscal incentive to maintain the status quo. Business and legislators also continue to oppose a move towards formulary apportionment. Path dependency is also apparent with a failure to recognize that the current model is just that: a model that was selected in the 1920s as one way to allocate income and expenses to particular jurisdictions. Traditionally, it has been argued that jurisdictions wish to maintain the arm's length approach, yet this is no longer a valid claim with countries like Brazil, China, and India all moving away from the traditional application of the arm's length system. Further, it is arguable that firms themselves are recognizing the problems associated with the traditional regime and would prefer greater certainty, especially where there are emerging businesses.

[B] Justifying a Sectoral Approach

Perhaps the most significant advantage of adopting an industry-specific approach is the ability to recognize the unique nature of that industry. When looking at national regimes, it is apparent that jurisdictional formulary apportionment models recognize that particular industries have unique products, services, and/or value chains, and for that reason, regimes are often varied according to different weighted factors or a special formula. These options are discussed below.

National regimes which apply specific rules to particular industries do not operate in a vacuum. Rather, the special rules apply as exceptions to the general formulary apportionment principles. However, the proposition of this chapter is that there are certain industries where formulary apportionment should be applied as an exception to the traditional transfer pricing regime. As such, a case needs to be made for any industry where a formulary apportionment model is proposed. The most obvious candidates are traditional industries where transfer pricing is increasingly difficult to apply and 'new' industries where the current rules fail to accurately and adequately function. Where the latter is generally the case, at a minimum the MNEs themselves are faced with uncertainty and jurisdictions have inadequate measures in place to deal with profit shifting. To this extent, prior studies have demonstrated that gains from formulary apportionment as compared to the separate accounting approach are greater where there is higher global profit and in situations where it is easier for an MNE to shift income.[6]

In previous articles, this author has argued for an industry-specific approach for the multinational financial sector on the basis that it is a unique industry for which the current transfer pricing rules fail to accurately allocate income.[7] Other authors have previously recognized that a discussion on the adoption of formulary apportionment requires a consideration of the key issue of identification of the potential anomalies in a standard formulary apportionment approach to the treatment of MNEs in two important sectors: institutions in the financial sector and firms engaged in the exploitation of natural resources.[8] Literature on the difficulties associated with the application of the current model to e-commerce business structures, along with the OECD's work in this area, also reflect many of the unique features of this industry and the difficulties in accurately taxing profits. The rationale for singling out specific industries is twofold. The primary rationale for singling out these sectors is the difficulty in applying the arm's length price methodologies predominantly because of the difficulties in finding comparables and also because of the ease of profit shifting. In any business, the arm's length price relies on certain assumptions in relation to any comparability analysis undertaken and, with certain industries, the need for assumptions becomes so extreme that the outcome is a complete fiction. The second reason these industries are often singled out is the ability to determine a taxable nexus as the

6. *See* Sara L. McGaughey & Pascalis Raimondos, *Shifting MNE Taxation from National to Global Profits: A Radical Reform Long Overdue*, 50(9) J. Int'l Bus. Stud. 1668, 1675 (2019), citing Søren Bo Nielsen, Pascalis Raimondos-Møller & Guttorm Schjelderup, *Company Taxation and Tax Spillovers: Separate Accounting versus Formula Apportionment*, 54(1) Eur. Econ. Rev. 121 (2010). In the latter study, though, the authors conclude that a move to formulary apportionment will not eliminate spillovers and may aggravate them.
7. Kerrie Sadiq, *Unitary Taxation of the Finance Sector*, in *Taxing Multinational Enterprises as Unitary Firms* 119 (Sol Picciotto ed., Institute of Development Studies 2017); Kerrie Sadiq, *The Case For Unitary Taxation With Formulary Apportionment in the Finance Sector and the Effect on Developing Nations*, 44(2) Austl. Tax Rev. 75 (2015); Kerrie Sadiq, *Taxation of Multinational Banks: Using Formulary Apportionment to Reflect Economic Reality (Part 2)*, 23(2) J. Int'l Tax'n 54 (2012); Kerrie Sadiq, *Taxation Of Multinational Banks: Using Formulary Apportionment to Reflect Economic Reality (Part 1)*, 22(5) J. Int'l Tax'n 46 (2011); Kerrie Sadiq, *The Taxation of Multinational Banks: Alternative Apportionment Through a Unitary Taxation Regime Aligning with Economic Reality*, N.Z. J. Tax'n L. & Pol'y 640 (2007).
8. Joe Andrus & Paul Oosterhuis, *Transfer Pricing After BEPS: Where Are We and Where Should We Be Going*, 95 Taxes 89, 96 (2017).

concept of a permanent establishment is one designed on physical presence with profits potentially not being taxed in the location of economic activity. Consequently, some industries may be more suited to formulary apportionment than others.

Two specific industries are ideal case studies to test the suggested framework. First, e-commerce can be considered on the basis that it is a 'new' type of international business model, and therefore the traditional system fails in many respects to deal with its distinct features. The second industry that can be analysed is the extractives industry which, while dating back to the beginning of civilization, is one that historically has been difficult to tax when undertaken by MNEs with the system failing to be reformed in a way to prevent well-known practices of profit shifting such as marketing hubs in low-tax jurisdictions. These two industries may seem to be very different in nature. However, suggesting that they should be considered to be at the extreme ends of a business sector continuum is far from correct. The extractive industry is one in which a jurisdiction's valuable resources are mined and sold globally. Broadly, the digital economy and e-commerce does the same as it mines raw data based on information provided by customers or users in a particular jurisdiction. The similarities do not end there. As the International Monetary Fund (IMF) points out, both the products of the extractive industry and the digital economy 'are excludable, both might be seen as collective national assets, and just as the value of crude oil increases as it is refined and processed, the value of raw data increases as it is refined by algorithms and analytics'.[9] More importantly from a taxing perspective, both products are unique to a particular location[10] raising issues around locational rents and location-specific advantages.

Digitalization of the economy is perhaps the most significant example of the traditional arm's length pricing requirement failing to tax income in the location of the economic activity or where value is created. Base erosion and profit shifting are amplified in the digital economy and the current regime has failed to provide a solution. Two distinct issues are exacerbated. First, the significant use of intangible assets that are highly mobile means that it is relatively easy for MNEs to shift profits via royalty payments. Second, digital businesses do not need a physical presence in a particular jurisdiction rendering the permanent establishment concept inadequate as both a prerequisite for jurisdictional nexus (who taxes) and basis for the source principle (what is taxed). As the IMF explains, 'with the increasing importance and salience of complex, intangible-and technology-heavy business models, these difficulties will only increase'.[11] The digital economy is front and centre of these issues. While Action 1 of the OECD BEPS programme of reform attempts to deal with many of the issues in relation to the digital economy, the outcome is one of essentially maintaining the status quo with unilateral measures being put in place while there is no common or global solution.

An MNE with a digital presence can engage with customers in countries in which it has no physical presence, rendering useless the concepts of both residency and

9. IMF, *Corporate Taxation in the Global Economy* 16 (IMF Policy Paper, March 2019).
10. *Ibid.*
11. *Ibid.*

source, the fundamental pillars of the international tax regime. This engagement with customers also extends beyond the traditional selling of goods and services with customers themselves providing significant value to the MNE in the form of content. The traditional arm's length pricing methodologies provide for a one-sided design model focusing on the local affiliate and its comparable transactions. Such an approach clearly fails to consider this new form a 'value add' resulting from user participation. Recent updates to the OECD's *Transfer Pricing Guidelines* (2017) do attempt to recognize such contributions through the profit split method. However, these business models profit from information gained from customers who are not remunerated directly. This may be through the process of engagement in the platform itself (e.g., Facebook collecting data on 'likes' and 'dislikes' for targeted advertising) or through a social contract whereby the customer provides reviews of goods and services (e.g., TripAdvisor reviews on restaurants and hotels).[12]

The digital economy and e-commerce have flourished not only because of technological advances but also because of the synergies created through an integrated network, thereby achieving economies of scale and global competitiveness.[13] E-commerce is the embodiment of the reason why MNEs exist. They are a single economic unit that decentralizes its operations and functions across jurisdictions in order to access the benefits from a presence in each of the localities.[14] As the OECD explains:

> Developments in ICT (information and communication technology) have thus accelerated and changed the spread of global value chains in which corporate legal structures and individual legal entities become less important and MNE groups move closer to the economist's conception of a single firm operating in a co-ordinated fashion to maximise opportunities in a global economy.[15]

As such, e-commerce can be easily recognized as a broad industry where the traditional transfer pricing regime is inadequate.

Extractive industries such as mining and mineral extraction and the production of oil and gas are generally regarded as traditional businesses with often easily comparable world market benchmark prices available. However, for some time, there has been concern around aggressive tax planning strategies used in the sector resulting in significant base erosion in the source jurisdiction. To this extent, the United Nations, in its *Handbook on Selected Issues for Taxation of the Extractive Industries by Developing Countries*, identifies five separate transfer pricing issues in relation to this market sector. These are:

---

12. While outside the scope of this chapter, it is also relevant that consumers who provide this data have some assurance in the tax system that their contributions are not going untaxed.
13. Paul W. Beamish & John C. Banks, *Equity Joint Ventures and the Theory of the Multinational Enterprise*, 18(2) J. Int'l Bus. Stud. 1 (1987); Elhanan Helpman, *A Simple Theory of International Trade with Multinational Corporations*, 92(3) J. Pol. Econ. 451 (1984); James R. Markusen, *The Boundaries of Multinational Enterprises and the Theory of International Trade*, 9(2) J. Econ. Persp. 169 (1995).
14. Richard Bird, *The Interjurisdictional Allocation of Income*, 3(3) Austl. Tax F. 333 (1986).
15. OECD, *Action 1 – 2015 Final Report: Addressing the Tax Challenges of the Digital Economy*, OECD/G20 Base Erosion and Profit Shifting Project 92 (OECD 2015).

(i) Fragmentation of the supply chain and ability to locate functions in order to allocate profits to:
    i. Marketing / procurement companies or branches; and
    ii. Offshore hedging companies;

(ii) Fragmentation of transactions (i.e., where MNEs enter into convoluted structures involving the inter-positioning of multiple companies, generally in low-tax jurisdictions (splitting out of functions and risks) to divide profits);

(iii) Thin capitalization;

(iv) Intra-group charges (e.g., technical fees and management fees); and

(v) Taxpayers using offshore marketing companies to divide profits, arguing that they are securing demand through customer relationships, 'smart contracting' and high-quality services - all of which are key to placing product in the market and to overall value creation.[16]

On one view, the extractive industry is a traditional business selling generic products for which, in theory, comparables are readily available. It is, however, an industry dominated by a few key players operating in an integrated manner, arguably being able to be classified as an oligopoly in which market prices are tightly controlled.[17] While market prices are available for finished products, data is limited along the supply chain. Sales and marketing hubs are also prominent in the extractive industries with those departments located in low-tax jurisdictions such as Singapore. Mining also has a long production phase with higher risks in the exploration and evaluation stage.[18] Interestingly, inaccurate reporting of volume for tax purposes is also a major issue in this sector,[19] although likely to be relevant in many industries.

Even with in-principle agreement on the adoption of formulary apportionment for particular sectors, technical issues around implementation are significant but not without the possibility of being resolved. A framework that provides guidance as to the technical issues, such as the one advocated for in this chapter, does allow a consideration of the components of such a model and could be applied on a sector-by-sector basis. In particular, a formulary apportionment model requires: (i) a taxable unit; (ii) jurisdiction to tax; (iii) the calculation of the tax base; and (iv) an apportionment formula. These matters would raise different questions for different sectors. Each of these is discussed below in §7.04-§7.06 for Steps 2 to 4.

16. United Nations, *United Nations Handbook on Selected Issues for Taxation of the Extractive Industries by Developing Countries* 219-220 (United Nations 2018).
17. James M. Otto, *Fiscal Decentralization and Mining Taxation* (paper prepared for the World Bank Group Mining Department, March 2001); Nick Mathiason, *Piping Profits* (Publish What You Pay 2011).
18. Philip Daniel, Michael Keen & Charles McPherson, *Introduction*, in *The Taxation of Petroleum and Minerals: Principles, Problems and Practice* 1 (Philip Daniel, Michael Keen & Charles McPherson eds., Routledge 2010).
19. Charles McPherson & Stephen MacSearraigh, *Corruption in the Petroleum Sector*, in *The Many Faces of Corruption: Tracking Vulnerabilities at the Sector Level* 191 (J. Edgardo Campos & Sanjay Pradhan eds., World Bank 2007).

§7.04 STEP 2: THE 'BUSINESS SECTOR'

The first question that needs to be addressed is the business unit to be taxed. That is, the 'group' used to determine consolidated income, to which a formula will be applied, needs to be defined. This leads to four interrelated questions around applying formulary apportionment in an industry-specific context: (1) first, the question of how a particular sector is defined and, within this, what makes it international; (2) second, the question of what falls within the scope of an MNE operating in the relevant sector and the various components of such operations; (3) third, the question of what the unitary business of the sector is; and (4) fourth, the question of which activities of the MNE should be included in the unitary business, in the context of both the different parts of the entity and the different activities undertaken. The first two questions are sector level, while the second two questions are entity-level questions.

The first question is perhaps the most difficult in terms of applying an industry-specific approach as it requires a definition of the industry itself. Some industries, such as the extractive industries, may be more easily defined than others, such as e-commerce. This question is much less a tax-related issue than a pure economic and commercial one. Many industries have regulatory regimes that already provide definitions; for example, financial institutions, extractive industries, and shipping, etc. are all clearly defined within other regulatory regimes. More modern sectors are not as easily defined but can either be determined by reference to current practices or specifically defined within a tax regime by reference to certain objective criteria.

For example, to implement a formulary apportionment approach for a sector broadly described as e-commerce, it is necessary to define what is meant by an 'e-commerce' business. This is likely to be a major hurdle in the design of such a model, as definitions are vague and generally capture any type of business or commercial transaction that involves the transfer of information across the Internet. This can include consumer-based retail sites, music and video sites, exchange of goods, and the provision of services, to name a few. Economic models may be business-to-business, consumer-to-consumer, and anything in between, meaning that defining the sector is difficult as are the activities within the sector. An alternative to defining the broad category of e-commerce is to identify unique industries within the broader grouping, with sector-specific rules applicable to a more narrowly defined set of industries. Such industries could be determined along with business models mentioned above, such as business-to-consumer, consumer-to-consumer, business-to-business, and consumer-to-business. Alternatively, industries could be categorized according to the goods and/or services provided such as, for example, digital products, intermediary services, or physical products.

Once a particular business sector is defined, it is necessary to consider whether the unique aspects of that industry can be segregated from other activities carried on by the entity. Many businesses are multifaceted and provide a range of different products and services that may be outside what is normally considered part of the industry so defined. For example, a traditional retail entity may also provide an online platform for consumers to purchase products, or the same entity may provide financial services to their customers. To work effectively, an industry-specific formulary apportionment approach needs to potentially ensure all relevant activities are captured and not quarantined into the traditional regime. This second question relating to the scope of an industry or market sector generally requires a broad and potentially inclusive definition of what activities the market participants undertake. Further, given the proposal of this chapter that formulary apportionment is suitable for non-traditional MNEs, it is likely that many of the activities which will be undertaken are not even currently imagined. Consequently, a broad principles-based approach is likely to be more suitable than a prescriptive one.

The third and fourth questions, relating to the unitary business of the sector and activities to be included, requires a definition of the unitary business. That is, which parts of the enterprise fall within the scope of the business for formulary apportionment purposes? These questions are entity-level questions applying to specific taxpayers and are both 'scope of group' and 'scope of business activities' questions. The wider any definition is, the more likely it is to achieve the objectives of formulary apportionment. However, this approach brings with it certain pragmatic problems.

There are two generally accepted models for determining the tax unit: either the unitary business or the unitary enterprise. The former involves defining the unitary business by way of business activities with jurisdictions able to claim a nexus to tax where activities are performed within the jurisdiction without a consideration of any form of legal affiliation such as a branch or subsidiary. The latter determines the tax base by more traditional means, with a determination of the commonly controlled group, taking into account subsidiaries and affiliates. Normally a unitary business is understood to be 'a business that has common control, common management, integrated operations, and, in general, a flow of value among the related entities'.[20] Usually, it will be obvious that structures falling within the scope of the traditional permanent establishment concept will come within the meaning of the unitary business. However, more modern MNEs, such as those engaging in e-commerce, pose challenges that ultimately will need to be settled by political agreement. To this end, a legal unity approach would seem flawed, with an economic unity approach which defines the unitary group by way of common economic activities closer to reality. Further, a legal unity approach is open to blatant manipulation as an entity can simply establish a subsidiary in a jurisdiction of choice. However, an economic unity approach would undoubtedly be more administratively challenging and lead to potential uncertainties.

Defining the taxable unit by reference to legal concepts of subsidiary and permanent establishment has an inherent appeal as it more closely aligns with the traditional regime and is readily applied and understood. However, it does little in the way of ensuring that all income is captured and that economic activity is recognized in locations where no such legal form exists but there is significant business activity. Defining a taxable unit by reference to the unitary business has greater appeal from a theoretical perspective and is consistent with the aim of a formulary apportionment model to tax profits in the location of the economic activity. This is because a unitary

20. Joann Martens-Weiner, *Company Tax Reform in the European Union: Guidance from the United States and Canada on Implementing Formulary Apportionment in the EU* 71 (Springer 2006).

business should include all contributions to the overall business enterprise being the operations and activities of the commonly controlled entities (rather than just the entities themselves), no matter what the structure is that is adopted by the MNE.

Once the unitary business is ascertained, it is necessary to consider the fourth question, the scope of the business activities. There are two possible approaches to determining the scope of the business activities. First, the formula should be applied to all the taxpayer's consolidated income from all sources without differentiating or categorizing income based on characterizations such as passive versus active or different activities.[21] However, to do so raises issues around affording scope to engage in aggressive tax planning strategies by pooling income from a core operation with unrelated and potentially unsuccessful business operations.[22] Two matters for consideration are whether passive and active (or business and non-business income) should be combined for the purposes of formula allocation and whether apportionment should be based on the consolidation along separate activity income lines rather than whole of business income. As to the former, despite the US models traditionally distinguishing between business and non-business income (while done so initially due to constitutional constraints), an approach that differentiates between different forms of income may prove difficult to administer and leave opportunities in place to reclassify income which undermines the rationale for a unitary taxation approach. The latter issue is also one which may prove difficult to administer and leave opportunities in place to reclassify income. Within this context, a combined income approach is one that more precisely captures all the activities of an entity globally, whereas an activity-by-activity approach would still require a methodology for sharing internal income and expenses where there are shared services such as, for example, marketing.

§7.05 STEP 3: JURISDICTION TO TAX

Step 2, discussed in §7.04 above, in the context of taxable unit and relating to how a particular sector is defined and whether an enterprise is multinational, raises a question around jurisdiction to tax. If it is determined that a business sector can be adequately distinguished from other business sectors so as to have a separate regime applied, and agreement is reached on the scope of the business group as well as the scope of the activities to which formulary apportionment will apply, it is necessary to consider a jurisdiction's right to tax. The current international tax regime with its adoption of the 'permanent establishment' concept to establish a taxable connection is consistent with traditional MNEs and the requirement to be multinational. Further, it accepts that a jurisdiction has the right to tax where there are components of the unitary enterprise present rather than the unitary business. This is because the unitary

21. Michael C. Durst, *Analysis of a Formulary System for Dividing Income, Part III: Comparative Assessment of Formulary, Arm's-Length Regimes*, 22(9) Tax Mgmt. Transfer Pricing Rep. 653 (2013).
22. Sol Picciotto, *Is the International Tax System Fit for Purpose, Especially for Developing Countries?* (International Centre for Tax and Development Working Paper 13, 2013); Sol Picciotto, *Towards Unitary Taxation of Transnational Corporations* (Tax Justice Network 2012).

enterprise captures physical presence, generally through a permanent establishment, whereas a unitary business extends beyond traditional measures to include what has become known as 'significant economic presence'.

The problems with the traditional permanent establishment rules need to be reconsidered in determining whether formulary apportionment is adopted or not. In the context of an industry-specific formulary apportionment approach, the issues are particularly significant where a 'unitary business' framework is adopted and a sales factor is used. The issues lie in the traditional approach to international business for which the traditional rules were designed. The distinction between an international enterprise (no foreign direct investment) and a multinational enterprise (foreign direct investment) was once significant from a taxing rights perspective. However, for many modern enterprises, true multinationality is no longer the case. The concept of the global company with a presence in numerous jurisdictions but a homogenized approach to business and a strong home base has also come to the fore. Structures are no longer a significant indicator of, or proxy for, jurisdictional nexus. Therefore, the traditional permanent establishment approach to determining nexus does not suffice for many industries and a potentially wider nexus test, such as significant economic presence, would be required. Further, its usefulness as a criterion for jurisdictional taxing rights under a formulary apportionment regime is questionable.[23] The presence of allocation keys is the indicator of business activities in a jurisdiction and therefore these keys provide a sound basis for jurisdiction to tax. For example, sales into a jurisdiction are a strong indicator of business activity. As evidenced by the US system, where a formulary apportionment model provides a physical presence for jurisdiction to tax, problems arise. For example, sales may be present without a permanent establishment. A 'throw-back' or 'throw-out' mechanism, as adopted in the United States may overcome this problem but is not an ideal solution.

A move from the traditional nexus of permanent establishment to a broader nexus of significant economic presence, as analysed in the Action 1 Final Report of the OECD BEPS programme, would provide a solution to the ability of a jurisdiction to tax profits allocated to that state because of sales. Factors are necessary to determine a significant economic presence, with the OECD describing this as providing a nexus for net taxation 'with the intent to reflect situations where an enterprise leverages digital technology to participate in the economic life of a country in a regular and sustained manner without having a physical presence in that country'.[24] This nexus would require factors to 'evidence a purposeful and sustained interaction with the economy of that country via technology and other automated tools',[25] with revenue generation offering the clearest potential indicator, potentially combined with digital factors such as a local domain name, digital platform, and payment options. User-based or user participation factors, such as feedback provided and data collected, monthly active users, and online contract conclusion, may also be considered important indicators.

23. Joann Martens Weiner, *Practical Aspects of Implementing Formulary Apportionment in the European Union*, 8(7) Fla. Tax Rev. 629 (2007).
24. OECD, *Addressing the Tax Challenges of the Digital Economy, supra* n. 15, at 107.
25. *Ibid.*

The OECD, in its Final Report on Action 1 of the BEPS programme, considered formulary apportionment as an option for apportioning profits of the whole enterprise to the locations of a digital presence where a 'significant economic presence' was found. However, this option was summarily dismissed on the basis that:

> fractional apportionment methods would be a departure from current international standards. Furthermore, pursuing such an approach in the case of application of the new nexus would produce very different tax results depending on whether business was conducted through a 'traditional' permanent establishment, a separate subsidiary or the new nexus.[26]

Where 'significant economic presence' is adopted as the test for jurisdiction to tax, the location of sales then potentially becomes an important allocation factor as those countries where there are significant sales, but no presence, have a share of the profits attributed to them. The advantage of a strong focus on sales is that decisions around investments and employment are not distorted by tax rates. However, there is a clear bias towards high consumption jurisdictions with reduced tax revenue for jurisdictions with a small market.

While jurisdiction to tax is fundamental to a formulary apportionment model, there necessarily must be income to allocate. As such, it becomes necessary to determine a group's unitary income. It is often suggested that international accounting standards could be the starting point for determining the income of the business enterprise. There is, however, no universally accepted set of international accounting standards, with International Financial Reporting Standards (IFRS) diverging from US GAAP and some other national standards and with all systems allowing for a degree of flexibility in reporting. If this hurdle can be overcome, each country using the formula could accept consolidated accounting figures as the starting point for allocating income using an agreed formula, and make adjustments to the allocated amount to determine local taxable income incorporating tax local incentives such as accelerated capital allowances or research and development incentives as well as penalties or restrictions in the national tax law.

Formulary apportionment does not impose tax rules on domestic jurisdictions and in this sense does not interfere with sovereignty. The regime merely allocates a proportion of the global income to a jurisdiction with that jurisdiction then electing how to tax its share, including refinements to the base and choice of rate. Retention of sovereignty over tax rates allows jurisdictions that believe they are adversely affected by resort to a common or standardized formula to adjust their tax rates accordingly.

Arguably, agreement on a financial accounting standard for specific industries may not be easier to attain industry-specific reporting standards are available. IFRS 6 *Exploration for and Evaluation of Mineral Resources*, applied to the extractives industry, is one such example.

---

26. *Ibid.*, 112.

§7.06 STEP 4: SELECTING AN APPORTIONMENT FORMULA

Once global profits are determined through consolidation, a formulary apportionment approach requires the assignment of a share of those profits to the relevant countries according to an accepted formula that traditionally, at a subnational level, has included a combination of property, payroll, and/or sales. The selection of an appropriate formula for allocating taxable profits to the relevant jurisdictions is perhaps the most controversial aspect of the unitary taxation debate.

Ultimately, the ideal suitable formula takes into account 'real' factors with jurisdictions having to consider the interaction between tax revenue and foreign direct investment.[27] Unlike the current system which takes into account book or paper transactions that allow corporate income to be reduced in a jurisdiction, multinational enterprise manipulation of formulary apportionment requires actual movement of the two factors, if used, of labour or property.

As alluded to in the discussion above, there are two aspects to a formula: first, the factors of the formula and, second, the relative weighting of each factor. A balanced formula generally takes into account both production factors (employment and assets) and consumption factors (sales based on destination). Current subnational formulary apportionment approaches provide examples of the different factors and weightings used, not only for traditional business sectors but also for those sectors which are considered an exception to a general application. Canada, the United States, Switzerland, and Germany all have subnational regimes which can be looked to for guidance. As previously noted, Canada is an often-cited example of a standard two-factor formula of payroll and sales, with modifications in nine different sectors.

The US subnational system is perhaps the most well known of the formulary apportionment regimes. States have different formulas which, over the years have included such factors as physical or intangible assets, employment, sales, manufacturing costs, purchases, expenditure for labour, accounts receivable, net cost of sales, capital assets, and stock of other companies.[28] Current formulas, however, adopt a combination (whether one or all) of what are now viewed as the acceptable factors of property, payroll, and sales. While each state applies its own formula, commonalities do exist. Historically, the well-known Massachusetts three-factor formula, consisting of equally weighted tangible property, payroll expense, and sales revenue factors, was the traditional approach. Today, instead of the traditional approach, greater emphasis is placed on sales, by either double-weighting the sales factor or adopting a single-sales factor formula.[29]

For the purposes of Germany's trade tax, a formula is used to allocate the tax to the relevant municipalities. The German system does not actually allocate income like more traditional formulary apportionment regimes, but it does offer insight into a

27. Picciotto, *Unitary Alternatives and Formulary Apportionment*, *supra* n. 3, at 34.
28. Joann M. Weiner, *Using the Experience in the US States to Evaluate Issues in Implementing Formula Apportionment at the International Level*, 13 Tax Notes Int'l 2113 (1996).
29. Michael C. Durst, *Analysis of a Formulary System for Dividing Income, Part II: Examining Current Formulary and Arm's-Length Approaches*, 22(5) Tax Mgmt. Transfer Pricing Rep. 27C (2013).

possible allocation formula. In the case of its trade tax, Germany uses a single factor of salaries and wages and, while the formula is now standard across all industries, historically it has had variations for two industries; first, retail, and, second, the banking, insurance, and loan industry. In the latter, a single factor formula of gross receipts is used.[30]

Switzerland provides the most flexible model for formulary apportionment with Swiss cantons maintaining a significant degree of autonomy from the federal state. Interestingly, both the tax bases and the object of apportionment can vary between cantons. The Swiss system is complex, with twenty-six cantons applying different formulas. Within those systems, different formulas are then potentially applied to different industries.[31]

The European Union's proposed Common Consolidated Corporate Tax Base (CCCTB) adopts a three-factor equally weighted formula with the allocation keys of labour, assets, and sales. However, unlike models discussed above, the labour factor is not merely based on payroll but rather calculated on the basis of an equal weighting between both payroll and the number of employees. There is also a safeguard clause allowing an alternative method where the outcome of the apportionment does not fairly represent the extent of business activity. Special apportionment rules for four industries are also included in the proposal: financial institutions; insurance; oil and gas and shipping; and inland waterway transport and air transport.

An industry-specific formula potentially needs to take into account the taxing rights of the place of origin and destination, i.e., both the supply side and demand side of income, to determine how each should be represented. Property and payroll generally reflect the supply side, while sales (at destination) represent the demand side. A formulary apportionment model also requires the relevant factors to be defined to determine their scope. Each of the three common factors is discussed below.

The payroll factor, included in the formula to reflect the contribution of labour to the generation of the income of the entity, is generally defined as total employee compensation including salaries, commissions, and bonuses. Agreement on the definition of the payroll factor requires a consideration of a lack of homogeneity in wages between jurisdictions with a solution proffered being the recognition of number of employees as part of the allocation key such as in the proposed EU model. Contract labour, that is, the outsourcing of labour functions, also presents difficulties as the payroll factor does not generally include independent contractors.

The property or asset factor, included in formulas on the basis that capital is an important income-producing factor, is complex in its definition and application. Intangible property is often used as part of tax planning strategies by MNEs and including this factor in any formula means that the same issues arise as intangible property is highly mobile. Where formulary apportionment is used at a subnational level and property is a factor taken into account, intangibles are generally weighted less heavily than other factors or are removed from the definition altogether. Alternatively,

30. For a detailed analysis of the Swiss system, *see* Stefan Mayer, *Formulary Apportionment for the Internal Market* 147-164 (IBFD Publications 2009).
31. For a detailed analysis of the Swiss system, *see ibid.*, 124-146.

as is the case in Canada, there is no property factor in the formula. Valuation is also an issue in relation to property with questions around whether historical cost or market value should be used.

The sales factor (by destination) is the predominant factor of existing formulas and is viewed as relatively easy to measure. However, identification of the location of sales can pose challenges, particularly in an industry-specific formula. While identification of the point of sale for tangible goods that are provided or delivered is relatively straightforward, finding the place of supply for intangible goods and services is more challenging, especially in the case of e-commerce businesses merely operate in an intermediary capacity. The solution usually suggested is one of an 'ultimate destination' test that looks to where the services are ultimately used. Retail services to individuals would readily lend themselves to such an approach; however, corporate clients would pose significant problems given their ability to establish subsidiaries anywhere.[32] A destination-based sales factor also needs to align with a jurisdiction's taxing connections to ensure income is only allocated to jurisdictions with taxing rights over the income.

In one of his series of articles on formulary apportionment, Durst undertakes an analysis of the sales factor and highlights the rationale for having this factor in a formula on the basis that it recognizes the market at play. That is, where there is a market for goods and services within a jurisdiction, at least some of the income should be apportioned to that jurisdiction due to that market.[33] Despite strongly advocating for a sales-based allocation key, Durst does recognize the difficulties associated with some industries, highlighting the financial services sector as one such example.

Often, it is argued that a heavily weighted destination-based sales factor is consistent with the economic substance of MNE transactions. There is inelasticity in ultimate destination-based sales[34] and, by reducing the emphasis on property and payroll, jurisdictions are able to attract investment without a proxy tax on those factors. As Clausing and Avi-Yonah explain:

> the key advantage of a sales-based formula is that sales are far less responsive to tax differences across markets, because the customers themselves are far less mobile than are firm assets or employment. Even in a high-tax country, firms still have an incentive to sell as much as possible.[35]

This discussion is consistent with the proposed EU CCCTB model which adopts a sales-by-destination approach.[36]

---

32. Ilan Benshalom, *The Quest to Tax Financial Income in a Global Economy: Emerging to an Allocation Phase*, 28(1) Va. Tax Rev. 165 (2008).
33. Michael C. Durst, *Analysis of a Formulary System, Part VII: The Sales Factor*, 22(22) Tax Mgmt. Transfer Pricing Rep. 1414 (2014).
34. Susan C. Morse, *Revisiting Global Formulary Apportionment*, 29(4) Va. Tax Rev. 593 (2010).
35. Kimberly A. Clausing & Reuven S. Avi-Yonah, *Reforming Corporate Taxation in a Global Economy: A Proposal to Adopt Formulary Apportionment* 12 (The Hamilton Project Discussion Paper, Brookings Institution, June 2007).
36. European Commission, *Proposal for a Council Directive on a Common Consolidated Corporate Tax Base (CCCTB)*, COM(2011) 121/4, 3 October 2011, Art. 96.

A formula which relies on sales results in the practical problem of identifying the location of consumers of the goods or services. In particular, there are questions around the practical difficulty in tracking sales in e-commerce. That is, the destination of the goods or services may not be able to be traced to the ultimate consumer with any degree of confidence. Yet, this problem arises with the traditional transfer pricing regime as well and is arguably facilitated through this system which allows the permanent establishment concept to be avoided and goods and/or services to be routed through intermediaries in low- or no-tax jurisdictions. However, the extractive industries involve a business sector where there is a strong argument against a heavily weighted sales factor. This industry is reliant on both capital- and labour-intensive activities in the original location of the product being sold.

Pragmatic arguments around jurisdiction-specific needs are also often put forward. The argument that labour-intensive jurisdictions would want a higher weighting of the labour factor becomes somewhat counterintuitive when analysed in the context of possible movement of that labour to another jurisdiction. That is, countries where labour is provided will want to keep the labour force employed. Support for such a proposition is found in the documented change to the US state system where most states over the last thirty years have moved from an equally weighted three-factor formula to an increase in the sales-factor weighting.[37] This move towards a sales-based formula is generally explained by way of tax competition, with investment in a jurisdiction discouraged where assets and employment are weighted. The counterargument for a formula with a heavily weighted sales factor is that there are industries and/or countries which are more reliant on foreign direct investment for production or extraction with very little in the way of local sales. This is particularly the case with developing nations where labour is cheap and natural resources are abundant.[38]

§7.07 CONCLUSION

This chapter has attempted to go beyond the traditional all-or-nothing proposals for formulary apportionment to be adopted on a global scale. Rather than proposing formulary apportionment as an alternative and complete substitute for the arm's length system of the generally adopted transfer pricing model, it is suggested that formulary apportionment may be adopted on a business sector basis provided appropriate steps are adhered to in order to assess its appropriateness. The assessment framework developed and analysed adopts a value-neutral approach to allow a considered appraisal of the overarching policy considerations along with pragmatic and implementation issues. In particular, challenges around the taxable unit, nexus, tax base, and appropriate formula, which may be compounded when an industry-specific approach is investigated, have been highlighted. The overarching purpose of the chapter has been ultimately to demonstrate that a practical transition to formulary

37. Kimberly A. Clausing, *The US State Experience Under Formulary Apportionment: Are There Lessons for International Reform?*, 69(2) Nat'l Tax J. 353 (2016).
38. For an extended discussion on these points, *see* Picciotto, *Unitary Alternatives and Formulary Apportionment*, *supra* n. 3.

apportionment could be achieved via industry-specific adoption. This, however, does not detract from the model developed, which can be used in any policy debate on the adoption of formulary apportionment.

Part III The Evolving Intersections of Arm's Length Pricing and Formulary Apportionment and Alternatives

CHAPTER 8

Between Arm's Length and Formulary Apportionment

Yariv Brauner

§8.01 INTRODUCTION

In the first half of the sixteenth century, the Italian artist, Girolamo Francesco Maria Mazzola, known as *Il Parmigianino,* painted what is perhaps the first 'selfie', the 'Self-Portrait in a Convex Mirror'.[1] Pulitzer prize-winning art critic Jerry Saltz made this observation in an article aptly named 'Art at Arm's Length: A History of the Selfie', in which he argued that the selfie had become a new visual genre, distinct, and with its own visual autonomy.[2] Anecdotally, the painting and Saltz's analysis can be very helpful, shedding light on some of the prominent features of one of the most fundamental bases of the current international tax regime, namely the arm's length standard.[3] As is well known, this universal standard is the basis for the (transfer pricing) rules that require firms to charge 'transfer prices' on intragroup transactions based on prices used by unrelated parties in comparable market transactions to prevent inappropriate shifting of profits by multinational enterprises (MNEs) from high to low tax jurisdictions.[4] Like the selfie, arm's length pricing is unreal, staged, and intended to

1. Circa 1523-1524, currently at the Kunsthistorisches Museum, Vienna. *See, e.g.*, Jonathan Jones, Self-Portrait in a Convex Mirror (c1523-24), Parmigianino, The Guardian (18 January 2003).
2. Jerry Saltz, Art at Arm's Length: A History of the Selfie, N.Y. Mag. (26 January 2014).
3. The arm's length standard has been effectively adopted by most nations, typically following the field's standard in Organisation for Economic Co-operation and Development (OECD), *OECD Transfer Pricing Guidelines for Multinational Enterprises and Tax Administrations* (OECD 2017).
4. *See, e.g.*, Hubert Hamaekers, *Arm's Length – How Long?*, in *International and Comparative Taxation: Essays in Honour of Klaus Vogel* 29, 30 (Kees van Raad ed. (English ed.), Kluwer Law International 2002). The formal origins of this standard are probably in the US legislation attempting to deal with domestic related-party transactions in the early twentieth century. *See* War Revenue Act of 1917, ch. 63, 40 Stat. 300 (1917). For a concise historical review of the

project an acceptable impression, and yet, also not unlike selfies, it is established based on a rigid set of essentially universal rules.[5] Arm's length prices are an *ersatz* version of market prices, much like the portrait of the artist as viewed in a convex mirror,[6] because the operations of MNEs are inherently different from market arrangements; they would not organize as such otherwise.[7] The transfer pricing rules attempt to adjust the comparable market prices to account for the differences between hierarchical and market arrangements, yet for the most part these adjustments are based primarily on the experience of a not unbiased (transfer pricing) expert rather than on any defensible principle, ironically drawing another parallel to *Il Parmigianino*, who was drawn to alchemy, an obsession that eventually led to his demise.[8]

The demise of the arm's length standard has similarly been predicted,[9] it has been constantly criticized for its variety of ailments, and alternative ideas for its replacement have been promoted, but the Organisation for Economic Co-operation and Development (OECD) and some of its most powerful member nations have consistently resisted reform. Even when they were forced to introduce changes to the transfer pricing rules, they stubbornly refused to change the terminology, insisting on bringing all operative rules under the umbrella of the arm's length standard. The protection of the arm's length standard tautology was so important for the OECD that it exposed itself to ample criticism, first, when it extended the arm's length standard analysis to intracompany, not just intragroup, transactions (so-called dealings between a company and its branch or permanent establishment (PE)), and, second, when it elevated the arm's length standard, with no warning, debate, or explanation, to the status of a legal 'principle'. The former move was rejected by both developing countries and many OECD members, while the latter is bluntly inconsistent with legal theory. The arm's length standard, renamed the arm's length principle,[10] continues to dominate the international tax discourse in the aftermath of the Base Erosion and Profit Shifting (BEPS) project, the constitutive document for which declared that in difficult cases the arm's length standard cannot provide satisfactory answers and hence requires reform, only to be forgotten over the course of the project when the OECD resorted to pragmatic tweaking of the rules and a keeping of the arm's length standard dominance façade.[11]

---

standard's origins, *see* Reuven S. Avi-Yonah, *The Rise and Fall of Arm's Length: A Study in the Evolution of US International Taxation*, 15(1) Va. Tax Rev. 89 (1995).

5. Hence Saltz's argument that the art of the selfie is becoming a new genre rather than an ephemeral style of portraiture. Saltz, *Art at Arm's Length*, *supra* n. 2.
6. *Supra* n. 1.
7. *See, e.g.*, Reuven S. Avi-Yonah & Ilan Benshalom, *Formulary Apportionment – Myths and Prospects: Promoting Better International Tax Policies by Utilizing the Misunderstood and Under-Theorized Formulary Alternative*, 3(3) World Tax J. 371, 379 (2011) ('the [arm's length standard] cannot break down the cost of what unrelated parties would have done – because the MNE setting is designed precisely to save the costs of doing business through unrelated transactions').
8. *See* Jones, *Self-Portrait in a Convex Mirror*, *supra* n. 1.
9. *See, e.g.*, Avi-Yonah, *The Rise and Fall of Arm's Length*, *supra* n. 4.
10. This chapter refers to the arm's length standard as such, ignoring the rhetoric of the OECD, unless the context otherwise requires.
11. *See* OECD, *Actions 8-10 – 2015 Final Reports: Aligning Transfer Pricing Outcomes with Value Creation*, OECD/G20 Base Erosion and Profit Shifting Project (OECD 2015). The reports and later work fail to respond to the original challenge presented by the original BEPS action plan. *See* OECD, *Action Plan on Base Erosion and Profit Shifting* 20 (OECD 2013) (stating that 'special

Transfer pricing reform proposals typically include formulary elements, which means that they do not rely on market comparatives but rather embrace the political roots of the transfer pricing problem (the wish of countries to divide tax bases among them without double taxation and without too much exposure to profit shifting or other avoidance schemes by MNEs) without the pretence of market justification, typically relying on one or more elements, such as asset location, sales, or personnel, connecting the income to the respective jurisdictions.[12] Such proposals are often presented, and criticized in the literature, together under the umbrella of formulary apportionment, presented in juxtaposition to arm's length standard-based transfer pricing[13] as if the choice is binary. The critique of formulary apportionment typically takes one of two paths: an outright, unargued dismissal of formulary apportionment as unfeasible because it requires an alleged utopian, universal consensus over the formula to be used,[14] or a pseudo theoretical opposition to the arbitrariness of formulary apportionment.[15] Scholars supporting formulary apportionment have demonstrated, however, that such critical representation is false and that arm's length standard analysis and formulary apportionment are parts of a continuum, meaning that a reform choice is really about where on such continuum a country wishes to be.[16] Moreover, transfer pricing reform does not need to be an all-or-nothing choice between arm's length standard and formulary apportionment, permitting mixed policies.[17]

The first contribution of this chapter is an elaboration on these observations and exposure of the harm that the binary approach inflicts on the international tax regime. This chapter then proceeds to examine the implications of defective analysis of transfer pricing on two key issues with which the international tax regime struggles: the taxation of the digital economy and the impact of the regime on developing countries demanding more source taxation for the fairer division of tax bases. This chapter puts forward an unorthodox, substantive approach to transfer pricing that is not confined to

---

measures, either within or beyond the arm's length principle, may be required', especially in the analysis of 'hard-to-value intangibles').

12. *See, e.g.*, Paul R. McDaniel, *Formulary Taxation in the North American Free Trade Zone*, 49(4) Tax L. Rev. 691 (1994); Walter Hellerstein, *Income Allocation in the 21st Century: The End of Transfer Pricing? The Case for Formulary Apportionment*, 12(3) Int'l Transfer Pricing J. 103 (2005); Reuven S. Avi-Yonah, Kimberly A. Clausing & Michael C. Durst, *Allocating Business Profits for Tax Purposes: A Proposal to Adopt a Formulary Profit Split*, 9(5) Fla. Tax Rev. 497 (2009); Yariv Brauner, *Formula Based Transfer Pricing*, in *The Proper Tax Base: Structural Fairness from an International and Comparative Perspective – Essays in Honor of Paul McDaniel* 149 (Yariv Brauner & Martin J. McMahon, Jr. eds., Kluwer Law International 2012).
13. William J. Wilkins & Kenneth W. Gideon, *Memorandum to Congress: You Wouldn't Like Worldwide Formulary Apportionment*, 69 Tax Notes 1259 (1994).
14. *See, e.g.*, Eric J. Coffill & Prentiss Willson, Jr., *Federal Formulary Apportionment as an Alternative to Arm's Length Pricing: From the Frying Pan to the Fire?*, 59 Tax Notes 1103 (1993).
15. *See, e.g.*, Elizabeth Chorvat, *Forcing Multinationals to Play Fair: Proposals for a Rigorous Transfer Pricing Theory*, 54(4) Ala. L. Rev. 1251 (2003).
16. *See, e.g.*, Avi-Yonah & Benshalom, *Formulary Apportionment – Myths and Prospects*, *supra* n. 7, at 372 ('Part of the solution is to stop viewing the [arm's length standard] and formulary arrangements as binary alternatives'); Eugene E. Lester, *International Transfer Pricing Rules: Unconventional Wisdom*, 2(1) ILSA J. Int'l & Comp. L. 283, 300-305 (1995).
17. *See, e.g.*, Lester, *supra* n. 16 (arguing that adopting a hybrid formulary-arm's length standard regime could be a viable, practical, and political option).

arm's length standard rhetoric and would be beneficial to progress on both matters. Removal of the convex mirror could provide a clearer picture of the issues at hand.

The rest of this chapter is organized as follows: §8.02 examines the real gap between the arm's length standard and formulary apportionment, supporting the argument that the choice between them is not binary but rather on a coherent continuum, demonstrating that this argument is already reflected in both practice and rule-making, and arguing that the terminological obscurity imposed by the OECD and a few of its members is costly and harmful for the evolution of the international tax regime. Section 8.03 focuses on the implications of the choice between the arm's length standard and formulary apportionment for the cooperation among nations in tax matters, elaborating on the benefits of a clearer discourse to all nations. Section 8.04 puts the discussion in context, demonstrating the pitfalls of the obscure discourse experienced by the international tax regime as it attempts to face the challenges presented by the ascent of the digital economy, while §8.05 similarly puts the discourse in the context of economic development. Section 8.06 concludes.

§8.02 BETWEEN ARM'S LENGTH AND FORMULARY APPORTIONMENT

Tax scholars should acknowledge by now that serious reform of the transfer pricing rules cannot be based on a simple choice between the arm's length standard and formulary apportionment. In a 2011 article, Avi-Yonah and Benshalom convincingly demonstrated that the choice between the arm's length standard and formulary apportionment is not binary, effectively explaining that the exclusivity of arm's length standard-based transfer pricing analysis is based on myths, which they easily dismissed and demonstrated that a mixed, perhaps compromise solution is feasible.[18] This chapter, agreeing with their analysis, builds on its argument that ignoring these insights is costly and prevents progress. This section reviews the debate over the arm's length standard and formulary apportionment and its contemporary implications. It begins, next, with the fundamentals, providing a clarification of the purpose of the transfer pricing rules which has been blurred over the years, causing confusion that has contributed to the mistaken, binary view of the arm's length standard and formulary apportionment debate.

[A] The Purpose of Transfer Pricing

The purpose of the transfer pricing rules is to prevent MNEs from easily shifting profits from high to low tax jurisdictions via intragroup transactions.[19] This purpose is reflected in most countries' transfer pricing regimes.[20] Yet, the origins of the arm's length standard, the US legislation from early in the twentieth century, failed to state its

18. See Avi-Yonah & Benshalom, *Formulary Apportionment – Myths and Prospects*, *supra* n. 7.
19. *See, e.g.*, Hamaekers, *supra* n. 4.
20. *See, e.g.*, Yariv Brauner, *Transfer Pricing and Tax Avoidance*, in *Tax Avoidance Revisited in the EU BEPS Context* 63 (Ana Paula Dourado ed., IBFD Publications 2017) (reporting based on multiple country reports, albeit primarily European country reports).

purpose, and follow-up guidance simply noted that it was self-explanatory.[21] From this void arose the argument that the arm's length standard has an allocative, rather than an anti-abuse, purpose.[22] Note that the argument is not that the outcome of arm's length standard transfer pricing is allocative, which is a given, but that it has a normative justification (i.e., that countries 'deserve' their arm's length standard-based share of the relevant tax base). Some have viewed this approach as the international manifestation of the arm's length standard in contrast to the domestic arm's length standard application, a nonsensical view since the international tax rules are domestic that may be amended by treaties for coordination but not elevated to the status of new international principles in the process.[23] From this false argument arose an equally misguided extension, claiming that the arm's length standard intends to create parity between market and non-market transactions.[24]

Understanding the falsity of both these arguments about the purpose of transfer pricing is critical for a serious analysis of the regime. The normative argument is patently false because the primary allocations of tax base rules, based on the residence/source paradigm, themselves are not normative, and hence a derivative rule, correcting for the inability of the primary residence/source based rule to allocate tax bases in cases of related-party transactions, cannot be considered normative. Moreover, the agreement to eliminate double taxation is at the heart of the arm's length standard. Such an agreement necessarily results in a compromise, not some maximal balance, between residence and source taxation. So, even if domestic law, based on either residence or source taxation, were to be normatively established, the final compromise could not be normatively justified.

Finally, the derivative argument that the purpose of transfer pricing (and the arm's length standard as the implementation standard) is to create parity among market and non-market (related-party) transactions, is especially problematic, equally false, and yet more destructive than the normative argument that most experts, unless completely blinded by the aura of market fundamentalism, would easily dismiss. The problem is that the parity argument carries with it the allure of efficiency as if the arm's length standard corrects for a market failure to ensure neutrality between market and non-market transactions. Transfer pricing does operate to eliminate a distortion. However it is not a market distortion; it is merely the legal opportunity for MNEs to minimize their effective taxes due to the lack of coordination of tax policy and

---

21. *See* Joseph H. Guttentag, *Passing the Torch on Transfer Pricing*, in *Liber Amicorum Sven-Olof Lodin* 119 (Krister Andersson, Peter Melz & Christer Silfverberg eds., Kluwer Law International 2001).
22. *See, e.g.*, Maarten F. de Wilde, *Some Thoughts on a Fair Allocation of Corporate Tax in a Globalizing Economy*, 38(5) Intertax 281, 282 (2010); Jens Wittendorff, *At Arm's Length: BEPS Actions 8-10: Birth of a New Arm's-Length Principle*, 81 Tax Notes Int'l 331 (2016) (lamenting the OECD's inclusion of 'new' anti-abuse elements in its post-BEPS interpretation of the arm's length standard).
23. *See, e.g.*, Mirjam Koomen, *Transfer Pricing in a BEPS Era: Rethinking the Arm's Length Principle – Part II*, 22(4) Int'l Transfer Pricing J. 230, 231-232 (2015).
24. A version of this argument is now embedded in OECD, *Transfer Pricing Guidelines*, *supra* n. 3, at 36.

enforcement among competing tax jurisdictions, an opportunity that all countries have decided should be considered as abusive, hence the transfer pricing rules.

The arm's length standard does not remove this distortion. Arm's length standard-based transfer pricing necessarily results in arm's length 'ranges' of acceptable transfer prices,[25] which means that MNEs, even under perfect arm's length standard analysis, still have an advantage in comparison to non-market transactions. The arm's length standard creates a tax bias that is always in favour of non-market transactions, and even more so in favour of intangibles-heavy MNEs.[26] The question of which method - arm's length standard or formulary apportionment - has more efficient results in this regard is nonsensical since it is an empirical question which cannot be preliminarily answered in favour of one or the other.[27] One may be biased in favour of the arm's length standard because it is a market-based methodology yet note that the arm's length standard is always biased in favour of non-market transactions while formulary apportionment could go both ways. But, even if one wished to examine the question empirically, it would be necessary to examine two concrete, detailed proposals (i.e., it would not be possible to 'prove' superiority of one methodology as such over the other).

In summary, the parity argument could only prevail if market and non-market transactions of MNEs and competing firms engaged in comparable transactions were actually in relevant competition with each other, i.e., put differently, that the transactions compared were substitutable. Yet, this is never tested by the arm's length standard.[28] It is implausible to argue that MNEs organize their affairs in the hierarchical mode to take advantage of the tax avoidance opportunities that related-party transactions present, while other market competitors of the MNEs are somehow disadvantaged by rules that are not arm's length standard-based.

The choice of business organization encompasses many considerations, tax being just one of them, and the option to organize hierarchically is open to all, taken only by those who wish to reap the benefits of such a mode of business organization (internalization of costs or monopolization) and willing to risk losing the quick and sure benefits of alternative business organization modes (primarily contracting with third parties). Consequently, the tax advantage targeted by the arm's length standard (even if the arm's length standard were the only method to address it) is unlikely to be significant in the choice of any firm, which pulls the rug out from under the parity argument.[29] Once the purpose of transfer pricing as an anti-abuse (or profit shifting)

25. *See, e.g.*, Treas. Reg. 1.482-1(e).
26. Yariv Brauner, *Value in the Eye of the Beholder: The Valuation of Intangibles for Transfer Pricing Purposes*, 28(1) Va. Tax Rev. 79 (2008).
27. *See* Thomas A. Gresik, *Assessing the Normative Differences Between Formula Apportionment and Separate Accounting*, in *Fundamentals of International Transfer Pricing in Law and Economics* 257 (Wolfgang Schön & Kai A. Konrad eds., Springer 2012).
28. And likely false in many, if not most, relevant cases since such competition rarely occurs in the above-mentioned simple form that generates a market failure when intangibles are involved, and in most difficult transfer pricing cases intangibles are involved. *See, e.g., ibid.*
29. Indirect evidence to support this may be found in Benjamin C. Ayers, C. Bryan Cloyd & John R. Robinson, *Organizational Form and Taxes: An Empirical Analysis of Small Businesses*, 18(2 Supp.) J. Am. Tax'n Ass'n 49 (1996).

norm is clear, one can consider the standards for its implementation, beginning, next, with the currently universal arm's length standard.

[B] The Limits of the Arm's Length Standard

The arm's length standard is an attractive standard for implementation of an anti-profit shifting norm because it seems to impose the impartial discipline of the market on the subject non-market transactions. The arm's length standard is indeed a reasonable rule for pricing non-market transactions when comparable (competing) market transactions exist and are easily observable. Its objective, market-based allure is justified in those conditions since the competing jurisdictions or the taxpayer cannot significantly influence the consequent allocation of the tax base among them and the taxpayer's impact on such allocation and the resulting effective tax rate is relatively limited. It is however always biased, and always 'in favour' of MNEs, since they elect the timing and stage most of the circumstances that will determine the comparability analysis, yet, even if such advantage were not significant, MNEs benefit from valuation difficulties (of synergies, intangibles, and risk), which gives them a range of reasonable transfer prices, a margin of benefit not available to other taxpayers.

This is the Achilles' heel of the arm's length standard: its inability to accommodate the unique value (or, expressed more directly, savings) generated by the hierarchical design of MNEs.[30] First, this is manifested in an advantage to intangibles-heavy MNEs that are impossible to effectively evaluate for transfer pricing purposes and, more specifically, are not easily matched with comparable market transactions. Second, this is manifested in the advantage to MNEs of the inability of arm's length standard methodology to capture synergies stemming from the very choice of corporate organization as an MNE, a value that is generated by intangibles that are impossible or very difficult to sever from the particular taxpayer and separately sell on the market, or value related to risk.[31]

The United States, followed by other countries and eventually the OECD, started to face these difficulties over half a century ago, by choosing to tweak the arm's length standard-based rules. After that had proven impossible, they added so-called profit-based transfer pricing methods that would pragmatically deal with difficult transactions without a declaration of fundamental reform. The key rhetorical interest was to preserve the overall dominance of the arm's length standard. The problem was that these profit-based methods that came to dominate the practice of transfer pricing were originally as controversial as formulary apportionment, since they lost the pretence of accuracy, particularly of market accuracy that generated much of the arm's length standard's appeal. Put simply, profit-based methods seek comparability not to specific, comparable market transactions, but rather to a category of transactions statistically similar to the tested one.[32] Once removed from the fiction of strict market discipline, the analysis is freed of the strict requirement to have good and available data pertaining

30. *See* OECD, *Transfer Pricing Guidelines*, *supra* n. 3.
31. *See, e.g.*, Brauner, *Value in the Eye of the Beholder*, *supra* n. 26.
32. *See* Treas. Reg. 1.482-5 and 1.482-6.

to the tested transaction. Because this is more readily available for wider categories of transactions than for particular transactions, at the same time a new challenge is created by the need to choose the appropriate, acceptable distance from the market and the factors (profitability indicators) that the taxpayer could use to establish such less-strict profitability.[33] Indeed, to this day, despite the awesome universality of transfer pricing analysis, the two most important sources of guidance on transfer pricing, the US regulations and the OECD Transfer Pricing Guidelines, conflict on this matter.

This concession to the practical challenge of data quality and availability could not therefore completely remove the challenge, and yet officially stakeholders seemed satisfied with it. It has not, however, solved the three key issues arising from the properties of MNE architecture: synergies, risk, and the valuation of intangibles. The BEPS project admitted as much and attempted to provide solutions to these issues.[34] However, it eventually reverted back to arm's length standard rhetoric and the old 'tweaking the rules' path rather than innovate and calling for a nonsensical solution to synergies (allocating them according to the parties 'contributions' to their creation)[35] eliminating risk from the analysis for most purposes (in vague language that hardly provides direct guidance). Despite the critical role risk plays in market analysis,[36] which is the basis and justification for the arm's length standard,[37] ignoring the difficulty of intangibles valuation by encouraging taxpayers to expand the use of profit-based methodology - especially profit split[38] - leads to the weakening of arm's length standard rhetoric when following such guidance and does not provide any assistance at all in cases where current methodology could not supply satisfactory answers (so-called hard-to-value intangibles),[39] despite admitting the existence of these cases.[40]

It is apparent therefore that the arm's length standard, even in its new, morphed version, finds it difficult (at best) to provide satisfactory solutions to the contemporary challenges faced by governments in the area of transfer pricing.[41] In response, scholars

---

33. *See, e.g.*, Céline Azémar & Gregory Corcos, *Multinational Firms' Heterogeneity in Tax Responsiveness: The Role of Transfer Pricing*, 32(9) World Economy 1291 (2009).
34. In BEPS action items 8-10. *See* OECD, *Action Plan on Base Erosion and Profit Shifting*, *supra* n. 11.
35. OECD, *Aligning Transfer Pricing Outcomes with Value Creation*, *supra* n. 11.
36. *Ibid.*
37. *See, e.g.*, Chorvat, *supra* n. 15.
38. *See ibid.*; OECD, *Inclusive Framework on BEPS: Action 10, Revised Guidance on the Application of the Transactional Profit Split Method* (OECD 2018).
39. *See* OECD, *Revised Guidance on the Application of the Transactional Profit Split Method*, *supra* n. 38; OECD, *OECD Releases New Guidance on the Application of the Approach to Hard-to-Value Intangibles and the Transactional Profit Split Method Under BEPS Actions 8-10*, press release (21 June 2018), https://www.oecd.org/tax/oecd-releases-new-guidance-on-the-application-of-the-approach-to-hard-to-value-intangibles-and-the-transactional-profit-split-method-under-beps-actions-8-10.htm (accessed 16 June 2019).
40. OECD, *OECD Releases New Guidance*, *supra* n. 39.
41. There are scholarly proposals to improve the implementation of the arm's length standard. However, such proposals do not cover all or even the most prevalent cases. Most importantly, they are highly complex and require expertise that will be available only to the largest and wealthiest taxpayers, itself a problem, and in any event could not be widely exercised by all

and others have suggested, as this chapter describes next, a reform that over the years has mainly involved some form of formulary apportionment.

[C] Formulary Apportionment and Its Advantages

Unlike the arm's length standard, formulary apportionment in principle seeks a political solution to a political problem. Countries wish to divide a single tax base among them without double taxation and without exposure to profit shifting by MNEs, and formulary apportionment provides them with a methodology to do just that: split the income into two (or more) shares in a legitimate manner. The key here is to establish legitimacy, which for the arm's length standard has already been established (even if based on questionable grounds) by its pseudo market analysis. For formulary apportionment to work, it must adopt a split that would be considered legitimate by both (or more) parties. Simple, arbitrary formulas, such as 50:50, are not very useful in this situation since rarely is there parity (economic, political, or otherwise) between the competing jurisdictions, and in any event, relative positions change over time, which makes a single split ratio unattractive. They also suffer from being 'easy targets' for the arbitrariness critique used by arm's length standard proponents against formulary apportionment. Therefore, most formulary apportionment proposals tend to rely on economic indicators as proxies to economic activity that legitimizes allocation of profit shares to the country within which jurisdiction such economic activity takes place (this is a natural intuition that many rules, including the residence/source paradigm, build on). Note that the use of the economic indicators is not intended for accuracy (an always false goal in this context) but rather for justification, flexibility, and resilience to abuse. For these same reasons, formulary apportionment often uses multiple factors, reducing the opportunities for both countries and taxpayers to manipulate the resulting split.

Many formulary apportionment proposals are based, in whole or in part on what many American scholars call the 'Massachusetts formula',[42] weighing assets, sales, and payroll to apportion a taxpayer's income to the state which is used in differing forms by US states to apply their corporate income taxes.[43] This is both helpful and distractive. It is helpful because it demonstrates that formulary taxation 'works' and that for the most part, a balanced formula is not simple to manipulate if universally applied. In recent years, however, the trend has been towards divergence rather than convergence in the design of the formulas, since states 'lose' from the use of the balanced formula or, even more so, states lose revenue from deciding to manipulate the

governments and, more importantly the courts that had consistently struggled with the challenge that the current, much less complex rule presented to them. *See, e.g.*, Robert Ackerman & Elizabeth A. Chorvat, *Modern Financial Theory and Transfer Pricing*, 10(4) Geo. Mason L. Rev. 637 (2002).

42. *See, e.g.*, Charles E. McLure, Jr., *Understanding Uniformity and Diversity in State Corporate Income Taxes*, 61(1) Nat'l Tax J. 141, 146-148 (2008).
43. *See, e.g.*, Jerome R. Hellerstein, Walter Hellerstein & John A. Swain, *State Taxation* (3rd ed., Thomson Reuters 2019 rev.).

formula to encourage investment without taxation and increasingly rely on the sales indicators.[44]

The relevant lesson from these developments is that the content of the formula is very important. Yet, one should note that the study of the story of US state taxation and their use of formulas is also distractive because the international tax regime is very different from US state corporate taxation. To begin with, the stakes are higher at the international level as national tax rates are significantly higher than those of US state taxes. Second, at the international level, there is an effective pact to eliminate double taxation that does not exist in state taxation. Third, the costs of moving from one jurisdiction to another in response to tax factors are much higher internationally.[45] Hence one should be careful in drawing parallels between the policy choices beyond the basic conclusions set out above. Most distracting is the assumption, almost unanimously made by formulary apportionment opponents, that formula-based transfer pricing reform at the international level will follow the Massachusetts formula.[46]

This assumption was fortified by the reliance on this formula in the European Union's Common Consolidated Corporate Tax Base (CCCTB) proposal. Note, however, that even that proposal that aims to operate in a single European market for most purposes tries to imitate a federal system (unsuccessfully at present), not a network of converging tax systems. Moreover, both state taxation and the CCCTB proposals apply to business taxation more generally rather than the transfer pricing rules alone that are resolved indirectly through the formulary taxation system. There is no serious discussion of universal reform and harmonization of the entire business taxation system in replacement of the current residence, source and permanent establishment rules, and therefore much of the critique of formulary apportionment made in the context of state taxation, the Massachusetts formula, and the CCCTB is misguided.[47]

The primary advantage of formulary apportionment over the arm's length standard is its straightforwardness and transparency: it divides tax bases among countries in a manner agreed upon by such countries without pretence of economic correctness or desert of the kinds that mar the application of the arm's length standard in practice. This argument may make some uncomfortable because pseudo-economic justifications are easier to sell politically, covering the simple political origins of the necessity to divide tax bases among competing jurisdictions. Furthermore, the exact argument is often used by opponents of formulary apportionment as its supposed key disadvantage. But, the transparency of the political arrangement embedded in the formula inherently eliminates claims of illegitimacy that are often, and mostly justifiably, raised against the current arm's length standard-based regime.

44. *See, e.g.*, *ibid.*
45. And therefore, the common reliance of market scholars on the Tiebout Model. Charles M. Tiebout, *A Pure Theory of Local Expenditures*, 64(5) J. Pol. Econ. 416 (1956) (making an analogy between state and local taxation to international taxation is misguided, at best). For more on the Tiebout Model and its conditions for useful policy guidance, *see, e.g.*, Jonathan Gruber, *Public Finance and Public Policy*, ch. 10 (6th ed., Worth Publishers 2019).
46. *See, e.g.*, Wilkins & Gideon, *supra* n. 13, at 1259.
47. *See, e.g.*, European Commission, *Common Consolidated Corporate Tax Base (CCCTB)*, https://ec.europa.eu/taxation_customs/business/company-tax/common-consolidated-corporate-tax-base-ccctb_en (accessed 16 June 2019).

The transparency of the formula simplifies the regime and reduces potential disparities in interpretation in comparison to the arm's length standard. It is easy to observe that disputes over comparability are much more significant, with disparate views (as is known from the current state of transfer pricing affairs), applications (or disputes over what counts or does not count as sales), and assets or payroll (or any similar indicator). Intangibles are of course difficult to value. Indeed, existing formulary apportionment applications simply ignore them - a practice that would not work for international tax law due to the centrality of intangibles in MNE operations. First, both the arm's length standard and formulary apportionment (if assets are included in the formula) equally require valuation of intangibles, so one cannot count the difficulty of their valuation against formulary apportionment. Second, formulary apportionment is more amenable than the arm's length standard to formulary solutions to link intangibles to particular tax jurisdictions, an inescapable solution that indeed has recently been found by the OECD itself as the only acceptable solution for what it calls 'hard-to-value-intangibles' in the context of residual profit split application.[48]

In conclusion, formulary apportionment cannot be viewed as inferior to the arm's length standard based on the difficulty in valuing intangibles. Formulary apportionment also simplifies the administration of transfer pricing, since it avoids the costly and complex comparability analysis, replacing it with compilation of data that the taxpayer should possess in any event. Opponents of formulary apportionment often counter this argument with the argument that the eventual rules applying formulary apportionment will be as complex as the arm's length standard rules, because they will need to fend off the inherent imprecision of definitions (of the formula factors), timing issues, and valuation much like the current arm's length standard rules. To some extent this critique is correct, yet one cannot avoid the fact that the 'degrees of freedom' in the comparability analysis and the inevitable reliance on external data (rather than internal firm data) that is often inaccurate and incomplete mandate unquestionably more complex and vague costlier norms for the arm's length standard.

A related issue is the manipulability of the various solutions. This chapter argues that the collapse of arm's length standard-based transfer pricing is sufficient evidence that it is simply incapable of meeting its anti-avoidance goals. The vagueness of the comparability analysis, the data quality, and the extent of proxies used cannot be compared to any reasonable formulary apportionment regime. The problem is that such a comparison is difficult to make without an actual, detailed proposal. Formulary apportionment opponents often refer therefore to the Massachusetts formula, arguing that firms could manipulate the formula by shifting of assets and personnel; sales are obviously less prone to manipulation but may be structured as if made in one country rather than the other.

While it is true that formulary apportionment is not perfectly immune from manipulation, it is easy to see that the costs of shifting assets, personnel, and sales are high, and certainly higher than the shifting of risks via arrangements with intangible

48. See OECD, *Inclusive Framework on BEPS: Action 8, Guidance for Tax Administrations on the Application of the Approach to Hard-to-Value Intangibles* (OECD 2018).

assets and obligations that leaves arm's length standard-based transfer pricing weaponless. Some have responded to the manipulability critique of formulary apportionment with ideas to limit the formulas to assets or sales.[49] These scholars typically give significant weight to resilience to manipulation in the design of tax rules applicable to MNEs. This chapter argues that a more sophisticated analysis is required to assess the impact of manipulation on the design of the formula, especially when weighed against the benefits of having a multifactor formula. In any event, formulary apportionment must be superior to the arm's length standard in terms of resilience to manipulation.

Lastly, a significant advantage of formulary apportionment is its superior compatibility with an international regime of tax norms. The arm's length standard is typically applied in every state unilaterally and with little interaction with the parallel application of the same general standard in the jurisdiction on the other side of the transaction. It is also for the most part limited to transactions with two sides involved. Formulary apportionment is not limited to particular transactions and definitely not to two sides, and its application normally presumes coordination in the application of the formula by the countries involved. Theoretically, the arm's length standard could also mandate bilateral application (a good idea in any event), and yet the already rooted practice is different and difficult to change. Similarly, one could argue that formulary apportionment could be applied by the parties separately, which is true, yet less likely after the parties have gone through the process of negotiation and compromise over the formula. Moreover, as already mentioned, the degrees of freedom in the application of formulary apportionment must be more limited than those of the arm's length standard.

Formulary apportionment has other, political advantages, on which this chapter expands in §8.05 that is dedicated to issues of development and international cooperation.

The common critique of formulary apportionment was largely disposed of by Avi-Yonah and Benshalom, repeated here for the sake of completeness.[50] First, of course, is the argument that formulary apportionment is arbitrary, as mentioned above, and therefore 'mimics' the operation of MNEs and does so too inaccurately, and since taxation should correspond to the manner profits are generated by MNEs,[51] formulary apportionment is not up to the task. Avi-Yonah and Benshalom respond that the arm's length standard is at least equally arbitrary, sensitive to the fictions of separate corporate personality and corporate residence, and completely divorced from the economic reality of highly integrated (multi-entity) firms.[52]

49. *See, e.g.*, Reuven S. Avi-Yonah & Kimberly A. Clausing, *Reforming Corporate Taxation in a Global Economy: A Proposal to Adopt Formulary Apportionment*, in *Path to Prosperity: Hamilton Project Ideas on Income Security, Education, and Taxes* 319 (Jason Furman & Jason E. Bordoff eds., Brookings Institution Press 2008).

50. *See* Avi-Yonah & Benshalom, *Formulary Apportionment – Myths and Prospects, supra* n. 7.

51. There is an interesting interaction between this argument and the recent 'value creation' rhetoric promoted by the OECD. *See supra* n. 11.

52. *See* Avi-Yonah & Benshalom, *Formulary Apportionment – Myths and Prospects, supra* n. 7, at 381-383.

Second is the critique that formulary apportionment would require an impossible universal agreement over a single formula. Such critique is obviously incorrect since any country can switch to formulary apportionment and apply it unilaterally (the US states do) and there is no reason why pairs or more of countries cannot agree to use it among themselves (this is actually the CCCTB proposal).[53] Moreover, Avi-Yonah and Benshalom remind us that formulary apportionment can be complementary to the arm's length standard since it is not contradictory to it as explained next, and therefore it could be used only in cases where the arm's length standard proves ineffective.[54] The BEPS project in effect points in this direction even though it maintains the rhetoric of the arm's length standard.

Third is the critique that formulary apportionment is disruptive of business practice since it does not follow the income (value) generation, but rather factors that may or not be proportionally contributing to it in proportion to their own value. This is effectively the same argument as the arbitrariness critique, and the response is that the arm's length standard cannot fare better in this respect. Note that the goal of transfer pricing is not to reflect the economics of non-market transactions but rather defend against tax avoidance in implementation of political agreements to divide tax bases among competing jurisdictions.

A different critique - that formulary apportionment is too inflexible in respect of its reliance on fixed and possibly inaccurate or inappropriate factors and therefore may have counterintuitive results - may be viewed as derivative of this critique and is more serious. Avi-Yonah and Benshalom acknowledge the issue yet argue that a hybrid arm's length standard and formulary apportionment regime should suffer less from this critique and that the regime could be designed in a manner that would remedy most of the potentially negative implications, through use of a default rule, for example.[55] This chapter agrees with this response, but one issue that remains is the adaptability of formulary apportionment to changes in relative positions among countries. This issue is less acute if a hybrid regime of the sort proposed by Avi-Yonah and Benshalom is adopted, but it does not disappear. Some countries may argue that they can agree on a certain formula today, but they worry about the implications of such agreement in the future when their economies and relative world stances change. Section 8.05 elaborates on this issue in the context of its discussion of development.

Fifth is the critique that formulary apportionment is highly manipulable, vulnerable to multinational enterprises recasting their structures to appear to alter the mix of factors in different jurisdictions.[56] Sixth is the argument that formulary apportionment is incompatible with tax treaties, international law, and generally harmful to international cooperation.[57] This chapter demonstrates that the opposite is the case, and, in any event, transfer pricing reform is inevitable and reform is better implemented by

53. Moreover, it has long been acknowledged that the proposal may be adopted also in the format of enhanced cooperation among a portion of the Union's members.
54. *See* Avi-Yonah & Benshalom, *Formulary Apportionment – Myths and Prospects*, *supra* n. 7, at 383-387.
55. *Ibid.*, 389-390.
56. *See also ibid.*, 390-392.
57. *See ibid.*, 390-395 (for complementary arguments).

clear rule changes and that is common to both the arm's length standard and formulary apportionment, as demonstrated by the BEPS project. Seventh is the argument that formulary apportionment will cause a shift of assets to low tax jurisdictions, which is essentially the same argument as the manipulability argument, but one should also note that the entire BEPS project was triggered by arm's length standard-based shifting of risks and assets, i.e., easily shifted assets, such as intangibles, while shifting of other assets and of personnel, which would be more devastating to formulary apportionment in comparison to the arm's length standard, is much costlier and realistically unlikely (one can hardly see Google, Microsoft, Amazon, or even Caterpillar moving their actual operations to the Caymans).

In the spirit of the hybrid proposal by Avi-Yonah and Benshalom, this chapter proceeds to explore the idea by first examining the idea in theory, conceptually, and then demonstrate that, despite the arm's length standard rhetoric, recent developments all move in this direction in practice.

[D] What Could a Mixed Arm's Length Standard/Formulary Apportionment Solution Look Like? The Theory

The debate between arm's length standard and formulary apportionment proponents has been going on in one form or another for almost the entire modern income tax era, but for the large part it has been corrupted by misconceptions and a lack of rigorous, clear analysis of the issues at stake. Even the 1930 study of the issue in the League of Nations, which famously commissioned Mitchell B. Carroll to study the practice of international taxation of business in different countries with a view to seeking a standard recommended solution, was biased, as is apparent from its recommendation to essentially adopt the arm's length standard, which the future model treaty did, consistently with the US Treasury position on the matter despite its inconsistency with the actual comparative study Carroll conducted. To date, the debate is based on several false premises, including: (1) that the choice is binary; (2) that the arm's length standard's current dominance requires overwhelming benefits involved with formulary apportionment for consideration of reform; (3) that formulary apportionment means apportionment according to the Massachusetts formula or its derivatives; and (4) that formulary apportionment requires wide international consensus about the formula, which makes it a non-starter. There are several other false objections to formulary apportionment, which Avi-Yonah and Benshalom have proved are 'myths'.[58] It has already been observed that a more serious debate is required, and as demonstrated in the following section, the practice of transfer pricing has already moved away from a pure arm's length standard, if such a notion has even ever existed; this section proceeds first, however, with clarifications of the issues at stake from a theoretical or conceptual perspective.

A preliminary issue that often escapes the debate is the scope of the issues. For the most part, the debate focuses on the choice of an implementation standard of the

58. *Ibid.*

transfer pricing norm that seeks to curb the ability of MNEs to shift profits intragroup among jurisdictions at will. Yet, the consequential apportionment of profits among jurisdictions is part of a wider regime that divides tax jurisdiction over business profits among jurisdictions. The latter regime is based on the concept of residence, source, and permanent establishment, which combine formal elements, such as legal residence, with economic or market elements. This means that market transactions are not taxed based on economic bases alone: the market prices, once established, are attributed to legal entities (and consequently to tax jurisdictions) largely, but not exclusively, based on formal rules of source and residence. Non-market (business) transactions are subject to the same regime, but in the absence of the market, a substitute mechanism for the determination of prices is required and filled by the transfer pricing rules. This regime has been subject to much critique primarily due to the dominance of the formal elements over the division of tax bases among jurisdictions[59] (assuming that all agree to eliminate double taxation), and one could see both arm's length standard and formulary apportionment principles recruited to reform this regime, but the regime as such is quite resilient, functions, and enjoys wide legitimacy, which leads to little or no actual prospects for its reform. It is the transfer pricing portion that is subject to the most heated debate. Providing the above context is important for a few reasons: first, it demonstrates that the discourse is not between purely arbitrary formulary apportionment and economically correct arm's length standard principles and, even if it were, the eventual taxation does not follow pure economic principles.[60] Second, it focuses on the function of the transfer pricing rules as determining solely intra-firm apportionment of profits, not directly allocating profits to jurisdictions. And third, it helps to put in context actual and proposed formulary apportionment regimes, and not blindly treat them, and a proposed reform of the transfer pricing rules as singular. An example of the latter is the parallels drawn to US state taxation that, unlike the international tax rules, do not follow an agreement to eliminate double taxation and uses nexus rather than residence and source concepts for taxing the profits once apportioned.

The key conceptual misunderstanding, however, is the binary view of the choice between the arm's length standard and formulary apportionment. Others have observed that these standards should more accurately be viewed as points on a continuum of policy options.[61] To explain this point, take by way of example USco, a Delaware corporation that produces agricultural equipment in the United States and sells it in country F, where the corporate tax rate is lower than the US tax rate of 21%, say 12%. Further assume that domestic sales in country F must effectively be done through a domestic corporation, for which purpose USco organizes Fco. Country F corporation performs all of the domestic functions in country F: sales, marketing, service, training, parts, customization, upgrades, and the various administrative

59. *See, e.g.*, Hugh J. Ault & David P. Bradford, *Taxing International Income: An Analysis of the US System and Its Economic Premises*, in *Taxation in the Global Economy* 11 (Assaf Razin & Joel Slemrod eds., University of Chicago Press 1990).
60. The simplest way of observing this is through the importance of residence taxation, residence being essentially meaningless from an economic perspective.
61. *See* Avi-Yonah & Benshalom, *Formulary Apportionment – Myths and Prospects*, *supra* n. 7.

functions (management, accounting, and legal). Assume also that Fco sells some of the product in neighbouring country B. Country B has a corporate tax rate of 20%. Without getting deeper into the details, it is simple to observe that the firm has an incentive to shift profits to F, whose tax rate is 12%. The transfer pricing rules apply to prevent such shifting. Note, however, that initial tax jurisdiction is established in the United States and in countries F and B (assuming that Fco's presence in country B is sufficient to trigger a permanent establishment and therefore corporate taxation in that country), based on primarily formal rules (residence and source), and the transfer pricing rules begin to apply only after the jurisdiction determination to divide the overall firm's profit among the entities (USco, Fco, and Fco's permanent establishment in country B that is typically taxed in the same manner as a separate subsidiary would have been taxed in the same circumstances), and consequently, among the tax jurisdictions involved.

The arm's length standard would base the appropriate transfer price (using which Fco appropriately purchases the equipment from USco) on the functions performed by the parties, the assets they use in the performance of such functions, and the risks each bears in such process. Recent OECD guidance which has generally been followed, at least at the rhetorical level, by most countries requires emphasis on the key people's functions, and, presumably less emphasis on the risks taken.[62] In contrast, formulary apportionment uses various economic indicators in the process of apportioning income to a jurisdiction, and the typical indicators proposed - payroll, assets, and sales related to operations in each country - are essentially the same indicators used in the arm's length standard functional analysis if one views risks as attached to other economic indicators. The most visible difference is the use of sales as a separate indicator. If sales were proportional to the investment in people and assets in a country, then the results would be the same. If not, such disproportionality would account for the difference between the arm's length standard and formulary apportionment, a quantitative rather than a qualitative difference justifying the continuum metaphor.[63]

62. *See* OECD, *Aligning Transfer Pricing Outcomes with Value Creation*, *supra* n. 11.
63. One may argue that this chapter's analysis is incorrect when a firm merely sells in a country without having people or assets 'on the ground' but note that scenario is not directly relevant to the issue at hand. Most of the sales-only scenarios are not taxed today by the country where the sales are commenced, because sales alone do not trigger a permanent establishment and permanent establishment taxation, so the transfer pricing question simply does not arise. A minimal permanent establishment does not change the analysis, because profits are attributed to permanent establishment based on the same principle: functions, assets, and risk. A more difficult objection to this analysis would be in the context of the digital economy where a permanent establishment is not created and when countries adopt virtual permanent establishment rules there are no assets or people, only sales, in the target country. Indeed, in such a situation, countries may impute the arm's length standard to allocate profits and tax virtual presence which, one may argue, would not appear in the formulary apportionment formula or will be disproportionately large in the formula (due to a large sales volume, for example). This argument should be rejected, because the entire debate over the digital economy is about the proper tax jurisdiction of countries where a firm has no physical presence. If a country chooses to tax virtual presence it would either impute presence, in which case there should not be difference between the arm's length standard and formulary apportionment, or use formulary apportionment in acknowledgment of its inability to apply the arm's length standard, which makes the debate moot. For more on this matter, *see infra* §8.05.

The technical use of the indicators differs, of course, among these standards: the arm's length standard uses the indicators to establish comparability between the tested transactions and comparable market transaction, while formulary apportionment uses them as a proxy to the economic presence or activity of the firm in the relevant country. This may seem to be a significant, conceptual difference, yet what determines market prices? The selling, producing firm would first wish to cover its expenses or costs, and then it would wish to earn a profit over such costs that is at least equivalent to the normal profit in its relevant market. If these were the only determinants of market prices, the difference between the arm's length standard and formulary apportionment would be small assuming that valuations and margins are acceptably within a narrow margin and publicly available as such.

The largest difference would be that under formulary apportionment the value of every dollar of cost is fixed, and in the case of an equally weighted formula such as the Massachusetts formula 'a dollar is a dollar' regardless of what it is expended for, while in the market it is possible for profits to increase disproportionately from increased expenditure on payroll or on certain assets or risks. Of course, this is just a crude description of the mechanism that does not reveal the interaction among the means of production, but it illustrates that the difference between the arm's length standard and formulary apportionment is not fundamental or conceptual, in support of the continuum metaphor. Now, of course, firms aspire to generate above normal profits and typically generate these with the use of intangibles, to which this chapter turns next. It is worth noting that above normal profits are not allocated differently than normal profits in market transactions and therefore would not change the analysis.

Intangibles are the enigma of transfer pricing analysis since traditional valuation methods are essentially useless in most cases due to their unique properties.[64] The simplification of analysis that lumps intangibles together, despite important differences, and that insists on strict analogy between the treatment of intangibles and tangible properties exacerbates the problem.[65] Various rounds of reform have attempted to focus on the economic reality of intangibles' creation, most recently following the 'people's functions' and particularly research and development activity in the spirit of the new OECD value creation mantra, which means that profit allocations should follow the location and efforts by the professional personnel of the firm and its productive assets (productive for both research and sales purposes). It is not difficult to observe, again, that such arm's length standard analysis is based on the same factors that a formulary apportionment analysis would track. The typical third element in formulary apportionment is of course reflected in the sales and people activities, but it is bound to more clearly be flushed out in the analysis if the virtual permanent establishment idea were to become widely accepted (as the case may likely be), since under such analysis profits would be allocated to a permanent establishment jurisdiction source based on sales in that jurisdiction even when no physical assets or

64. *See* Brauner, *Value in the Eye of the Beholder, supra* n. 26.
65. *Ibid.*

personnel are locally located.[66] The sole distinct conceptual difference between arm's length standard and formulary apportionment analysis of intangibles remains therefore the treatment of risk as a distinct factor under the arm's length standard, a treatment that came under much criticism and which importance has been demoted, even if vaguely by the OECD itself post-BEPS.[67] In conclusion, once taken apart to its components, there is little fundamental difference at the theoretical level between the arm's length standard and formulary apportionment, further demonstrating the superiority of viewing them as points on a continuum rather than two opposite, binary policy choices.

[E] The Reality of Formulary Rules That Cannot Be Called Formulary

Formulas are already extensively used in the tax laws of many countries, but, even more importantly, they have become an important feature of much of the more recent OECD work on transfer pricing, albeit in the latter case that the organization seems to be welcoming them but only so long as one does not use the formulary apportionment terminology. This section demonstrates this phenomenon with some prominent examples.

[1] US Tax Law's Use of Formulary Apportionment

Formulaic taxation is not new for US tax law. Interest expense allocation, for example (e.g., to domestic and foreign source income), is done based on the ratio of domestic to foreign (when this is the relevant distinction) assets,[68] rather than based on the normal expense allocation rule.[69] More recently, Internal Revenue Code section 951A,[70] enacted in 2017, and known as the Global Intangibles Low-Taxed Income (GILTI) provision, uses a formula to capture a hypothetical amount of not-otherwise-taxed income related to US investment in tangible property in the calculation of the residual GILTI (10% yield on the adjusted basis of the taxpayer's investment in business and depreciable tangible property, named net deemed tangible income return).[71] Finally, US transfer pricing practice is dominated by methodologies introduced by the 1994 regulations known as Comparable Profits Method (CPM) and profit split, both of which, though primarily CPM, came under attack at the OECD as violations of the

66. *See* OECD, *Addressing the Tax Challenges of the Digitalisation of the Economy: Public Consultation Document, 13 February – 6 March 2019*, OECD/G20 Base Erosion and Profit Shifting Project (OECD 2019).
67. *See* OECD, *Aligning Transfer Pricing Outcomes with Value Creation*, *supra* n. 11. *See also, e.g.*, Rutger Hafkenscheid, *International – The BEPS Report on Risk Allocation: Not So Functional*, 24(1) Int'l Transfer Pricing J. 1 (2017); Richard J. Vann, *Taxing International Business Income: Hard-Boiled Wonderland and the End of the World*, 2(3) World Tax J. 291, sec. 4.1 (2010) (one of the most respectable defenders of the arm's length standard advocating *inter alia* de-emphasizing risk in the analysis).
68. 26 C.F.R. § 1.861-9T(f)-(g).
69. 26 C.F.R. § 1.861-8.
70. 26 U.S.C. § 951A.
71. 26 U.S.C. § 951A(b)(2) and (d).

arm's length standard.[72] The two methods were introduced since the government acknowledged the inability of traditional arm's length standard methods to adequately apply to more complex transactions, especially transactions involving intangibles.[73] The United States continues to use CPM, while the rest of the world, via the OECD Transfer Pricing Guidelines, eventually adopted a variant of CPM, known as the Transactional Net Margin Method (TNMM).[74]

[2] The European CCCTB Proposal

Although most of the opposition to US dabbling with formulary apportionment has come from Europe, the European Union itself has been struggling with the application of corporate taxes in the single market. The most prominent reform proposal in that respect, still a proposal but one that has dominated the discourse for many years now in Europe, is the CCCTB proposal originating in the European Commission.[75] This proposal is boldly and directly formulary, using for allocation of the common base what is known as the Massachusetts formula. The European context is somewhat different from the global one because in Europe the Member States on the one hand agreed not to harmonize direct income taxation, but on the other subjected themselves to constitutional-like constraints that were interpreted by the Court of Justice of the European Union to require at least some harmonization of these rules. Being a smaller and perhaps more homogeneous group than all the countries of the world, they had, so the argument went, perhaps a better chance of agreeing on a formula that would be fair to them all. An earlier initiative along similar lines was commonly called 'home state taxation'.[76] The idea was that each European corporate group would be taxed under the tax rules of the Member State where it resided.[77] All Member States would have then mutually recognized each other's laws. Joann Weiner and others produced multiple assessments of potential adoption of formulary taxation among European Member States, drawing lessons *inter alia* from the United States.[78]

72. *See, e.g.*, Helmut Becker, *Comments on Profit Methods proposed by the OECD Discussion Report*, 23(5) Intertax 256 (1995) (summarizing comments of industry, governments, and scholars on various reforms, including CPM); Sven-Olof Lodin, *Is the American Approach Fair? – Some Critical Views on the Transfer Pricing Issues*, 23(5) Intertax 240 (1995).
73. *See* US Treasury Dept., *White Paper: A Study of Intercompany Pricing*, I.R.S. Notice 88-123, 1988-2 C.B. 458.
74. Currently in OECD, *Transfer Pricing Guidelines*, *supra* n. 3, at 117-132. *See also* Robert E. Culbertson, *A Rose by Any Other Name: Smelling the Flowers at the OECD's (Last) Resort*, Worldwide Tax Daily (1995).
75. *See* European Commission, *Common Consolidated Corporate Tax Base (CCCTB)*, *supra* n. 47.
76. Sven-Olof Lodin & Malcolm Gammie, *Home State Taxation: Tax Treaty Aspects* (IBFD Publications 2001).
77. Specifically, the proposal was for an election to be taxed where the parent had its headquarters.
78. Joann M. Weiner, *Practical Aspects of Implementing Formulary Apportionment in the European Union*, 8(7) Fla. Tax Rev. 629 (2007); Joann M. Weiner, *Formulary Apportionment and Group Taxation in the European Union: Insights from the United States and Canada* (European Commission, Taxation and Customs Union, Working Paper No. 8, 2005); Patrick Weninger, *Formulary Apportionment in the EU* (Intersentia 2009).

[3] OECD BEPS Work

Much of the transfer pricing work done by the OECD in the context of BEPS is formulary in nature. The origins of such work are in the original BEPS commitment:

> [A]lternative income allocation systems, including formula based systems, are sometimes suggested ... special measures, either within or beyond the arm's length principle, may be required with respect to intangible assets, risk and over-capitalisation ... .[79]

This promise was essentially abandoned during the project, resulting in very anaemic substantive reforms in the transfer pricing area.[80] This need did not disappear, however, leading to the post-BEPS work, which has focused primarily on strengthening the use of residual profit splits, including, explicitly, a place made for formulas in cases where allocation simply cannot be based on objective criteria.[81] Finally, a BEPS minimum standard, country-by-country reporting presents countries with various financial and other indicators that closely correspond to indicators typically used in formulary apportionment application, such as the US states' taxation formulas.[82] BEPS emphasized that country-by-country reporting should only be used for risk assessment purposes and could never be used to directly assess taxation, surely not by formulary apportionment,[83] and yet such limitations are toothless and at best naïve when many of the users of these reports could not expect to tax most MNEs operating within their jurisdiction in any other way.[84]

[4] The Rhetoric of Non-formulary Apportionment

By now, it is clear that formulary elements are required for the effective operation of the transfer pricing rules, even when such rules are based primarily on the arm's length standard. Although the evidence is merely anecdotal, experience and all available evidence points to the dominance of transactional methods (CPM/TNMM/profit split) rather than classic arm's length standard methods (Comparable Uncontrolled Price/Cost Plus/Resale Price Minus) in the practice of transfer pricing.[85] In BEPS, the OECD has signalled that the future lies in the use of residual profit splits that focus on

79. OECD, *Action Plan on Base Erosion and Profit Shifting*, *supra* n. 11, at 20.
80. OECD, *Aligning Transfer Pricing Outcomes with Value Creation*, *supra* n. 11.
81. OECD, *Revised Guidance on the Application of the Transactional Profit Split Method*, *supra* n. 38; OECD, *Guidance for Tax Administrations on the Application of the Approach to Hard-to-Value Intangibles*, *supra* n. 48.
82. *See* OECD, *Action 13 – 2015 Final Report: Transfer Pricing Documentation and Country-by-Country Reporting*, OECD/G20 Base Erosion and Profit Shifting Project (OECD 2015).
83. *Ibid.*
84. *See also* Reuven S. Avi-Yonah & Zachée Pouga Tinhaga, *Formulary Apportionment and International Tax Rules*, in *Taxing Multinational Enterprises as Unitary Firms* 67, 69-70 (Sol Picciotto ed., Institute of Development Studies 2017).
85. In the United States, *see, e.g.*, Internal Revenue Service, *Announcement and Report Concerning Advance Pricing Agreements* (27 March 2017), https://www.irs.gov/pub/irs-utl/2016_apma_statutory_report.pdf (accessed 6 March 2019). The IRS does not release statistics about the use of transfer pricing methods more generally.

the allocation of profits rather than the traditional focus on gross sales proceeds to resolve the difficulties it had admitted to have with application of the arm's length standard to transactions involving intangibles.[86] Similarly, the de facto opening of the door to simple formulary apportionment using country-by-country reporting demonstrates the overwhelming need for simplification of the transfer pricing rules by the use of formulary elements.[87] All these developments are permitted under what seems like an embargo on the use of the terminology associated with formulary apportionment. Every update of the Transfer Pricing Guidelines includes multiple repeats of the mantra that formulary apportionment is unacceptable and that all countries reject it, a strong rhetorical signal that this is a matter of concern to the political forces attempting to preserve the dominance of the arm's length standard.[88] The mix of firm arm's length standard rhetoric and different, mixed actions results in vague and often useless guidance, which is one of the most important costs of the binary rhetoric demonstrated by this chapter. Next, this chapter explains the negative impact of such rhetoric and legal obscurity on the understanding of the optimal level of international tax cooperation.

§8.03 INTERNATIONAL COOPERATION, TAX COMPETITION, AND THE TRANSFER PRICING DEBATE

We live in turbulent times, of an unprecedented multinational effort to coordinate tax policies,[89] culminating in the first true multilateral tax treaty - the Multilateral Instrument.[90] In addition, many of the same countries are uncooperative with each other, 'jumping the gun' with legislation that pre-empts cooperative efforts to standardize the international tax rules,[91] or simply deviating from supposed consensus measures out of frustration with the outcomes of the cooperative efforts.[92] Some of the turmoil could be attributed to the ongoing, mostly unfruitful cooperation versus

86. *Supra* text accompanying n. 81.
87. In the 2017 IFA Congress in Rio de Janeiro, for example, an overwhelming majority (over 95%) of the general assembly voted (informally) in favour of such contention, while only a few participants voted in favour of the traditional OECD analysis.
88. *See, e.g.*, OECD, *Transfer Pricing Guidelines*, *supra* n. 3, at 38-39, 43.
89. Currently in the format of the OECD/G20 Inclusive Framework on Base Erosion and Profit Shifting ('Inclusive Framework') that includes 129 countries and jurisdictions (as on March 2019). *See* OECD, *About the Inclusive Framework on BEPS*, http://www.oecd.org/tax/beps/beps-about.htm (accessed 6 March 2019).
90. Formally, the Multilateral Convention to Implement Tax Treaty Related Measures to Prevent BEPS (entered into force 1 July 2018). For the full text, supporting documents and an updated list of signatories, *see* OECD, *Multilateral Convention to Implement Tax Treaty Related Measures to Prevent BEPS*, http://www.oecd.org/tax/treaties/multilateral-convention-to-implement-tax-treaty-related-measures-to-prevent-beps.htm (accessed 16 June 2019).
91. *E.g.*, the UK's 'google tax'. *See* Finance Act (FA) 2015 (UK); *see also* HM Revenue and Customs, *Diverted Profits Tax: Guidance* (December 2018), https://assets.publishing.service.gov.uk/government/uploads/system/uploads/attachment_data/file/768204/Diverted_Profits_Tax_-_Guidance__December_2018_.pdf (accessed 16 June 2019).
92. *See, e.g.*, India's Equalisation Levy Rules. Chapter VIII of Finance Act, 2016. *See also, e.g.*, Sagar Wagh, *The Taxation of Digital Transactions in India: The New Equalization Levy*, 70(9) Bull.

competition discourse, which is really a debate over the appropriate level of international coordination of tax policies,[93] in which interest in the standardization of the international tax norms[94] competes with fears of power grabs by the richest nations, or cartelization of the process, resulting in inefficient, uncompetitive consequences.[95] The transfer pricing rules are naturally at the centre of the discourse, the arm's length standard being an essentially universal norm, and a struggling norm that all countries find difficult to apply in important, difficult cases.

There is no question that effective transfer pricing rules are, first, essential for all countries and, second, inherently multilateral, requiring standardization and some level of coordination among countries, because the impact of the rules is to practically divide a 'single' economic profit among two (or more) competing jurisdictions. The arm's length standard gave countries a pretence of division based on economic truths or desert as if the economics of related-party transactions somehow mandate division of the tax base in one rather than another manner.

The application of the arm's length-based transfer pricing rules demonstrates more than anything the competitive nature of the regime with each jurisdiction calculating separately profits sourced within the jurisdiction. These rules respond to the inability of states to rely on market disciplined transactions and actual market prices to (unilaterally) calculate taxes on related-party transactions. Alternatively, essentially all countries adhere to the market imitating arm's length standard to establish 'transfer prices' that allow them to legitimately apply their long-established tax rules to the resultant profits as if they were real. The unreal nature of the profits is irrelevant since the allocation of profits generated by firms is required solely due to the fact that more than a single political jurisdiction wishes to tax them; the profits do not 'belong' to any of the jurisdictions, and none of them 'deserve' to tax such profits. The states involved simply agree on a legitimate division rule that will prevent double taxation on the one hand and abuse of the system by MNEs on the other. The game here is simple and basically zero sum: we know the profit, we know it should all be taxed, and we agree on the division rule. A person who is unfamiliar with international taxation would therefore be surprised to learn that, despite the simplicity of the game, it is played with essentially no contact, no positive coordination between the states that were supposed to divide the said profit, that each of the states applies the arm's length standard by itself, often in manners different from each other, often with no remedy in cases of suspected violation of the rules of the game, and usually with complete disregard for what the other state does. It is not surprising therefore that transfer pricing disputes overwhelm all other international tax issues today.[96]

Int'l Tax'n 538 (2016); Amar Mehta, *'Equalization Levy' Proposal in Indian Finance Bill 2016: Is It Legitimate Tax Policy or an Attempt of Treaty Dodging?*, 22(2) Asia-Pac. Tax Bull. online (2016).

93. Yariv Brauner, *The Multilateral Instrument as a Platform for Coordination of International Tax Policies*, Brit. Tax Rev. (forthcoming 2019).
94. *Ibid.*
95. *See, e.g.*, Tsilly Dagan, *International Tax Policy: Between Competition and Cooperation* (Cambridge University Press 2019 forthcoming).
96. *See, e.g.*, OECD, *Mutual Agreement Procedure Statistics for 2017*, http://www.oecd.org/tax/dispute/mutual-agreement-procedure-statistics.htm (accessed 16 June 2019).

It is of course possible to reform the arm's length standard-based system and require consistency of transfer prices determined in both (or more) competing jurisdictions,[97] and effective communication and dispute resolution among such jurisdictions, but such reform seems unachievable at the present time. Partial reforms that would include pre-agreed solutions such as safe harbours and predetermined margins are more likely yet still highly contested without the support of the OECD. This chapter argues that the high stakes involved, the perceived advantage that the more powerful countries seem to have, and the acquired comfort with the system gained by now by MNEs will make it highly unlikely that cooperative reforms of the arm's length standard-based transfer pricing rules will be implemented in the near future. The false normative support for the arm's length standard will continue to hinder progress in such direction as it has to date, even in the BEPS project.[98]

The advantage of formulary apportionment reform over the arm's length standard is twofold. First, it cannot be easily corrupted by arguments such as the above-mentioned normative argument since it is apportionment rather than 'valuation' based. Of course, conflicts over interpretation and implementation may arise under formulary apportionment, but these are limited to questions regarding classification in categories such as assets, people, and sales, which are naturally much simpler than questions involving vague concepts like comparability. Second, the transparency of the formulary application makes it much easier to compare and enforce consistency and, hopefully, the disagreement and compromise among the relevant jurisdictions would be concluded prior to the establishment of the rules rather than (or more so than in arm's length standard analysis) in the application stages. Effective dispute resolution is as important for formulary apportionment as it is for arm's length standard-based transfer pricing. In conclusion, the transparency and simplicity of formulary apportionment and its mechanism should be more supportive of enhanced cooperation among nations in tax matters in contrast to the interference with such processes caused by the current arm's length standard-based transfer pricing regime.

§8.04 AUGMENTED REALITY? ON TRANSFER PRICING AND THE CHALLENGES PRESENTED BY THE DIGITAL ECONOMY

With digital, augmented reality tools, commonly known as filters, people can elevate their staged selfies beyond perceptions of authenticity. Digital transactions, however, produce real profits that should be taxed by the income tax like every other item of income. By now, there is a (justified) consensus also that digital transactions cannot be ring-fenced from the rest of the economy for tax purposes since they are an inseparable part of the economy, especially in the cross-border context.[99] Income from digital transactions is different, however, as they do not simply fit the residence/source

97. The inclusion of OECD Model article 9, para. 2 in the MLI is a step forward towards this goal of weakening the dominance of one-sided analyses.
98. *See* discussion *supra* §8.02[A].
99. *See, e.g.*, OECD, *Action 1 – 2015 Final Report: Addressing the Tax Challenges of the Digital Economy*, OECD/G20 Base Erosion and Profit Shifting Project 11 (OECD 2015).

paradigm that dominates the international tax regime. As many have explained, digital economy firms often may perform similar functions to traditional economy firms without physical presence in the target jurisdictions, avoiding the traditional taxation triggers in such jurisdictions.[100] The different treatment of digital and non-digital firms (having used these terms simplistically) requires a choice between one of two conservative responses (assuming that countries have no appetite for a complete overhaul of the international tax regime): tweak the rules so that they could apply and tax the digital firms, or legitimize the current situation of no source taxation in the case of digital firms. At present, it is quite clear that the latter approach would not be acceptable and that in the absence of a universal solution along the lines of the former response, individual jurisdictions will adopt it unilaterally in any event.[101]

The key technical questions raised by the ascent of the digital economy in this framework of pragmatic rather than holistic solutions pertain to source taxation and its extension to the taxation of permanent establishments. It is easy to observe that without physical presence a non-resident firm would not be taxed in a jurisdiction because it would not have a permanent establishment there. The most straightforward solution to this problem has been therefore to deem taxable presence through relevant presence indicators other than physical presence, a solution known as the significant economic presence or virtual permanent establishment.[102] This solution was not immediately promoted, however, as despite the intuitive appeal, it is much more difficult to agree on acceptable virtual indicators than on observable (and now long-established) physical presence indicators.[103] The permanent establishment question is not alone, however, in this context because even less significant transactions in digitalized content face the question of source: at the location of the consumer or the provider? Answering this question is difficult and in any event insufficient because the administrative difficulties involved with taxing such transactions overwhelm the legal conundrums.

It is not surprising therefore that the application of the transfer pricing rules to such transactions is in a state of uncertainty as well. It is so at two different levels: first, at the comparability level, as it is difficult to establish comparability with digital transactions that represent perhaps the most difficult cases of transactions involving intangibles, transactions with which the transfer pricing rules struggle unrelated to the digital economy,[104] and, second, at the solutions level, since several seriously discussed proposals involve reliance on profit allocation methods (i.e., transfer pricing

100. *See, e.g., ibid.*
101. Hence the continuous work is dominated by the efforts at the OECD. *See, e.g.*, the dedicated website for the matter OECD, *Digital Economy*, http://www.oecd.org/sti/ieconomy/.
102. *See, e.g.*, Peter Hongler & Pasquale Pistone, *Blueprints for a New PE Nexus to Tax Business Income in the Era of the Digital Economy* (WU International Taxation Research Paper Series No. 2015-15, 2015), https://ssrn.com/abstract=2591829.
103. For more, *see* Andres Baez & Yariv Brauner, *Taxing the Digital Economy Post BEPS . . . seriously*, 58 Colum. J. Transnat'l L. (forthcoming 2019).
104. *See, e.g.*, OECD, *Aligning Transfer Pricing Outcomes with Value Creation, supra* n. 11; Brauner, *Value in the Eye of the Beholder, supra* n. 26.

methods) for the division of tax bases among competing jurisdictions in the context of the digital economy.[105]

The application of the arm's length standard to digital transactions is notoriously difficult. Take the most basic transaction: a related-party business-to-business transfer of digitalized content (a piece of software).[106] Application of the arm's length standard would require a comparability analysis that is rarely fruitful since such transfers are almost always unique, and, not less important, the data for good comparability analysis is rarely available or satisfactory. Alternative arm's length standard analysis would attempt to isolate the part of the profit that cannot be allocated based on traditional functional and comparability analyses (the 'upside') and allocate it on a basis other than the market. In the pre-BEPS world, the upside was most frequently allocated to the legal owner of an intangible, which led to obvious opportunities for tax planning and in any event to little or no taxation at source. BEPS promoted analysis based on less formal and more substantive indicia, known as development, enhancement, maintenance, protection, and exploitation of intangibles (DEMPE) factors, consistent with the 'value creation' idea.[107] DEMPE analysis clarifies that mere legal ownership should not be allocated profits, and it hardly provides a clear allocation tool due to the lack of a device for division among the factors and the vagueness of some of them, mainly the exploitation factor. The sole resort for a source jurisdiction under this framework is to maximize profits allocated to them under the exploitation factor, an exercise that is understandably different from the parallel allocations in the residence jurisdictions where the entire research, development, and management functions are performed. The OECD work and the global tendency to follow it focus more on people's functions and less on risk and formal ownership in the analysis, which is understandable in terms of broad strokes but hardly useful for actual implementation, an issue that all tax practitioners face at the present.

Note, however, that regardless of what one views as the optimal solution to the challenges above, the most important part of the analysis – the allocation of the upside – cannot be done based on the arm's length standard; it will always be formulary, either via a multifactor functional analysis and allocation or otherwise (i.e., based on formulary apportionment of some kind, an option that the recent OECD guidance on hard-to-value-intangibles specifically prescribes, even if via vague language).[108] Note that this work and the recent guidance on profit splits are consistent with the Avi-Yonah and Benshalom proposal of a compromise between the arm's length standard and formulary apportionment which would use formulary elements in the difficult cases of intangibles transfers.[109] In conclusion, the ascent of the digital economy has made the difficulty of applying the arm's length standard to transactions

105. *See also* OECD, *Addressing the Tax Challenges of the Digitalisation of the Economy*, *supra* n. 66.
106. Note that the debate tends to focus on more visible transactions (business-to-consumer sale of digitalized content, such as song files), yet these specifically are not the concern of the transfer pricing rules.
107. *See* OECD, *Aligning Transfer Pricing Outcomes with Value Creation*, *supra* n. 11.
108. *See* OECD, *Guidance for Tax Administrations on the Application of the Approach to Hard-to-Value Intangibles*, *supra* n. 48.
109. *See* Avi-Yonah & Benshalom, *Formulary Apportionment – Myths and Prospects*, *supra* n. 7.

involving intangibles clearer and most obvious. Pure arm's length standard application has become impossible, leaving the stage to transactional methods to reign, but the insistence of the OECD to gown them as arm's length standard has made them incapable of fully solving the problem, resulting in the current resort to more expressly formulaic solutions as complements, especially profit splits.[110]

A second dimension of the interaction between the transfer pricing rules and the debate over the taxation of the digital economy is the proposition by some players to use transfer pricing methodologies to more generally tax business income generated by the digital economy. The least dramatic interaction between the transfer pricing rules and reform proposals involves the above-mentioned virtual permanent establishment proposals. Once nexus or the permanent establishment treatment is triggered under whatever proposal prevails, one must allocate profits to such nexus or permanent establishment. The current profit allocation rules generally follow the arm's length standard, more or less strictly (depending on one's interpretation or version of Model Treaty Article 7). However, regardless of the course taken, the result is unsatisfactory when intangibles are involved and can be expected to be worse for pure digital presence (one would presumably be required to allocate profits to the digital presence indicators: sales and users), at least without global consensus on the matter. Note again that once digital presence triggers taxation at the source, the solution becomes very similar to formulary apportionment: reliance on sales, users, and other digital indicators in a purely formulaic manner. Most importantly, sales in a country are factored in, and the location of sales most importantly distinguished the arm's length standard from most formulary apportionment proposals.

The more dramatic reform proposals that implement transfer pricing or arm's length standard methodology have been the 'user participation' and 'marketing intangibles' proposals advanced in the last year or so by the United Kingdom and the United States, respectively.[111] The user participation proposal calls for an amendment of the profit allocation rules to take account of user participation in the user's country.[112] The proposal is to permit countries where certain users truly provide a benefit to certain businesses of the type that significantly benefit from the contribution of users, such as social media platforms, to automatically declare nexus and require allocation of some profits to such nexus with the view of having consequent jurisdiction to tax such profits.

The proposal does not extend the rule to all businesses but rather only to those significantly benefiting from such user participation, which is an obvious ring-fencing that violates the first principle established by the OECD.[113] For the purposes of this

110. *See* OECD, *Revised Guidance on the Application of the Transactional Profit Split Method*, *supra* n. 38.
111. *See* OECD, *Addressing the Tax Challenges of the Digitalisation of the Economy*, *supra* n. 66.
112. For its origins, *see* HM Treasury, *Corporate Tax and the Digital Economy: Position Paper Update* (March 2018), https://assets.publishing.service.gov.uk/government/uploads/system/uploads/attachment_data/file/689240/corporate_tax_and_the_digital_economy_update_web.pdf.
113. There are multiple other issues with this proposal, yet these are beyond the scope of this chapter. For more, *see* Baez & Brauner, *Taxing the Digital Economy Post BEPS*, *supra* n. 103.

chapter, one immediately notes that this proposal essentially eliminates the two-step analysis currently required for taxation of business profits in a non-resident jurisdiction, permitting business income taxation at the source based on factors such as user participation, and not based on comparability, functions, assets, or risks (i.e., more formulary apportionment than arm's length standard).

The marketing intangibles proposal avoids the ring-fencing pitfall of the user participation proposal by applying it to all businesses and is based on a similar logic, relating tax jurisdiction at the source to marketing intangibles developed by the non-resident business in the source (market) country. The proposal is not yet developed, but it would essentially avoid the question of nexus or permanent establishment by directly allocating profits to the said marketing intangibles. The difficulty is in the allocation: how much of the profits to allocate? (this is separate from the vagueness and controversy over how to determine and define a marketing intangible, a question beyond the scope of this chapter). The proposal remains vague at the present, but it acknowledges that current arm's length standard rules may not suffice (again, there is no way to establish viable comparables, and it is very hard to hang allocation to marketing intangibles on easily identifiable factors, namely people's functions, and assets). Therefore, the proposal calls for further study of 'formulaic approaches' based on 'mechanical approximations'.[114] The above proposals are only the proposals promoted by the OECD, the most vigorous opponent of formulary apportionment. This is observed again and again as one observes the inevitability of resort to formulaic solutions in the most difficult situations.

The debate over the taxation of the digital economy also exposes the behind the scenes conflict between residence and source jurisdictions, when the former wish to maintain as much of the current regime that limits most source taxation and the latter demand expansion of source taxation. This conflict is discussed more directly in the next section.

§8.05 THE ARM'S LENGTH STANDARD, FORMULARY APPORTIONMENT, AND DEVELOPING COUNTRIES

The transfer pricing discourse has been on the agenda of the international tax regime for a long time. At present, it must share the limelight with some contemporary policy challenges, including the changes in the markets, primarily the increasing importance of intangibles and the digital economy, and also dramatic geopolitical changes, that make the fair allocation of tax bases a primary concern in the BEPS project.[115] The ascent of the emerging economies, loosely organized in the BRICS or the G20 formats, has resulted in the OECD – that rich countries club – to accept their inclusion in various international tax policy fora culminating with the creation of the Inclusive Framework

114. *See* OECD, *Addressing the Tax Challenges of the Digitalisation of the Economy*, *supra* n. 66, at 15.
115. Yariv Brauner & Pasquale Pistone (eds), *BRICS and the Emergence of International Tax Coordination* (IBFD Publications 2015).

for the implementation of the BEPS project.[116] For the most part, the claim of developing countries (viewed together for simplicity) has been for more source taxation, because such a claim does not easily translate in the context of transfer pricing. The rhetoric here has typically followed a demand for more attribution to the market economies (again, a similar argument to that made in the context of the taxation of the digital economy), inevitably at the expense of the residence countries of MNEs. Perhaps the most notable innovation promoted in this context has been the campaign led by China within the BEPS project to recognize allocation of profits based on location savings, the notion that the profits of a multinational enterprise are attributable to some extent to the proximity to other factors resulting from presence in the jurisdiction, an idea considered and rejected by the BEPS project, yet nonetheless immediately implemented in any event by China, a BEPS stakeholder.[117]

Any reform of transfer pricing must therefore consider its implications on this conflict and the shifting balance of power in the international tax regime. The present arm's length standard-based transfer pricing regime is unacceptable to developing countries for two distinct sets of reasons: first, it has an inherent bias in favour of the most powerful economies, and, to some extent, in favour of low tax jurisdictions. Second, its complexity and costliness deepen the imbalance against developing countries. The arm's length standard provides an inherent benefit for MNEs, especially for the largest and most intangible-heavy MNEs. These MNEs reside almost exclusively in the most powerful developed countries. Moreover, key economic factors that dictate the terms of the comparability exercise are concentrated in such countries: management and similar high-paid personnel, key research and development, the most valuable tangible assets, and, naturally, most of the capital. Much of the value of such MNEs stems from intangibles they own, and in the absence of a clear 'tangible' location for such property it is regularly attributed to the source of capital invested (risked) in its development, the location of research and development, the location of key personnel whose actions and interaction account for much of the intangible value, and to the domestic legal protection and enforcement regime that ensures the preservation of its value, all of which naturally concentrate in the most developed countries. 'Leakages' of value, resulting from the unresolved deficiencies of the arm's length standard-based rules, increasingly find themselves in low tax jurisdictions, primarily based on risks and legal ownership properties that are highly manipulable. Such leakages hurt both developed and developing countries, which explain the cooperation of both groups in the BEPS project, but it is obvious that the more powerful countries are better able to fight them. The magnitude of a market impacts not only the cost of compliance and enforcement but also the availability and quality of data, and when the data is problematic (fewer transactions lead to fewer comparables, naturally), the opportunity typically presents itself to the MNE, strengthening it vis-à-vis the less developed country government. Finally, the notorious complexity and costliness of arm's length standard-based transfer pricing is prohibitive for developing countries.

---

116. *Supra* text accompanying n. 89.
117. *See, e.g.*, Diheng Xu, *The Convergence and Divergence Between China's Implementation and OECD/G20 BEPS Minimum Standards*, 10(3) World Tax J. 471 (2018).

Standardization and assistance with data, which improves exponentially with automatic exchange of information and country-by-country reporting, are simply insufficient to bring developing countries even close to a level playing field.

The question becomes whether developing countries should fare better under formulary apportionment. This question is impossible to answer in a comprehensive manner because serious comparison must be against a specific proposal, and only a few observations point to a positive answer. First, formulary apportionment does not have an embedded bias in favour of MNEs and their residence countries. Its basic neutrality does not put developing countries with smaller or less sophisticated markets at an initial disadvantage in the way the arm's length standard does. Second, the elusive risks should not factor in (at least not much) the division of tax bases under formulary apportionment. Third, the more transparent nature of formulary apportionment, and the larger likelihood of the application of formulary apportionment through bilateral or multilateral agreement, not permitting one-sided application that dominates arm's length standard-based transfer pricing, should be significantly advantageous to developing countries. Formulas, of course, could be applied unilaterally and, in the formulary apportionment context, developing countries have a few cards to play. They may apply differing formulas or different interpretations of formulas, which may result in double taxation, and this would not be tolerated by MNEs which would in turn apply considerably greater power for resolution of the situation, and MNEs should not be able to argue that unilateral application by a developing country is in violation of some pseudo-economic principle in the same way they do with the arm's length standard. Formulary apportionment may also allow developing countries a better competitive position (although tax competition is generally detrimental to developing countries), for example by adopting a sales-only formula in a similar fashion to many US states, not including assets in the formula which is effectively a tax incentive to invest. Fourth, formulary apportionment should generally be less subject to manipulability, although one cannot expect none, and a realistic, hybrid solution is perhaps the most resilient to manipulation (as well as the most politically likely). Consequently, formulary apportionment should be much less complex and costly than the arm's length standard, which reduces the disadvantage that developing countries' tax authorities have vis-à-vis the richer countries. Accounting and even valuation practices are much more universal than comparability analyses, and for the most part must be made anyway, which directly reduces the costs of administering transfer pricing. It has already been possible to see the importance of this observation and its feasibility in the strong push for simplified methods and safe harbours that even the OECD has begun to recognize. Anecdotally, in the 2018 annual meeting of the International Fiscal Association in Rio de Janeiro, an overwhelming majority of the members expressed support for acceptability of these methods, impacted, admittedly, by the leadership of Brazil in this regard, but the Brazilian effect cannot account for the entire tendency.

A more accurate comparison must be made with a specific formulary apportionment proposal that has yet to even be considered by the international tax regime due to the dominance of the reluctant OECD and, again, only a few observations are possible on the components of a future formula. A small number of studies have been carried out to examine the impact of a move from the arm's length standard tc formulary apportionment, typically based on the CCCTB proposal, which is an articulation of the Massachusetts formula. For example, a 2014 study by the International Monetary Fund[118] noted the asymmetric allocation of the formula factors among developed and developing countries. As expected, developing countries benefit from employment factors (low cost of labour), but lose from payroll factors (again, low cost of labour). They also lose from asset factors, but the outcome depends on the treatment of intangibles. Sales factors benefit both developed and developing countries, if more the former. Yet both benefit at the expense of 'conduit' countries, as the study calls them - low tax jurisdictions or tax havens, in other words. Study of the actual consequences of various reforms could build a consensus over an optimal formulary apportionment method, likely hybrid with some arm's length standard elements that could benefit all productive countries at the expense of 'conduit' countries.

§8.06 CONCLUSION

This chapter has exposed the costs of the misguided rhetoric that dominates the international transfer pricing discourse, emphasizing the particular mistake in the binary approach to the policy options available for reformers. This chapter demonstrates the potential benefits of a more focused discourse, removing the convex mirror of the arm's length standard, through the analysis of the most contemporary challenges faced by the international tax regime, concluding that such an approach is both desirable and feasible, being as a practical matter prevented solely by the OECD's rhetoric rather than its actions.

118. International Monetary Fund (IMF), *Spillovers in International Corporate Taxation* (IMF Policy Paper, 9 May 2014); IMF, *Corporate Taxation in the Global Economy* 33 (IMF Policy Paper, March 2019).

CHAPTER 9

Is Arm's Length Profit Split Methodology Morphing into a Formulary Apportionment Hybrid: The Chinese Example

Fei Gao & Antony Ting

§9.01 INTRODUCTION

There are signs that the Profit Split Method (PSM) may become more widely used, and 'market' may play an increasingly important role as a factor in the allocation of profits of multinational enterprises (MNEs). For instance, in response to the rise of the digital economy, the Organisation for Economic Co-operation and Development (OECD) and its broader Inclusive Framework of jurisdictions participating in the Base Erosion and Profit Shifting (BEPS) project are considering, among other things, the marketing intangible proposal under which 'the market jurisdiction would be entitled to tax some or all of the non-routine income properly associated with [marketing] intangibles ... even in the absence of a taxable presence'.[1] The allocation method of such income being considered includes a revised residual PSM.[2]

The marketing intangible proposal deviates from the traditional position of the OECD, which has otherwise recognized marketing intangibles as a 'unique and valuable contribution' only in very limited scenarios.[3] This new position arguably represents a shift towards the arguments that China has been making with respect to its

1. OECD, *Addressing the Tax Challenges of the Digitalisation of the Economy: Public Consultation Document, 13 February – 6 March 2019* OECD/G20 Base Erosion and Profit Shifting Project, para. 32 (OECD 2019).
2. *Ibid.*, para. 47.
3. OECD, *Revised Guidance on the Application of the Transactional Profit Split Method, Inclusive Framework on BEPS Action 10* Examples 2, 3 and 13 (OECD 2018).

transfer pricing policies, in particular, the concepts of location-specific advantages (LSAs) and marketing intangibles, as well as a wider application of the PSM.[4]

In the course of its involvement in the BEPS project, China consistently, but unsuccessfully, advocated the inclusion of LSAs in profit split calculations,[5] and when that effort proved unsuccessful, it unilaterally incorporated LSAs into its own transfer pricing rules.[6] Those rules, while largely based on the OECD *Transfer Pricing Guidelines*, were modified by China primarily in response to key problems identified by the State Administration of Taxation (SAT) in the application of the traditional transfer pricing methods, including the lack of comparable local transactions, and the desirability of identification, valuation and allocation of LSAs and marketing intangibles in the determination of the share of income attributable to a jurisdiction.[7]

The PSM is arguably similar to the global formulary apportionment model in concept, as both allocate profits of an MNE based on a formula involving various factors such as assets, employees and sales.[8] Of course, there are key differences between the two methods. In particular, the PSM adopts a formula that is tailor-made for each MNE, while the formulary apportionment model, in general, adopts a predetermined and mechanistic formula for all MNEs.[9] Nevertheless, an analysis of China's policies with respect to the PSM may provide some useful insights into the development of the formulary apportionment model.

This chapter in §9.02 first analyses the core principles and policies of China's PSM, aiming to set the stage for a detailed discussion in §9.03 of the concepts of LSAs and marketing intangibles. The conclusion in §9.04 summarizes the findings and insights into the development of a modern formulary apportionment model.

4. United Nations, *United Nations Practical Manual on Transfer Pricing for Developing Countries* Part D.2 China Country Practice (United Nations 2017).
5. Diheng Xu, *The Convergence and Divergence between China's Implementation and OECD/G20 BEPS Minimum Standards*, 10(3) World Tax J. 471, 485 (2018).
6. *Ibid.*
7. Sophie Ashley, *SAT's Liao Tizhong Discusses China's Transfer Pricing Position: Part One*, question 2, TP Week (10 April 2013), https://www.tpweek.com/articles/sats-liao-tizhong-discusses-chinas-transfer-pricing-position-part-one/araejlcu (accessed 11 June 2019).
8. Both the formulary apportionment and the PSM models take group synergies into consideration, whereas the traditional transfer pricing methods do not. According to transactional cost theory, internal transactions are much less costly than comparable external transactions: Mitchell A. Kane, *Transfer Pricing, Integration and Synergy Intangibles: A Consensus Approach to the Arm's Length Standard*, 6(3) World Tax J. 282, 282 (2014). Also, an MNE group is a single enterprise, so the group members are willing to sacrifice their benefits for a more substantial group benefit ('enterprise approach'): Milton Friedman, *The Social Responsibility of Business is to Increase its Profits*, N.Y. Times Mag. (13 September 1970), http://umich.edu/~thecore/doc/Friedman.pdf (accessed 11 June 2019). It means that an integrated corporate group is more profitable than an aggregation of individual members. The additional profit that arises from a corporate group being a group is labelled 'group synergies'. By contrast, the arm's length principle assumes that an MNE group is merely an aggregation of separate entities. The group members try to maximize their own profits separately ('separate entity approach').
9. OECD, *OECD Transfer Pricing Guidelines for Multinational Enterprises and Tax Administrations* paras 1.16 and 1.17 (OECD 2017).

§9.02 CHINA'S PROFIT SPLIT METHODOLOGY

[A] Core Principles

The OECD defines the PSM as a 'method that identifies the relevant profits to be split for the associated enterprises from a controlled transaction ... and then splits those profits between the associated enterprises on an economically valid basis that approximates the division of profits that would have been agreed at arm's length'.[10] While China largely adopts this definition, it has developed its PSM approach premised on a number of principles.

First, China's transfer pricing practice emphasizes the importance of the market. China believes that MNEs require fast-growing markets, such as China's, and the contributions of local subsidiaries to realize the value of their trade intangibles.[11] Profits are generated from taking advantages of the emerging market and create value for the MNE.[12] Therefore, it is not considered fair to allocate most or all of the residual profits of an MNE to the residence jurisdictions of parties with trade intangibles. In response to these concerns, China has argued for the application of the concepts of LSAs and marketing intangibles in comparability analysis and profit allocation.[13]

Although China does not specify the economic theory underlying its transfer pricing practice, its emphasis on LSAs is most closely aligned with comparative advantage theory.[14] The simplest model of this theory consists of two countries, such as China and the United States. Assume that China has a comparative advantage in low-cost labour and the United States in research and development. The two countries perform their functions at relatively low cost and use fewer resources than if they carried out both functions. An MNE will choose to perform functions in a country with a lower cost to benefit from the comparative advantages of each country and maximize its profits. If this is the case, it is not fair to allocate all or most of the residual profits to one particular state only because its comparative advantages give rise to trade intangibles. The MNEs involved enjoy the benefits as single enterprises, so the two countries should share the benefits of the cost savings.

China repeatedly uses the term 'comparative advantages' in its Country Practice chapter of the United Nations *Practical Manual on Transfer Pricing*:

> In a globalising economy, MNEs usually set up operations in developing countries to take advantage of *comparative advantages* that these countries offer. For

---

10. OECD, *Revised Guidance on the Application of the Transactional Profit Split Method*, *supra* n. 3, at 11, Glossary.
11. United Nations, *Practical Manual on Transfer Pricing for Developing Countries*, *supra* n. 4, at para. D.2.4.5.1.
12. Jinyan Li & Stephen Ji, *Location-Specific Advantages: A Rising Disruptive Factor in Transfer Pricing*, 71(5) Bull. Int'l Tax'n 259, 260 (2017).
13. China is likely the first major country that recognizes LSAs in its transfer pricing regulations. For an overview of Chinese transfer pricing regime and LSAs, *see ibid.*, 259.
14. Comparative advantage theory was built on the absolute advantage concept alluded to by Adam Smith in his well-known *The Wealth of Nations* (1776). The theory was developed by Robert Torrens, and refined by David Ricardo in David Ricardo, *On the Principles of Political Economy, and Taxation* (1st Am. ed., J. Milligan 1819).

> example, they set up manufacturing operations to take advantage of the abundant cheap labour or natural resources to supply products for overseas markets, R&D to take advantage of local talent for overseas principals, and distribution of imported products to the local market. These operations often take the form of contract or toll manufacturing, contract R&D, and limited risk distribution to leave little profit to the local country, despite the fact that many such *comparative advantages* contribute significant profits to the MNE group.[15]

Second, China has a stronger application of the enterprise approach in its transfer pricing regime. Under the enterprise approach, a company group is in general treated as one single enterprise, instead of as separate entities, for tax purposes. The SAT has observed that uncontrolled 'comparable transactions are often hard to find in real life'.[16] In response, China argues that 'it is nearly impossible to take out one piece of a value chain of an MNE group and try to match it to comparable transactions/companies'.[17] Instead of trying to find third-party comparable transactions, it is often necessary to analyse the global value chain and allocate profits based on the contributions of intangibles and assets used, functions performed and risks assumed, as well as the LSAs and group synergies.[18] The application of the enterprise approach in China's policies as to when and how the PSM should be applied is discussed in the following section.

[B] When Should the PSM Be Applied?

China, in general, follows the OECD *Transfer Pricing Guidelines* with respect to the application of the PSM. In particular, it applies the PSM in a three-step approach:

(1) determine whether the PSM is the most appropriate transfer pricing method;
(2) calculate the relevant profit to be split; and
(3) split the profit to the parties of the controlled transaction.[19]

Sections 9.02[B][1] and 9.02[B][2] analyse the first step, and §9.02[C] the other two steps.

[1] The Most Appropriate Method

The OECD stipulates the following general rule for choosing the most appropriate transfer pricing method:

---

15. United Nations, *Practical Manual on Transfer Pricing for Developing Countries*, *supra* n. 4, at para. D.2.4.6.1 (emphasis added).
16. *Ibid.*, para. D.2.4.2.1.
17. *Ibid.*, para. D.2.4.2.3.
18. SAT, *Consultation Draft Circular: Implementation Measures for Special Tax Adjustments*, Art. 73 (2015).
19. SAT, *Public Notice [2017] No.6: Public Notice of the State Administration of Taxation on Issuing the 'Administrative Measures of Special Tax Investigation and Adjustment and Mutual Agreement Procedure'*, Arts. 15, 16 and 21 (2017) (Bulletin 6).

> the selection of ... the most appropriate method for a particular case [should take] into account the respective strengths and weaknesses of each method, its appropriateness in view of the nature of the accurately delineated controlled transaction, the availability of reliable information (in particular on uncontrolled comparables) ... and the degree of comparability between the controlled and uncontrolled transactions.[20]

To determine whether the PSM is the most appropriate method, the OECD states that the presence of any of the following indicators is relevant:

- each party makes unique and valuable contributions;
- the business operations are highly integrated such that the contributions of the parties cannot be reliably evaluated in isolation from each other;
- the parties share the assumption of economically significant risks or separately assume closely related risks.[21]

China currently recognizes only the first two indicators.[22] The absence of the third indicator is possibly because China released its most recent transfer pricing regulations in early April 2017, which was before the OECD introduced the third indicator in its Revised Guidance on the PSM in June 2017.[23]

While the two indicators that the OECD and China have both identified may appear similar, the application of these indicators in practice may be quite different. In particular, the OECD emphasizes the importance of the first indicator to determine when the PSM is the most appropriate method: '[t]he existence of unique and valuable contributions by each party ... is perhaps the *clearest* indicator that a transactional profit split may be appropriate'.[24]

Following this logic, the OECD indicates that, in general, the PSM is unlikely to be appropriate for a typical limited risk distributor structure:

> where ... one party to the transaction performs only simple functions, does not assume economically significant risks in relation to the transaction and does not otherwise make any contribution which is unique and valuable, a [PSM] typically would not be appropriate.[25]

20. OECD, *Revised Guidance on the Application of the Transactional Profit Split Method, supra* n. 3, at para. 2.116.
21. *Ibid.*, 9, Executive summary.
22. SAT, Bulletin 6, *supra* n. 19, Art. 21.
23. Possibly for the same reason, the UN in general only recognizes the first two indicators for the PSM: United Nations, *Practical Manual on Transfer Pricing for Developing Countries, supra* n. 4, at para. B.1.6.16 (2017).
24. OECD, *Revised Guidance on the Application of the Transactional Profit Split Method, supra* n. 3, at para. 2.126 (emphasis added). The OECD defines unique and valuable contributions to be those that '(i) ... are not comparable to contributions made by uncontrolled parties in comparable circumstances, and (ii) ... represent a key source of actual or potential economic benefits in the business operations': para. 2.130.
25. OECD, *Revised Guidance on the Application of the Transactional Profit Split Method, supra* n. 3, at para. 2.127.

In contrast, China argues that the contributions from marketing and distribution functions in developing countries are often underestimated, even for the typical limited risk distributor structure:

> The Chinese experience shows that many MNEs treat their Chinese distribution entities as limited risk distributors, and use a set of simple distributors performing limited functions in a mature market such as Japan as the comparables... There are a couple of obvious deficiencies ... First, there is often a mismatch in terms of functional profile, as the Chinese entity may perform significantly more functions ... which is evident if it incurs significantly more operating expenses relative to sales. Second, it does not account for market differences, with China being a fast growing economy with strong demand and requiring relatively less selling effort, which can therefore achieve higher efficiency and profitability. *Other LSAs such as country premium and any marketing intangibles that are created by the Chinese entity* are also commonly ignored.[26]

To rectify these deficiencies, China may apply the PSM as a 'more appropriate transfer pricing method ... in cases where there are significant local marketing intangibles or LSAs'.[27] As the presence of these intangibles is critical to the application of the PSM in China, they are analysed in more detail in §9.03 below.

Contract research and development (R&D) is another area where China believes that the contribution of developing countries is often underestimated.[28] The transfer pricing method commonly used to reward R&D activities performed by a subsidiary of an MNE in China is cost plus.[29] However, China argues that the PSM is more appropriate in the following example:

> the Chinese entity has obtained 'high and new technology status' in Chinese law and therefore enjoys tax incentives on the basis of ownership of valuable core technology. However, it also claims to be a contract R&D service provider with no valuable intangibles. [In this case,] a cost plus approach would not be adequate, and a different method such as profit split would be more appropriate.[30]

Another telling example in which China argues that the PSM method is more appropriate is contract manufacturing, between related parties under which typically the 'profits of the Chinese manufacturer are stripped away as much as possible on the basis that [it has] a very low risk profile'.[31] With an example of the electronic manufacturing services (EMS) sector, China effectively applies the enterprise approach and argues for a 'global formulary approach' with more weighting for assets and headcounts in the allocation of profits:

> China takes the view that a risk based approach may have insufficient regard for the fact that there are sizeable assets located in China (i.e. the workforce and factory plants). In many cases, the majority of the headcount of the EMS group is

26. United Nations, *Practical Manual on Transfer Pricing for Developing Countries*, *supra* n. 4, at paras D.2.4.6.11 and D.2.4.6.12 (emphasis added).
27. *Ibid.*, para. D.2.4.6.13.
28. *Ibid.*, para. D.2.4.6.5.
29. *Ibid.*, para. D.2.4.6.5.
30. *Ibid.*, para. D.2.4.6.5.
31. *Ibid.*, paras D.2.4.7.1 and D.2.4.7.2.

> based in China ... remuneration to each party involved would be commensurate with its role and contribution to the value chain in the group. In this case, the assets and the people should largely dictate where the group's profits should stay, and a global formulary approach should be a realistic and appropriate option.[32]

[2] Do Reliable Comparables Exist?

The OECD emphasizes the importance of 'reliable comparables', the presence of which may limit the scope of application of the PSM: '... while a lack of comparables is, by itself, insufficient to warrant the use of the [PSM], if ... reliable comparables *are* available it is unlikely that the method will be the most appropriate'.[33]

China has consistently argued that it is very difficult to find reliable comparables in practice:

> In a developing country, there are usually only a small number of public companies, while information on domestic private companies is lacking or inadequate. This limits the amount of publicly available information on domestic companies that can be used for transfer pricing analysis. Take China as an example. As of September 2016, there are 2952 listed companies in China whereas the private companies are not bound by law to disclose financial information to the public ... It is unrealistic to expect that reliable comparables to the tested companies can be found in less than 3000 listed companies.[34]

The United Nations states that comparable data may not be available in many developing countries and foreign comparables, with proper adjustments, may have to be used.[35] On this issue, China regards itself as an emerging market with comparative advantages, including large market size, and low-cost land and labour. Therefore, foreign comparables from developed countries should be subject to significant comparability adjustments for these LSAs.[36] It follows on with this logic and argues that the PSM may be the more appropriate method in such situations: 'In some cases, it may require a different methodology such as a profit split as no sufficiently reliable comparability adjustment may be feasible.'[37]

For a detailed analysis of the concept of LSAs and how they may affect the allocation of profits, *see* §9.03 below.

32. *Ibid.*, para. D.2.4.7.3.
33. OECD, *Revised Guidance on the Application of the Transactional Profit Split Method, supra* n. 3, at 9, Executive summary.
34. United Nations, *Practical Manual on Transfer Pricing for Developing Countries, supra* n. 4, at paras D.2.4.2.1 and D.2.4.3.2.
35. *Ibid.*, para. B.2.4.3.5.
36. *Ibid.*, paras D.2.2.17 and D.2.4.3.4–D.2.4.3.6.
37. *Ibid.*, para. D.2.4.3.4. The SAT has stipulated this policy in the latest transfer pricing regulations: SAT, Bulletin 6, *supra* n. 19, Art. 27.

[C] How Should the PSM Be Applied?

Once the PSM is determined to be the most appropriate method, the next step is to determine the relevant profit or loss to be split and the allocation method. The OECD admits that the PSM is difficult to apply in practice and it is necessary to rely heavily on 'judgment':

> associated enterprises and tax administrations alike may have difficulty accessing the detailed information required to apply a [PSM] reliably. It may be difficult to measure the relevant revenue and costs for all the associated enterprises participating in the controlled transactions ... [leading to] the necessity of *judgement* in determining each of the parameters for the application of the [PSM].[38]

As such, the OECD allows significant flexibility in the application of the PSM:

> These Guidelines [on the application of the PSM] do not seek to provide an exhaustive catalogue of ways in which the ... method may be applied. Application of the method will depend on the facts and circumstances of the case and the information available...[39]

Bearing in mind the above caveats, the OECD provides that, to compute the profit to be split, the relevant segregated financial data, including income and expenses for each party to the controlled transaction, needs to be identified and combined.[40] The financial data needs to be built on a common basis as to accounting practice and currency.[41] The choice of different types of profits (for example, actual profit or anticipated profit) and different measures of profits (for example, gross profit or operating profit) should be consistent with the accurate delineation of the transaction.[42]

The OECD guidance on how to split the profits is similarly flexible:

> the criteria used to achieve an arm's length division of the profits *depend on the facts and circumstances of the case.* It is therefore not desirable to establish a prescriptive list of criteria or profit splitting factors.[43]

Possible allocation factors that are acceptable to the OECD include:

---

38. OECD, *Revised Guidance on the Application of the Transactional Profit Split Method*, *supra* n. 3, at para. 2.123 (emphasis added). Similar concern has been raised in respect of the difficulty in determining the relative value of the contribution by each associated enterprise, as well as the identification and valuation of intangibles: paras 2.151 and 2.181.
39. *Ibid.*, para. 2.146.
40. *Ibid.*, para. 2.155.
41. *Ibid.*, para. 2.155.
42. *Ibid.*, paras 2.158 and 2.162.
43. *Ibid.*, para. 2.166 (emphasis added). The profit may be split under a contribution analysis or a residual analysis depending on whether 'at least one party ... makes some less complex contributions which are capable of being benchmarked by reference to comparable, uncontrolled transactions': para. 2.149. Detailed technical discussion of these two methods is beyond the scope of this chapter.

> a figure (e.g. a 30%-70% split...) or a variable (e.g. relative value of participant's marketing contributions...) which could be calculated on the basis of a single profit splitting factor or a weighting of multiple factors.[44]

Interestingly, the OECD leaves the door wide open for possible profit splitting factors:

> Profit splitting factors [may be] based on assets or capital (e.g. ... fixed assets ... intangibles), or costs ... Other profit splitting factors that could be appropriate ... include incremental sales, or employee compensation ... The guidance in this section *should not be considered as an exhaustive list* of potential profit splitting factors. *Other profit splitting factors may be acceptable* provided they result in arm's length outcomes for all relevant parties.[45]

In particular, the OECD does not specifically exclude LSAs from the PSM method. It follows that China's PSM methodology can arguably be regarded as being largely in line with the OECD guidance, even though China specifically highlights LSAs as relevant factors in the application of the PSM:

> The comparability analysis under the [PSM] should examine ... the functions performed, risks assumed, and assets used by each party, allocation of revenue, cost, expenses and assets to each party, *location savings, market premium and other location specific factors*, together with other value creating factors [for the purpose of evaluating] the contribution of each related party to the residual profit.[46]

The next section analyses the concept of LSAs and how they may affect the allocation of profits under the PSM.

§9.03 LOCATION-SPECIFIC ADVANTAGES

[A] The Concept of LSAs

China defines LSAs to be 'advantages for production arising from assets, resource endowments, government industry policies and incentives, etc., which exist in specific localities'.[47] The concept was first introduced by China in its Country chapter in the 2012 UN *Transfer Pricing Manual*.[48] Since then, the concept of LSAs has become a focus of the SAT for transfer pricing audit and advance pricing agreement (APA)

44. *Ibid.*, para. 2.170.
45. *Ibid.*, paras 2.171 and 2.172 (emphasis added).
46. SAT, Bulletin 6, *supra* n. 19, Art. 21 (emphasis added).
47. United Nations, *Practical Manual on Transfer Pricing for Developing Countries*, *supra* n. 4, at para. D.2.4.4.1.
48. Deloitte, *Location-Specific Advantages* in *The New Transfer Pricing Landscape: A Practical Guide to the BEPS Changes* (November 2015), https://www2.deloitte.com/content/dam/Deloitte/us/Documents/Tax/us-tax-beps-changes-transfer-pricing-location-specific-advantages.pdf (accessed 11 June 2019).

negotiations.[49] Identifying LSA leads to allocation of more profits to the LSA host country.[50]

By contrast, the concept of LSAs was not formally recognized by the OECD until the revision of its *Transfer Pricing Guidelines* in 2017 after the BEPS project. The 2017 *Guidelines* do not formally define LSAs but instead refer to the concept in terms of 'location savings' and 'other local market features'.[51] They are relevant factors in comparability analysis if the difference is material.[52] China believes that LSAs arise more frequently in developing countries and are comprised of two main categories: location savings and market premium.[53]

Location savings are defined to be 'the net cost savings derived by an MNE when it sets up its operations in a low cost jurisdiction'.[54] They represent the net savings due to lower costs for labour, rent, raw materials and infrastructure, etc., after offsetting against additional expenses due to the relocation, such as increased training costs.[55]

Conversely, market premiums are defined to be 'additional profit derived by an MNE by operating in a jurisdiction with unique qualities impacting on the sale and demand of a service or product'.[56] In China's view, the relevant market conditions that may give rise to premiums are market size or scale, market access, government incentives for certain industries, substitution of products or services in a market, and inelasticity of demand for certain products or services.[57] They are often seen in the luxury goods, pharmaceutical and automotive industries in China.[58]

[B] Linkage with Marketing Intangibles

It is important to note that China argues that, for developing countries, LSAs are often closely integrated with marketing intangibles, which can be an important factor in the

49. United Nations, *Practical Manual on Transfer Pricing for Developing Countries, supra* n. 4, at para. D.2.2.17. For instance, LSAs are specifically mentioned as relevant factors in comparability analysis of a transfer pricing investigation: SAT, Bulletin 6, *supra* n. 19, Art. 15.
50. For a worked example showing the effect of LSAs from the perspective of China, *see* United Nations, *Practical Manual on Transfer Pricing for Developing Countries, supra* n. 4, at para. D.2.4.4.9.
51. OECD, *Transfer Pricing Guidelines, supra* n. 9, Ch. 1, D.6.
52. *Ibid.*, Part D.6.
53. An illustration of the calculations of location savings may be found in United Nations, *Practical Manual on Transfer Pricing for Developing Countries, supra* n. 4, at para. D.2.4.4.2.
54. *Ibid.*, para. D.2.4.4.3. The OECD defines the term in a similar way: OECD, *Transfer Pricing Guidelines, supra* n. 9, at para. 1.139.
55. United Nations, *Practical Manual on Transfer Pricing for Developing Countries, supra* n. 4, at para. D.2.4.4.3.
56. *Ibid.*, para. D.2.4.4.4.
57. SAT, *Public Notice [2016] No.42: Public Notice of the State Administration of Taxation on Issuing the 'Public Notice on Matters Regarding Refining the Filing of Related Party Transactions and Administration of Contemporaneous Transfer Pricing Documentation'*, Art. 14(iii)(a)(4) (2016); Ashley, *supra* n. 7, question 5.
58. United Nations, *Practical Manual on Transfer Pricing for Developing Countries, supra* n. 4, at para. D.2.4.4.10.

allocation of profits.[59] The following example provided in China's Country chapter in the 2017 UN *Transfer Pricing Manual* is telling:

> the Chinese subsidiaries of some luxury brands have undertaken significant promotion activities to educate Chinese customers who had known nothing about the brands before. With more and more Chinese customers now familiar with the brands and products, sales revenue has experienced a great increase for the Chinese subsidiaries. In this case, China argues that, according to the principle that 'taxation should follow value creation', the additional profits arising from the marketing intangibles created in the country should be taxed in China.[60]

While this position may not be surprising, China continues with this example and has taken an arguably aggressive stand by extending the logic to impose taxing rights on sales of *overseas* associated enterprises:

> deterred by the high prices set by the MNE groups in the Chinese stores, some Chinese customers who would have gone to luxury stores in China have instead chosen to go abroad. The money spent by Chinese shoppers in overseas luxury stores ... has constituted a sizeable portion of the sales revenue of overseas affiliates ... This portion of the sales revenue and the profits realized should be attributed to the marketing contribution made by Chinese subsidiaries and taxed in China.[61]

In other words, China argues that the marketing activities of the Chinese subsidiaries in the country have created valuable marketing intangibles which contribute not only to local sales of the Chinese subsidiaries but also to the foreign sales of the overseas associates.

The concept of marketing intangibles has become more important as the OECD, and the Inclusive Framework jurisdictions have considered the marketing intangible proposal to be one of the possible reforms in response to the rise of the digital economy.[62] The OECD defines marketing intangibles as follows:[63]

> An intangible ... that relates to marketing activities, aids in the commercial exploitation of a product or service and/or has an important promotional value for the product concerned ... marketing intangibles may include ... trademarks, trade names, customer lists, customer relationships, and proprietary market and customer data that is used or aids in marketing and selling goods or services to customers.[64]

The OECD recognizes marketing intangibles as a 'unique and valuable contribution' in limited scenarios.[65] However, as the core concept of one of the three proposals being considered by the OECD and the Inclusive Framework in the Digital Economy discussion document, and given the OECD's further clarification that the marketing

59. *Ibid.*, para. D.2.4.5.1.
60. *Ibid.*, para. D.2.4.4.11 (emphasis added).
61. *Ibid.*, para. D.2.4.4.12 (emphasis added).
62. OECD, *Addressing the Tax Challenges of the Digitalisation of the Economy*, *supra* n. 1, Part 2.2.2
63. OECD, *Transfer Pricing Guidelines*, *supra* n. 9, at 27.
64. *Ibid.*, Glossary.
65. OECD, *Revised Guidance on the Application of the Transactional Profit Split Method*, *supra* n. 3, examples 2, 3 and 13.

intangibles proposal would be applied not only to highly digitalized businesses but also to other businesses as a response to 'the broader impact of the digitalisation on the economy', marketing intangibles have the potential to play a key role in expanding the taxing rights of the market jurisdiction.[66]

The policy rationale of the marketing intangible proposal seems to be aligned with China's argument in the above-mentioned example and arguably represents a shift of position towards that of China in respect of the importance of market jurisdictions:

> The marketing intangible proposal addresses a situation where an MNE group can essentially 'reach into' a jurisdiction ... to develop a user/customer base and other marketing intangibles. It sees an intrinsic functional link between marketing intangibles and the market jurisdiction ... some marketing intangibles, such as brand and trade name, are reflected in the favourable attitudes in the minds of customers and so can be seen to have been created in the market jurisdiction. Taking into account this link between marketing intangibles and the market jurisdiction, the proposal ... considers that the market jurisdiction would be entitled to tax some or all of the non-routine income properly associated with such intangibles and their attendant risks ... The proposal is intended to be consistent with the principle of allocating profit based on the value creation by firms in that this positive attitude in the minds of customers is created by ... the active intervention of the firm in the market.[67]

Though the OECD seems to be more accepting of greater allocation of taxing rights to market jurisdictions, it insists that the marketing intangible must be created by active actions of an MNE and specifically excludes from the proposal some of the LSA factors that China has been arguing for:

> The proposal ... is ... different from favourable demand conditions in the market jurisdiction that exist independent of the actions of the firm – such as the existence of a stable population benefitting from a successful economy that provides them with the financial means to be able to buy the relevant product. While these aspects of demand obviously have economic relevance, *they are not relevant for the allocation of a firm's profits* under the general tax framework, which is based on a determination of how different activities by the firm contribute to its profits.[68]

It should also be noted that, possibly as an anti-BEPS measure, under the marketing intangible proposal, the allocation of non-routine returns from marketing intangibles would apply regardless of which entity in the MNE group owns the legal title to the marketing intangibles.[69]

As the concept of LSAs plays a critical role in China's PSM approach, the following section provides an overview of the LSA factors in China's transfer pricing regime.

---

66. OECD, *Addressing the Tax Challenges of the Digitalisation of the Economy*, *supra* n. 1, at paras 16 and 29.
67. *Ibid.*, paras 30-32.
68. *Ibid.*, para. 33 (emphasis added).
69. *Ibid.*, para. 44.

[C] LSA Factors

[1] Labour Costs

Labour cost is a classic example of location savings, and both the OECD and UN recognize this factor in the comparability analysis.[70]

China does not provide details to guide the recognition and allocation of the LSAs arising from labour costs, but the Jiangsu Provincial Office of the SAT, one of China's leading local tax offices in international tax avoidance campaigns against BEPS, specifies that:

> China has a large growing number of technicians of high value-added labour force in R&D, and software design. ... Many Chinese subsidiaries of MNEs have undertaken R&D activities for the group but paid comparatively low salaries *compared to the technicians in developed countries*. MNEs should consider the cost savings of this factor...[71]

In contrast, the OECD has a more restrictive position and argues that the LSA arising from low labour costs will not lead to greater profit allocation to the market jurisdiction if the MNE can find a third party to perform the same functions for the same low price.[72] For a more detailed discussion of this issue, *see* §9.03[C][4] below.

[2] Market Size

The OECD includes market size as a potential item for comparability adjustment but does not mention it in the discussion of LSAs.[73]

In contrast, China specifically identifies 'huge ... demand in China due to the large population and growing wealth of the population' as one of the LSAs 'that ha[s] led to extraordinarily high profits that are rightly earned by Chinese taxpayers'.[74] This LSA factor may arise due to the fact that China is an expanding market, so that MNEs spend less effort to sell.[75] It may also arise due to a large number of high-quality, low-cost suppliers, which give rise to location savings.[76]

70. OECD, *Transfer Pricing Guidelines, supra* n. 9, at para. 9.128; United Nations, *Practical Manual on Transfer Pricing for Developing Countries, supra* n. 4, at para. B.2.3.2.51.
71. Jiangsu Provincial Office, *2016 - 2018 Compliance Plan on International Tax Administration, Su Guoshuifa [2016] No. 125*, Part 2(3) (2016) (emphasis added).
72. OECD, *Transfer Pricing Guidelines, supra* n. 9, at paras 9.128 and 9.129.
73. *Ibid.*, para 1.110. The UN takes a similar position: United Nations, *Practical Manual on Transfer Pricing for Developing Countries, supra* n. 4, at para. B.2.3.2.48.
74. United Nations, *Practical Manual on Transfer Pricing for Developing Countries, supra* n. 4, at para. D.2.2.17.
75. *Ibid.*, para D.2.4.6.12.
76. *Ibid.*, para D.2.4.4.7.

[3] *Consumer Purchasing Power*

The OECD recognizes 'purchasing power and product preferences of households in that market' as one of the factors in 'other local market features'.[77]

China believes that Chinese customers have a general preference for foreign brands and imported goods.[78] It is not a firm-specific advantage, such as being loyal to a specific brand, but a general trend attributable to many social factors. Consequently, those foreign brands and imported goods that have the same quality as the local ones can charge a premium. This position was illustrated with an example of automotive products sold in China in the UN Country Practice discussion.[79]

[4] *Degree of Competition in the Market*

From an economic perspective, the stronger the competition in a market, the more likely that value will be passed on to customers. The OECD in general views it as a negative factor that tends to deny profit share to Chinese subsidiaries, unless the MNE has gained firm-specific advantages through competition, such as dominant market share.[80]

China follows the OECD's logic to a large extent but also argues that the degree of competition in the country can often give rise to LSAs. This is due to the fact that the degree of competition in the Chinese market is relatively low in many sectors, such as automotive and luxury goods.[81] For instance, the 'market-for-technology' industry policy requires foreign automotive manufacturers to form joint ventures before they can assemble automobiles in China, thus significantly limiting market access opportunities for other foreign car manufacturers.[82]

[5] *Availability of Substitutes for Goods/Services*

The OECD includes the availability of substitute goods and services as an item to be adjusted for in comparability analysis but does not refer in particular to it as an LSA factor.[83]

China specifically identifies this item as an LSA factor. For instance, the automotive industry in the country has been benefiting from 'many LSAs that have led to

77. OECD, *Transfer Pricing Guidelines*, *supra* n. 9, at para. 1.144. The UN also recognizes 'large customer base with increased spending capacity' as a factor of 'other LSAs': United Nations, *Practical Manual on Transfer Pricing for Developing Countries*, *supra* n. 4, at para. B.2.3.2.53.
78. *Ibid.*, para D.2.4.4.7.
79. *Ibid.*, para D.2.4.4.7.
80. OECD, *Transfer Pricing Guidelines*, *supra* n. 9, at para. 1.144. *See also* United Nations, *Practical Manual on Transfer Pricing for Developing Countries*, *supra* n. 4, at para. B.2.3.2.55.
81. United Nations, *Practical Manual on Transfer Pricing for Developing Countries*, *supra* n. 4, at para. D.2.4.4.3.
82. *Ibid.*, para D.2.4.4.7.
83. OECD, *Transfer Pricing Guidelines*, *supra* n. 9, at para. 1.110. The UN has a similar position: United Nations, *Practical Manual on Transfer Pricing for Developing Countries*, *supra* n. 4, at para. B.2.3.2.48.

extraordinarily high profits ... [including] a large supply of high quality, low cost parts manufactured by suppliers in China'.[84]

[6] Government Regulations

The OECD, again, includes 'the nature and extent of government regulation of the market' as an item to be adjusted for in comparability analysis but does not include it specifically as an LSA factor.[85]

As mentioned in §9.03[C][4] above, China argues that government regulations can have the effect of limiting competition for MNEs in the country and thus should be regarded as an LSA factor. Furthermore, some local governments in China provide special concessions and financial incentives to attract foreign investments and reduce MNEs' manufacturing costs, which will also be considered to give rise to LSAs. For example, Guangdong province offers up to CNY 100 million in financial incentives to eligible overseas investments.[86]

[7] Duty Savings

While the OECD is silent on this item, China regards the duty saving of MNEs in China as an LSA factor and illustrates this view with an example from the automotive industry:

> [D]uty savings from the lower duty rates on automotive parts (e.g. 10%) compared to imported vehicles (e.g. 25%) ... [mean that] when MNEs manufacture products in China as opposed to importing the products from outside of China, they are able to generate overall savings from the lower duty rates, even if the MNEs incur manufacturing costs and sell their domestically-manufactured products at a lower sales price compared to a foreign-manufactured vehicle ... .[87]

[D] Allocation of LSAs

As mentioned in §9.02[C] above, the OECD does not stipulate a prescriptive approach to the allocation of LSAs. Instead, it stipulates the following broader approach to determine whether and how the LSAs should be allocated:[88]

84. United Nations, *Practical Manual on Transfer Pricing for Developing Countries*, *supra* n. 4, at para. D.2.4.4.7.
85. OECD, *Transfer Pricing Guidelines*, *supra* n. 9, at para. 1.110 (2017). *See also* United Nations, *Practical Manual on Transfer Pricing for Developing Countries*, *supra* n. 4, at para. B.2.3.2.58.
86. Guangdong Provincial Government, *Notice Issued by Guangdong Provincial Government Regarding Reduce the Cost for Manufacturing Sector and Support the Development of Real Economy* (2017).
87. United Nations, *Practical Manual on Transfer Pricing for Developing Countries*, *supra* n. 4, at para. D.2.4.4.7.
88. OECD, *Transfer Pricing Guidelines*, *supra* n. 9, at para. 1.141. A similar approach is set out for 'other local market features': para. 1.146.

- determine the amount of LSAs;
- determine the extent to which LSAs are passed on to independent customers or suppliers;
- where LSAs are not fully passed on to independent customers or suppliers, determine the manner in which independent enterprises operating under similar circumstances would allocate any retained LSAs.

The OECD illustrates this approach with an example in which an MNE reallocates its clothing manufacturing activities - which are basic and can be readily performed by a third party - to Country B for a lower cost, while the group member (Co.A) in Country A retains the brand name and continues performing the design function. The company in Country B (Co.B) manufactures the clothes under a contract manufacturing arrangement and sells the products to Co.A which in turn sells to third-party customers. In this case, the OECD's position is that the LSA benefits arising from the low cost should not be allocated to Country B:

> [G]iven that the relocated activity is a highly competitive one, it is likely that the enterprise in Country A has the option realistically available to it to use either the affiliate in Country B or a third party manufacturer. As a consequence, *it should be possible to find comparables data* to determine the conditions in which a third party would be willing at arm's length to manufacture the clothes for the enterprise. In such a situation, *a contract manufacturer at arm's length would generally be attributed very little, if any, part of the location savings.*[89]

The OECD provides another example to illustrate when and how LSAs may lead to a greater allocation of profits.[90] This example is similar to the one above except that the MNE is in the business of providing highly specialized engineering services, and Co.B is the only entity in a lower-cost country that can provide the same quality services for substantially lower wages. In this case, the OECD agrees that Co.B should enjoy the benefits arising from the LSAs and the PSM may be the appropriate method to provide for this:[91]

> [Co.A] does not have many other options available to it than to use this service provider. The remuneration payable by [Co.A] to [Co.B] should take into account the location savings created by [Co.B] ... In some instances, the nature of the contributions made by the [two companies] may meet the criteria for the use of a [PSM].

China has a different focus with respect to the allocation of LSAs:

- determine whether the LSA generates additional profit;
- quantify and measure the additional profits arising from the LSA; and

89. *Ibid.*, para. 9.129 (emphasis added).
90. *Ibid.*, para. 9.130.
91. *Ibid.*, para. 9.131.

- determine the transfer pricing method to allocate the profits arising from the LSA.[92]

This approach focuses on whether the LSAs generate additional profits for an MNE, instead of whether they are passed on to independent customers or suppliers and thus is more likely to result in a greater profit allocation to market jurisdictions.

§9.04 CONCLUSION

China observes that the BEPS project is unique due to the significant involvement of developing countries:[93]

> A distinguishing factor ... is the involvement of many developing countries in both the early stage when the various measures were developed and the later implementation phase ... This unprecedented event has provided developing countries with an opportunity to begin at the same starting line as their developed counterparts.

With respect to the PSM and the concept of LSAs, China in fact arguably has already begun even before the OECD has arrived at the starting line. China has been arguing for the recognition of LSAs and thus the application of the PSM since 2012, while the OECD formally recognized the LSA concept in 2017.

There are a number of key differences between the positions of China and the OECD. First, the OECD insists that the PSM should not be applied if reliable comparables exist. In contrast, China argues that it is common for developing countries to suffer from the lack of reliable comparables, often due to the presence of LSAs. This issue dictates that the PSM may be the more appropriate transfer pricing method. Second, while the OECD imposes a greater number of limitations for LSAs to be allocated to market jurisdictions, China specifically highlights LSAs as factors in the application of the PSM.

China believes that marketing intangibles are closely integrated with the concept of LSAs and should lead to greater taxing rights to market jurisdictions. This position is arguably reflected in the marketing intangible proposal of the OECD and Inclusive Framework jurisdictions, under which the PSM is a possible allocation method for the profits arising from marketing intangibles.

It is difficult to predict whether or not the marketing intangible proposal will ultimately be adopted as a generally accepted principle. In any case, the final destiny of the proposal may provide a clearer signal as to whether China's early jump from the starting line with respect to the PSM and the concept of LSAs will lead to substantial reform of the international tax regime.

92. United Nations, *Practical Manual on Transfer Pricing for Developing Countries*, *supra* n. 4, at para. D.2.4.4.5 (emphasis added).
93. *Ibid.*, para. D.2.1.1.

Part IV Formulary Apportionment in an Evolving International Tax System

CHAPTER 10

Value Creation and the Allocation of Profits under a Formulary Apportionment System

John Vella[*]

§10.01 INTRODUCTION

Allocation formulas are of first-order importance for formulary apportionment systems. They determine the distribution of revenues among participating states, thus affecting both the perceived equity of the systems and their political viability. But they also matter because different formulary factors – and combinations of factors – have different consequences in terms of economic efficiency, robustness to avoidance, ease of administration and stability.

The allocation factors commonly used in practice and discussed in the literature are labour, assets and sales, often as part of an equally weighted three-factor formula. The formulary apportionment system proposed by the Commission of the European Union – the Common Consolidated Corporate Tax Base (CCCTB) – featured this formula. It was also used extensively in the United States for state corporate taxation, reaching a high point in 1978 when forty-three of the forty-five states adopted it.[1] Since then, an increasing number of US states have moved to formulas giving a greater weight to the sales factor or even to a sales-only formula,[2] and this has been accompanied by an increased interest in the academic literature in the properties and

* I would like to thank Michael P. Devereux for his suggestions and many illuminating discussions on the issues covered in this chapter. I would also like to thank Richard Krever, François Vaillancourt, Michael Smart and the other participants at the Formulary Apportionment Workshop held in Montreal in April 2019 for their helpful comments. The usual disclaimers apply.

1. Walter Hellerstein, *A US Subnational Perspective on the 'Logic' of Taxing Income on a 'Market' Basis*, 72(4/5) Bull. Int'l Tax'n 293, 294 (2018).
2. *Ibid.*

viability of sales-based formulary apportionment.[3] Other factors have been considered in the academic literature and in policy discussions, including macro factors and value added, but have thus far not been used.[4]

This chapter asks whether the factors used to allocate profits in a formulary apportionment system could, in appropriate weightings, correctly attribute profits to countries according to the value created in those countries (the 'value creation' principle). This is an important question to consider. There appears to be widespread agreement among many policymakers, campaigners, academics and others in the international tax community that corporate profits *should* be taxed where value is created. Failing to allocate profits in this way would be viewed by many as a weakness that militates against the adoption of formulary apportionment systems.

Formulary apportionment has been dismissed on these grounds in the past, although the criticism was framed in different terms. It was argued that formulary apportionment systems lead to an 'arbitrary' allocation of profits rather than an allocation that is (more) in line with the 'true' economic sources of profits. The OECD Transfer Pricing Guidelines, for example, argue that: '*predetermined formulae are arbitrary* and disregard market conditions, the particular circumstances of the individual enterprises, and management's own allocation of resources, thus producing an allocation of profits that may bear no sound relationship to the specific facts surrounding the transaction'.[5]

While the value creation principle – and indeed its consideration in the context of formulary apportionment systems – may not be new, the increased prominence of and support for the principle following the G20/OECD's Base Erosion and Profit Shifting (BEPS) project makes a reconsideration of the issue timely. Much academic writing[6]

3. *See for example* Martti Nieminen, *Destination-with-Credit Formula: A Simple Add-On that Would Make the CCCTB More Resilient in the Face of Tax Competition and Tax Planning*, 47(5) Intertax 490 (2019) (and the responses in the same issue by Christoph Spengel & Kathrin Stutzenberger, *Comment on M. Nieminen, 'Destination with Credit Formula': A Simple Add on that Would Make the CCCTB More Resilient to Tax Competition and Tax Planning*, 47(5) Intertax 496 (2019) and Krister Andersson, *Comment on M. Nieminen, 'Destination with Credit Formula': A Simple Add on that Would Make the CCCTB More Resilient to Tax Competition and Tax Planning*, 47(5) Intertax 499 (2019)); Jeff Ferry, *Revenue Gains From Sales Factor Apportionment Corp Income Tax*, 157 Tax Notes 1313 (2017).
4. These factors were considered in the context of the CCCTB but were dismissed due to 'important flaws'. *See* CCCTB Working Group, *Report and Overview of the Main Issues that Emerged During the Discussion on the Sharing Mechanism, SG6 Second Meeting – 11 June 2007*, Brussels, 20 August 2007, CCCTB\WP\056\doc\en.
5. Organisation for Economic Co-operation and Development (OECD), *OECD Transfer Pricing Guidelines for Multinational Enterprises and Tax Administrations 2017* para 1.25 (OECD Publishing 2017) (emphasis added). The OECD Transfer Pricing Guidelines also state, at para 1.29: 'global formulary apportionment cannot, as a practical matter, recognise important geographical differences, separate company efficiencies, and other factors specific to one company or sub-grouping within the MNE group that may legitimately play a role in determining the division of profits between enterprises in different tax jurisdictions'.
6. On this principle, *see* Michael Devereux & John Vella, *Are We Heading Towards a Corporate Tax System Fit for the 21st Century?*, 35(4) Fiscal Stud. 449 (2014); Michael P. Devereux & John Vella, *Value Creation as the Fundamental Principle of the International Corporate Tax System* (European Tax Policy Forum Policy Paper, July 2018); Michael P. Devereux & John Vella, *Taxing the Digitalised Economy: Targeted or System-Wide Reform?*, [2018] 4 Brit. Tax Rev. 301; Johanna Hey, *'Taxation Where Value is Created' and the OECD/G20 Base Erosion and Profit Shifting Initiative*,

and even entire conferences[7] are now devoted to this principle. Many political and policy documents accept value creation as the undisputed guiding principle for the allocation of taxing rights over corporate profits among countries. Now, more than ever, any proposal for international corporate tax reform will be measured against this principle.

This chapter argues that formulary apportionment systems cannot give effect to the value creation principle. They cannot allocate taxing rights to countries according to where value is created. In fact, one can easily think of circumstances where factors commonly used in formulary apportionment systems cause a reduction in value. This conclusion is backed by empirical economic research undertaken by James R. Hines Jr. Hines tested whether the magnitude of property, employment and sales can explain the variation in profits among European firms and concluded: '[p]ut simply, the formulas do not apportion income accurately among the jurisdictions in which it is earned'.[8]

This is not surprising. Businesses are complex endeavours, and many fail to successfully generate a profit. Those that generate a profit do so for a variety of internal and external reasons, be it the brilliance of a particular group of employees, the prime location of a retail store, sourcing raw material at a favourable price or market conditions affecting competitors. Researchers in this area devote their academic careers trying to identify why some businesses are successful and generate profits, while others are not and generate losses. It turns out to be an extremely difficult question to answer even ex post facto. For example, there is still some disagreement as to what led to Honda's success in the US motorcycle market in the 1950s (Honda became the leading supplier of motorbikes within five years of entering the market).[9] It would be truly remarkable if a simple factor formula would correctly capture the true economic source of a company's profit. The true economic source of profit varies from business to business; an economy-wide or even sector-wide formula cannot identify the source for a particular business in any meaningful sense. As Hines explains:

> profits are not simple scalar functions of employment, sales or tangible property. Instead, profits are produced by many factors, including managerial inputs, that are difficult to measure or subject to reporting manipulation, and therefore omitted from the formulas that governments use.[10]

72(4/5) Bull. Int'l Tax'n 203 (2018); Susan Morse, *Value Creation: A Standard in Search of a Process*, 72(4/5) Bull. Int'l Tax'n 196 (2018); Itai Grinberg, *User Participation in Value Creation*, [2018] 4 Brit. Tax Rev. 407; Michael Lennard, *Act of Creation: The OECD/G20 Test of 'Value Creation' as a Basis for Taxing Rights and its Relevance to Developing Countries*, 25(3) Transnat'l Corp. 55 (2018); Allison Christians & Laurens van Apeldoorn, *Taxing Income Where Value is Created*, 22(1) Fla. Tax Rev. 1 (2018). For a more positive view of this principle, *see* Stanley I. Langbein & Max R. Fuss, *The OECD/G20-BEPS-Project and the Value Creation Paradigm: Economic Reality Disemboguing into the Interpretation of the 'Arm's Length' Standard*, 51(2) Int'l Law. 259 (2018).

7. For example, the 2020 European Association of Tax Law Professors Congress will be on 'Taxation and Value Creation'.
8. James R. Hines, Jr., *Income Misattribution Under Formula Apportionment*, 54(1) Eur. Econ. Rev. 108, 109 (2010).
9. John Kay, *Foundations of Corporate Success: How Business Strategies Add Value* 7-9 (Oxford University Press 1993).
10. Hines, *supra* n. 8, at 109.

However, and critically, this chapter also argues that failure to allocate taxing rights in line with value creation should *not* be counted against formulary apportionment systems. The existing system – which allocates taxing rights between residence and source countries and adopts separate accounting – cannot be said to allocate taxing rights in line with value creation either. Again, this follows naturally from the observation that it is hard (and at times impossible) to identify how and where value is created for each particular business. This was true of traditional bricks and mortar businesses, but it is even truer in a digitalized economy. As recent debates on international tax reform have demonstrated, countries – as well as commentators – even disagree on which factors create value in this setting.

Systems for taxing corporate profits in an international setting should not be judged on whether they are able to allocate taxing rights in line with the value creation principle. This is partly because it is an impossible task, but also, to the extent that it is possible, because it would lead to an economically inefficient and unstable system which is not easily justified on the basis of fairness. There certainly are valid arguments against – as there are arguments in favour of – formulary apportionment, but failure to allocate taxing rights in accordance with value creation is not one.[11]

This chapter proceeds as follows. Section 10.2 examines the value creation principle. It first charts the rise to prominence of this principle in the ongoing debates on international tax reform, as well as its use in earlier debates on formulary apportionment. It then questions the meaning of the principle and, in particular, whether the market country is deemed to create value. Finally, it provides a brief critique of the principle. Section 10.3 examines more closely whether allocation formulas can allocate profits in accordance with the value creation principle. This is done in two steps. In the first step, it asks whether all the factors that create value can be included in an allocation formula. In the second step, it asks whether the factors can be weighted in line with the value they create. Given that the conclusion is reached that value creation should not – indeed cannot – guide the choice of an allocation formula, §10.04 provides some brief thoughts on alternative principles that can be used as guidance. Section 10.05 concludes.

11. The view taken in this chapter appears to align with the views of Walter Hellerstein, the doyen of formulary apportionment systems. After surveying different views on whether the objective of income allocation is to determine the 'true' geographic source of income – the resolution to which, he opines, 'may be more a question of faith than of logic' – he concludes: '[t]he purported superiority of arm's length/separate geographic-accounting standard over formulary apportionment as a method of income allocation frequently rests on a questionable premise, namely that the purpose of income allocation is to determine the "true" geographic source of income. If it is not, as many believe, then at least one argument purportedly favouring the arm's length/separate geographic accounting standard over formulary apportionment as an income allocation method is substantially undermined': Walter Hellerstein, *The Case for Formulary Apportionment*, 12(3) Intl. Transfer Pricing J. 103 (2005).

§10.02 THE VALUE CREATION PRINCIPLE

[A] The Use of the Principle in Tax Debates

[1] Current International Corporation Tax Debates

It is now widely taken as axiomatic that the existing international corporate tax system is based on the principle that corporate profits are taxed where value is created (the 'value creation principle'). There also appears to be widespread agreement, at least amongst policymakers, that the system should be based on this principle.[12]

The ascendency of the value creation principle has been remarkable, as has its influence. The precise historical origins of this principle are not investigated here, but it was certainly articulated and put centre stage in the BEPS project led by the G20/OECD between 2013 and 2015.[13] The value creation principle was adopted as the guiding principle of the BEPS project but quickly became widely accepted as the guiding principle for taxing corporate profits in an international setting more generally.

The OECD, the European Commission and Parliament, many finance ministries around the world and many academics now repeat the mantra that profits should be taxed where value is created without question. Recent European Commission documents, for example, explain that '[s]ince the start of its mandate, this Commission has taken action to ensure the principle that all businesses operating in the EU pay their taxes *where profits are made and thus where value is created*'[14] and that '[i]t is an internationally agreed principle that profits should be taxed where value is created'.[15] The UK Treasury confidently asserted both descriptive and normative claims: '[t]he international tax framework is based on a principle that the profits of a business should be taxed in the countries in which it creates value. The UK continues to support that principle'.[16] Even the Addis Ababa Action Agenda of the Third International Conference on Financing for Development adopted the principle: '[W]e will make sure that all companies, including multinationals, pay taxes to the governments of countries where economic activity occurs and value is created, in accordance with national and international laws and policies.'[17] Finally, a number of multinational companies have

12. This section is based on Devereux & Vella, *Value Creation as the Fundamental Principle, supra* n. 6 and Devereux & Vella, *Taxing the Digitalised Economy, supra* n. 6.
13. Herzfeld considers it a 'brand new standard': Mindy Herzfeld, *The Case Against BEPS: Lessons for Tax Coordination*, 21(1) Fla. Tax Rev. 1, 42 (2017).
14. European Commission, *Impact Assessment Accompanying the Document Proposal for a Council Directive Laying Down Rules Relating to the Corporate Taxation of a Significant Digital Presence and Proposal for a Council Directive on the Common System of a Digital Services Tax on Revenues Resulting from the Provision of Certain Digital Services*, 21.03.2018, SWD (2018) 81 final/2, 5 (emphasis added).
15. European Commission, *Time to Establish a Modern, Fair and Efficient Taxation Standard for the Digital Economy, Communication from the Commission to the European Parliament and the Council*, Brussels, 21.03.2018, COM(2018) 146 final.
16. HM Treasury, *Corporate Tax and the Digital Economy: Position Paper Update* (March 2018).
17. *Addis Ababa Action Agenda of the Third International Conference on Financing for Development*, 27 July 2015, para. 23.

referred to this principle in their tax strategies.[18] The FTSE4Good Index and the Dow Jones Sustainability Index assess, among other things, whether companies make declarations on paying taxes according to where value is created.[19]

The value creation principle has been embraced broadly and its influence is being felt keenly, as can be seen in the ongoing debate on how to respond to the challenges posed by digitalization. The European Commission and a number of Member States, including the United Kingdom, have used this principle to justify proposals extending the permanent establishment (PE) concept and profit attribution rules in the context of certain highly digitalized businesses. Indeed, astonishingly, the principle is also used to justify proposals for *turnover* taxes on certain highly digitalized businesses: '[the proposal for a turnover tax] remains fully grounded on the most basic principle of corporate taxation – namely, that profits should be taxed where value is created'.[20]

[2] Formulary Apportionment Debates

The value creation principle featured in debates on formulary apportionment systems, albeit in a different formulation. A number of commentators assumed it to be the guiding principle for allocation formulas. McLure and Weiner, for example, stated that: '[i]n principle, the choice of apportionment formula should be guided by the objective of determining the geographic source of income of a group of companies in more than one jurisdiction',[21] although they went on to note that this theory does not provide much guidance in practice. Similarly, Hines noted that: '[i]t is far from clear what factors properly enter an apportionment formula ... if the goal is to allocate income roughly according to where it is earned'.[22]

Certain policymakers also embraced the value creation principle in the context of formulary apportionment systems. The European Commission, for example, adopted it as its guiding principle when designing its CCCTB proposal: the principle is to 'assign[s] a proportionate share of the company's or associated companies' corporate tax base to the state by reference to a factor or factors that reflect (or are deemed to reflect) the underlying income-producing activities within the state'.[23]

18. For example, Sky Group's 2019 Tax Strategy explains: 'Sky aims to pay the appropriate amount of tax in each of the jurisdictions in which it operates, in accordance with where value is created.' https://static.skyassets.com/contentstack/assets/bltdc2476c7b6b194dd/blt74158a7776081aa2/5d728be86b141a30e6ef1969/Sky's%20Tax%20strategy%202019.pdf.

19. *See, e.g.*, Maya Forstater, *Publishing Corporate Tax Strategies*, 1320 Tax J. 10 (2016).

20. European Commission, *Questions and Answers on a Fair and Efficient Tax System in the EU for the Digital Single Market*, Brussels, 21 March 2018.

21. Charles E. McLure, Jr. & Joann M. Weiner, *Deciding Whether the European Union Should Adopt Formula Apportionment of Company Income*, in *Taxing Capital Income in the European Union: Issues and Options for Reform* 243, 266-267 (Sijbren Cnossen ed., Oxford University Press 2000).

22. Hines, *supra* n. 8, at 109. *See also* the discussion in Hellerstein, *The Case for Formulary Apportionment*, *supra* n. 11, at 104 and 107-108.

23. CCCTB Working Group, *The Mechanism for Sharing the CCCTB*, Brussels, 17 November 2006, CCCTB\WP\047\doc\en, 5.

[B] The Meaning of Value Creation

[1] In the Current International Corporation Tax Debate

The concept of value creation has never been satisfactorily defined in any of the OECD BEPS publications, nor do any of these publications explain why it should be the underlying principle of the international allocation of taxing rights. Despite the uncertainty about the meaning of the principle, there appears to be a general understanding among its proponents that value is created by activities on the 'supply' side (including research and development, production and marketing) but not those on the 'demand' side (purchasing the resulting good or service). The UK's Treasury Department best summarized this view:

> The overall principle underpinning that framework is to tax a multinational group's profits in the countries in which it undertakes its value generating activities, such as where major operating decisions are made and where important assets and risks are controlled. That is a principle that the government continues to support. It does not, for example, believe that another country should have a general right to tax profits that a UK business generates from a product that is designed in the UK, manufactured in the UK, marketed in the UK and then sold remotely to that country's customers ... Instead countries should have the right to tax business profits derived from productive activities, enterprise and human innovation in their jurisdiction, irrespective of where shareholders and customers are located.[24]

The OECD similarly explained that, while aspects of demand – such as the existence of a stable population benefitting from a successful economy – obviously have economic relevance, 'they are not relevant for the allocation of a firm's profits under the general tax framework, which is based on a determination of how different activities by the firm contribute to its profits'.[25]

The current debate on international tax reform has revealed some tension among countries on this point. The orthodoxy, supported by countries such as the United Kingdom, Germany and France, is that the market does not create value and therefore corporate profits should not be allocated to market countries following this allocative principle. But this orthodox view is being challenged by other countries, including India.[26]

At the time of writing, and despite this disagreement, the 137 members of the OECD's Inclusive Framework are considering international corporate tax reform that allocates some taxing rights to the market country (and/or, possibly, to the country where users of certain highly digitalized businesses are found). This departure from the

24. HM Treasury, *Corporate Tax and the Digital Economy: Position Paper* (November 2017).
25. OECD, *Public Consultation Document: Addressing the Tax Challenges of the Digitalisation of the Economy*, para. 33 (February 2019).
26. *See* Committee to Examine the issues related to Profit Attribution to Permanent Establishment (PE) in India and Amendment of Rule 10 of Income-tax Rules, 1962, *Proposal for Amendment of Rules for Profit Attribution to Permanent Establishment (Report on Profit Attribution to Permanent Establishments)*, released for consultation on April 2019.

existing system appears to be justified by the value creation principle and is limited by the understanding that the market does not create value. Under the proposed changes, it seems that taxing rights would be allocated to the market country in recognition of the value created by the company in the market country. It does not seem to be done on the basis that the market itself creates value.[27]

[2] In Formulary Apportionment Debates

In the US the courts accepted sales as being one of the sources of income.[28] However, the current disagreement among countries over whether markets create value previously arose in the debates over formulary apportionment in the European Union. Indeed, sales proved to be the 'most controversial'[29] factor and 'generated the greatest divisions between experts'[30] in the run-up to the European Commission's 2011 CCCTB proposal. Some experts argued that the sales factor was the 'most important factor',[31] while others opposed its inclusion altogether. It would not be surprising to find an overlap between countries (and some of their experts) that argued against the inclusion of sales as a factor in the CCCTB formula and countries (and some of their experts) that are now arguing against allocating taxing rights to the market country. It is worth revisiting this previous debate, not least because of its relevance to the current debate on international corporate tax reform.

As a start, note that sales could be included as a factor on an origin or a destination basis. Opponents of the inclusion of sales argued that, if a sales factor is to be included, it should be included on an origin and not a destination basis.[32] But, of course, this simply reaffirms their preference for not allocating taxing rights to a market country as they do not believe that demand creates value. If a sales factor is to be included to reflect the contribution to the generation of profits made by the market, it should be included on a destination basis. Furthermore, sales by origin would duplicate the role of the labour and assets factors in the origin country. The remainder of this section concerns the allocation to sales on a destination basis.

---

27. The OECD's Inclusive Framework is considering reform under two pillars, Pillars I and II. A number of proposals were put forward by countries for consideration under Pillar I. The OECD explained that these proposals 'all allocate more taxing rights to the jurisdiction of the customer and/or user – hereafter, the "market jurisdictions" – in situations where value is created by a business activity through (possibly remote) participation in that jurisdiction that is not recognised in the current framework for allocating profits': OECD, *Programme of Work to Develop a Consensus Solution to the Tax Challenges Arising from the Digitalisation of the Economy*, OECD/G20 Inclusive Framework on BEPS, para. 23 (OECD Publishing 2019). In October 2019 the OECD Secretariat put forward a 'Unified Approach' for consideration by the Inclusive Framework. OECD, *Secretariat Proposal for a 'Unified Approach' under Pillar I* (OECD Publishing 2019).
28. *See, for example*, *Container Corp. of Am. v. Franchise Tax Bd.*, 463 US 159 (1983) and *General Motors Corp. v. District of Columbia*, 380 US 533 (1965).
29. CCCTB Working Group, *Report and Overview of the Main Issues*, *supra* n. 4, at 7.
30. CCCTB Working Group, *An Overview of the Main Issues that Emerged during the Discussion on the Mechanism for Sharing the CCCTB*, Brussels, 27 February 2007, CCCTB\WP\052\doc\en, 8.
31. *Ibid.*
32. *Ibid.*, 9.

Experts who opposed the inclusion of sales questioned whether demand is an income-generating factor.[33] Some years earlier, for example, Schäfer and Spengel stated that: 'it is in principle questionable whether the mere demand constitutes an income-producing factor and, as a consequence, whether a part of the taxable income shall be assigned to the demand jurisdiction solely for providing a consumer market'.[34] However, they did not provide arguments in this discussion paper to back their statement. This position is questionable. The profits being allocated among countries owe as much to the market as they owe to the various parts of a supply chain. Profit depends on the price charged at the point where supply and demand meet; it simply would not have arisen in the absence of a market. This is true of intermediate sales as it is of final sales.

Consumers' contribution to the production of income is seen particularly clearly where businesses generate a higher income simply because of consumer preferences. For example, due to higher demand in Japan for high-quality blue fin tuna, businesses can sell such tuna at a higher price in Japan than anywhere else.[35] This higher consumer demand clearly is a factor that generates value for the supplier. It is not entirely clear why the allocation of taxing rights among countries should adopt an understanding of value creation that departs from this simple and uncontroversial economic understanding. Arguing that consumers in market countries do not create value – and therefore corporate profits should not be allocated to countries where they are located – because consumers merely consume, simply ignores the role of consumers in the generation of profits.

Further arguments were marshalled against the inclusion of sales in the CCCTB formula. We can consider them briefly in turn.

First, opponents argued that the inclusion of sales would 'represent a big change from current practice' with manufacturing and distributing countries' share of the base reducing and that of destination countries increasing.[36] This is true, but it would only be a problem if the existing allocation was justified and an allocation which included the market was not. Second, it was argued that the sales factor should not be allocated to the market country because the function of corporation tax is 'to tax production' and not consumption.[37] This is not convincing. A corporation tax is a tax on the return to

33. CCCTB Working Group, *Report and Overview of the Main Issues*, *supra* n. 4, at 7.
34. Anne Schäfer & Christoph Spengel, *The Impact of ICT on Profit Allocation within Multinational Groups: Arm's Length Pricing or Formula Apportionment?* (ZEW Discussion Paper No. 03-53, 2003). *See also* the discussion in Peggy B. Musgrave, *Principles for Dividing the State Corporate Tax Base*, in *The State Corporation Income Tax: Issues in Worldwide Unitary Combination* 228 (Charles E. McLure, Jr. ed., Hoover Institution Press 1984).
35. The highest price paid on record for a giant blue fin tuna is GBP 2.4 million. Kiyoshi Kimura paid this price in Tokyo's main fish market in 2019 for a 278-kilo tuna fish. He also paid the second highest price on record – GBP 1.37 million for a tuna fish weighing 276 kilos in 2020. *See* Didi Tang, 'That's a lot of sushi! Restaurant king pays £1.3m for giant tuna', *The Times of London* (6 January 2020), https://www.thetimes.co.uk/article/thats-a-lot-of-sushi-restaurant-king-pays-1-3m-for-giant-tuna-t8w7hvvj9 (accessed 7 Jan. 2020).
36. CCCTB Working Group, *The Mechanism for Sharing the CCCTB*, *supra* n. 23, at 8.
37. CCCTB Working Group, *Report and Overview of the Main Issues*, *supra* n. 4, at 9.

equity[38] that requires a market to generate it. Third, it was argued that sales should not be included because market countries already levy value added taxes (VATs) or sales taxes on the same activity. As the Commission noted, this is unpersuasive as it ignores the fact that countries where assets and labour are found also tax these factors through a variety of taxes including income taxes, social security contributions and business rates.[39] Fourth, a more persuasive argument was made by noting that the sales factor could be manipulated through sales routed via an independent agent in a low tax country. This is an important and significant problem. However, assets and labour can also be manipulated, although, perhaps, not with the same ease.

Overall the case against including sales in the allocation formula appears weak.

[C] Brief Critique of the Value Creation Principle

As seen in §10.02[A][1] above, it is commonly held that the existing system is based on the value creation principle. This descriptive claim is questionable. Note, for example, that under the existing system a country can - and some countries still do - tax the foreign business income of resident companies. It might give a credit for tax paid at source, but even then, it could still tax the foreign source income. The point here is that no one would object to a residence-based tax on the grounds that it contravenes the principle on which the existing international tax framework is based. Note also, for example, that the minimum taxes currently being considered under Pillar II by the OECD's Inclusive Framework are a form of residence-based taxation that again cannot be easily reconciled with the value creation principle.

The normative claim seen in §10.02[A] - that the value creation *should* guide the allocation of taxing rights - is also questionable. The main reason is that it is hard, even impossible, to determine which factors generate value for a business. This guiding principle thus fails to provide much guidance. This point is examined at some length, in the context of formulary apportionment systems, in §10.03 below.

It is also difficult to justify value creation as a normative principle on efficiency or fairness grounds. Taxing businesses where supply-side activities take place (for example, research and development, production, marketing and management) distorts the location of real activities as companies have an incentive to move these activities in response to the tax. Taxing businesses in the market country (if markets are deemed to create value) should distort real activities less, to the extent that sales are made to consumers. Overall, the distortions created by following the principle would lead to considerable economic inefficiency.

Fairness, in a tax context, is generally understood in terms of either (or both) the ability to pay or benefit principles. The ability to pay principle justifies taxing business

38. *See, for example,* the discussion in Michael Devereux, *Debating Proposed Reforms of the Taxation of Corporate Income in the European Union*, 11(1) Int'l Tax & Pub. Fin. 71 (2004).
39. CCCTB Working Group, *Report and Overview of the Main Issues, supra* n. 4, at 9.

profits in the parent company's country of residence and not where value is created.[40] In theory, a tax system could be designed to allocate taxing rights in accordance with the benefit received in each country, although that would be hard to achieve in practice. In any event, such a system would not be fair, in terms of the benefit principle, because value creation is not commensurate with benefit. Note, also that the benefit principle certainly does not justify interpreting value creation as excluding the market country. Benefit is undoubtedly provided by market countries – not least because of the legal system which allows them to conclude contracts with consumers and protects them against counterfeit products through trademarks – just as it is provided by countries where supply-side activities are found.

§10.03 VALUE CREATION AND ALLOCATION FORMULAS

This section considers in more depth the application of the value creation principle in designing an allocation formula. For an allocation formula to allocate profit in line with this principle – in other words to allocate profit to its true economic source – at least two steps are required. All the factors that create value must be in the allocation formula (factor choice), and the factors must be weighted to allocate profit in proportion to the value created (factor weighting).

[A] Factor Choice: Can All Sources of Value Creation Be Included as Factors in an Allocation Formula?

Failure to include all factors that create value for a business necessarily means that the resulting allocation formula does not allocate profits according to value creation.

At least two issues arise here. First, there may be different views on whether a factor creates value for a business at all. Sales, as seen in §10.02 above, are deemed to create value by some countries but not others. It follows, therefore, that if sales are (not) included in the allocation formula, the formula would allocate taxing rights in accordance with the value creation principle according to some countries but not others.

The contribution of users of certain highly digitalized businesses is similarly contentious. In the recent debates on how to tax the digitalized economy, a group of countries, including the United Kingdom, and the European Commission argued that 'user participation is an important value driver for certain types of digital businesses, and one that deserves recognition in the rules for allocating taxing rights and taxable profits between countries'.[41] Users are believed to create value through at least four channels: the generation of content; the depth of engagement with the platform;

40. For a discussion of this principle in the context of international taxation, see J. Clifton Fleming, Jr., Robert J. Peroni & Steven E. Shay, *Fairness in International Taxation: The Ability-to-Pay Case for Taxing Worldwide Income*, 5(4) Fla. Tax Rev. 299 (2001).

41. HM Treasury, *Corporate Tax and the Digital Economy: Position Paper Update*, *supra* n. 16.

network effects and externalities; and contribution to the brand.[42] If one accepts that users create value, then they should be included in the allocation formula. In fact, the European Parliament has proposed adding users to the CCCTB allocation formula,[43] and the Commission has described the Parliament's work on this point as a 'good base for further work'.[44] However, some countries do not agree that users create value,[45] and, therefore, the problem again arises that countries will disagree on whether a formula allocates income in line with value creation whether or not it includes users in the allocation formula.

Second, even if everyone agrees that a particular factor creates value, it might not be possible to include it in a formula because of practical or related constraints. Intangible assets are the most significant example here as they are generally excluded from allocation formulas, making them a 'major chink in the armour of formulary apportionment'.[46] They are excluded due to the difficulties entailed in valuing them and the tax planning opportunities that would follow their inclusion. However, their exclusion necessarily means that the formula fails to allocate profit to its true economic source. This is particularly problematic given the increasing importance of intangibles as a source of value to business. One recent study, for example, suggests that intellectual property and other intangibles add twice as much value to products as tangible capital.[47] To the extent that intangibles are developed by employees using physical facilities of a business, they can be partly captured by assets and labour factors.[48] However this would not be true of intangibles that are purchased from third parties, and, in any case, it seems unlikely that the value of an intangible as a source of income for a business is proportionate to these costs.

[B] Factor Weighting: Can the Value Created by Each Factor Be Determined?

Even if the allocation formula included all factors that create value, it would then be necessary to devise broadly applicable weightings that allocated profits to the factors in proportion to the value they created. This appears to be impossible.

42. Through these channels 'users can be seen participating in a non-traditional value chain and performing supply-side functions that would historically have been undertaken by the business itself': *ibid.*, para. 2.30.
43. European Parliament Legislative Resolution of 15 March 2018 on the Proposal for a Council Directive on a Common Corporate Tax Base (COM(2016)0685 - C8-0472/2016 - 2016/0337(CNS)); and European Parliament Legislative Resolution of 15 March 2018 on the Proposal for a Council Directive on a Common Consolidated Corporate Tax Base (CCCTB) (COM(2016)0683 - C8-0471/2016 - 2016/0336(CNS)).
44. European Commission, *Time to Establish a Modern, Fair and Efficient Taxation Standard for the Digital Economy*, *supra* n. 15, at 18.
45. OECD, *Tax Challenges Arising from Digitalisation – Interim Report 2018: Inclusive Framework on BEPS*, OECD/G20 Base Erosion and Profit Shifting Project 25-26 (OECD Publishing 2018).
46. McLure & Weiner, *supra* n. 21, at 270.
47. World Intellectual Property Organization, *World Intellectual Property Report 2017: Intangible Capital in Global Value Chains* (2017).
48. International Monetary Fund (IMF), *Corporate Taxation in the Global Economy* 32 (IMF Policy Paper, May 2019).

For a start, part of a multinational's profit arises because of synergies created from the combination of different factors. Determining how much profit arises from such synergies is a difficult task in itself, but, furthermore, by definition such profit cannot be accurately attributed to particular factors.

Second, determining the true economic contribution made by each factor is an impossible task. Businesses are successful and thus profitable for many different reasons.[49] It may even be difficult to explain ex post facto which factor led to a particular company's success and profitability. It certainly seems impossible to correctly allocate profit to its true economic source (or according to value creation) through the use of a formula weighted for the economy as a whole or even for specific sectors.

Consider two companies running restaurants, with identical assets, labour, sales and profits. Both companies earn economic rent. Company A runs a restaurant outside town. It is inconvenient to get to but still attracts guests because it has secured the services of a young chef on relatively low wages who turned out to be a star. Company B runs a restaurant in a prime location in the centre of town which it acquired at a favourable price. It serves mediocre food but still attracts guests because of its location. Labour appears to be a more significant source of profits for A than for B, and assets appear to be a more significant source of profits for B than for A, but a formula would not correctly attribute profits to the two factors because they are undervalued on the books of the restaurants.[50] The relative size of labour costs or asset values does not give a clear indication of the contribution they make to the profits generated.

Note that it would not suffice to know the value created by different factors on average. Assume that on average value is created by assets, labour and sales in equal measure. Applying an equally weighted three-factor formula would still lead to allocations of profits in particular cases that are not in line with value creation. An extreme example can be taken to make this point. Three companies operate in a country and it is observed that 100% of profit is due to labour in company A, assets in company B and sales in company C. On average one can say that labour, assets and sales each contribute to one-third of corporate profit in this country. However, an equally weighted three-factor formula would fail to allocate profit in line with value creation in the case of all three companies.

A third point follows from the second. Allocation formulas assume that the size of a factor in a particular country is positively related to profit. But this is not necessarily true. In fact, the size of a factor can be negatively related to profit. Under a formulary apportionment system with labour (measured by wages) as a factor, high

49. As Kay explains: '[t]here are no recipes, and generic strategies, for corporate success. There cannot be, because if there were their general adoption would eliminate any competitive advantage which might be derived. The foundations of corporate success are unique to each successful company. The uniqueness is a product of the firm's contracts and relationships. I see the firm as a set of relationships between its various stakeholders – employees, customers, investors, shareholders. The successful firm is one which creates a distinctive character in these relationships and which operates in an environment which maximizes the value of that distinctiveness': Kay, *supra* n. 9, vi-vii.

50. Economic rent would not arise under perfect market conditions. However, they arise, and are observed, in the real world where perfect market conditions do not hold.

labour costs in a particular country lead to a higher allocation of profit to that country, but the high labour costs might actually reduce the MNE's profit. Consider the application of a three-factor formulary apportionment system (with labour measured by wages) to the following fact pattern. An MNE with assets, labour and sales in countries A and B hires a superstar chief executive officer in A. Following the CEO's appointment, the MNE's global profit increases from $10 million to $12 million, excluding the CEO's wages:

- If the MNE pays the CEO $2 million in wages, the global profit (post-wages) does not increase. But the increase in wages in A leads to a different allocation of the same profit between A and B. Despite the global profit remaining the same following the appointment, the profit allocated to A increases and that allocated to B decreases.
- If the MNE pays the CEO $1 million in wages, the global profit (post-wages) increases by $1 million. Despite being attributable to the CEO's activities in A, the additional $1 million is shared between countries A and B.
- If the MNE overenthusiastically pays the CEO $3 million, the global profit (post-wages) decreases. Even if the decrease in profit is attributable to a factor in A, the proportion of (reduced) profit allocated to A actually increases.

This simple example shows that formulary apportionment systems can do worse than failing to allocate profit in line with value creation. In fact, they can allocate profit to countries where profit-reducing factors are located.

The conclusion reached in this section is backed by empirical evidence.[51] Using data for just over 11,000 European companies, Hines finds that apportionment formulas:

> significantly misattribute income, since employment and other factors in which they are based do a very poor job of explaining a firm's profits. For example, the magnitude of property, employment and sales explains less than 22% of the variation in profits between firms.[52]

Labour costs, in particular, are very poor at predicting income.[53]

Finally, note that, while identifying the factors that create value and establishing how much value they each create in traditional bricks and mortar businesses may be hard, it is even harder in a digitalized economy. And, of course, over time, most companies are becoming increasingly digitalized. Despite its unstinting support of value creation as a guiding principle for allocating income among countries, the European Commission conceded that: '[i]n a digitalised world, it is not always very

51. Hines, *supra* n. 8, at 117-118.
52. *Ibid.*, 108.
53. Hines notes that '[i]t may not be surprising that labor cost factors do a very poor job of predicting income, given that labor expenses are deductible in calculating income; whereas capital expenses are typically only partially deductible, and greater sales conditional on factor inputs contribute to income': *ibid.*, 116.

clear what that value is, how to measure it, or where it is created'.[54] Similarly, and as noted above, the United Kingdom and others argued that users of certain highly digitalized businesses create value. At the same time, however, the United Kingdom conceded that it is all but impossible to measure the value created by such users.[55]

[C] Is the Existing System Better at Allocating Profits in Line with Value Creation?

It is often claimed that one of the relative merits of the existing system over formulary apportionment is that the former is more successful at allocating income to its true economic source. But if the true economic source of income is often unknown, as argued above, then this relative comparison is meaningless. Both systems result in an arbitrary allocation of income.

It is useful to make a few further points about the ability of the existing system to allocate income according to value creation.[56] First, as noted in §10.02[C] above, under the existing system residence countries are allowed to tax. This can lead to situations where tax is levied by countries in which there is very little real activity. It certainly allows residence countries to tax income disproportionately to the contribution made to its generation. Second, again as argued above, in §10.02[B], the existing system does not allocate taxing rights to the market country, thus ignoring a critical source of income. Third, the arm's length standard[57] and the profit attribution rules for permanent establishments – which are at the heart of the existing system – also lead to an arbitrary allocation of taxable profit. The proxies used in transfer pricing and profit attribution rules for permanent establishments, especially 'significant people functions', lead to an allocation of profit that is clearly not in line with value creation – unless it is thought that significant value in a business comes from middle management.[58] Finally, although steps have been taken to make the existing system more robust to profit shifting, opportunities remain to shift profit away from countries where real activities are found to low tax jurisdictions.

54. European Commission, European Parliament and European Council, *A Fair and Efficient Tax System in the European Union for the Digital Single Market*, Brussels, 21.9.2017 COM(2017) 547 final.
55. HM Treasury, *Corporate Tax and the Digital Economy: Position Paper Update*, *supra* n. 16, at 16-17.
56. *See* the discussion in Hellerstein, *The Case for Formulary Apportionment*, *supra* n. 11, at 108.
57. *See* Reuven Avi-Yonah & Ilan Benshalom, *Formulary Apportionment: Myths and Prospects – Promoting Better International Tax Policies by Utilizing the Misunderstood and Under-Theorized Formulary Alternative*, 3(3) World Tax J. 371 (2011). The authors dismiss as a myth the broader argument that formulary apportionment cannot replace the arm's length standard because it is a mere approximation which cannot penetrate the MNE profit-generating process. *See also* Michael Kobetsky, *The Case for the Unitary Taxation of International Enterprises*, 62(5) Bull. Int'l Tax'n 201, 203 (2008).
58. On the issues arising from the use of these proxies, *see* Richard Collier & John Vella, *Five Core Problems in the Attribution of Profits to Permanent Establishments*, 11(2) World Tax J. (2019).

§10.04 ALTERNATIVE GUIDING PRINCIPLES TO CHOOSE ALLOCATION FACTORS

Given the impossibility of designing an allocation formula which allocates profits in line with value creation, how then should the choice of formula be made? In practice, of course, the choice may be based on political considerations. However, two more principled options can be considered.

[A] The Nature of Corporation Tax

A corporation tax is a tax on the return to capital, or, to be more precise, equity investment. This suggests that it would be theoretically justified to allocate the corporate tax base among countries where equity investors are found. Note that the justification here would not be that the sole economic source of corporate profits is equity investment. As argued in §10.03[B] above, many factors contribute to the generation of corporate profits. The justification is that the corporation tax is a tax on the return to equity (independently of what factors contribute to the generation of that profits). Two immediate problems arise. One is its apparent infeasibility.[59] The other is that countries where equity holders are found are already able to tax the returns to equity when dividends are paid or the shares are transferred. Proxies may then be considered as an alternative, and it may be argued that tangible property can be a valid proxy for equity investment. This may have been true for a wide range of companies in the past, but it appears to be increasingly problematic in the current digitalized economy where equity investment may be used to fund labour engaged in research and development in the hope of creating valuable intangible property. In conclusion, therefore, this route is principled but it does not offer much promise.

[B] Criteria for Good Tax Design

The best option to guide the design of an allocation formula in a principled way is to use criteria for good tax design.[60] There is no definitive list of criteria, and different lists of criteria have been proposed over the years.[61] However, these lists generally include a number of core criteria. Possible criteria include: economic efficiency, fairness, robustness to avoidance, ease of administration and stability/incentive compatibility.[62] Once

59. It has been argued that such a tax would be practically infeasible because of most corporations' need to make pro rata distributions: Wei Cui, *Residence-Based Formulary Apportionment: (In)feasibility and Implications*, 71(3) Tax L. Rev. 551 (2018).
60. This approach is broadly followed in Ana Agúndez-García, *The Delineation and Apportionment of an EU Consolidated Tax Base for Multi-Jurisdictional Corporate Income Taxation: A Review of Issues and Options* (European Commission Directorate-General for Taxation and Customs Union Working Paper No 9/2006).
61. Adam Smith's Canons of Taxation are probably the best-known set of criteria: Adam Smith, *An Inquiry into the Nature and Causes of the Wealth of Nations* (W. Strahan 1776).
62. *See* Michael Devereux, Alan Auerbach, Michael Keen, Paul Oosterhuis, Wolfgang Schön & John Vella, *Taxing Multinational Profit* (Oxford University Press forthcoming).

a set of criteria are agreed, allocation factors and combinations of factors can be assessed against this set of criteria using the information garnered from academic research and practical experience. Some factors are more easily assessed under particular criteria than others. For example, it is relatively uncontroversial to state that assets and labour distort real-location decisions, thus causing economic inefficiency, more than retail sales. But it is harder to assess all three factors against their susceptibility to avoidance or fairness. Also, difficult trade-offs might arise between the different factors and combinations of factors. For example, fairness might have to be traded off against efficiency and ease of administration. While this process is not without difficulty, it ought to allow for a better-informed and principled choice of allocation formula.

§10.05 CONCLUSION

Formulary apportionment systems have been long criticized for failing to allocate profit in line with value creation (or to allocate profit to its true economic source). This criticism has gained importance in recent years with the growing consensus that, as a normative matter, companies should be taxed where value is created.

This chapter argued that formulary apportionment systems do not allocate profits in line with this principle. But this should not be deemed to be a weakness. The question of whether formulary apportionment or the existing system is better at allocating income in line with value creation is simply the wrong question to ask. International tax systems should not be judged on whether they allocate corporate profits in line with value creation. Value creation cannot assume this normative role, as it is very hard, if not impossible, to know where value is created in a business, particularly complex multinational businesses. Furthermore, this principle would lead to an international tax system that distorts real economic decisions while not being easily justified in terms of standard definitions of fairness. A more principled approach is to identify criteria for good tax design - which could include economic efficiency, fairness, ease of administration, robustness to avoidance and incentive compatibility - and assess different existing and proposed tax systems against these criteria.

CHAPTER 11

Formulating the International Tax Debate: Where Does Formulary Apportionment Fit?

Itai Grinberg

§11.01 INTRODUCTION

As the contributions in this volume are being written, the Inclusive Framework nations, a group drawn together by the Organisation for Economic Co-operation and Development (OECD) as part of its Base Erosion and Profit Shifting (BEPS) project, are in the midst of a consultation process intended to revise the international corporate tax profit allocation and nexus rules. At the end of May 2019, the OECD released its *Programme of Work to Develop a Consensus Solution to the Tax Challenges Arising from the Digitalisation of the Economy*.[1] At the beginning of June 2019, this Programme was endorsed by the G20 Finance Ministers during their ministerial meeting in Fukuoka, Japan.[2]

To use the OECD's terminology, the proposals under consideration to revise the current nexus and profit allocation rules would create a 'new taxing right' to be allocated to the 'market jurisdiction'.[3] The Programme of Work describes certain technical issues that must be considered when making such fundamental changes to the international tax architecture.[4]

The OECD's work on these major revisions to international tax norms is being undertaken under the auspices of the Inclusive Framework. The Inclusive Framework arose out of a G20 request that the OECD create a body in which all interested countries

1. OECD, *Programme of Work to Develop a Consensus Solution to the Tax Challenges Arising from the Digitalisation of the Economy*, OECD/G20 Inclusive Framework on BEPS (OECD 2019).
2. Communiqué, G20 Finance Ministers and Central Bank Governors Meeting, Fukuoka, Japan, 9 June 2019, [11] (Fukuoka Communiqué).
3. OECD, *Programme of Work*, *supra* n. 1, at 11.
4. *Ibid.*, [24].

– regardless of G20 or OECD membership – could participate in the BEPS project on an equal footing.[5] The subsequently developed Inclusive Framework allows interested countries to work with the OECD/G20 on developing standards on BEPS-related issues.[6] As of this writing, over 125 countries have joined the Inclusive Framework[7] and committed to implementing the comprehensive BEPS package.[8] It was clear from the outset that the Inclusive Framework could be used as a stand-in for a world tax organization. In the current OECD project on profit allocation, it is in effect being used in that manner for the first time.

The Inclusive Framework is not currently considering a full move to formulary apportionment, as that term is understood in this volume. Yet evaluation of the proposals under consideration by the Inclusive Framework suggests that each and every one can be improved by reappraising formulary apportionment. Accordingly, the purpose of this chapter is to highlight the relationships between the options under consideration in the current OECD-led process and 'formulary apportionment', as that term is used elsewhere in this volume.

Section 11.02 of the chapter briefly offers some background on the major developments – arguably, tectonic shifts – of the last few years in the international tax arena. Section 11.03 describes the proposals for revising the profit allocation rules that are currently under consideration by the Inclusive Framework. Section 11.04 fleshes out 'straw men' that develop these ideas in greater detail, with the purpose of highlighting that the proposals that are under consideration by the Inclusive Framework at the time of this writing are partially formulary approaches and that lessons from formulary apportionment likely carry over to any partially formulary system that may be developed multilaterally in the future.

§11.02 BACKGROUND: THE ROAD TO FUKUOKA

In the summer of 2019, the G20 endorsed the OECD's *Programme of Work to Develop a Consensus Solution to the Tax Challenges Arising from the Digitalisation of the Economy* intended to develop a new taxing right to change the international tax architecture. The Programme of Work is a continuation of the OECD's Base Erosion and Profit Shifting (BEPS) project, another G20-endorsed international tax effort which ran principally from 2013 to 2015. One of the Final Reports associated with that project noted that the digitalization of the economy exacerbated BEPS issues, while also raising broader tax challenges.[9] At the same time, the top-line conclusion of the OECD's 2015

5. G20 Leaders' Communiqué, Antalya Summit, 15-16 November 2015, [15] (Antalya Communiqué); *see also* OECD, *Background Brief: Inclusive Framework on BEPS* (OECD 2017).
6. *Ibid.*, section 2.1.
7. OECD, *About the Inclusive Framework on BEPS*, https://www.oecd.org/tax/beps/beps-about.htm (accessed 12 Jun. 2019).
8. *See* OECD, *Background Brief: Inclusive Framework on BEPS*, *supra* n. 5, section 2.1, requiring that countries commit to the BEPS package and its consistent implementation in order to join the Inclusive Framework.
9. OECD, *Action 1 – 2015 Final Report: Addressing the Tax Challenges of the Digital Economy*, OECD/G20 Base Erosion and Profit Shifting Project 135 (OECD 2015).

project on the digital economy was that there was no such thing as a 'digital economy' that could be ring-fenced from the broader economy. Rather, the OECD came to the view that the entire economy was in the process of 'digitalizing'.[10]

Nevertheless, in 2015 the OECD committed to continue working on issues related to the so-called digital economy, and to deliver an interim report to the G20 in 2018, and a final report in 2020.[11]

In the work undertaken in the three years following the 2015 Final Reports of the BEPS project, the Inclusive Framework again underscored that certain characteristics of highly digitalized business models allow multinational enterprises (MNEs) to create value through activities closely linked with a domestic economy, without needing to establish a taxable physical presence in that economy.[12] This conclusion was not initially intended to disturb the earlier conclusion that the digital economy could not be 'ring-fenced', because the entire economy was digitalizing, albeit with different parts of the economy digitalizing at different speeds.

Despite this conclusion, many jurisdictions that had hoped to collect more revenues from specific companies in the digital sector decided quite quickly that they were not satisfied with the relevant BEPS transfer pricing outcomes. Illustrative examples of the companies of interest were often mentioned in documents issued by governments either by name or by transparent references to specific business models, and almost always included Google, Apple, Facebook, and Amazon, as well as some other US-headquartered companies.[13]

10. *See* Erik Cederwall, *Making Sense of Profit Shifting: Pascal Saint-Amans*, Tax Foundation (22 May 2015), https://taxfoundation.org/making-sense-profit-shifting-pascal-saint-amans/ (accessed 28 Jun. 2019); OECD, *Addressing the Tax Challenges of the Digital Economy*, *supra* n. 9.
11. *OECD, Addressing the Tax Challenges of the Digital Economy*, *supra* n. 9; *see also* PricewaterhouseCoopers, *OECD Consultation to Reshape the International Tax System for the Digitalised Age Commences*, Tax Policy Bulletin (15 February 2019), https://www.pwc.com/gx/en/tax/newsletters/tax-policy-bulletin/assets/pwc-oecd-consultation-reshape-international-tax-for-digital.pdf (accessed 29 Jun. 2019).
12. OECD, *Tax Challenges Arising from Digitalisation – Interim Report 2018*, Inclusive Framework on BEPS (OECD 2018); *see also* OECD, *Addressing the Tax Challenges of the Digitalisation of the Economy: Public Consultation Document, 13 February – 6 March 2019*, OECD/G20 Base Erosion and Profit Shifting Project 11-13 (OECD 2019).
13. Itai Grinberg, *International Taxation in an Era of Digital Disruption: Analyzing the Current Debate*, 97 Taxes: The Tax Mag. 73, 79 (2019); European Commission, *Digital Taxation: Commission Proposes New Measures to Ensure That All Companies Pay Fair Tax in the EU*, press release (21 March 2018), http://europa.eu/rapid/press-release_IP-18-2041_en.htm; European Commission, *Questions and Answers on a Fair and Efficient Tax System in the EU for the Digital Single Market*, fact sheet (21 March 2018), http://europa.eu/rapid/press-release_MEMO-18-2141_en.htm; HM Treasury & HM Revenue and Customs (UK), *Digital Services Tax: Consultation* (November 2018), https://assets.publishing.service.gov.uk/government/uploads/system/uploads/attachment_data/file/754975/Digital_Services_Tax_-_Consultation_Document_FINAL_PDF.pdf; Government of France, *GAFA Tax: A Major Step Towards a Fairer and More Efficient Tax System*, press release (9 April 2019), https://www.gouvernement.fr/en/gafa-tax-a-major-step-towards-a-fairer-and-more-efficient-tax-system (accessed 29 Jun. 2019); Federal Ministry of Finance, Austria, Digitalsteuergesetz 2020, draft Bill to amend Turnover Tax Law 1994 (5 April 2019), https://www.parlament.gv.at/PAKT/VHG/XXVI/ME/ME_00132/index.shtml, discussed in Ernst & Young, *Austria Publishes Draft Digital Advertising Tax Bill*, Indirect Tax Alert (8 April 2019), https://www.ey.com/gl/en/services/tax/international-tax/alert--austria-publishes-draft-digital-advertising-tax-bill.

In March 2018, the European Commission called for new international rules that would alter the application of permanent establishment (PE) and transfer pricing rules to the digital economy alone.[14] The Commission released two digital tax proposals: an interim digital services tax (DST) which would be based on turnover or a withholding mechanism, and would be imposed on digital platform companies,[15] and a long-term proposal that would create a new digital PE based on 'significant digital presence'.[16]

A number of individual EU Member States, as well as countries in other parts of the world, went ahead and proposed their own digital services taxes, separate and apart from the European proposal put forward by the Commission. European countries moving forward included France, Italy, Spain, and the United Kingdom, while major non-EU countries taking steps to enact DSTs included Australia, India, Mexico, New Zealand, and South Korea.[17]

Even before the DSTs were proposed, countries had begun taking unilateral steps inconsistent with the BEPS outcomes that targeted digital business. The first such action, which arguably opened the floodgates because it was proposed by a jurisdiction (the United Kingdom) which helped lead the BEPS project, was the United Kingdom's diverted profits tax (DPT). The DPT enacted on 26 March 2015 with effect from 1 April 2015 a 25% tax on profits deemed to be artificially diverted away from the United Kingdom. The DPT targets instances where, under the existing PE rules, an MNE legitimately avoids establishing a taxable presence in the United Kingdom, despite the fact that the MNE supplies goods or services to UK customers. The United Kingdom's decision to enact the DPT while simultaneously helping lead the BEPS project treated sovereignty as a licence for organized hypocrisy. But for the DPT, one could imagine that a more cooperative international tax environment might have evolved out of the BEPS project.

Shortly after the United Kingdom moved forward with its DPT, India went ahead and targeted the so-called digital economy by imposing a 6% 'equalization levy' on outbound payments to non-resident companies for all digital services, and by expanding its taxing rights over non-residents to cover profits arising from a 'significant economic presence'.[18] Other countries that undertook unilateral actions other than DSTs, but not limited by or consistent with the BEPS agreements, include Australia,

---

14. European Commission, *Communication from the Commission to the European Parliament and the Council: A Fair and Efficient Tax System in the European Union for the Digital Single Market*, COM(2017)547 final 9 (21 September 2017).
15. *Ibid.*, 10; Ernst & Young, *European Commission Issues Proposals for Taxation of Digitalized Activity*, Global Tax Alert (21 March 2018), https://www.ey.com/gl/en/services/tax/international-tax/alert--european-commission-issues-proposals-for-taxation-of-digitalized-activity (accessed 29 Jun. 2019).
16. *See* Ernst & Young, *New Digital Tax Policies: What, When, Where, How and By Whom?*, Global Tax Policy and Controversy Briefing (August 2018), https://www.ey.com/Publication/vwLUAssets/EY-new-digital-tax-policies-what-when-where-how-and-by-whom/$FILE/EY-new-digital-tax-policies-what-when-where-how-and-by-whom.pdf (accessed 29 Jun. 2019).
17. *See* Grinberg, *International Taxation in an Era of Digital Disruption*, *supra* n. 13, at 79.
18. Deloitte, *Taxation of Non-Residents Through a Significant Economic Presence: Widened Scope Under the Indian Income Tax Law* (2018), https://www2.deloitte.com/content/dam/Deloitte/in/Documents/technology-media-telecommunications/in-tmt-significant-economic-presence-1-noexp.pdf (accessed 29 Jun. 2019).

Argentina, Chile, France, Israel, Italy, Japan, Mexico, New Zealand, Poland, Spain, and Uruguay.[19]

The proliferation of unilateral measures targeting digital business had the unintended effect of bringing together an unusual coalition of traditional 'source' countries and the United States and China (major 'digital business' headquarter countries). Beginning in 2017 some countries (such as Brazil and India) that had long advocated major change to the international tax system, and others (such as the United States) that were historically seen as the vanguard of OECD traditionalism, came to believe that any discussion of changing profit allocation rules could not be limited to a narrowly defined digital sector.[20] They therefore pushed for multilateral work on profit allocation generally, rather than a specific focus on digital economy companies. Given the earlier conclusion that it was not possible to ring-fence the digital economy, this request was hard to deny on the basis of any logic of appropriateness. Thus, a multilateral project that was initially spearheaded by countries that wanted to tax the digital economy more heavily was in effect converted into a project sponsored by a wider range of states in which all states found themselves forced to confront basic conflicts regarding profit allocation that they had managed to set aside in the original BEPS project.

The Inclusive Framework then went through a difficult period, mostly as a consequence of disagreements between countries that believed that the serious problems in the international tax regime were limited to the taxation of social media companies, search engines, and online marketplaces and those countries that believed that the profit allocation issues raised by those business models were just particularly noteworthy examples of much more widespread issues.

In February 2019, cognizant of the looming 2020 deadline and the OECD's newfound commitment to consult broad groups of stakeholders, the OECD distilled these intra-governmental tensions into a public consultation document that outlined three substantially irreconcilable proposals grouped under two 'pillars'. The first pillar addressed proposals to revise the nexus and profit allocation rules; the second addressed the so-called remaining BEPS issues.[21] The Inclusive Framework acknowledged that all three of the proposals it was considering in the consultation document under the first pillar would 'go beyond the arm's length principle'[22] and came to call

19. For a more robust discussion on the rise of international tax unilateralism, *see* Grinberg, *International Taxation in an Era of Digital Disruption*, *supra* n. 13.
20. Remarks of Brian Jenn, Deputy International Tax Counsel, US Treasury, at the US Council for International Business (USCIB) 2018 OECD International Tax Conference, Washington, DC, 4-5 June 2018 (all major economies believe either the first or the second of the options).
21. OECD, *Addressing the Tax Challenges of the Digitalisation of the Economy – Policy Note, As Approved by the Inclusive Framework on BEPS on 23 January 2019*, OECD/G20 Base Erosion and Profit Shifting Project 1 (OECD 2019).
22. *Ibid.*, 2. Both the 'marketing intangibles' and 'user participation' proposals that were described in the consultation document were different 'flavours' of a modified residual profit split method, while the significant economic presence proposal took a worldwide formulary apportionment approach: OECD, *Addressing the Tax Challenges of the Digitalisation of the Economy: Public Consultation Document*, *supra* n. 12, at 11-13. Under the first two proposals, routine returns are calculated at arm's length. The marketing intangibles approach then carves out the portion of residual profits that can be deemed attributable to 'marketing intangibles'. Under the marketing

these ideas the 'new taxing right'. Two of the 'new taxing right' proposals continued to utilize the arm's length principle in allocating routine returns. One of the proposals – the so-called significant economic presence proposal – contemplated an approach which allocated profit to a significant economic presence in a jurisdiction, based on a 'fractional apportionment' method. Fractional apportionment was the term used to describe formulary apportionment regimes in the multilateral context in earlier generations.[23] There is no substantive difference between the two ideas.

After inviting public input on the consultation document proposals, the OECD received over 200 submissions. In March 2019, the OECD hosted a one and a half-day public consultation at which key members of the Task Force on the Digital Economy discussed the possible directions for future work.[24] In the months after the publication of the consultation document, it became clear that the majority of governments would not support a full move to fractional apportionment based on a significant economic presence concept.[25] Nevertheless, three alternative proposals for revising the international tax profit allocation and nexus rules were advanced by the Inclusive Framework. Each required that a significant portion of an MNE's returns be allocated using a formulary method. The Inclusive Framework produced a Programme of Work to further study these ideas and move towards a new international tax consensus for profit allocation. In the summer of 2019, the G20 Finance Ministers approved the Programme, with the (unrealistic) hope that the work would be completed by the end of 2020.[26]

---

intangibles concept, affiliates of an MNC were to be compensated for their functions on a cost-plus or return on assets basis using the arm's length principle. The 'residual return' would then be divided between marketing or customer-based intangibles and other intangibles. Residual returns deemed attributable to 'marketing intangibles' would be allocated in part or in whole to the market – the jurisdictions where the customers reside. Residual returns deemed attributable to other intangibles would be allocated based on current transfer pricing rules: Public Consultation Document, *supra* n. 12, at 14 [43]. In contrast, whereas the marketing intangibles approach did not ring-fence the 'digital economy', a user participation approach would be limited to social media platforms, search engines, and online marketplaces. The user participation proposal also required that profits deemed attributable to user participation would somehow be separated from other non-routine profits.

23. *See, e.g.*, Mitchell B. Carroll, *Taxation of Foreign and National Enterprises: A Study of the Tax Systems and the Methods of Allocation of the Profits of Enterprises Operating in More Than One Country, Vol. IV: Methods of Allocating Taxable Income*, League of Nations Document No. C.425(b). M.217(b).1933.II.A. (League of Nations 1933); Stanley I. Langbein, *A Modified Fractional Apportionment Proposal for Tax Transfer Pricing*, 54 Tax Notes 719 (1992); Vinay Kumar Singh, *Interaction of Transfer Pricing and Profit Attribution: Conceptual and Policy Issues for Developing Countries*, South Centre Tax Cooperation Policy Brief No. 3 (August 2018), https://www.southcentre.int/wp-content/uploads/2018/08/TCPB3_Interaction-of-Transfer-Pricing-Profit-Attribution_EN.pdf (accessed 29 Jun. 2019); Joann M. Weiner, *Using the Experience in the US States to Evaluate Issues in Implementing Formula Apportionment at the International Level* 3 n. 7 (US Treasury Office of Tax Analysis Paper 83, April 1999).
24. Ernst & Young, *OECD Hosts Public Consultation on Document Proposing Significant Changes to the International Tax System*, Tax News Update (19 March 2019), https://taxnews.ey.com/news/2019-0563-oecd-hosts-public-consultation-on-document-proposing-significant-changes-to-the-international-tax-system (accessed 29 Jun. 2019).
25. Remarks of L. G. 'Chip' Harter, Deputy Assistant Secretary (International Tax Affairs), US Treasury, at the USCIB 2019 OECD International Tax Conference, Washington, DC, 3-4 June 2019.
26. *See* Fukuoka Communiqué, *supra* n. 2, at [11].

§11.03 INCLUSIVE FRAMEWORK PROPOSALS

The Programme of Work endorsed by the G20 Finance Ministers advanced two key methods for quantifying the amount of an MNE's profits to be reallocated to market jurisdictions under the new taxing right, and determining how those profits are to be allocated among the market jurisdictions.[27] These methods are labelled in the Programme of Work as a modified residual profit split (MRPS) and a distribution-based (DB) approach.[28]

The Work Programme identified three technical issues to be resolved when designing the new taxing right, regardless of whether an MRPS or DB approach was taken:

(1) how to determine the amount of an MNE's profits that are subject to this 'new taxing right' and how those profits are allocated among the relevant jurisdictions;
(2) how to design a new nexus rule that establishes a business presence in a market jurisdiction without the need for a physical presence; and
(3) creating instruments that ensure full implementation and efficient administration of the 'new taxing right'.[29]

Reappraisals of lessons learned in the debate over formulary apportionment can assist with all three of these questions. However, describing the relationship of these issues in the new taxing right to lessons learned in studying formulary apportionment first requires describing the OECD's modified residual profit split and distribution-based approaches to creating a new taxing right in greater depth. Accordingly, the next subsection turns to that task. The task remains useful even if the OECD process moves beyond these particular proposals in the immediate term, because this debate is likely to continue for a number of years.

[A] Modified Residual Profit Split Method

According to the Programme of Work, a modified residual profit split method would allocate a portion of an MNE's non-routine profits that 'reflects the value created in markets' to market jurisdictions.[30] This allocation of taxing rights would take place in four steps: (i) determine the parameters of the total profits to be split; (ii) remove routine profits from total profits; (iii) determine the portion of non-routine profit that is within the new taxing right, and (iv) use an allocation key to allocate that portion to the relevant market jurisdictions.[31] In the modified residual profit split method, three allocations and/or apportionments are therefore required. First, a distinction between

27. OECD, *Programme of Work*, *supra* n. 1, at 12.
28. *See ibid.*, 12-16.
29. *Ibid.*, 11.
30. *Ibid.*, 12.
31. *Ibid.*

routine and non-routine profits must be made; then the non-routine profit must be divided between an amount that is subject to the new taxing right and an amount that is not subject to the new taxing right; and finally the amount subject to the new taxing right must be allocated among jurisdictions. This final allocation between jurisdictions where the customers reside would be based on an 'agreed allocation metric (e.g. revenues)'.[32] Importantly, the Programme of Work specifies that any modified residual profit split method must be calibrated to run alongside the current arm's length transfer pricing rules. Therefore, it is clear that at least part of the arm's length standard is intended to be preserved.[33]

[B] A Distribution-Based Approach

In contrast to a modified residual profit split method, a distribution-based approach likely would not be limited in application to non-routine profits. It might, for example, also address profits arising from routine activities associated with marketing and distribution, or all routine profits.[34] One way to design a distribution-based system would be to specify a baseline profit in the market jurisdiction for marketing, distribution, and user-related activities. For example, the Programme suggests that a baseline profit allocation to market jurisdictions could be increased based on the MNE group's overall profitability or modified to accommodate additional variables that may also indicate value such as the relevant industry sector. The result would be a reallocation of some of the MNE group's profit - both routine and non-routine - to market jurisdictions.[35]

One professed appeal of the distribution-based approach is its potential for simplicity and ease of administration, including for developing countries. The distribution-based approach is thus intended to allocate more profit to market jurisdictions while also reducing the ongoing controversies associated with the current transfer pricing system.[36]

However, despite its superficial simplicity, the Programme acknowledges that such a distribution-based system raises complex issues. Some concerns include considering whether the system's allocation to market jurisdictions is a final allocation or one that would allow for post-allocation re-evaluation; how reallocations could be applied where the MNE has no established tax presence in the market jurisdiction; and how this approach would run alongside the current transfer pricing system without resulting in double taxation or double non-taxation.[37]

32. OECD, *Addressing the Tax Challenges of the Digitalisation of the Economy: Public Consultation Document*, *supra* n. 12, at 10, [24.3]; *see also* OECD, *Programme of Work*, *supra* n. 1, at 14.
33. OECD, *Programme of Work*, *supra* n. 1, at 13.
34. *Ibid.*, 15 [32].
35. *Ibid.*, 15 [33].
36. *Ibid.*, 15 [32].
37. *Ibid.*, 16, section 1.4.

§11.04 'STRAW MEN' FOR PARTIALLY FORMULARY APPROACHES TO PROFIT ALLOCATION

The parameters of the two approaches that were laid out by the Inclusive Framework in the 2019 Programme of Work are ill-defined. As a result, both to consider what reappraising formulary apportionment might teach us about the Programme, and to make the lessons of this chapter relevant to periods after that Programme is complete, it is helpful to specify 'straw man' proposals that add content to the proposals.

The straw man discussed in §11.04[A] below builds out a modified residual profit split-type profit allocation approach and is termed in this chapter the capitalized expenditure method (CE Method), while the straw man discussed subsequently in §11.04[B] builds out the distribution-based type of profit allocation approach and is termed the operating margins method (OM Method). While the CE Method and the OM Method serve as more detailed illustrations of a modified residual profit split and a distribution-based approach respectively, they are not intended to be descriptive of what the OECD is actually developing as this chapter goes to publication. Indeed, by the time this volume is published, the specifics of the straw men will almost certainly be shown to differ from what the OECD in fact is working towards. Nevertheless, the straw men are fully consistent with the language in the OECD's public consultation document; the general direction of the Inclusive Framework's public consultation in March 2019;[38] the Inclusive Framework's Programme of Work published on 29 May 2019;[39] and public remarks made in various venues by the leading international tax officials of the OECD and of the largest economies participating in the Inclusive Framework through the summer of 2019.

[A] The Capitalized Expenditure Method

The CE Method would begin by separating 'excess' or 'residual' returns from 'routine returns'.[40] The CE Method provides a normal rate of return to productive economic functions. It uses arm's length methods to determine this return, on the theory that the arm's length method works reasonably well in the context of determining appropriate 'non-entrepreneurial' returns for specific economic activities. Then, to allocate the remaining 'entrepreneurial', 'non-routine', or 'residual' returns, the CE Method in effect deems the country in which customer sales take place to be an 'entrepreneurial'

38. *See* Ernst & Young, *OECD Hosts Public Consultation, supra* n. 24.
39. OECD, *Programme of Work, supra* n. 1.
40. The CE Method raises various technical challenges. My prior article (Grinberg, *supra* n. 13) focused on pragmatic administrative issues associated with implementing the proposal. In contrast, this chapter focuses only on *stabilizing* a marketing intangibles proposal internationally. Thus, my description of the method in this section does not restate the pragmatic administrative issues I believe are raised by the CE Method, except to the extent these are relevant to stabilizing the proposal within the international tax system.

affiliate with respect to local market sales. The CE Method treats part of the 'non-routine' or 'residual' profits to be due to 'market intangibles' and allocates that part of the non-routine profits to the affiliate in the market country.[41]

Thus, splitting the residual profit between profits being allocated to market intangibles and profits being allocated to other intangibles is necessary in the CE Method. The CE Method for arriving at that split would involve specifying which expenditures contribute to developing market intangibles and which expenditures contribute to developing other intangibles. Governments would then establish (presumably on a presumptive basis) 'useful lives' for various 'buckets' of expenditure. The resulting relative 'capitalized values' associated with functional costs incurred for market intangibles as compared to other intangibles would produce a ratio. The ratio would change each year as a result of both new expenditures by the MNE and the operation of whatever 'amortization schedule' was adopted for the various buckets of expenditure. The 'amortization schedule' would not produce actual deductions; it would simply establish the annual ratio of 'market intangibles' to 'other intangibles' (the CE Method Ratio). The CE Method Ratio would determine the ratio of excess return to be allocated through the current arm's length system as opposed to being assigned to market jurisdictions in the CE Method.[42] Other mechanisms could be utilized to calculate the CE Method Ratio. For purposes of the analysis in this chapter, all that matters is that a CE Method Ratio is somehow established.

CE Method analyses could be undertaken on a consolidated MNE basis or (with substantially increased complexity) on a business unit or product line basis. The amount of residual return deemed attributable to market intangibles would then be allocated among market jurisdictions based on the percentage of gross sales revenue by country.

This method requires global consolidation because there must be a measure of taxable income at the consolidated level in order to identify the amount of residual return. Most discussion of market intangibles and residual profit allocation more

41. *See* Michael Devereux, *Residual Profit Allocation Proposal* (presentation to the Urban Institute and Brookings Institution Tax Policy Center Conference, '*A Corporate Tax for the 21st Century*', Washington, DC, 14 July 2016), https://www.taxpolicycenter.org/sites/default/files/residual-profit-allocation-proposal_2.pdf.

42. In theory, the CE Method Ratio – especially an approach to calculating the CE Method Ratio involving preset presumptive useful lives for marketing intangibles, on the one hand, and trade intangibles, on the other, and calculations at the consolidated entity level – could function as a safe harbour. Some have suggested MNCs might be allowed to elect either the safe harbour method or a pure facts and circumstances transfer pricing valuation method for marketing intangibles and trade intangibles respectively as an alternative means to compute their CE Method Ratio. Skadden, Arps, Slate, Meagher & Flom LLP, *Comments on Public Consultation Document: Addressing the Tax Challenges of the Digitalization of the Economy* (6 March 2019), https://www.dropbox.com/s/hou6dvuckmahoft/OECD-Comments-Received-Digital-March-2019.zip?dl=0&file_subpath=%2FSkadden.pdf (accessed 21 Sep. 2019). However, it is unclear what would motivate governments to provide this election. The already high risk of controversy would increase without obvious systemic revenue or compliance gains. As a result, governments would need a truly deep conviction around the clarity of the distinction between marketing intangibles and trade intangibles, combined with a high tolerance for controversy with other tax administrations, in order to believe that such an election is justified.

generally in the OECD process assumes 'top down' calculations, and therefore implicitly requires this form of global consolidation.[43]

The CE Method is a compromise between a destination-based residual profit allocation (DBRPA) and the current transfer pricing system. Thus, analysing the relationship between the CE Method and formulary apportionment is easier if one first understands the relationship between formulary apportionment and the destination-based residual profit allocation. In turn, explaining the relationship between formulary apportionment and the destination-based residual profit allocation first requires defining what we mean by formulary apportionment and what we mean by destination-based residual profit allocation. This section addresses those questions in order.

[1] What is Formulary Apportionment?

Most analysts tend to agree on the two first-order features of formulary apportionment. Formulary apportionment involves: 1) a unitary system of taxation and 2) agreed upon apportionment factors that allocate taxing rights over the unitary tax base across jurisdictions.

Beyond those two features, consensus as to what 'formulary apportionment' entails breaks down. One key reason that there is no perfectly shared definition of what 'formulary apportionment' means in the context of cross-border transactions between related entities is that, while there is no existing global formulary apportionment system, there are two existing subnational formulary systems to apportion corporate income tax rights, namely those in Canada and the United States. Moreover, there is a proposed intra-EU system – the common consolidated corporate tax base (CCCTB)[44] – that is based on a formulary approach as well. Finally, academics have proposed

43. In theory, an alternative mechanism for determining the amount of residual income allocable to each jurisdiction could be developed from the 'bottom up': *see* description of such an approach as an alternative in Michael P. Devereux, Alan J. Auerbach, Michael Keen, Paul Oosterhuis, Wolfgang Schön & John Vella, *Residual Profit Allocation by Income* (Oxford International Tax Group Working Paper No. 19/01, March 2019), https://www.sbs.ox.ac.uk/sites/default/files/2019-03/WP1901_0.pdf (accessed 29 Jun. 2019). The details of the Oxford Working Paper 'bottom up' system are not essential to the analysis in this chapter. Nevertheless, it is worth observing, first, that the Oxford Working Paper 'bottom up' system remains unitary in the sense that it requires a unitary definition of indirect expenses (notably including interest expense, global non-allocable sales and marketing expenses, research and development expenses, and other general and administrative expenses) that must then be allocated out according to a consistent and agreed multilateral system. Second, the 'bottom up' system would only be workable if the concept of 'residual gross income' developed in the Oxford Working Paper were adopted by all jurisdictions consistently and used by each of them as the allocation key for indirect expenses. Third, and most importantly, the 'bottom up' method results in an allocation of all residual profits to the destination jurisdiction. In contrast, in a marketing intangibles concept, some mechanism is needed to split residual profits being allocated to marketing intangibles from residual profits being allocated to the destination jurisdiction. Methodologically, a bottom-up approach (unlike a top-down approach) for the CE Method would have to 'take away' profits initially allocated to the destination country from that market country. Given the politics of the marketing intangibles debate, that last result seems untenable.
44. European Commission, *Common Consolidated Corporate Tax Base (CCCTB)*, https://ec.europa.eu/taxation_customs/business/company-tax/common-consolidated-corporate-tax-base-ccctb_en (accessed 20 Jun. 2019).

allocating only 'residual profits' using a residual formulary apportionment (RFA) regime. In residual formulary apportionment, apportionment factors are complemented by a rule that assigns a return related to a fixed percentage of costs to the jurisdiction where the costs are incurred. None of these systems is entirely alike. Nor do they all use the same apportionment factors. Indeed, some US states use only one factor – the destination of sales.

Nevertheless, using even the thinnest consensus definition of formulary apportionment brings certain quintessential features into focus.[45] In particular, taxation under a formulary apportionment regime takes place in three steps.[46] First, the integrated business whose income is subject to apportionment is defined. Second, the global income of the defined integrated business is aggregated. Third, the aggregated income is divided among the members of the integrated business, using a formula based (at least in the main) on certain apportionment factors.[47] Dividing aggregated income using apportionment factors is an alternative to arm's length pricing because it generally dispenses with the need to recognize transactions among related entities within the integrated business.

Defining an integrated business whose income is aggregated entails unitary taxation which generally disregards the independence of related entities.[48] Such a system necessarily involves consolidation for tax purposes[49] across the integrated business using a shared single definition of the taxable base. That is, the measurement of the MNE's total income is undertaken 'using a consistent set of accounting and income recognition principles'.[50] That income is then divided using apportionment factors and weights given to each factor that are meant to be common across all participating jurisdictions.

---

45. Julie Roin, *Can the Income Tax Be Saved? The Promise and Pitfalls of Adopting Worldwide Formulary Apportionment*, 61(3) Tax L. Rev. 169, 172-173 (2008); Joann Martens-Weiner, *Company Tax Reform in the European Union: Guidance from the United States and Canada on Implementing Formulary Apportionment in the EU* 1 (Springer 2006).
46. Joseph L. Andrus, Mary C. Bennett & Caroline Silberztein, *The Arm's-Length Principle and Developing Economies*, 20(12) Tax Mgmt. Transfer Pricing Rept. 495, 496-501 (2011).
47. *Ibid.*; Roin, *supra* n. 45, at 172-173.
48. In fact, Canadian apportionment does not allow a multi-provincial corporation, operating through subsidiaries in different provinces, to consolidate its income for tax purposes. However, it does require such consolidation across permanent establishments in different provinces. Weiner, *supra* n. 45, at 69. Nevertheless, there is a general consensus that this feature of Canadian formulary apportionment would not make sense in the global context (or in any situation where there was not a supranational authority recognized by all participating jurisdictions).
49. Consolidation itself can mean various things. For instance, it could mean 'worldwide consolidation', under which commonly owned corporations which meet an appropriate control threshold would be treated as a single taxpayer. Weiner, *supra* n. 45, at 70; *See also* James W. Wetzler, *Is It Time to Consider Worldwide Consolidation?*, 163 Tax Notes 253 (2019). It could also mean 'unitary combined reporting', which is applied by many US states, and defines the consolidated base at the unitary business level, with less pressure on the definition of common control. In addition, the US implements, and the European Commission has proposed, 'water's edge consolidation', which limits the consolidated tax base to entities and income within their respective territorial boundaries. But such a system does not, by definition, make sense at the international level. Weiner, *supra* n. 45, at 70-71.
50. Andrus, Bennett & Silberztein, *supra* n. 46, at 499.

[2] What is Destination-Based Residual Profit Allocation?

The destination-based residual profit allocation proposal was developed by a group consisting of Alan Auerbach, Michael Devereux, Michael Keen, Paul Oosterhuis, Wolfgang Schön, and John Vella. The idea is most extensively explained in their working paper *Residual Profit Allocation by Income*.[51] The destination-based residual profit allocation proposal represents an attempt to move to a destination-basis corporate income tax system by means that can be described as remaining consistent with some of the principles of the current arm's length transfer pricing architecture.

Like single factor sales-based formulary apportionment, the destination-based residual profit allocation proposal is animated by the understanding that the location of consumers is less mobile than the location of booked profits, intellectual property, corporate assets, corporate employees, or any other element that purportedly creates value. However, the destination-based residual profit allocation attempts to separate 'excess' or 'residual' returns from 'routine returns' and provide a normal rate of return to productive functions.

Although destination-based residual profit allocation is not a sales-based formulary apportionment proposal, in many circumstances destination-based residual profit allocation could produce results that are similar to a sales-based residual formulary apportionment proposal put forth by Avi-Yonah, Clausing, and Durst in 2011.[52] Avi-Yonah, Clausing, and Durst would allocate a fixed markup on costs to entities that undertake activity within an MNE. All other profits would then be allocated to the destination/market country. In contrast, the destination-based residual profit allocation tries to salvage the existing arm's length system with respect to routine returns while using a sales-based system to allocate residual returns.

To allocate excess/residual returns, the destination-based residual profit allocation in effect deems the country in which customer sales take place to be an 'entrepreneurial' affiliate with respect to local market sales and ascribes the part of the 'non-routine' profits allocated to marketing intangibles to the entrepreneurial affiliate in the market country.[53] Destination-based residual profit allocation requires global consolidation because there must be a measure of taxable income at the consolidated level in order to measure the excess return to be allocated as among market jurisdictions. The tax base harmonization conundrum associated with unitary taxation is, of course, most well known in the context of formulary apportionment.

Achieving a destination-based residual profit allocation of non-routine profits to the market jurisdiction would also require MNEs to measure gross revenues on a country-by-country basis and on a product-by-product basis using some concept of

51. Devereux, Auerbach, Oosterhuis, Keen, Schön & Vella, *supra* n. 43.
52. Reuven S. Avi-Yonah, Kimberly A. Clausing & Michael C. Durst, *Allocating Business Profits for Tax Purposes: A Proposal to Adopt a Formulary Profit Split*, 9(5) Fla. Tax Rev. 497, 540-541 (2009).
53. *See* Devereux, *supra* n. 41.

'destination' or 'place of supply'. Of course, the sales factor of a traditional formulary apportionment system confronts this same issue.[54]

[3] The Relationship Between the CE Method and Formulary Apportionment

Importantly, each of the formulary apportionment-like issues that arises in the destination-based residual profit allocation method also arises in the CE Method, because the CE Method has the same starting point as a destination-based residual profit allocation. Affiliates in an MNE are compensated for their functions on a cost-plus or return on assets basis using arm's length principles. Unlike in the destination-based residual profit allocation, however, the 'residual return' must then be divided between returns allocated to the 'new taxing right' and returns allocated to the arm's length standard system. The portion of the residual return deemed to arise from market intangibles is then allocated to the market of destination for the good or service; the remaining residual return is allocated under existing transfer pricing principles.

The CE Method therefore raises three basic administrative concerns. First, it retains all of the problems of current transfer pricing law because, with respect to residual returns that are not attributed to market intangibles, current law applies. Second, the proposal imposes a hard-to-administer distinction between residual returns associated with marketing intangibles and other residual returns. Third, since the CE Method allocates residual returns subject to the new taxing right to the market jurisdiction, all the challenges associated with any sales-based formulary proposal are present in the CE Method.

The problems of current transfer pricing law and historical evidence suggesting that attempting to split a residual return between some allocation to 'market-based' intangibles and some allocation to 'other intangibles' continue to exist. However, those two issues are beyond the scope of this chapter. They have been discussed by this author elsewhere.[55]

The most important overlaps between the CE Method and formulary apportionment relate to determining destination and using a unitary approach. A further discussion of those issues follows below.

54. Other technical questions that arise in thinking about the DBRPA also have analogues in the formulary context. Such issues include the treatment of losses, the treatment of flow-through entities, the treatment of certain financial transactions, and the treatment of mergers and acquisitions. Unlike traditional formulary apportionment, global costs in the DBRPA would need to be measured at a product line level, and then either traced or apportioned out to revenues from specific countries. *Cf.* Mitchell Kane, *Transfer Pricing, Integration and Synergy Intangibles: A Consensus Approach to the Arm's Length Standard*, 6(3) World Tax J. 282 (2014).

55. *See* Grinberg, *International Taxation in an Era of Digital Disruption*, *supra* n. 13.

[4] Determining Destination under the CE Method

In any system that allocates part of the return to the market (in other words, any 'destination-basis' system), the tax burden is meant to rest in the jurisdiction of the final consumer, rather than the jurisdiction of residence of any intermediaries in the supply chain. The economic rationale for this result is that the final consumer is thought to be the least mobile factor. Thus, from a theoretical economic perspective, a destination-basis system is less economically distortive than other more mobile bases for assessing corporate tax.[56]

However, if the administrative mechanism for measuring the location of sales does not conform to the location of the final consumer, this justification for attempting to tax at destination is undermined. Importantly, MNEs can easily structure their transfer pricing arrangements to book sales income in a jurisdiction other than the residence of the final consumer and are incentivized to do so if they can lower their tax burden as a result.

The most common destination-basis tax (and likely the most important tax on Earth (measured by revenue raised) is the value added tax (VAT). The VAT generally resolves the issue of determining destination using the credit-invoice mechanism. Two of the most important features of the credit-invoice mechanism are taxation on gross amounts and imposition of tax on every transfer, both intra-firm and inter-firm. An income tax cannot adopt the credit-invoice mechanism for one key reason: income taxes tax net income, rather than gross revenues. In an income tax, cross-border business input purchases are generally deductible. By contrast, the VAT establishes destination, in large measure, by affording cross-border business input purchases, a treatment that is the equivalent of non-deductibility.[57]

Destination of Goods

For tangible goods, VAT laws generally assess VAT using frontier or border controls[58] – imported goods are in effect treated as having the destination of the jurisdiction where they clear customs. VAT is assessed on the full value of the good as it enters the jurisdiction. VAT laws then free exports of VAT through a combination of non-inclusion of proceeds and a refund mechanism for VAT previously paid. As a result, the VAT avoids the difficulties a destination-basis income tax would have with cross-border sales through third-party intermediaries.

---

56. *See, e.g.*, Alan J. Auerbach, Michael Devereux, Michael Keen & John Vella, *Destination-Based Cash Flow Taxation* (University of Oxford Saïd Business School Research Paper 2017-09, February 2017).
57. The VAT mechanism works cross-border and is not equivalent to a tariff because the VAT credit mechanism then provides a credit to registered businesses (and not to consumers). The whole tax is passed on to consumers; businesses bear none of it. In contrast, in an income tax, businesses are intended to pay tax. As a result, the full credit mechanism is not an option in an income tax.
58. VAT on imports is generally collected at the same time as customs duties, although in some countries collection is postponed until declared on the importer's next VAT return.

The reason third-party cross-border intermediation does not obscure destination in the VAT is that the intermediary pays a full tax on its purchases and has the full amount refunded on re-export. Exports are not included in the tax base, and then a tax based on the sales price of the good is collected at the jurisdiction of (further) destination. A similar result applies with respect to the importation of intermediate inputs (whether raw materials, components, or intermediate goods) that are subsequently exported as part of a different tangible good. Due to expensing, the result even applies to capital goods that are purchased to allow for the manufacture of other products for export.[59] In all cases, the credit-input system thereby moves the tax burden to the final buyer.

The VAT system for ensuring that tax is collected only at the destination of the good works because the system taxes on a gross basis and provides refunds on every intra-firm and inter-firm transfer. An income tax cannot adopt this basic element of the credit-invoice mechanism as it operates in cross-border situations and remain a tax on net income. As a result, the VAT does not provide useful guidance for determining the destination of goods in an income tax system. Formulary apportionment and the CE Method thus share the problem of being unable to use the VAT credit-invoice mechanism to determine destination.

Location of Services

Determining the destination of cross-border services is a highly significant issue in the international formulary apportionment and CE Method contexts. One important and challenging sub-issue is the destination of cross-border services provided to MNEs. Determining the destination of these services raises especially difficult issues.[60] In many cases, MNE service recipients utilize the services of a service provider in multiple jurisdictions.

In the VAT context, charge-out mechanisms of the kind used in today's income tax system can, and do, conceptually resolve the problem of determining the destination of services an MNE recipient receives and uses in multiple locations.[61] However, tax administrations attempting to employ this solution in the formulary apportionment and CE Method contexts would encounter distinct problems. Tax administrations would need to audit service recipients to determine whether charge-outs had been made appropriately in order to inform their audit of the service provider. While charge-outs can be a subject of audit in today's income tax system, tax administrators never need to ask whether charge-outs by an unrelated party change the tax result for

59. Of course, income taxes cannot provide expensing treatment in all cases while maintaining their status as income taxes.
60. *See* Roin, *supra* n. 45, at 208 and Walter Hellerstein, *A US Subnational Perspective on the 'Logic' of Taxing Income on a 'Market' Basis*, 72(4/5) Bull. Int'l Tax'n 9 (2018) for a discussion of these issues.
61. Note also that to solve the problem of determining where globally provided MNC to MNC services are 'consumed', most VATs today generally follow the result achieved for the purpose of corporate income tax charge-outs. It is obviously no answer to rely on the VAT to solve an income tax problem if the present law VAT solution is to rely on the income tax answer to solve that same problem.

a separate, unrelated taxpayer. The level of internal coordination such a system would require of government auditors simply does not exist today.

Since the administrative features of the VAT do not help, other anti-abuse rules would be needed in a CE Method, just as they would be needed in a formulary apportionment system. Indeed, US states - which manage to operate a formulary apportionment regime in a country without a VAT - have had to live with this problem and its consequences for many years. Understanding their approach to the problem and the potential distortions it can cause is therefore a potentially useful means to considering the issue in the CE Method context.

[5] Unitary Approach under the CE Method

The CE Method calculates most revenues at a country level. However, just like the 'unitary' aspect of formulary apportionment, the CE Method calculates costs on a global consolidated basis. In other words, one needs a single measurement of apportionable income. The CE Method may not require a common measure of gross income, but it would require common rules regarding costs. The most obvious category of costs that need common allocation rules is so-called indirect costs, such as research and development, interest expense, and stewardship expenses.[62]

Moreover, for the CE Method to work well, schedules for depreciation or amortization of tangible and intangible property and treatment of original issue discount - and perhaps even issues like the method used to inventory costs or the treatment of fines and penalties - would ideally be standardized across jurisdictions. As one commentator explained a decade ago with respect to formulary apportionment, unitary systems become inadministrable if global costs must be measured for purposes of determining income in each jurisdiction, but each jurisdiction has its own rules with respect to when those global costs are taken into account.[63]

Pressure to Move Towards 100% Allocation to Sales

Issues raised by determining destination and addressing unitary taxation are technical in nature. In addition to these technical issues, the history of US subnational formulary apportionment highlights an obvious policy concern with the CE Method - in the era of globalization, business activity is mobile. By contrast, sales are much less mobile. As a result, any formula that allocates less than 100% of the residual profit to sales would find itself under policy pressure.

Over the years, the US states have shifted - in inconsistent ways - away from traditional three-factor apportionment towards sales-only apportionment factors to

62. *Cf.* OECD, *Revised Guidance on the Application of the Transactional Profit Split Method*, OECD/G20 Base Erosion and Profit Shifting Project [2.154]-[2.157] (June 2018) (describing the importance of aligning accounting rules in transactional profit splits). The problems of indirect cost allocation are familiar to US practitioners from the foreign tax credit system and current debates about the Global Intangible Low-Taxed Income (GILTI) rules.

63. Roin, *supra* n. 45, at 200.

gain a competitive advantage in attracting tangible investment and jobs.[64] In the international setting, with higher tax rates than state income taxes and fewer coordination mechanisms to limit competition, most commentators agree that this competitive dynamic would be more intense. Moreover, customers are much less mobile than employment in the cross-border setting, so economic theory would suggest that a sales-based apportionment should produce fewer economic distortions than an apportionment formula that takes the location of employment into account.[65]

In the context of fixed ratio formulas, the inclusion of an apportionment factor that is immobile and an apportionment factor that is highly mobile creates an implicit excise tax on the mobile factor. That reality would likely push countries in the direction of unilaterally choosing a 100% allocation to the immobile factor (the location of the consumer), in order to eliminate the implicit excise tax on high-skilled jobs that the 50:50 split would create, just as US states have overweighted sales and abandoned the payroll factor to encourage job creation in their jurisdictions.

[B] The Operating Margins Method

[1] General Remarks

Even though the OM Method may be characterized as a part of the market intangibles genre, it departs from the conceptual motivation for 'market intangibles' proposals in the interest of administrative ease.[66] Importantly, advocates of simplified approaches might suggest that an appropriately calibrated OM Method could, in practice, produce results are no more or less likely than the capitalized expenditure method to allocate only profits attributable to 'market intangibles' to market jurisdictions.[67]

The OM Method also has a conceptual relationship with the deemed profit methods that were common in Latin America a generation ago.[68] The OM Method would specify a minimum taxable income due from an MNE in a given jurisdiction. The main variable that would determine this minimum market jurisdiction taxable amount is a measure of the global operating margin, either overall or by business line. A fixed return on sales would then be allocated to market jurisdictions in general. The fixed return percentage would vary based on operating margins. The global minimum

64. *See* Hellerstein, *supra* n. 60.
65. For similar reasons, most academic observers agree that formulary apportionment employed internationally would probably be implemented (sooner or later) under a single factor sales-based formulary apportionment system.
66. However, the OECD Transfer Pricing Guidelines already hint that sometimes it is worth considering the 'trade-off between strict compliance with the arm's length principle and administrability': OECD, *OECD Transfer Pricing Guidelines for Multinational Enterprises and Tax Administrations 2017* [4.112] (2017).
67. In other words, advocates would say the OM Method usually would in practice allocate only residual returns and returns that are the result of functions in market jurisdictions to market jurisdictions.
68. *See, e.g.*, Lewin & Wills, *Managing Corporate Taxation in Latin American Countries: An Overview of Main Corporate Taxes in Selected Jurisdictions 2013* (Lataxnet 2013), http://lewinywills.com/wp-content/uploads/2017/03/2013_Managing_Corporate_Taxation_in_Latin_American_Countries.pdf (accessed 27 Jun. 2019).

market profit amount deemed allocable to market jurisdictions would be calculated by multiplying the fixed return percentage by revenues. The global minimum market profit amount would then be apportioned among market jurisdictions on the basis of local revenues (sales).

The return on sales percentage that determines the global minimum market profit amount would increase (or decrease) for businesses or business lines with operating margins above (or below) an empirically determined average operating margin (the Margin Adjustment Factor). When a business has very low, zero per cent, or negative operating margins, the deemed minimum allocation to market jurisdictions would be zero. Since the OM Method is not limited to residual returns, without a properly calibrated Margin Adjustment Factor, the market profit amount would disproportionately allocate profit to market jurisdictions for low margin businesses. To avoid double taxation in the OM Method, it would be necessary to specify the 'surrender jurisdiction' that would give up the right to tax the market profit amount.

[2] The Relationship Between the OM Method and Formulary Apportionment

The OM Method is clearly dominated by formulas. Yet the OM Method's relationship to formulary apportionment as that term is commonly understood is more tenuous than that of the CE Method. What that tension reveals is that the key distinguishing features of formulary apportionment from an analytical perspective are actually unitary taxation and an apportionment factor that requires defining destination.

Notwithstanding the fact that it does not use an apportionment factor, the OM Method faces exactly the same issues regarding defining destination as the CE Method (described in §11.04[A][4] above). The reason is that the fixed return percentage is allocated among jurisdictions by comparative sales revenues, and this calculation requires determining where sales occur. Thus all the concerns described above with regard to the CE Method apply to the OM Method.

In contrast, the unitary taxation questions raised in §11.04[A][5] above with respect to the CE Method are less of a concern in the OM Method. The basic reason is not that the OM Method does not require global consolidation. To the contrary, calculating global operating margins either by business line or overall requires global consolidation. The reason the OM Method differs from the CE Method on this dimension is only because it explicitly relies on financial accounting conventions to provide the consolidated results. In doing so, the method accepts book-tax conformity as the price of administrability. The question then becomes what is sacrificed by giving up or attempting to give up the segregation between tax accounting and financial accounting as developed by the two major self-regulating accounting bodies (US Generally Accepted Accounting Principles (GAAP) and International Financial Reporting Standards (IFRS)). While this is an important issue to consider, historically, the literature has suggested that the problems of book-tax conformity would be less severe in a formulary apportionment regime than in regimes based on recognition of the legal independence of related entities and use of the arm's length standard.[69] As this volume goes to press, an OM Method-type approach seems to be the focus of discussions at the OECD. Thus, further work on the consequences of book-tax conformity in formulary taxation regimes may well be required in the international tax policy debate going forward.

§11.05 CONCLUSION

The contributions in this volume attempt to reappraise formulary apportionment at a time when international tax policymakers are considering proposals to develop a hybrid system for allocating taxing rights internationally that combines some features of the arm's length standard with some formulary features. This chapter highlights the relationship between the current debate being undertaken within the Inclusive Framework of the OECD and the various issues involved in formulary apportionment considered in this volume. Evaluation of the proposals under consideration by the Inclusive Framework suggests that each and everyone can be improved by reappraising formulary apportionment.

69. Michelle Hanlon & Edward Maydew, *Book-Tax Conformity: Implications for Multinational Firms*, 62(1) Nat'l Tax J. 127, 139-140 (2009).

Part V Can International Tax Sharing Become Reality?

CHAPTER 12

International Tax Sharing: Can the Dream Become Reality?

Richard Bird & Jack Mintz

§12.01 INTRODUCTION

The Holy Grail of corporate taxation for many in recent years has been to develop an international arrangement for corporate tax sharing. Much has been written about the need for, and ways to achieve, international cooperation with respect to the corporate income tax.[1] Policymakers have taken up some of these issues in numerous forums, for example, at the Organisation for Economic Co-operation and Development (OECD) through the major Base Erosion and Profit Shifting (BEPS) project, and new proposals on how to achieve this goal continue to emerge.[2]

Although much of the discussion of international corporate income tax issues has focused on economic efficiency, the distributional issue – who gets how much – is equally if not more important. Developing countries, especially those with important resource sectors, have long sought a greater share of corporate tax revenues.[3] Many developed countries are now seeking the same goal with respect to the increasingly important digital sector, and some, especially in Europe, are moving towards imposing special digital service taxes. Every country (apart from a few tax havens) may have

1. For a useful recent discussion, *see* Allison Christians, Wolfgang Schön & Stephen E. Shay, *Foreword: International Tax Policy in a Disruptive Environment*, 72(4/5) Bull. Int'l Tax'n 191 (2018), and the other articles in the same special issue of that journal.
2. For examples, *see* Michael Durst, *Taxing Multinational Business in Lower-Income Countries: Economics, Politics and Social Responsibility* (Institute for Development Studies 2019); Michael Devereux, Alan Auerbach, Michael Keen, Paul Oosterhuis, Wolfgang Schön & John Vella, *Residual Profit Allocation by Income* (Oxford University Saïd Business School Working Paper WP 19/01, 2019).
3. Erika Siu, Sol Picciotto, Jack Mintz & Akilagpa Sawyer, *Unitary Taxation in the Extractive Sector* (International Centre for Tax and Development Working Paper 35, 2015).

something to gain from coordinating corporate taxes to minimize spillovers. But many see the division of the potential revenue pie to be a zero-sum game and, in the absence of any institutions for global governance when it comes to coordinating taxes imposed by sovereign nations, only soft (voluntary) cooperation is possible. Sometimes, this approach may work, as in the interesting case of a royalty charged for resource exploitation outside the 200 nautical mile limit under Article 82 of the United Nations Convention on the Law of the Sea (UNCLOS). Nonetheless, even for this rather tiny 'global tax' many questions remain to be settled - who determines and shapes policy, who administers the levy, how the revenue is distributed and how the system is enforced.[4] Such issues are much more difficult when it comes to sharing the much larger global revenue from corporate income taxes - potentially in the order of USD 2.5 trillion.[5]

The plan of this chapter is as follows. In the next section (§12.02), we discuss taxing corporate incomes in federations which have constitutional governing bodies with independent taxation powers. The following section (§12.03) takes up the European Union's attempt at corporate tax base sharing as a lesson about the real problems in developing an international approach to formulary allocation. Section 12.04 considers how we might, so to speak, pull a rabbit out of the international hat with a proposal that, while far from ideal because of its non-uniform approach, may perhaps achieve much of what is needed. A brief final section (§12.05) concludes.

§12.02 TAXING CORPORATE INCOMES IN FEDERATIONS

As Table 12.1 shows (reflecting our discussion below), several federations with sovereign central and subnational governments have developed methods to share the corporate income tax. Cooperation is obviously more likely in federal countries, in which both central and subnational governments have some constitutional fiscal sovereignty than it is internationally in the absence of any global government. However, it has not been a simple or easy process to work out even the existing imperfect corporate tax sharing arrangements in any country, no matter how well governed or how long established.

---

4. *See* Richard Bird & Jack Mintz, *Sharing the Wealth: Article 82 of UNCLOS – The First Global Tax?*, 4 Brit. Tax Rev. 537 (2019).
5. Current world GDP is USD 90 trillion and, on average in 2016, corporate tax yielded 2.7% of GDP (data from OECD Tax Database, https://www.oecd.org/tax/tax-policy/tax-database/). The number reported in the text assumes the same ratio applied worldwide. For comparison, Zucman estimates that perhaps USD 6 trillion of unreported personal wealth is in tax havens: Gabriel Zucman, *The Missing Wealth of Nations: Are Europe and the US Net Debtors or Net Creditors?*, 128(3) Q.J. Econ. 1321 (2013).

Table 12.1 Taxing Corporate Income in Federations: Alternative Solutions

	Canada	*United States*	*Switzerland*	*Germany*
Who decides to tax?	Provinces	States	Cantons	Constitution
Who sets tax base?	Provinces – but within limits, if federal-provincial tax agreement	States	Cantons; some federal limits	Federal
Who sets tax rates?	Provinces	States	Cantons	Federal
Who administers?	Federal for agreeing provinces, or themselves	States	Cantons	States
Who decides how harmonized?	Provinces	States	Federal to some extent (citizen vote)	Federal
How is base allocated?	Payroll; sales	Varies by state	Varies by sector and income type	Payroll
Who decides formula?	Voluntary cooperation	States; courts	Cantons	Federal

[A] Canada[6]

In Canada, where the federal government has the constitutional power to levy both direct and indirect taxes, the 1867 Constitution limited provinces to direct taxes only. However, because income taxes, including those on corporations, are considered to be direct taxes, both federal and provincial governments can and do tax corporate income.[7] After the federal (Dominion) government introduced the first federal corporate income tax under the Income War Tax Act of 1917, those provinces that did not already have such taxes soon implemented them, largely based on the Dominion definition of corporate income. Because the determination of income allocated to any

6. For a more detailed examination of the Canadian case, *see* Michael Smart & François Vaillancourt, *Formulary Apportionment in Canada and Taxation of Corporate Income in 2019: Current Practice, Origins and Evaluation* (this volume).
7. For a fuller discussion of the constitutional and subsequent judicial interpretations, *see* Benjamin Alarie & Richard Bird, *Tax Aspects of Canadian Fiscal Federalism*, in *Tax Aspects of Fiscal Federalism: A Comparative Analysis* 77 (Gianluigi Bizioli & Claudio Sacchetto eds., IBFD Publications 2011); the underlying political developments are set out in Elspeth Heaman, *Tax, Order and Good Government: A New Political History of Canada, 1867-1917* (McGill-Queens University Press 2017), for the first fifty years (up to 1917) and in Shirley Tillotson, *Give and Take: The Citizen-Taxpayer and the Rise of Canadian Democracy* (UBC Press 2017) for the next half-century.

province depended on provincial legislation, however, the result was both inconsistency and overlap.[8] For example, a province could recognize that income earned by a corporation came from out-of-province sources either by simply providing a credit for other provincial taxes (e.g., British Columbia) or by applying its own rules for allocating income within and without their province and for taxing and crediting (Ontario and Quebec). Importantly, each province limited its credit for other provincial taxes to the amount of tax that would be paid to the province with respect to the same income. Only two provinces (Prince Edward Island and Manitoba) provided a deduction for the proportion of Dominion tax applicable to net income earned in the province.[9] Neither the federal nor any provincial government made any attempt to consolidate subsidiaries in corporate groups – as is still the case today.

After the Depression of the 1930s resulted in significant provincial deficits, with the onset of World War II all provinces agreed to 'rent' their own powers over income and estate taxes to the federal government in exchange for grants and debt relief. After the war, however, the provinces wanted to resume control over their own corporate income tax. After considerable discussion, in 1947 a new tax rental agreement was reached with seven out of the then nine provinces that contained the seeds of federal-provincial corporate tax sharing in later years. The federal government provided a credit of 5 (percentage) points for provincial taxes levied at that rate on net income as determined by federal legislation.[10] Corporate income was allocated to the provinces according to equally weighted shares of payroll and gross receipts (with special rules applied to finance and transportation companies). The alternative of using only gross receipts as a weighting factor was rejected because it was considered to give too much of the corporate tax base to the province in which the headquarters were located. Assets were also rejected as a factor in the allocation formula, apart from special cases such as finance. Each province agreed to tax only the income allocated to it, so there were no gaps or overlaps in the tax base at the provincial level. The federal government agreed to collect the corporate income tax without charging the agreeing provinces an administrative fee.

However, the two large provinces, Ontario and Quebec, decided not to join the 1947 tax collection agreement. Instead, these two provinces levied a 7% tax on the total profits of a corporation headquartered in the province, with a credit for provincial taxes applied on corporate income allocated to non-headquarters provinces. The corporate tax bases in Ontario or Quebec were similar to each other but differed from that in the agreeing provinces. Moreover, Quebec based its allocation formula on sales and not payroll. To avoid conflict with Quebec, the other provinces agreed to maintain a sales factor on a destination basis. Because British Columbia was concerned about losing corporate tax revenues since exports to other countries were often made through sales

8. For a full discussion of the evolution of the system over time, *see* Ernest Smith, *Federal-Provincial Tax Sharing and Centralized Tax Collections in Canada* (Canadian Tax Foundation 1998).
9. In 1939, both these provinces entered into a tax collection agreement with the Dominion to collect their corporate income taxes.
10. In contrast to the case in the United States, provincial corporate income taxes were not deductible against the federal base except for mining profit taxes and other specific profit-insensitive corporate taxes.

offices in other provinces, all provinces agreed to allocate export sales based on the province of production or manufacture, similar to the Quebec rule for exports. By 1957, when Ontario accepted the same allocation factors as other provinces, taxable income was commonly measured across all the provinces except Québec.

In 1962 the tax rental agreements were replaced by tax sharing agreements which gave provinces greater freedom to choose their corporate tax policies. The federal government agreed to 'abate' (reduce) federal taxes at a standard rate (9 points) to give provinces 'room' to assess their own tax rate on corporate income. Agreeing provinces were also given the flexibility to vary effective rates through surtaxes and tax credits. The federal government agreed to eliminate previous caps on the deductibility of specific corporation taxes on paid-up capital and other profit-insensitive taxes. In addition, Quebec adopted the same allocation formula as other provinces so that common payroll and sales factors were used to allocate corporate income across all provinces.

The Canadian approach to corporate tax sharing has thus provided provinces considerable flexibility to choose rates, surtaxes and credits, as well as other specific corporation taxes, while gradually, over time, moving them closer to using the same tax base and the same allocation formula. Since Ontario agreed in 2006 to let the federal government collect its corporate income tax, only Quebec and Alberta currently collect their own corporate income tax. However, even these two non-agreeing provinces have largely followed the federal corporate tax base – but not always. Quebec, for instance, has often introduced accelerated depreciation, tax holidays and regional preferences that would not be permitted under a tax collection agreement with the federal government. Recently, however, after the federal government adopted accelerated depreciation provisions on 21 November 2018 – provisions that were automatically adopted by the agreeing provinces – Quebec scaled back an additional capital cost allowance it had previously introduced and adopted the federal provisions on 3 December. In contrast, Alberta's new government in May 2019 decided to reduce the provincial tax rate from 12% to 8%, only announcing accelerated depreciation in its 2019 Fall Budget.[11]

On the whole, however, the common allocation formula to apportion corporate income across provinces has remained amazingly stable with few adjustments since 1962. Complaints have been made at times about fairness. In the 1970s, for example, the resource provinces argued that they would receive more revenues if more weight was placed on an origin basis such as assets or gross receipts rather than a destination basis associated with sales. However, no changes were made, in part, it seems, because renegotiating fixed shares in a revenue pie even when – or perhaps especially when – the size of the pie changes is inevitably a costly and difficult exercise and one that may open up many questions that no one really wants to deal with again. In addition, as

11. *See* https://www.alberta.ca/budget-highlights.aspx#p19765s1. Initially, it was unknown whether Alberta would adopt accelerated depreciation. Philip Bazel & Jack Mintz, *Corporate Tax Policy: Alberta Goes its Own Way* (Tax Policy Trends paper, School of Public Policy, University of Calgary, 2019), https://journalhosting.ucalgary.ca/index.php/sppp/article/view/68524/53168.

Smart and Vaillancourt note elsewhere in this volume, Canada's fiscal equalization system largely offsets the redistributional effects of formulary apportionment for equalization-recipient provinces.[12]

[B] The United States[13]

As in Canada, the US federal government has constitutional powers over direct taxes and can levy an income tax so long as it is uniform across states. State governments can also tax corporations, and some states began to impose capital taxes on corporations in the late 19th century on the basis of a 'unitary' corporation that included subsidiaries under a holding company. This concept, although not unambiguous, continues to be the basis for apportioning income across states as well as defining corporate groups in the US where a consolidated company has no option but to be subject to apportionment, unlike Canada where it can simply reorganize into separate provincial subsidiaries to avoid allocation and reduce taxes.

The approach to apportionment in the United States is to separate certain forms of income, typically investment income, from the corporate tax base to be attributed to only one jurisdiction (this is called 'allocation') and then to apportion the rest according to a formula.[14] Initially, the Massachusetts formula, equally weighting payroll, property and sales factors to determine a state's share of multistate business income was favoured. By 1978, almost all states levying corporate income taxes had adopted the Massachusetts formula for apportionment except Iowa, which used sales only. In a 1978 case (*Moorman Mfg. Co. v. Bair*, 437 US 267), the US Supreme Court found that the Iowa apportionment formula was not invalid, an outcome that over time led many other states to put more weight on the sales factor to apportion income.[15] Most states have now moved away from the Massachusetts formula for apportionment.

---

12. Michael Smart & François Vaillancourt, *Formulary Apportionment in Canada and Taxation of Corporate Income in 2019: Current Practice, Origins and Evaluation* (this volume). *See* Daniel Béland, André Lecours, Gregory P. Marchildon, Haizhen Mou & M. Rose Olfert, *Fiscal Federalism and Equalization Policy in Canada: Political and Economic Dimensions* (University of Toronto Press 2017) for an account of the evolution of the equalization system over the last half-century and Richard Bird, *Equalization and Canada's Fiscal Constitution – The Tie that Binds?*, 66(4) Can. Tax J. 847 (2018) for a recent evaluation of the system.
13. For a detailed treatment of the US case, *see* Walter Hellerstein, *The Application of Formulary Apportionment to Related Entities: Lessons from the US Experience* (this volume). On the evolution of the US corporate tax, see Steven A. Bank, *From Sword to Shield: The Transformation of the Corporate Income Tax, 1861 to Present* (Oxford University Press 2010); the broader political context is discussed more fully in Ajay K. Mehrotra, *Making the Modern American Fiscal State: Law, Politics, and the Rise of Progressive Taxation, 1877-1929* (Cambridge University Press 2013). See also the tabular review of multistate taxation in R. B. Johnson, *History of Multistate Income Tax Apportionment* (2013), http://www.utahtaxpayers.org/wp-content/uploads/2013/05/Bruce-Johnson-2History-of-Multistate-Income-Tax-Apportionment.pdf (accessed 21 Mar. 2019).
14. Joann Martens-Weiner, *Company Tax Reform in the European Union: Guidance from the United States and Canada on Implementing Formulary Apportionment in the EU* (Springer 2006).
15. For an extensive discussion of these and other issues with respect to unitary taxation and apportionment, including the treatment of foreign source income, *see The State Corporation Income Tax: Issues in Worldwide Unitary Combination* (Charles E. McLure, Jr. ed., Hoover Institution Press 1984).

States choose their own factors and weights in apportioning the consolidated corporate income of permanent establishments in their jurisdictions. Thirteen states use a single factor – sales – to apportion income to their state. Another twenty-one continue to use the traditional three factors but put a higher weight on sales (as much as 93% in the case of Minnesota). Only ten states now weight all three factors equally, as in the original Massachusetts formula.[16]

At present, all but six states (Nevada, Ohio, South Dakota, Texas, Washington and Wyoming) levy their own corporate income tax.[17] States may choose whether and how they harmonize the tax base with federal rules.[18] Twenty-five states begin with federal taxable income before special deductions and twenty begin with federal taxable income.[19] But all make adjustments – additions and subtractions – as they desire. For example, fifteen states have adopted the federal bonus depreciation rule with the balance adding back deductions to capital expenditures. Some automatically adopt federal base changes (with some exclusions) while others do so on a selective basis. State corporate income tax rates are as high as 12% in Iowa.[20] State corporate income taxes are treated as an expense for federal tax purposes and therefore deductible in determining federal tax liabilities.

Subnational governments in the United States thus have considerable flexibility in designing their corporate taxes. They may choose rates, tax bases and credits and even apportionment rules. Most harmonize their corporate tax bases with the federal base to reduce administrative and compliance costs, but they are not required to do so. The resulting system is thus far from uniform but nonetheless achieves a certain degree of coordination.

[C] Germany

Few federal countries allow as much leeway to their subnational corporate taxing units as does Canada, let alone the United States. In Germany, for example, the national corporate income tax rate is uniform and set by the federal level government, and all states are strictly governed by the constitutional provision that taxes must be administered uniformly even though the corporate tax is administered by the states (with the

16. Based on data derived from Judith Lohman, *Corporation Tax Income Apportionment Factors* (Connecticut General Assembly Office of Legislative Research report, 26 September 2012), https://www.cga.ct.gov/2012/rpt/2012-R-0414.htm (accessed 21 Mar. 2019).
17. Nevada, Ohio, Texas and Washington have gross receipts taxes instead. For a recent comprehensive review of state and local taxes, see *The Oxford Handbook of State and Local Government Finance* (Robert D. Ebel & John E. Petersen eds., Oxford University Press 2012).
18. David Brunori, *State Corporate Income Taxes*, in *The Oxford Handbook of State and Local Government Finance* 332 (Robert D. Ebel & John E. Petersen eds., Oxford University Press 2012).
19. Andrew Phillips & Steve Wlodychak, *The Impact of Federal Tax Reform on State Corporate Income Taxes* (Ernst & Young for the State Tax Research Institute, March 2018), https://www.ey.com/Publication/vwLUAssets/ey-the-impact-of-federal-tax-reform-on-state-corporate-income-taxes/$File/ey-the-impact-of-federal-tax-reform-on-state-corporate-income-taxes.pdf.
20. *See* Morgan Scarboro, *State Corporate Income Tax Rates and Brackets for 2018, Tax Foundation* (7 February 2018), https://taxfoundation.org/state-corporate-income-tax-rates-brackets-2018/ (accessed 21 Mar. 2019). Some local governments (such as New York City) also have corporate income taxes.

federal government assuming the costs of administering federal taxes). Corporate income tax revenues are split equally between the federal and state levels, with the state share allocated essentially on the basis of payroll.[21] Although there is some evidence that one result of this system is to discourage the richer states - those that contribute to fiscal equalization - from enforcing taxes as fully as they should ideally do, there appears to be little interest in Germany in changing its very decentralized tax administrative system.[22]

Since 1950, municipalities in Germany have been able to levy their own corporate income taxes (the municipal trade tax), which generally follow federal rules with some adjustments, particularly with the partial deductibility of interest, leasing and royalty expense.[23] The trade tax, collected by the municipalities, is a minimum tax rate of 3.5% plus the municipal rate (varying from 7% to 17.5%) that can be charged by those municipalities with more than 80,000 inhabitants. Income is apportioned to a municipality according to the location of employees.

[D] Switzerland

In contrast, neighbouring Switzerland is from a fiscal perspective perhaps even more federal than the United States: not only does every canton have its own tax policy and tax administration but so do most communes (local governments). Cantons establish whatever taxes they wish on corporations at whatever rates they decide. The resulting variations from canton to canton in applying independent taxes - sometimes at rates much higher than the (low) federal rate - to (essentially) a source tax base have doubtless increased administrative and compliance costs and led to allocative inefficiency, although over the years various judicial and federal interventions have provided some guidance and resolved some conflicts.[24]

Although considerable attempts have been made in recent decades to harmonize many aspects of cantonal taxation, there remain many variations not only in rate but also to some extent on the details of how the tax base is determined and how (and when) taxes are administered. Inter-cantonal double taxation is constitutionally prohibited, but it was only in 1991 that a federal tax harmonization law required the cantons to harmonize (by 2001) some key aspects of corporate taxation such as

---

21. Alexander Ulbricht, *The Decentralization of Tax Administration in Germany: The Consequences*, in *Fiscal Federalism and Political Decentralization* 193 (Núria Bosch & José Durán eds., Edward Elgar 2008).
22. *See* Timm Bönke, Beate Joachimsen & Carsten Schröder, *Fiscal Federalism and Tax Enforcement* (ZBW Discussion Paper No. 2015/15, 2015). For further discussion of the relationship between who sets bases and rates (tax policy) and who administers the taxes in decentralized countries, *see* Richard Bird, *Fiscal Decentralisation and Decentralising Tax Administration: Different Questions, Different Answers*, in *Comparing Fiscal Federalism* 190 (Alice Valdesalici & Francesco Palermo eds., Brill Nijhoff 2018).
23. For further details, *see* Consultinghouse, *A Guide to the German Trade Tax* (2017), http://blog.consultinghouse.eu/compliance/a-guide-to-the-german-trade-tax (accessed 21 Mar. 2019).
24. The historical development of the system may be found in Bernard Dafflon, *Federal Finance in Theory and Practice with Special Reference to Switzerland* (Verlag Paul Haupt 1977). For a brief current overview, *see, e.g.*, Ernst & Young, *Swiss Parliament Approves Tax Reform Package*, Global Tax Alert (28 September 2018).

procedural law and tax penalties. However, cantons may still set rates, exemptions, credits and other features as they wish. Corporations are taxed where they are domiciled, which usually means where they are registered, with income being apportioned to other cantons considered to be permanent establishments - that is, with either a physical facility or a substantial material part of their activities.

Corporate income is first allocated to the canton of domicile and then apportioned to other cantons in a number of different ways, either through separate accounting (used mainly for banks) or, most commonly, in proportion to the ratio of production factors (gross receipts, payroll, assets).[25] Different formulae may be used for different lines of business (e.g., insurance sector by premium receipts and transportation by activities), and certain income is apportioned in specific ways (e.g., interest income in proportion to the value of assets). There are no standard formulae, although some general rules for specific sectors have been established judicially, and individual firms often negotiate with their cantons of domicile. The system works successfully in part because, within the shelter of a strongly enforced prohibition against inter-cantonal double taxation, the basic tax framework is uniform, accounting and tax records are virtually identical and taxing authorities at all levels have access to the same records. Perhaps most importantly, not only do these authorities generally trust each other but also they all work within a general culture of negotiation that encourages consultation before escalation. The Swiss can make this largely self-enforcing system work; others may have more problems.

Considering only the twenty-six cantonal corporate income taxes, at present, the effective tax rates (including federal tax of 8.5%) range from a low of 11.5% to a high of 24.2%.[26] A major tax reform approved at the federal level in September 2018, in part in response to years of pressure from the EU and the OECD, is supposed to enter into effect in 2020. Since the federal reform has now been passed by voters in May 2019[27] it will now be implemented by legislative changes in every canton. Two major features of this reform are to repeal the currently widespread special cantonal corporate tax regimes, replacing them to a considerable extent with various provisions including a mandatory patent box (up to 90% exemption on qualifying income), a 150% super-deduction of research and development (R&D) costs combined with a 70% maximum limitation on total reduction in taxable income at the cantonal level and an optional allowance for equity financing (only expected to be taken up by the canton of Zurich to maintain company headquarters). Other measures are included in the reform package to diminish its revenue impact: for instance, the cantonal share (now 17%) of federal total tax revenues is to be increased to 21%. Many cantons are expected to lower their taxes, and some have already done so: one estimate is that the average combined

25. This description is based largely on Erika Dayle Siu, Milly Isingoma Nalukwago, Rachmanto Surahmat & Marcos Aurélio Pereira Valadão, *Unitary Taxation in Federal and Regional Integrated Markets* (International Centre for Tax and Development Research Report 3, 2014).
26. PricewaterhouseCoopers (PwC), *Worldwide Tax Summaries*, http://tax summaries.pwc.com (accessed 25 Mar. 2019).
27. *See* EY, *Adoption of Swiss Tax Reform*, News Alert (20 May 2019), https://switzerlandblog.ey.com/2019/05/18/unternehmenssteuerreform-resultat-der-bundesabstimmung/.

federal and cantonal rates will decline from 19.6% at present to perhaps 14.5% when the full reform comes into effect.[28]

§12.03 THE EU ATTEMPTS TO GET ITS ACT TOGETHER[29]

Almost two decades ago, the European Commission published a proposal to adopt a unitary corporate income tax by consolidating the tax base using a set of single tax rules.[30] The recommendations followed earlier proposals to implement a common corporate income tax in Europe.

In 2001, four optional proposals for a consolidated European corporate tax were discussed. One approach included a European Corporate Income Tax to replace national systems that multinational companies could choose to adopt. A second approach was Home State taxation, which would involve mutual recognition whereby the tax rules of the home country would be used to determine the tax base for member EU countries with a tax rate being applied to the base allocated to each jurisdiction. A third approach was an optional Common Consolidated Base Taxation system whereby each EU Member State would be able to set its own tax rate on the portion of the consolidated company's base allocated to the Member States based on a common definition of taxable profits – companies would be able to opt into the system. A final approach was a compulsory European corporate tax with formulary apportionment. Under both the Home State and common consolidated income tax approaches, the portions allocated to each state were also to be calculated by a formula. The formula, to be determined by negotiation, would be based on a distribution of company assets, payroll or sales – like those in Canada and United States or perhaps on value added, for which there is already a common tax base in the EU.

The Commission argued that corporate tax harmonization would bring several economic benefits. It would relieve businesses from compliance with many different European corporate tax systems. It would reduce tax obstacles interfering with the flow of capital across borders. Profits and losses would be consolidated for EU companies enabling them to reduce effective tax rates. Although transfer pricing would remain an issue for income earned outside Europe, a common tax base would reduce the need to administer transfer pricing within Europe and lessen the scope for profit shifting by

28. Maurus Winzap & Robert Desax, *Swiss Parliament Approves Corporate Tax Reform*, *Walder Wyss & International Law Office* (28 September 2018), https://www.internationallawoffice.com/Newsletters/Corporate-Tax/Switzerland/Walder-Wyss/Swiss-Parliament-approves-corporate-tax-reform (accessed 25 Mar. 2019).
29. For a more detailed (and positive) review of EU experience, *see* Joann M. Weiner, *The Dream is Alive: EU Tax Policy with a Common Consolidated Corporate Tax Base and Formulary Apportionment* (this volume).
30. The studies were released in 2001 and published as European Commission, *Company Taxation in the Internal Market* (Office of Official Publications of the European Communities 2002).

shifting intangible income into low-tax EU countries and costs into high tax jurisdictions. However, it was not apparent that economic efficiency gains would be significant.[31] Effective tax rates on capital could still vary across businesses in fundamental ways. Since countries could choose their tax rate, companies could reduce tax payments by investing more heavily or hiring more workers in countries with lower tax rates so that the weights used to distribute income would be affected by economic decisions.[32] Efficiency gains would be muted if the consolidated corporate tax base were optional, applied to only some companies. Moreover, although an EU-consolidated corporate tax base would help curtail transfer pricing and other profit-shifting strategies among EU countries, it would not deal with tax strategies involving third countries, especially since each EU member would maintain its distinctive treatment of international income under the corporate income tax. Although there would certainly be efficiency gains from adopting a consolidated corporate tax, they may not have been substantial. The principal gain from a consolidated corporate tax base may well be to reduce compliance costs for taxpayers and administrative costs for governments as well as reducing the scope for tax avoidance.[33]

After years of deliberations, including a new proposal issued in 2011 which allowed multinational enterprises to decide to use the common base or not, negotiations effectively stalled until 2016, when the Commission relaunched a proposal to adopt a common consolidated corporate tax base in Europe.[34] Unlike the 2011 proposals, the common base proposed in 2016 would be mandatory for companies with more than EUR 750 million in revenues and would be apportioned by a formula taking into account three equally weighted factors: sales, labour (based equally on payroll and employment) and assets. The rules for determining the corporate tax base would be based on unanimous decisions taken by the EU members. This is clearly a more uniform approach than discussed previously, providing less flexibility to each Member State to establish country-specific provisions under their own corporate tax. Countries signing on to the proposed agreement would be unable to introduce any incentives unless unanimously agreed by all members.[35]

---

31. On efficiency gains, *see* the interesting analysis by Marco Runkel & Guttorm Schjelderup, *The Choice of Apportionment Factors under Formula Apportionment*, 52(3) Int'l Econ. Rev. 913 (2011) and, for an earlier discussion, Jack M. Mintz, *Globalization of the Corporate Income Tax: The Role of Allocation*, 56(3/4) Finanzarchiv 389 (1999).
32. Mintz, *Globalization of the Corporate Income Tax*, *supra* n. 31; Jack Mintz & Joann M. Weiner, *An Exploration of Formula Apportionment in the European Union*, 42(8) Eur. Tax'n 346 (2002).
33. Jack Mintz, *Corporate Tax Harmonization in Europe: It's All About Compliance*, 11(2) Int'l Tax & Pub. Fin. 221 (2004).
34. Besides relaunching of negotiations over the common consolidated tax base, the EU will adopt measures to resolve tax disputes more expeditiously and address mismatches with non-EU countries such as hybrid financing. *See* European Commission, *Commission Proposes Major Corporate Tax Reform for the EU*, press release (25 October 2016), http://europa.eu/rapid/press-release_IP-16-3471_en.htm (accessed 10 Apr. 2019). *See also* the explanatory memorandum in European Commission, *Proposal for a Council Directive on a Common Corporate Tax Base*, COM(2016) 685 final, 25 October 2016, https://ec.europa.eu/taxation_customs/sites/taxation/files/com_2016_685_en.pdf (accessed 10 Apr. 2019).
35. Interestingly, the proposal did provide two new EU-wide incentives for equity financing and research and development, as mentioned below (text at *infra* n. 36), which arguably both muddy the waters and narrow the tax base.

In June 2018, France and Germany announced a proposal to move ahead with the consolidated corporate income tax applied to all taxpayers, regardless of size and legal form, similar to the 2016 proposals but without either the EU-wide incentive for research and development or an allowance for new equity financing costs.[36] The two countries also proposed a minimum tax on profits to limit the deduction of losses. While France and Germany are among the largest members of the EU, it is far from clear whether countries such as Ireland and Luxembourg will agree with the Franco-German proposal. The EU as a whole still seems to be a long way from reaching an agreed way to deal with corporate income taxes.

This is perhaps not surprising. In contrast to a federation, in which both sovereign central and subnational governments have specific responsibilities and powers with policies legitimized by an electoral process, the EU, even with its elected Parliament, has no taxing powers and its budget essentially depends on grants from the member countries. So far, its Member States have proved quite resistant to encroachment on their own tax sovereignty. Unlike the EU, Canada, the United States and Switzerland have much stronger central governments. Nonetheless, they afford much more flexibility to their subnational governments, not necessarily because they like the results but because, after decades of experience, they have learned that providing such leeway is essential to maintain the federation. In contrast, the EU seems to have learned the opposite lesson since it is trying to achieve a considerably greater level of uniformity among the corporate tax systems of its Member States compared to what most federal states have been able to achieve with substantial subnational corporate taxes. Trying to do more in a considerably weaker institutional framework has so far, unsurprisingly, not proved successful.

§12.04 CAN INTERNATIONAL TAX SHARING BE DONE THROUGH VOLUNTARY COOPERATION?

People have been trying to pull the 'rabbit' – a rational and feasible way to share the corporate tax base – out of the international 'hat' for over a century, with little success. Different approaches have been taken to this problem. Some have stressed a particular goal such as (world) efficiency or (interpersonal or intercountry) equity. But even those who agree that a particular objective is worthwhile have not been able to agree on just what it means or how best to get there. Others have stressed a particular approach – finding the right rules or the right institutional structure, again usually running up against the barrier of lack of insufficient agreement or trust. Some have argued that what is needed is a global tax enforcement agency, but no one has agreed on who should (could) do this or how to do it. Many have stressed that business arrangements are so integrated globally that only an apportionment rule (or the split-profit method, which is effectively an apportionment rule) can really determine

36. Michael Nienaber, *Germany, France Agree On Harmonization of Corporate Tax Systems*, *Reuters.com* (20 June 2018), https://www.reuters.com/article/us-germany-france-tax-harmonisation/germany-france-agree-on-harmonization-of-corporate-tax-systems-idUSKBN1JG1RB (accessed 10 Apr. 2019).

the income earned by each state. More modestly, some have stressed simply the need and desirability of providing a better information base to all involved so that we could begin to see how an agreement might be reached.

This last approach has had some success in recent years as the United States, driven by its own goals, first imposed information exchange arrangements (the Foreign Account Tax Compliance Act, FATCA) on many countries,[37] and most countries in response have fallen in line with the country-by-country reporting agreement that emerged from the OECD/Group of 20 BEPS initiative. However, it is not yet clear what difference this emerging increase in transparency may make in terms of results if and as it becomes more fully operational.[38] Any international tax sharing plan will necessarily depend on the voluntary cooperation of fully sovereign national tax authorities, most of which now do not trust each other, let alone their taxpayers, sufficiently to make such a system very likely. Such cooperation is unlikely to emerge if an international solution is sought by following the EU's model of laying down stronger uniform rules for its members than most federal countries with subnational corporate taxes have imposed.[39] Moreover, it seems unlikely that any agreement likely to be reached in the near future, even if embodied in some kind of United Nations (or other) Convention like UNCLOS, will include any kind of judicial body to enforce whatever rules may be agreed.[40]

To some, formulary allocation (of an agreed unitary tax base) seems a desirable, feasible and relatively simple solution.[41] For this approach to succeed, however, requires more agreement on both objectives and means than seems attainable in this heterogeneous world. Moreover, it is far from clear that every country should have to follow exactly the same rules. It is equally unclear how, when the voice of each sovereign country is not heard with equal weight in the discussions, one can expect the relatively voiceless to accept the results as fair. Many long and continuing negotiations will be needed to reach any feasible solution, and everybody involved is going to have

37. Itai Grinberg, *Taxing Capital Income in Emerging Countries: Will FATCA Open the Door?*, 5(3) World Tax J. 325 (2013).
38. Country-by-country reporting is not as simple as it might seem when it comes to transparency. It requires companies to report income and various components (such as revenue) but many judgments must still be made about cost apportionment, related transaction pricing and so on. For a detailed discussion and analysis of the common reporting standard adopted for the automatic exchange of information, *see* Elisa Casi, Sara Nenadic, Mark Dinko Orlic & Christoph Spengel, *A Call to Action: From Evolution to Revolution on the Common Reporting Standard*, [2019] 2 Brit. Tax Rev. 166, and Elisa Casi, Christoph Spengel & Barbara M. B. Stage, *Cross-Border Tax Evasion After the Common Reporting Standard: Game Over?* (ZEW Discussion Paper No. 18-036, 2019).
39. A recent analysis (Robert Inman & Daniel Rubenfeld, *Democratic Federalism: The Economics, Politics, and Law of Federal Governance* (Princeton University Press, forthcoming)) of the attempts at corporate tax reform in the EU concludes - as we suggest - that, although there is little case for continued decentralization of corporate taxation, there is also little reason, in the absence of any appropriate EU-wide taxing institution, to expect any real reform beyond, perhaps, some further base harmonization.
40. This remains a problem with UNCLOS, as discussed in Bird & Mintz, *Sharing the Wealth: Article 82 of UNCLOS*, *supra* n. 4.
41. Indeed, both the present authors argued this case in earlier work: Richard Bird, *Shaping a New International Tax Order*, 42(7) Bull. Int'l Tax'n 292 (1988); Mintz, *Globalization of the Corporate Income Tax*, supra n. 31.

to compromise to some extent to achieve sufficient consensus to reach a feasible (sufficiently widely acceptable) solution that is sustainable. Some countries, perhaps even important countries, may prove unwilling to sign on or, if they sign, they may not fulfil their agreed obligations. Since no once-and-for-all solution is likely to be sustainable because adjustments will need to be made in the face of changing realities, any solution reached will doubtless continue to be the subject of much future discussion.

As we argued some years ago in terms of cooperative game theory and as federal experience suggests, cooperation is hard to achieve in the absence of transfers between governments because the set of gains resulting from cooperation without transfers is too small for all to see a net gain.[42] It is difficult to achieve international cooperation because there is no central government that can use other policies to help achieve a cooperative outcome. When it comes to corporate tax cooperation, the bargaining is more complex. Actions include choosing rates, factors for apportioning income, tax base parameters and exemptions. The more decisions that have to be made, the more complex the game, requiring each participant to have more information about outcomes from different strategies. It is likely to be the case that no cooperative solution may exist that cannot be superseded by a smaller set of actions that would yield a better payoff to an individual or coalition of participants. Further, cooperative games require a binding agreement to avoid cheating - and more complex agreements are harder to police to ensure cooperation. Moreover, the larger the number of countries, the smaller the share of the potential joint gains. It becomes easier for a country to choose not to cooperate to improve its own position or for a few countries to form a coalition to block the gains that would be received by a grand coalition.

International tax cooperation will thus occur only if willing participants decide reform is necessary. Countries have different objectives or trade-offs of objectives such as growth (investment and job creation) and acquiring source-based revenues to fund public services. They also have different political considerations that can impact on objectives. To reach an international agreement to reform corporate taxes requires at a minimum that participating nations feel they have more to gain than lose. Perhaps paradoxically, for a cooperative agreement to be binding and enforced, it must first be sufficiently flexible that countries are willing to accept it in the first place.

Is it possible to set up such a club - a coalition of the willing, as it were - to reform international corporate taxes?[43] It may be. Several such 'clubs' now exist such as NATO, the World Health Organization, the UN Convention on the Law of Sea (UNCLOS) and, perhaps especially relevant, the World Trade Organization (WTO) as well as the EU and a number of regional trade agreements. For such an alliance not only

42. Richard Bird & Jack Mintz, *Sharing the International Tax Base in a Changing World*, in *Public Finance and Public Policy in the New Century* 405 (Sijbren Cnossen & Hans-Werner Sinn eds., MIT Press 2003).

43. Another name for such a club is a Coasian alliance. The original idea is set out in R. H. Coase, *The Problem of Social Cost*, 3 J.L. & Econ. 1 (1960) and the theory is discussed in detail in Richard Cornes & Todd Sandler, *The Theory of Externalities, Public Goods and Club Goods* (2nd ed., Cambridge University Press 1996). The present discussion has benefited from the discussion of 'cooperative federalism' in Inman & Rubenfeld, *Democratic Federalism*, *supra* n. 39.

to be created but also to succeed in achieving its objectives and be sustainable over time, there must be explicit rules about how members behave as well as clear and available information permitting everyone to see what everyone else is doing and some agreed way to enforce the rules. The record of most international clubs like those mentioned above – let alone the various attempts recently made to create international environmental alliances – is at best mixed: not all members are always willing to reveal all they should, and when they do not comply or someone breaks the rules, enforcement is usually lax or lacking.[44]

An additional element in many successful clubs is that all members receive something they value as a result of their membership.[45] One important reason the WTO proved to be by far the most successful tax reformer ever in world terms – the real prime mover behind many of the VATs so widely adopted around the world – was because most countries were convinced they would benefit from more trade and were therefore willing not only to reduce tariffs but also to make them more uniform and apply them in an agreed standardized way in order to join the club.[46] The WTO also has a clear enforcement mechanism, importantly including provision for retaliation by other members if agreement is not reached. As recent events have shown, this system may not always be sufficient to restrain important players from pushing the limits. In the case of China, for example, many have argued WTO membership did not lead to the opening up of its market. Nonetheless, on the whole the WTO has worked relatively well for the last few decades.[47]

Although even the best international club is unlikely to be fully efficient in terms of achieving the efficient level of international public goods, let alone ensuring that benefits are distributed to the satisfaction of every member, the WTO and other examples suggest that at least sometimes a system based on voluntary cooperation may work sufficiently well to be better than the alternatives of unrestricted independent action or monopoly control (however well intentioned initially). Over the last half-century, few countries have acted as though they were alone in the world. Most have, to varying extents, broadly and often explicitly accepted the need to cooperate with

---

44. As shown by Kai Konrad & Marcel Thun, *The Better Route to Global Tax Coordination: Gradualism or Multilateralism?* (CESifo Working Paper 7305, October 2018), with incomplete information global coordination is most likely to emerge if everything is negotiated at once with everyone. If negotiations must be sequential, then they should begin with the country where the potential net benefits are most uncertain. This analysis usefully sets out some of the inherent problems of international negotiation. However, since it necessarily assumes not only that all those negotiating are fully rational but also that the groups and interests that shape national policy decisions are equally rational, it is inevitably far removed from the real world of international taxation.
45. Mancur Olson, *The Logic of Collective Action* (Harvard University Press 1965).
46. Kathryn James, *The Rise of the Value-Added Tax* (Cambridge University Press 2015).
47. Some may dispute this categorization of the WTO, and there is certainly a large literature cataloguing its defects and failures. Still, as William Niskanen, *Building on the WTO's Success*, 19(3) Cato J. 459 (1999) and others have noted, as international clubs go, the WTO is certainly one of the most successful: *see also* Robert Read, *Trade Dispute Settlement Mechanisms: The WTO Dispute Settlement Understanding in the Wake of GATT*, in *The WTO and the Regulation of International Trade* 41 (Nicholas Perdikis & Robert Read eds., Edward Elgar 2005); Brendan Ruddy, *The Critical Success of the WTO: Trade Policies of the Current Economic Crisis*, 13(2) J. Int'l Econ. L. 475 (2010).

other countries and to do so within a generally accepted framework. None may be willing to turn over any significant element of their fiscal sovereignty to any kind of international body. But many may be willing to go at least a bit further down the road of soft cooperation when it comes to international taxation.

[A] International Tax Sharing in Practice

To create an international tax alliance, one necessary condition may be to make it plain that the basic aim is for all to benefit and not simply to redistribute income. Federal countries can go down the redistributive road to some extent because they have both important central fiscal systems and an array of methods to provide compensatory offsets to those who might feel they have little or nothing to gain from sharing their corporate tax base with other governments. Although the EU does not have any real tax system, it too can and does redistribute to a limited extent through its agricultural and regional policies. However, it has not so far been able to do much to reshape Member State's corporate taxes, in part perhaps because some Member States are unwilling to confer what they see as unearned gains on others, and none is eager to give up national tax sovereignty. UNCLOS, like the WTO and the EU, was sold as having something for everyone and succeeded in putting in place a small global tax; however, it remains to be seen whether it will continue to be widely supported once it becomes more explicitly redistributive from the perspective of those who may consider themselves to be on the 'giving' side. Few people seem willing to make personal financial sacrifices for the benefit of those in other countries, and as yet there is no global political ethos strong enough to support international tax sharing.[48]

Even if substantial redistribution is ruled out, to establish any form of international tax sharing, one must persuade those in the countries that gain most from the existing system not only that the potential efficiency gains from a more rational international tax system will be shared fairly (as they see it) but also that any agreement reached can and will be enforced fairly and effectively in countries in which they have little trust. To do so will not be easy. Impelled in part by the earlier US FATCA initiative, considerable progress has been made under the BEPS initiative to put into place arrangements to make what is at stake more transparently clear to all. Perversely, however, increased transparency may perhaps damage the cause of international tax sharing by making potential losers even less willing to act in the interests of all unless and until they can be persuaded that they have more to lose by staying out than by joining. An important reason for restraining more ambitious aims and seeking the minimal level of cooperation needed to provide some improvement for all (compared to the current system) is that it will be difficult enough to secure that level of agreement, let alone to push for any more utopian uniform global solution. And even if an international agreement can be reached, it will not last long without the

48. On UNCLOS, *see* Bird & Mintz, *Sharing the Wealth: Article 82 of UNCLOS*, *supra* n. 4; for a fuller discussion of global taxes, *see* Richard M. Bird, *Are Global Taxes Feasible?*, 25(5) Int'l Tax & Pub. Fin. 1372 (2018).

development of a sufficiently credible enforcement system to restrain those who will inevitably seek to opt out by channelling activities through non-member jurisdictions.

The EU example illustrates both the possibilities and the limitations of the club approach to transnational governance. The origins of the EU were clearly political, as European countries tried to develop institutions that provided some protection against the terrible prospect of future continent-wide wars. Building a transnational institutional structure began in a specific, limited economic area in the form of the European Coal and Steel Community (ECSC) which itself began with a two-country agreement between France and Germany, subsequently expanded by the addition of three small neighbouring countries and Italy, with decisions being made unanimously by all members. The recent financial crisis was not a devastating war, and the current concern with developing some more effective way to tax the digital service sector in Europe is far less clearly linked to economic survival than coal and steel was thought to be in the post-war period, but perhaps, as with the ECSC, the combination of the two – the crisis and the concern especially in France and Germany with taxing (mostly foreign) digital companies – may pave the way to broader international cooperation on corporate taxes in the EU. When the ECSC was later expanded and deepened into the EU, an essential ingredient was the provision of substantial compensation for regions and industries that would otherwise have lost. One way or another for most EU residents, the union was an economic success, despite the efficiency costs of many of these politically necessary arrangements – at least until the crisis a decade or so ago shook the foundations of the Euro area in large part because the European Monetary Union created in 2001 was not matched by any kind of fiscal union, so there was no institutional way to offset the differential effects of enforcing the uniform budget rules of the EU (let alone the EMU with no exchange rate flexibility) across its heterogeneous membership.

This history suggests two lessons with respect to international tax cooperation, one positive and one negative. The positive lesson is that starting small – say, with the digital sector – and building trust into success may perhaps open the door to subsequent institutional building and, up to a point, more success.[49] The negative lesson is simply that one cannot redistribute across nations to any extent without first building up more trust and institutional resilience than Europe has so far managed to do in the last sixty years. The likelihood that the world as a whole can do better in this respect in the near future is, absent a massive catastrophe, exceedingly small. The most that can perhaps be hoped for is to begin to build the elements needed to establish a more fair and efficient international tax system. No uniform solution, however desirable it may be in principle (and even potentially workable in practice), seems feasible in this heterogeneous world.

49. The 'starting small' option is explored further in Kerrie Sadiq, *A Framework for Assessing Business Sector Formulary Apportionment* (this volume).

[B] Towards a Workable Solution

Building a transnational alliance is neither a simple nor a quick process. To begin with, one often needs a system-wide shock. As suggested above in the context of the EU, the financial crisis of a decade ago provided a good starting point, moving the discussion about international taxation onto the front pages and the desks of decision makers. The next step is to decide what exactly one wants to achieve and how best to achieve it. No matter what one wants to do, however, the most critical aspect is that whatever is done should be sufficiently widely acceptable and workable that it proves feasible. Although all this is far too complex to discuss in detail here, the simple diagram set out in Figure 12.1 outlines the argument.

First, and most importantly, *feasibility* must be the main concern in building any international alliance. If any scheme is not widely enough accepted to come into existence, it will not work. The major condition for feasibility is that the system must be acceptable to at least its critical (and preferably to most) potential members. If it is not acceptable, it will not be accepted.[50]

Figure 12.1 Building a Transnational Alliance

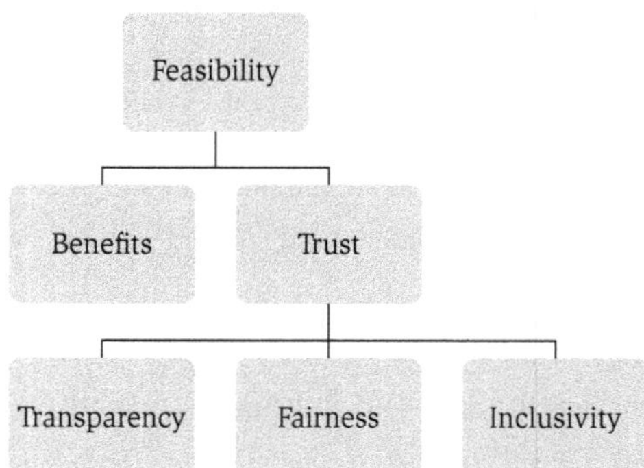

Experience (and theory) suggest that an acceptable package requires both the perception that each party will gain some private benefits from joining and sufficient belief that other parties can be trusted and that the institutional arrangements will credibly ensure that everyone keeps their word or will be penalized if they fail to do so. This is where the efficiency concerns of economists are clearly relevant: unless there is sufficient *benefit* – for example, a net gain in the form of increased revenue either

50. As shown by Christophe Farquet, *Explaining the Failure of International Tax Regulations throughout the 20th Century* (Université de Genève Working Paper, 2016), http://archive-ouverte.unige.ch/unige:88348, every international tax agreement has always been shaped by a few critical countries: one may deplore this, but the need for agreement from the powerful few remains a central concern. Although not discussed further here, an additional success criterion in building any system is that it should be sustainable, which requires both resiliency (ability to adjust to change) and, critically, enforceability. If it is not sustainable, it will not last and if it cannot accommodate change and be credibly enforceable, it is not sustainable.

directly from the existing 'pot' on the table or indirectly from the increased activity attributable to an improved tax system - for everyone to expect at least some perceptible benefit from taking part, few are likely to do so.

Even if everyone can be convinced there is some benefit in an alliance, the most important and difficult problem in constructing any transnational voluntary association is to build *trust* not only between countries but also across and within countries between such groups as domestic and transnational businesses, labour and capital, regions, sectors, etc. An essential element in building trust is *transparency*. Although this is one front on which progress has been made over the last few years, ensuring the right numbers are made available and getting everyone to accept the same numbers with respect to what is at stake are major and ongoing tasks.

Another key ingredient in building trust is that all participants must think the underlying decision processes both in shaping the alliance and in operating it are sufficiently *inclusive* for their concerns to be fairly heard and taken into account. While not perfect, the expanded discussions undertaken in the course of the BEPS project arguably constituted a major step in the right direction.[51] But much more needs to be done within most countries as well as at the international level to strengthen this dimension of trust. Many long, involved and no doubt often heated discussions lie ahead if we are to succeed in improving the international tax system.

While much remains to be done in improving both transparency and inclusivity when it comes to international tax sharing, some progress has been made on both fronts in recent decades. Perhaps the major barrier still to be resolved is the extent to which any revenue redistribution resulting from changing the existing system is seen as *fair* both from the perspective of those who may gain and from the perspective of those who may perceive that they lose. Earlier attempts to 'tax' (from their perspective) people in one country to benefit those elsewhere suggest strongly that focusing on redistribution is a good way to kill any global tax proposal.[52] If the real problem is how to share the wealth, in the absence of any global government, the only solution possible is through voluntary or cooperation. To date, the only tax resulting in any small redistribution seems to have been Article 82 of UNCLOS - an instance in which everyone came to think that they had something to gain although as yet has led to no real redistribution.[53]

Previous attempts to reform international taxation have understandably focused on reaching agreement on a set of common rules rather than on the distributive outcomes of applying those rules. When most of those involved were capital exporters, their interests dominated the process, leading to the system we now have. But the world has become more complex in recent decades, and a much more diverse set of countries are now involved in the process. To reach a successful outcome, everyone - or at least most - must find it broadly acceptable. Some redistribution, even if considerably less than what they consider really fair, may be acceptable to those who

51. Richard M. Bird, *Reforming International Taxation: Is the Process the Real Product?*, 216(2) Hacienda Pública Español/Rev. Pub. Econ. 155 (2016).
52. Bird, *Are Global Taxes Feasible?*, *supra* n. 48.
53. Bird & Mintz, *Sharing the Wealth: Article 82 of UNCLOS*, *supra* n. 4.

gain because it is better than nothing.[54] In addition, however, the results must also be acceptable to those who perceive themselves to be losers. The real problem in reforming how international taxes are shared is thus how to improve world outcomes - presumably by increasing the size of the pie - sufficiently for everyone involved to be able to see they have something to gain by signing on. The WTO managed to do this with respect to most trade (if not all agriculture or services), but even in the long-standing and generally successful EU, it has proved difficult to secure a similar degree of agreement with respect to financial and real capital flows. One may hope that if enough people keep talking together - and really listening to each other - about these issues long enough, sufficient trust may be built up to do something, but EU experience is not all that encouraging.

The three federal countries discussed in some detail earlier achieved better results, but of course they all share some important common features. Most importantly, these countries have effective central governments which can (and do) provide both some guidance and help in developing more uniform subnational systems and some compensatory measures to offset perceived politically untenable results. The EU has tried to do the same but with little success because its central governing structure does not have enough clout (taxing power). Second, in federations, the main emphasis has been simplifying the corporate tax world by standardizing and (to varying extents) harmonizing the tax base while leaving considerable discretion to subnational governments when it comes to tax rates. None of these countries has tried to impose a centrally designed uniform system. Nonetheless, it took many years, and numerous adjustments, even to reach their present degree of tax coordination. On efficiency grounds, ideally subnational governments should not tax corporate income, so the present position is definitely not economically optimal. But because it has proved to be politically sustainable, and perhaps even politically essential, federal countries have learned to live with a degree of imperfection.

In contrast, the EU's attempts to deal with the different corporate tax regimes in its Member States have from the beginning attempted to reach a degree of harmony - even uniformity - that none of the federal countries reviewed earlier, apart from Germany, has even attempted, let alone achieved. Moreover, it did so without having an overriding central government fiscal policy allowing it to compensate for the gains and losses that harmonization would impose on Member States. It is little surprise that to date these efforts have not been very successful. Indeed, it would be astonishing if they were.

The world as a whole surely cannot do what the EU could not do. There is no world government to guide or facilitate (through other measures) tax harmonization in any depth across the very diverse jurisdictions and realities that constitute the world economy. No doubt it is useful, perhaps even necessary, to develop and advocate better and more satisfactory solutions. Without a vision of the ideal, it is not always clear in which direction one should best move from today's messy reality. However,

54. This point is related to the discussion of the importance of recognizing popular as well as expert opinions when it comes to tax policy in Steven Sheffrin, *Tax Fairness and Folk Justice* (Cambridge University Press 2013).

the important question is not so much what we - the countries of the world - should ideally do. It is what we can do. Postulating an ideal solution may sometimes provide a useful target, but experience suggests that offering the adoption of a uniform formula allocating a unitary worldwide base as the solution is to ask for too much. Aiming lower may be a better strategy if one really wants to improve matters.

Sovereign countries will always want to maintain a very substantial amount of control over corporate taxes not only for revenue purposes but also because the corporate income tax is an important policy instrument in terms of both its regulatory effects (control, incentives) on the corporate sector[55] and its perceived (if not always realistic) role from a political perspective as a way of taxing capital and the rich.[56] A critical element in any acceptable solution is thus likely to be to leave not only statutory but also effective tax rates as matters for national decision alone. At best, it may perhaps be possible, as some regional trade agreements have tried (not very successfully) to do, to obtain some agreement on how to tax transnational activities and establish some agreed limit for maximum allowable variations to encompass divergent national preferences for certain activities or regions. But even this may be reaching too far for success.

Assuming some agreement can be reached on the appropriate base - admittedly a big assumption but one that should in principle, if countries become fully engaged in making the necessary information available (as many have now agreed in principle), be possible - this step should over time lead them to come to trust each other to some extent. Perhaps it would be easier to agree to a common base but allow each country to take exception to the common base (such as the current practice followed by US states starting with the federal base as the common base) or (as in Canada) to choose credits that effectively change the base. The more flexible the arrangements, the easier it will be to come to an agreement. Agreement on the starting point for a common base would be difficult to achieve, but if a few large countries did agree, past experience suggests that others could be willing to follow their lead.

An obvious next step would be to try to agree on the formula used to apportion the base among the relevant countries, assuming again that the necessary information is available to all. The main thing that needs to be agreed is the allowable components (e.g., sales, payrolls, assets) in the formula, leaving it up to countries (like US states) to choose the mix and weights (which, incidentally, need not be equal on each component of the formula). A key to getting agreement may be to, as it were, let countries choose their own 'poison' in taxing the agreed base. Ideally, some limits may be needed to avoid misbehaviour, for example, requiring that at least some minimum rate should be applied to each element of the general formula. But what matters most is to establish a functioning system with as broad a membership as possible that all members come to view it as 'their' system. Of course, if one starts with a system that is imperfect one will likely have to live with imperfections for many years. Perhaps a partial solution may be found by establishing a periodic review mechanism - say, every five or ten years - to consider possible future adjustments and, one may hope,

55. Reuven S. Avi-Yonah, *The Three Goals of Taxation*, 60(1) Tax L. Rev. 1 (2006).
56. Geoffrey Hale, *The Politics of Taxation in Canada* (Broadview Press 2002); Bank, *supra* n. 13.

improvements. What matters may be less the precise form of any international agreement than the simple fact that there is such an agreement – that enough countries agree sufficiently on broad principles to set out a framework allowing for some (limited) national differences that can be clarified and developed further over time.

Any agreement that can be reached on a formulary apportionment system should have the benefit of making it possible to reallocate at least some of the resources now devoted to tax planning (and countering tax planning) to the task of making the system work by generating and verifying the needed information and by developing a mechanism – if only a 'naming and shaming' one – to ensure that all countries live up to their obligations to provide information and follow the rules. No such system would be perfect, of course, and it might be neither uniformly applied nor economically optimal. But it might work better and be considered fairer than the existing system and it may, once launched, be subsequently improved to some extent. Ultimately, any system rests on the willingness of countries to provide information even to those untrustworthy people in other countries. Some may fudge the data and try to get around the rules in various ways. Others may shoot themselves in the foot by trying to impose rates that are too high. The first problem requires vigilance and some kind of trusted monitoring system that would doubtless be difficult to enforce. The second problem mentioned is not really a problem because the countries themselves would pay the price even if, presumably for domestic political reasons, they may sometimes be willing to do so.

There are other possible approaches besides formulary apportionment. Recently, governments have discussed applying a minimum tax to multinational enterprises resident of a specific country to ensure global income is taxed and denying certain deductions not subject to the minimum tax.[57] Both of these proposals have elements of the new US provisions with respect to a minimum tax on global intangible income (defined as taxable income in excess of a presumed rate of return on tangible assets) earned by US companies and the Base-Erosion Anti-Avoidance tax that operates as a minimum tax on income gross of disallowed payments.[58] This approach, which leaves international income belonging to the jurisdictions where the company resides, would

57. See *Organisation for Economic Co-operation and Development Secretary-General Report to G20 Finance Ministers and Central Bank Governors*, Fukuoka, Japan, June 2019, 48, http://www.oecd.org/tax/oecd-secretary-general-tax-report-g20-finance-ministers-june-2019.pdf (accessed 23 Jul. 2019), which '... seeks to address the remaining BEPS challenges through the development of two inter-related rules:

(1) an *income inclusion rule* that would tax the income of a foreign branch or a controlled entity if that income was subject to tax at an effective rate that is below a minimum rate; and
(2) a *tax on base eroding payments* that would operate by way of a denial of a deduction or imposition of source-based taxation (including withholding tax), together with any necessary changes to double tax treaties, for certain payments unless that payment was subject to tax at or above a minimum rate'.

58. For a further discussion of these provisions *see* Jack Mintz, *Global Implications of US Tax Reform* (CESIfo Lecture, Munich, Germany, January 2018), https://www.ifo.de/DocDL/sd-2018-07-mintz-us-tax-reform-2018-04-12.pdf (accessed 23 Jul. 2019).

be more consistent with current separate accounting practices rather than formulary apportionment.

In addition, countries that baulk at any international tax cooperation may of course also fall back on taxes on business other than the corporate income tax to raise revenues.

§12.05 CONCLUSION

No perfect system for the international sharing of the corporate tax base seems feasible today. Nonetheless, it may perhaps be possible to establish an imperfect system beginning with existing tax systems as a starting point. Of course, any system will require governments to recognize the necessity of some cooperation and to accept an arrangement. To do so, they must see that it will make them better off in some visible way even if it does not get them all they would ideally like. Attempting to pursue a degree of economic and administrative perfection that successful federal countries have not managed over the last century is decidedly not the right path to achieve some form of international cooperation, especially given the lack of a central coordinating governing body.

Perhaps, as we suggest, the big players in the international tax game might be able to start the process by agreeing on a common base and establishing an agreement that allows any country to diverge from it, including choosing their own apportionment formula, subject perhaps to some constraints. A modest proposal along these lines, which leaves far more room for differential national policies than most other contenders, is of course not ideal. But it might prove to be acceptable and thus provide the essential framework for the ongoing, and perhaps endless, task of improving the present system. Life is never perfect, but it is better to do something that might work than to do nothing at all.

Index

V

SERIES ON INTERNATIONAL TAXATION

1. Alberto Xavier, *The Taxation of Foreign Investment in Brazil*, 1980 (ISBN 90-200-0582-0).
2. Hugh J. Ault & Albert J. Rädler, *The German Corporation Tax Law with 1980 Amendments*, 1981 (ISBN 90-200-0642-8).
3. Paul R. McDaniel & Hugh J. Ault, *Introduction to United States International Taxation*, 1981 (ISBN 90-6544-004-6).
4. Albert J. Rädler, *German Transfer Pricing/Prix de Transfer en Allemagne*, 1984 (ISBN 90-6544-143-3).
5. Paul R. McDaniel & Stanley S. Surrey, *International Aspects of Tax Expenditures: A Comparative Study*, 1985 (ISBN 90-654-4163-8).
6. Kees van Raad, *Nondiscrimination in International Tax Law*, 1986 (ISBN 90-6544-266-9).
7. Sijbren Cnossen (ed.), *Tax Coordination in the European Community*, 1987 (ISBN 90-6544-272-3).
8. Ben Terra, *Sales Taxation. The Case of Value Added Tax in the European Community*, 1989 (ISBN 90-6544-381-9).
9. Rutsel S.J. Martha, *The Jurisdiction to Tax in International Law: Theory and Practice of Legislative Fiscal Jurisdiction*, 1989 (ISBN 90-654-4416-5).
10. Paul R. McDaniel & Hugh J. Ault, *Introduction to United States International Taxation* (3rd revised edition), 1989 (ISBN 90-6544-423-8).
11. Manuel Pires, *International Juridicial Double Taxation of Income*, 1989 (ISBN 90-6544-426-2).
12. A.H.M. Daniels, *Issues in International Partnership Taxation*, 1991 (ISBN 90-654-4577-3).
13. Arvid A. Skaar, *Permanent Establishment: Erosion of a Tax Treaty Principle*, 1992 (ISBN 90-6544-594-3).
14. Cyrille David & Geerten M.M. Michielse (eds), *Tax Treatment of Financial Instruments*, 1996 (ISBN 90-654-4666-4).
15. Herbert H. Alpert & Kees van Raad (eds), *Essays on International Taxation*, 1993 (ISBN 90-654-4781-4).
16. Wolfgang Gassner, Michael Lang & Eduard Lechner (eds), *Tax Treaties and EC Law*, 1997 (ISBN 90-411-0680-4).
17. Glória Teixeira, *Taxing Corporate Profits in the EU*, 1997 (ISBN 90-411-0703-7).
18. Michael Lang et al. (eds), *Multilateral Tax Treaties*, 1998 (ISBN 90-411-0704-5).
19. Stef van Weeghel, *The Improper Use of Tax Treaties*, 1998 (ISBN 90-411-0737-1).
20. Klaus Vogel (ed.), *Interpretation of Tax Law and Treaties and Transfer Pricing in Japan and Germany*, 1998 (ISBN 90-411-9655-2).
21. Bertil Wiman (ed.), *International Studies in Taxation: Law and Economics; Liber Amicorum Leif Mutén*, 1999 (ISBN 90-411-9692-7).
22. Alfonso J. Martín Jiménez, *Towards Corporate Tax Harmonization in the European Community*, 1999 (ISBN 90-411-9690-0).

23. Ramon J. Jeffery, *The Impact of State Sovereignty on Global Trade and International Taxation*, 1999 (ISBN 90-411-9703-6).
24. A.J. Easson, *Taxation of Foreign Direct Investment*, 1999 (ISBN 90-411-9741-9).
25. Marjaana Helminen, *The Dividend Concept in International Tax Law: Dividend Payments Between Corporate Entities*, 1999 (ISBN 90-411-9765-6).
26. Paul Kirchhof, Moris Lehner, Kees van Raad, Arndt Raupach & Michael-Rodi (eds), *International and Comparative Taxation: Essays in Honour of Klaus Vogel*, 2002 (ISBN 90-411-9841-5).
27. Krister Andersson, Peter Melz & Christer Silfverberg (eds), *Liber Amicorum Sven-Olof Lodin*, 2001 (ISBN 90-411-9850-4).
28. Juan Martín Jovanovich, *Customs Valuation and Transfer Pricing: Is It Possible to Harmonize Customs and Tax Rules?*, Second Edition, 2018 (ISBN 978-90-411-6134-5).
29. Stefano Simontacchi, *Taxation of Capital Gains under the OECD Model Convention: With Special Regard to Immovable Property*, 2007 (ISBN 978-90-411-2549-1).
30. Michael Lang, Josef Schuch, & Claus Staringer (eds), *Tax Treaty Law and EC Law*, 2007 (ISBN 978-90-411-2629-0).
31. Duncan Bentley, *Taxpayers' Rights: Theory Origin and Implementation*, 2007 (ISBN 978-90-411-2650-4).
32. Sergio André Rocha, *Interpretation of Double Taxation Conventions: General Theory and Brazilian Perspective*, 2008 (ISBN 978-90-411-2822-5).
33. Robert F. van Brederode, *Systems of General Sales Taxation: Theory, Policy and Practice*, 2009 (ISBN 978-90-411-2832-4).
34. John G. Head & Richard Krever (eds), *Tax Reform in the 21st Century: A Volume in Memory of Richard Musgrave*, 2009 (ISBN 978-90-411-2829-4).
35. Jens Wittendorff, *Transfer Pricing and the Arm's Length Principle in International Tax Law*, 2010 (ISBN 978-90-411-3270-3).
36. Marjaana Helminen, *The International Tax Law Concept of Dividend*, Second Edition, 2017 (ISBN 978-90-411-8394-1).
37. Robert F. van Brederode (ed.), *Immovable Property under VAT: A Comparative Global Analysis*, 2011 (ISBN 978-90-411-3126-3).
38. Dennis Weber & Stef van Weeghel, *The 2010 OECD Updates: Model Tax Convention & Transfer Pricing Guidelines - A Critical Review*, 2011 (ISBN 978-90-411-3812-5).
39. Yariv Brauner & Martin James McMahon, Jr. (eds), *The Proper Tax Base: Structural Fairness from an International and Comparative Perspective—Essays in Honour of Paul McDaniel*, 2012 (ISBN 978-90-411-3286-4).
40. Robert F. van Brederode (ed.), *Science, Technology and Taxation*, 2012 (ISBN 978-90-411-3125-6).
41. Oskar Henkow, *The VAT/GST Treatment of Public Bodies*, 2013 (ISBN 978-90-411-4663-2).
42. Jean Schaffner, *How Fixed Is a Permanent Establishment?*, 2013 (ISBN 978-90-411-4662-5).

43. Miguel Correia, *Taxation of Corporate Groups*, 2013 (ISBN 978-90-411-4841-4).
44. Veronika Daurer, *Tax Treaties and Developing Countries*, 2014 (ISBN 978-90-411-4982-4).
45. Claire Micheau, *State Aid, Subsidy and Tax Incentives under EU and WTO Law*, 2014 (ISBN 978-90-411-4555-0).
46. Robert F. van Brederode & Richard Krever (eds), *Legal Interpretation of Tax Law*, 2014 (ISBN 978-90-411-4945-9).
47. Radhakishan Rawal, *Taxation of Cross-border Services*, 2014 (ISBN 978-90-411-4947-3).
48. João Dácio Rolim, *Proportionality and Fair Taxation*, 2014 (ISBN 978-90-411-5838-3).
49. Paulo Rosenblatt, *General Anti-avoidance Rules for Major Developing Countries*, 2015 (ISBN 978-90-411-5839-0).
50. Gaspar Lopes Dias V.S., *Tax Arbitrage through Cross-Border Financial Engineering*, 2015 (ISBN 978-90-411-5875-8).
51. Geerten M.M. Michielse & Victor Thuronyi (eds), *Tax Design Issues Worldwide*, 2015 (ISBN 978-90-411-5610-5).
52. Oktavia Weidmann, *Taxation of Derivatives*, 2015 (ISBN 978-90-411-5977-9).
53. Chris Evans, Richard Krever & Peter Mellor (eds), *Tax Simplification*, 2015 (ISBN 978-90-411-5976-2).
54. Reuven Avi-Yonah & Joel Slemrod (eds), *Taxation and Migration*, 2015 (ISBN 978-90-411-6136-9).
55. Alexander Bosman, *Other Income under Tax Treaties: An Analysis of Article 21 of the OECD Model Convention*, 2015 (ISBN 978-90-411-6610-4).
56. John Abrahamson, *International Taxation of Manufacturing and Distribution*, 2016 (ISBN 978-90-411-6664-7).
57. Frederik Boulogne, *Shortcomings in the EU Merger Directive*, 2016 (ISBN 978-90-411-6713-2).
58. Angelika Meindl-Ringler, *Beneficial Ownership in International Tax Law*, 2016 (ISBN 978-90-411-6833-7).
59. Andreas Waltrich, *Cross-Border Taxation of Permanent Establishments: An International Comparison*, 2016 (ISBN 978-90-411-6832-0).
60. Sergio André Rocha & Allison Christians (eds), *Tax Sovereignty in the BEPS Era*, 2017 (ISBN 978-90-411-6707-1).
61. Peter Antony Wilson, *BRICS and International Tax Law*, 2018 (ISBN 978-90-411-9435-0).
62. Louise Otis, Brigitte Alepin & Blanca Moreno-Dodson (eds), *Winning the Tax Wars: Tax Competition and Cooperation*, 2018 (ISBN 978-90-411-9460-2).
63. Marta Castelon, *International Taxation of Income from Services under Double Taxation Conventions: Development, Practice and Policy*, 2018 (ISBN 978-90-411-9594-4).
64. D.M. Broekhuijsen, *A Multilateral Tax Treaty: Designing an Instrument to Modernise International Tax Law*, 2018 (ISBN 978-90-411-9872-3).

65. John Abrahamson, *International Taxation of Energy Production and Distribution*, 2018 (ISBN 978-90-411-9101-4).
66. Leopoldo Parada, *Double Non-taxation and the Use of Hybrid Entities: An Alternative Approach in the New Era of BEPS*, 2018 (ISBN 978-90-411-9991-1).
67. Richard Snoeij, *International Tax Aspects of Sovereign Wealth Investors: A Source State Perspective*, 2018 (ISBN 978-90-411-9431-2).
68. Aleksandra Bal, *Taxation, Virtual Currency and Blockchain*, 2019 (ISBN 978-94-035-0103-1).
69. Werner Haslehner, Georg Kofler, Katerina Pantazatou & Alexander Rust (eds), *Tax and the Digital Economy: Challenges and Proposals for Reform*, 2019 (ISBN 978-94-035-0361-5).
70. Eva Escribano, *Jurisdiction to Tax Corporate Income Pursuant to the Presumptive Benefit Principle: A Critical Analysis of Structural Paradigms Underlying Corporate Income Taxation and Proposals for Reform*, 2019 (ISBN 978-94-035-0640-1).
71. Jérôme Monsenego & Jan Bjuvberg (eds), *International Taxation in a Changing Landscape: Liber Amicorum in Honour of Bertil Wiman*, 2019 (ISBN 978-90-411-9234-9).
72. Kasper Dziurdź, *Non-discrimination in Tax Treaty Law and World Trade Law: The Impact of Formal, Substantive and Subjective Approaches*, 2019 (ISBN 978-94-035-0904-4).
73. Félix Daniel Martínez Laguna, *Hybrid Financial Instruments, Double Non-taxation and Linking Rules*, 2019 (ISBN 978-94-035-1074-3).
74. Jan Gooijer, *Tax Treaty Residence of Entities*, 2019 (ISBN 978-94-035-1301-0).
75. John Abrahamson, *International Taxation of Banking*, 2020 (ISBN 978-94-035-1094-1).
76. Richard Krever & François Vaillancourt (eds), *The Allocation of Multinational Business Income: Reassessing the Formulary Apportionment Option*, 2020 (ISBN 978-94-035-0614-2).

www.ingramcontent.com/pod-product-compliance
Ingram Content Group UK Ltd.
Pitfield, Milton Keynes, MK11 3LW, UK
UKHW020235290926
15470UKWH00002B/547

9 789403 506142